Proceedings
Comparative Literature Symposium
Texas Tech University
Volume IX

ETHNIC LITERATURES SINCE 1776:
THE MANY VOICES OF AMERICA

Part 1

Edited by
Wolodymyr T. Zyla
Wendell M. Aycock

Texas Tech Press
Lubbock, Texas
1978

INTERDEPARTMENTAL COMMITTEE ON COMPARATIVE LITERATURE
TEXAS TECH UNIVERSITY

Editorial Board for Volume IX

Roberto Bravo-Villarroel
Vivian I. Davis
Carl Hammer, Jr.

Proceedings of the Comparative Literature Symposium result from annual symposia organized by Texas Tech University's Interdepartmental Committee on Comparative Literature. *Ethnic Literatures Since 1776: The Many Voices of America* is the proceedings of a symposium held on 27 to 31 January 1976 in commemoration of our nation's bicentennial. Copies of the Proceedings may be obtained on an exchange basis from, or purchased through, the Exchange Librarian, Texas Tech University Library, Lubbock, Texas 79409.

ISSN: 0084-9103
ISBN: 0-89672-059-4
Library of Congress Catalog Card Number: 78-52073
Texas Tech Press
Texas Tech University, Lubbock, Texas 79409
Printed in the United States of America

Table of Contents

Part 1

Poetry

Symposium Lectures

Preface

The Bicentennial provides a major opportunity for recognition of "ethnic America." During this time significant studies and evaluations have been produced to clarify hitherto obscure or neglected contributions of many ethnic groups to the nation's birth and development.

Two hundred years of American statehood have given us an American civilization that has grown with contributions of millions of immigrants from over one hundred different cultures producing our nation's pluralistic heritage. This American heritage is not accidental; its roots are in the diversity of the American experience and in the freedom to foster the many voices of that experience.

The American society was already a "mosaic of peoples" at its beginning, as reflected by the first United States Census in 1790. Germans, Dutch, French, Swedish together with people of British origin were building a new nation. At that time, as today, settling in America did not result in erasing cultures but in relocating them. Therefore, significant progress was possible, and major gains were made toward gradually making American democracy a living reality for each settler. It is not easy to comprehend the heterogeneity of American society and its cultural, social, and economic forces that influence the behavior of many ethnic groups. For this one needs a sound knowledge of the actual accomplishments of each group in order to see in its totality the problem that America faces.

It is easy to argue, as some distinguished scholars do, that ethnic diversity is "bad" and that it can be "dangerously divisive." But this argument does not contribute to the solution of the problem, because ethnic groups will not vanish. We have to acknowledge the ethnic groups because they do exist in our society, develop, grow culturally and therefore present a unique social problem. And this is the ethnic diversity because America is a varied nation—"a nation richer in its heritage by the very fact of its variability."[1] We are fortunate to live at a time when American society is no longer infatuated with the unrealistic "melting pot" theory and recognizes the value of every ethnic group's contribution to the society. Here mention should be made of the passage of the Ethnic Heritage Studies Programs Act of 1972. Its "Title IX—Ethnic Heritage Program: Statement of Policy" reads:

> In recognition of the heterogeneous composition of the Nation and of the fact that in a multi-ethnic society a greater understanding of the contributions on one's own heritage and those of one's fellow citizens can contribute to a more

5

harmonious, patriotic, and committed populace, and in recognition of the principle that all persons in the educational institutions of the Nation should have an opportunity to learn about the differing and unique contributions to the national heritage made by each ethnic group, it is the purpose of this title to provide assistance designed to afford to students opportunities to learn about the nature of their own cultural heritage, and to study the contributions of the cultural heritages of the other ethnic groups in the Nation.[2]

Senator Richard S. Schweiker, sponsor of the Ethnic Heritage Studies Programs Act, called it "an important new Federal commitment to ethnicity and pluralism as positive forces in America." In particular he said: "By passing this ethnic studies legislation, the Congress is for the first time providing official national recognition to ethnicity. . . . The 'melting pot' theory of assimilation in our society is no longer working, and too many people in modern society have lost the important values of community, identity, traditions, and family solidarity."[3]

This legislation, in my opinion, transcends in importance a mere amendment to an educational bill. And one may hope that homogenization of the population will never again be a stated national goal.

With these facts in mind and careful study of many ethnic literatures, we decided some three years ago that the best way to commemorate the nation's Bicentennial would be to examine the richness of American society as it is found in the diversity of its cultures and in the American experience of its many peoples. The result of these considerations was the Ninth Annual Comparative Literature Symposium, entitled "Ethnic Literatures Since 1776: The Many Voices of America," that Texas Tech University presented 27-31 January 1976, in commemoration of the American Revolution on its 200th Anniversary.

The symposium, which included leading literary scholars of this country, discussed and compared some of the many ethnic literatures and learned about the differences and similarities in the experiences of American ethnic groups and their respective cultural contributions to American pluralistic society. The approach at the symposium was scholarly. The discussions centered on ethnic works produced in ethnic languages or in English by immigrants or descendants of immigrants and also on works with an ethnic theme regardless of the author's nationality. In some cases stress was placed on the historical beginnings of the ethnic literatures. Most attention, however, was devoted to literary and cultural study of works in order to exhibit their emotional effects, excellence of form, ethnic distinction, and permanent cultural value.

During the discussions that followed each paper, it became obvious that much of American literature has been written by members of ethnic groups. Creative immigrants and their descendants, sometimes socially assimilated as time passed, remained culturally ethnic, and their ethnicity was expressed in their works.

Thus ethnicity as such was never a dead letter in America. The immigrants and their descendants at all times of American history retained a sense of ethnicity that was based upon their ancestry, their national roots, their religion, and their language. They did not lose their identity, nor did they cease to exist. They remained who they were.

In most cases the literature was considered as historical source material and was analyzed by combined methods of historical analysis and literary criticism. References were also made to the linguistic skills necessary to understand the treasures of ethnic thought and feeling and to avoid concentrating upon a single group but to study instead the total ethnic experience that too often is overlooked by scholars. The linguistic problem, as was rightly stressed, is not to be exaggerated because this nation has a great capacity, and its scholars can easily master more than one language and thereby develop tools to understand and properly research ethnic literatures.

Perhaps it is a significant prophetic vision that Brom Weber recently expressed: "Americanists should become multi-lingual as a group, minimally bi-lingual as individuals. They should become sensitive to the pecularities of an ethnic culture, of an ethnic group, of an immigrant experience. . . . Comparative literary studies conducted competently may become an everyday affair for Americanists. It should be obvious that multilingualism and multi-culturalism are but one future direction for American literary studies."[4]

Every paper and the discussions that followed opened an exciting perspective and made a serious impact on the participating audience. Lawrence L. Graves, Dean of the College of Art and Sciences of Texas Tech University, in his concluding remarks, summed up the proceedings of the symposium as follows:

> It is true, unfortunately, that for a long series of decades this country paid very little attention to the contributions of those whose ancestry was not Anglo-Saxon. We were occupied with other things: conquering the wilderness, building our industrial base, populating our cities. But now we have done these things, and, in a way, paused to reflect upon our past. And now in our own day we are beginning to realize the richness of the fabric of the society we have woven. It would be tedious and redundant to review what has transpired during this symposium. Suffice it to say that in its way this gathering has examined the texture of our linguistic heritage. And you who have attended and participated in the deliberations have made for the success that has been achieved.[5]

* * *

Prior to the lectures concerning ethnic literatures, the symposium program featured a special session devoted to the commemoration of ethnic literatures on the two hundredth anniversary of the American Revolution.

The commemorative address was presented by Alwyn Barr, Professor of History, Texas Tech University.

The symposium lectures were followed by panel discussions and comments from the audience. The observations made by the panelists and members of the audience were indicative of their interest in ethnic literatures and in the papers that were presented. The symposium panel discussion members were Francis Bulhof, The University of Texas at Austin, Robert G. Collmer, Baylor University, Sergio D. Elizondo, New Mexico State University, Mary E. Davis, University of Oklahoma, Adam F. González, South Plains College, Bart Lewis, Texas A&M University, guest panelists; and Peter L. Abernethy, Beatrice W. Alexander, Theodor W. Alexander, James G. Allen, Norwood H. Andrews, Jr., William L. Andrews, Wendell M. Aycock, Thomas I. Bacon, Laura Ballew, Roberto Bravo-Villarroel, Mary Kay Bray, Mary Louise Brewer, Peter D. Bubresko, Mary Sue Carlock, Peder G. Christiansen, Alfred Cismaru, Sydney P. Cravens, J. Richard Crider, Ann A. Daghistany, Vivian I. Davis, Floyd E. Eddleman, Edward V. George, Everett A. Gillis, David Leon Higdon, Patricia M. Hopkins, Leonid A. Jirgensons, J. James Johnson, Daryl E. Jones, Leo J. Juarez, Theodore M. Klein, Jean S. Koh, Vadim Komkov, Michael T. Kopetzky, Magne Kristiansen, Henry J. Maxwell, Marion C. Michael, Walter R. McDonald, Evelyn I. Montgomery, Robert J. Morris, Lynn Novak, Harley D. Oberhelman, William T. Patterson, Rosemarie E. Petrich, Donald W. Rude, Elizabeth Rylander, Jeffrey R. Smitten, Lorum H. Stratton, Dahlia J. Terrell, Jack D. Wages, Warren S. Walker, Joel C. Weinsheimer, Joe N. Weixlmann, Wolodymyr T. Zyla, faculty members at Texas Tech University; Christian J. W. Kloesel, Research Associate, Institute for Studies in Pragmaticism, Texas Tech University; Paul R. Milosevich, professional artist and former Texas Tech faculty member; and Harry W. Storey, graduate student at Texas Tech University. In all its sessions the symposium was attended by approximately 3,291 persons, including faculty members, graduate students, and undergraduates from Texas Tech University and from forty-nine universities and colleges.

In addition to the lectures, the symposium program included theatrical and musical performances and three exhibits. Texas Tech Dance Division of the Department of Health, Physical Education and Recreation presented an Evening of Dance that consisted of "The Shaker Way," "Canto Chicano," selections from "Coppelia" and "Primitive Fire." These performances were directed by Diana Moore, Texas Tech University. Peggy Lockwood in cooperation with David Hamm, Tom Moore, Ricardo Pérez, Margarita Rodríguez, and Debbie Waghorn, students at Texas Tech University presented two Chicano short plays by Luis Valdez, *Los Chicanos* and *Los Vendidos.* The Black Players, Marsha Beaman, Denise Bradford, Cora Guinn, Mythe Kervin, and Christopher Thomas, performed an oral interpretation of "An Idea of Ancestry." The symposium program included also a concert with performances of Texas Tech Symphony Orchestra, Concert Band, and Texas Tech Women Singers. The concert, co-sponsored by the Twenty-Fifth Symposium of Contemporary Music and the Ninth Annual Comparative Literature Symposium, presented "Echoes of Time and the River," a major composition by George Crumb, a noted contemporary American composer. It also included "Darest Thou Now, O Soul," a work by Tech composer Mary Jeanne van Appledorn, performed by the Tech Women Singers and Judson D. Maynard, organist, under the direction of William Hartwell, Texas Tech University.

A new attraction of the symposium was a literary forum featuring the Chicano author Tomás Rivera who presented "Life in Search of Form" and read a few of his poems, among them "The Searchers." The symposium musical program of the commemorative session included a solo performance, "I Hear America Singing," music by Mary Jeanne van Appledorn, presented by Mary R. Kelly, soprano and Trudi Post, pianist.

The University Bookstore featured a display of visiting lecturers' works, and the University Library presented "Voices of Freedom—American Ethnic Literature." The main symposium exhibit "Ethnic Literatures: Manuscripts, First Editions, and Photographs" was on display in The Museum of Texas Tech University. This exhibit contained material provided by Calvin Library, Calvin College; Franco-American Materials Project at Assumption College and Franco-American Institute of New England; Istituto Italiano di Cultura; Instituto de Cultura Puertorriqueña (the Instituto donated its exhibit to Texas Tech University Library); Latvian Writers' Association in the United States; Slovenian Research Center of America, Inc.; Texas Tech University Library; The Charles Patterson Van Pelt Library, University of Pennsylvania; The Humanities Research Center of the University of Texas at Austin; the Norwegian-American Historical Association; University of Illinois at Urbana-Champaign; U.S. Population Ethnohistorical Research Center, Phoenix; Professors Branimir Anzulovic, Armand B. Chartier, David Hsin-Fu Wand, Walter Lagerwey, William J. Lynch, Valters Nollendorfs, Tomás Rivera, Francis M. Rogers, Dmytro M. Shtohryn, Rudolf Sturm, Victor Terras, Gerald Thorson, Daniel Walden, guest speakers; Professors Rolando R. Hinojosa-S., Texas A&I University, Lisa Kahn, Texas Southern University, Frank Pino, The University of Texas at San Antonio; Professors Thomas I. Bacon, Peter D. Bubresko, Aldo Finco, Edmundo García-Girón, Carl Hammer, Jr. and Mrs. Laura Ballew, Texas Tech University.

During the symposium lectures, there was on display a large acrylic painting "The Immigrants" created by Paul R. Milosevich, professional artist and former Texas Tech faculty member. There were also two television programs devoted to the symposium theme and presented on the

Texas Tech Television Station (KTXT-TV), in which the participants were Francis M. Rogers, Brom Weber, guest speakers; and James G. Allen, Mary Louise Brewer, Vivian I. Davis, Edmundo García-Girón, Leo J. Juarez, Wolodymyr T. Zyla, faculty members at Texas Tech University.

This volume of the Proceedings is divided into five parts: A Commemoration, Poetry, Symposium Lectures, Luncheon Presentation, and Selected Bibliography. We begin the commemorative part with a letter of commendation from John W. Warner, Administrator of the American Revolution Bicentennial Administration. The lectures appear in alphabetical order with the exception of the first lecture, which is a general introduction to the topic. The cover for this work is based on the artistic design of the symposium poster, and pamphlet, created by Jerry D. Kelly. This volume contains a photograph of an acrylic painting "The Immigrants" by Paul R. Milosevich, two photographs of the dance program, three photographs of The Museum exhibit and other photographs of the symposium activities. An exchange publication, this volume is placed in various libraries throughout the world in order to stimulate the growth of comparative literature studies.

In conclusion I should like to express my gratitude to Mr. Warner for his letter of commendation and the Certificate of Appreciation to the University and to the Interdepartmental Committee on Comparative Literature regarding the symposium. My deep appreciation and gratitude is due to the distinguished guest speakers, speakers from the University, guest panelists, and panelists from Texas Tech, who made this symposium possible. Thanks are due to all guests from other universities and colleges who attended this symposium. I thank the Departments of Music, Health, Physical Education, and Recreation, and The Museum of Texas Tech University, the University Library, and the University Bookstore for their helpful cooperation. I am indebted to the Lubbock Chamber of Commerce for its help in registration. Thanks are due to all colleagues at Texas Tech University who helped in this symposium by working on various committees. My sincerest thanks go to those who served as chairmen of various symposium meetings: C. Leonard Ainsworth, James J. Allen, Norwood H. Andrews, Jr., Glenn E. Barnett, J. Wilkes Berry, Alfred Cismaru, J. Richard Crider, James W. Culp, Ann A. Daghistany, Floyd E. Eddleman, Edmundo García-Girón, Lawrence L. Graves, Carl Hammer, Jr., Ray C. Janeway, William R. Johnson, J. Knox Jones, Jr., Thomas A. Langford, Harold Luce, Henry J. Maxwell, Marion C. Michael, Harley D. Oberhelman, Idris R. Traylor, Warren S. Walker, Margaret E. Wilson. I wish to express my appreciation to Ray C. Janeway, Dean of Library Services at Texas Tech University and to Charles M. McLaughlin, Acting Administrative Officer, The Museum of Texas Tech University, for their help and assistance.

The financing for this Bicentennial Symposium was borne by Texas Tech University, with a grant from the National Endowment for the Humanities. I am especially grateful to Grover E. Murray, then President of Texas Tech University, and J. Knox Jones, Jr., Vice President for Research and Graduate Studies, for their generous support of the comparative Literature symposium project.

Wolodymyr T. Zyla

NOTES

[1] Francis J. Brown and Joseph S. Roucek, ed., *One America*, 3rd ed. (New York: Prentice-Hall, Inc., 1952), p. 4.

[2] *Congressional Record*, Proceedings and Debates of the 92nd Congress, Second Session, 118, No. 96 (14 June 1972), 1.

[3] Ibid.

[4] Brom Weber, "Our Multi-Ethnic Origins and American Literary Studies," paper read at the Annual Meeting of the Society for the Study of the Multi-Ethnic Literature of the United States, held in conjunction with the Modern Language Association of America, 28 December 1974, p. 13.

[5] Lawrence L. Graves, "Concluding Remarks," 31 January 1976. Text taken from recorded tape.

Ethnic Literatures on the Two Hundredth Anniversary of the American Revolution: A Commemoration

American Revolution
Bicentennial Administration
2401 E Street, N.W.
Washington, D.C. 20276

Dr. Wolodymyr T. Zyla
Chairman, Interdepartmental Committee
  on Comparative Literature
Texas Tech University
Lubbock, Texas 79409

Dear Dr. Zyla:

Americans across our entire nation are commemorating with
individuality and diversity the two-hundredth anniversary
of the founding of our nation. The contributions of our
many ethnic and racial peoples to the formation and
development of our nation is of such great significance
that the recognition and reflection of those contributions
is essential.

Texas Tech University's Ninth Annual Comparative Literature
Symposium emphasized the importance of the many literatures
which form the bases of American literature and examined
the differences and similarities in the experiences of our
peoples and their cultural contributions to our pluralistic
society. The pluralism which has marked American society
throughout our history as a nation will continue to be a
source of vitality and strength in the century ahead.

Texas Tech's Interdepartmental Committee on Comparative
Literature is to be highly commended for recognizing that
the most appropriate examination of the richness and
stability of American society is found through the expression
of the rich diversity of backgrounds and the special American
experience of our myriad peoples.

On behalf of the American Revolution Bicentennial Administration,
I am pleased to express appreciation for the significant and
substantive contribution to the national Bicentennial commemoration made by Texas Tech University.

                    In the Spirit of '76,

                    John W. Warner
                    Administrator

AMERICAN REVOLUTION BICENTENNIAL 1776-1976

Certificate of Appreciation

Accorded to

Interdepartmental Committee on Comparative Literature

Texas Tech University

for meritorious contribution to the Nation's Bicentennial Observance

By the
American Revolution
Bicentennial Administration

John W. Warner

John W. Warner, Administrator

Ethnic Literature in America: A Commemorative Address

Alwyn Barr

The Bicentennial of the American Revolution provides us with a unique opportunity and a powerful motivation to explore and expand our understanding of the diverse peoples who struggled to create the United States and constantly sought to revitalize and perfect its ideals over the past two hundred years. We know this is primarily a nation of immigrants because of the great waves of new settlers from Europe, Asia, Africa, and Latin America who flooded its shores, some as slaves but most by choice, throughout the nineteenth and early twentieth centuries. But we should not forget that the varied ethnic backgrounds of those who came earlier in the colonial period may have contributed to the creation of a new American, rather than English, sense of identity which strengthened the drive for independence through the American Revolution. Nor should we fail to recall that the contributions of diverse ethnic groups to the revolutionary cause gave greater force to the successful movements for religious toleration in all states and to the emancipation of slaves in the North.

This comparative literature symposium on the ethnic literatures of the United States would seem to be an especially appropriate celebration of the bicentennial because of its emphasis upon "the many voices of America" and upon one of the most crucial ideals of all Americans, the freedom to express diverse views. Writers of different cultural backgrounds have enriched our knowledge of this nation in several ways. The beliefs and hopes they expressed concerning the United States, both before and after they arrived, helped to renew American ideals of individual freedom, economic opportunity and religious toleration. For literary dissenters from less democratic societies, the United States frequently provided a refuge from which to speak out on behalf of freedom.

17

We must acknowledge the darker side of American society, however, for a major theme of ethnic literature in the United States has been the struggle to overcome cultural or racial prejudice. Such efforts to advance the cause of basic human rights by ethnic minorities ultimately became a major contribution to the preservation of those rights for all Americans. Another theme of conflict for writers of many ethnic groups in the United States has been the struggle for identity because of a dual cultural heritage. Ethnic literature often describes pressures for conformity to dominant Anglo-American cultural values, countered by strong ties to ethnic traditions. These writings suggest no simple solutions to the problem, but rather a variety of experiences. For the descendants of European immigrants the experience might approximate a "melting pot," a term coined by a Jewish immigrant playwright to describe a blending of cultures, though the human ingredients often were limited by religion and race. For non-white ethnic groups the best hope often appeared to be a growing acceptance of "cultural pluralism," which usually meant participating in the political and economic life of the nation while retaining some ethnic social patterns. But despite these tensions, certain broad values seem to emerge. Ethnic writings about the problems of identity should provide insights for later generations of Americans undergoing other forms of "future shock." And surely a major result of increased interest in diverse ethnic literatures will be an expanded American literary tradition.

To promote an awareness of the ethnic variety in American literature is clearly in keeping with the ideals of the bicentennial and also with the goals of Texas Tech University. In recent years Texas Tech has developed an interdisciplinary Ethnic Studies program, which includes several courses in ethnic literature and emphasizes understanding and respect for ethnic diversity. This symposium undoubtedly will serve as a vital stimulant to the efforts of the university in ethnic studies.

Texas Tech University

Photograph of an original acrylic on canvas painting (40″ x 50″) of "The Immigrants," displayed during the symposium. (Artist, Paul R. Milosevich)

Poetry

Pioneer*
1776-1976

Everett A. Gillis

Out of many nations,
many voices,
the miracle of unity:
one heritage.

Nameless, without history,
straddling a wilderness globe,
his wagons creaking
over the mountain passes.

Sowing his cabins
like seeds in snug valleys,
planting his schools and churches
at every crossroad.

Shaping a destiny
with axe and rifle,
racing the sun,
fording the rivers.

Plowing a continent,
forging a nation
from the fires of the sunrise,
the rock of the mountains.

Gone with the bison
and the passenger pigeon,
his monuments map-lines
on the American landscape.

Texas Tech University

*Dedicated to the scholars and to the bicentennial spirit of the Ninth Annual Comparative Literature Symposium: "Ethnic Literatures Since 1776: The Many Voices of America," 27-31 January 1976.

The Searchers

Tomás Rivera

I

How long
how long
have we been searchers?

We have been
behind the door
Always
behind screens and eyes
of other eyes
We longed to search
Always
longed to search

"naranja dulce
limón partido
dame un abrazo
que yo te pido"

We searched through
our own voices
and through
our own minds
We sought with our words

A la víbora, víbora
de la mar
de la mar
por aquí pueden pasar

How those words
lighted our eyes
From within came
the passions to create
of every clod and stone
a new life
a new dream
each day
In these very things
we searched
as we crumbled
dust, our very own
imaginary beings

Hey, ese vato, chíngate

A terrón lighted our eyes
and we watered it and made
mud-clay
to create others in

II

The search begun
so many years ago only
to feel the loneliness
of centuries
Hollow—soundless centuries
without earth

How can we be alone
How can we be alone
if we are so close to the earth?

Tierra eres
Tierra serás
Tierra te volverás

Una noche caminando
una sombra negra vi
Yo me separaba de ella
y ella se acercaba a mí.

¿Qué anda haciendo caballero?
¿Qué anda haciendo por aquí?
Ando en busca de mi esposa
que se separó de mí.

Su esposa ya no está aquí,
su esposa ya se murió
Cuatro candeleros blancos
son los que alumbran allí.

III

Death
We searched in Death
We contemplated the original
and searched
and savored it
only to find profound
beckoning
A source that continued the search
beyond creation and death
The mystery
The mystery of our eyes
The eyes we have as
spiritual reflection
and we found we were
not alone

In our solitude
we found our very being
We moved into each other's
almost carefully, deliberately

Had we been here before?
What do we have you and I?
Only our touch, our feeling
shared, that is all that we have
life in such ways, way
again, again, again
We found ourselves in ourselves
and while touching
we found other mysteries
that lay beneath
every layer of truth
unwinding each finding
another lonely vigil
another want, desire
to find
to find what?

What we always had?
Did anyone know that we
were searching?
That every look toward the earth
was a penetrating search that
had lasted for years
the mystery of time halted
and unknown without
itself discovery

IV

At night we searched each other
Somewhere was the soul
Somewhere in there was the heart
Somewhere in the night
was the lonely eye of the soul
Motionless
Waiting

Sometimes we found it
and slept with our lips
on it till the light fractured
everything

Can we find something every day
and every night?
We believed
yes, we had been finding
for centuries

Other beings?
We,
one,
the very same flavor
the very same
We looked behind heads
at the back of heads
The back of white heads
was less dangerous
Sometimes we turned the
heads around only to find
eyes that didn't see
who dared not see

who dared not be
within our own

No estamos solos.

V

We are not alone
if we remember and
recollect our passions
through the years
the giving of hands and backs
"dale los hombros a tus hijos"
We are not alone
Our eyes still meet with the passion
of continuity and prophecy

We are not alone
when we were whipped
in school for losing
the place in the book
or for speaking Spanish
on the school grounds
or
when Chona,
dear Chona,
a mythic Chicana,
died in the sugar beet fields
with her eight month
child
buried deep within her
still
or
when that truck
filled with us
went off the mountain road
in Utah
with screams
eternally etched among
the mountain snows

We were not alone in death

VI

We were not alone in Iowa
When we slept in wet ditches
frightened by salamanders
at night
reclaiming their territory
and we
killing them
to maintain it as our—
then, our only—possession
or
in San Angelo
when we visited the desiccated
tubercular bodies of
aunts and uncles
friends and lovers

We were not alone
when we created children
and looked into their eyes
and searched for perfection
We were not alone
when taught
the magic of a smile, a kiss
an embrace each morning
and to feel the warmth
and quiver of a human
being

We were not alone
murmuring the novenas,
los rosarios, each night,
los rosarios we hoped
would bring joy and lasting peace
for Kiko
killed and buried in Italy in 1943
or
when we gathered each night
before bed
and waited
for the nightly sound

of the familiar cough
and the sweet/pan dulce
that it brought
Warm milk/pan dulce
opened the evening door
or
when we walked
all over Minnesota
looking for work
No one seemed to care
we did not expect them to care

VII

We were not alone
after many centuries
How could we be alone
We searched together
We were seekers
We are searchers
and we will continue
to search
because our eyes
still have
the passion of prophecy.

The University of Texas at San Antonio

Ethnic exhibit opening: From left to right Wendell M. Aycock, Wolodymyr T. Zyla, James V. Reese (Chairman of Texas Tech University Bicentennial Program), and Kenneth May (Chairman of the Lubbock Bicentennial Committee). (Photographed by Pat Broyles)

Mary R. Kelly, soprano, Texas Tech University, performing "I Hear America Singing," a composition by Mary Jeanne van Appledorn, Texas Tech University. From left to right seated: Alwyn Barr and Wolodymyr T. Zyla. (Photographed by Paul Tittle)

Symposium Lectures

Ethnic Literatures in Pre-Revolutionary America

Brom Weber

ABSTRACT

The concept of American literature as literature written by Anglo-Americans has its origins in a colonial American experience dominated by English-speaking immigrants. This concept long governed American literary scholarship and is reflected in most full-scale anthologies of American literature. Geographical and sociopolitical factors isolated the Spanish and French from the English-oriented Atlantic seaboard and stimulated assimilation of those—such as the Dutch, Swedes, Germans and French—who settled in the seaboard colonies. The American Revolution was led in the main by Anglo-Americans, and its central documents were composed in English. Subsequent cultural nationalism and the linguistic hegemony of American English fostered the unilingual view of American literature, with consequent relative neglect of non-English literary expression in both colonial America and the new nation and similar neglect of the diverse cultural components in English-language literature written by members of non-English ethnic groups. Nevertheless, a valuable ethnicity was sustained by non-English colonial immigrants and revealed itself in the diverse languages, spiritual beliefs, cultural values, and behavior patterns discernible in ethnic enclaves as well as in social conditions of apparent cultural uniformity. Increased contemporary concern with the cultural life and worth of these immigrants suggests that a necessary prerequisite for incorporation of neglected ethnic literatures into the corpus of American literature is a synthetic review of the existing state of scholarly knowledge concerning their existence prior to 1776. A good deal has been accomplished with respect to some ethnic literatures, notably the Pennsylvania German literature, but it has not been brought together with a predominant literary focus and frequently is concealed in studies of non-literary cultural phenomena. This paper, after consideration of non-English ethnicity in colonial America, will provide an introductory review concerned with the form and significance of the known literatures and with such special scholarly problems as bibliography, accessibility of materials, and linguistic requirements for further inquiry. (BW)

I shall hypothesize that, late in August 1776, a unilingual German immigrant not long resident in Pennsylvania was handed an English-language broadside entitled "The Unanimous Declaration of the Thirteen United States of America." The keeper of the tavern in which the German-American farmer had stopped for a few hours of rest assured him that the document was highly important.

Indeed it was! The Continental Congress had approved the Declaration of Independence in July as a collective expression of the total population of the rebellious colonies, including their German-speaking inhabitants in Pennsylvania, Maryland, Georgia, and elsewhere. Soon after approval, Congress ordered that the text be engrossed on parchment. The engrossed copy then formally was signed by members of Congress and made available to the citizenry.

Regrettably, however, the German-American farmer could not read English. No one in the tavern—including its proprietor—could translate the Declaration into German. The farmer stuffed the broadside into one of his saddle-bags, intending to ask a neighbor to translate it after arriving at home. But he had many other matters on his mind. By the time he had completed his journey, the paper had vanished from his belongings and thoughts.

Like his neighbors, the farmer was soon caught up in the turbulence of civil war. If he was a neutralist or a Loyalist, would scrutiny of the Declaration have led him to adopt a revolutionary position? Or, contrariwise, would a reading have stimulated him to become more adamantly neutral or loyal? From a political point of view, these questions may appear too peripheral for serious consideration. A German in eastern Pennsylvania, where Loyalism was strong, might not have changed his Loyalist stance. On the other hand, western Pennsylvania was generally antagonistic to British rule, so that a German in that region probably would have been reinforced in his pro-revolutionary attitude.

If the same two questions had been put to John Hancock, President of the Continental Congress, he might have replied that Pennsylvania's citizenry—including the farmer hypothesized above—had been represented in the gathering of congressional members who drafted and approved the Declaration of Independence. Implicitly, therefore, the German immigrant knew of the document's major thrust and more than a little about its details. At any rate, he was bound by it. Why worry about the language in which the Declaration reached the populace? After all, Congress, though setting forth the Declaration as a letter to the world explaining the inevitability of severing political ties with Great Britain, had not deemed it essential to order translations into the major European tongues for distribution in continental Europe.

From a literary point of view, however, the anomalous situation of the Pennsylvania German farmer cannot be dismissed as frivolous or inconsequential. Disregard or repression of linguistic diversity is symptomatic of modern nationalism's readiness to suspect any diversity as inimical to political unity. From its beginnings, the first new nation of modern times—the United States of America—emphasized one national language, English, and one national culture, Anglo-American. Subsequently, millions of immigrants would be encouraged to blur or forget their cultural identities by deculturative insistence upon one language and one culture.

One eighteenth-century American writer who enthusiastically and memorably expressed the culture's unitary ethos prior to 1776 was James Hector St. John de Crèvecoeur. Born in France in 1735 as Michel-Guillaume-Jean de Crèvecoeur, he lived briefly in England, then spent several years in Canada as a French soldier. In 1759 he settled in the British province of New York, where he was naturalized in 1765 and purchased land for a farm. Crèvecoeur's literary reputation since the late eighteenth-century rests primarily upon his *Letters from an American Farmer*, published in London in 1782 after he had fled North America in 1780 because of his antipathy to the revolution.[1]

The American, as Crèvecoeur envisioned him in the oft-reprinted and cited Letter III ("What Is an American"), was a former European who yielded up his language, kinship, and associated cultural traditions in order to acquire material, social, and political security in the New World. "What attachment can a poor European emigrant have for a country where he had nothing? " Crèvecoeur inquired. His answer was unhesitating: "The knowledge of the language, the love of a few kindred as poor as himself, were the only cords that tied him: his country is now that which gives him land, bread, protection, and consequence: *Ubi panis ibi patria*, is the motto of all emigrants." American experience was wholly transforming: "Individuals of all nations are melted into a new race of men . . . . " Illustratively Crèvecoeur referred to "a family whose grandfather was an Englishman, whose wife was Dutch, whose son married a French woman, and whose present four sons have now four wives of different nations."[2]

Crèvecoeur qualified these remarks somewhat later in Letter III with assurances that "no sooner does an European arrive . . . than his eyes are opened on the fair prospect; he hears his language spoken, he retraces many of his own country manners, he perpetually hears the names of families and towns with which he is acquainted . . . . " But this was only transitory as "Europeans become Americans."[3] Essentially, Crèvecoeur was an enthusiastic assimilationist for whom British culture was the core of life in British America. His letters are ostensibly composed by an English-speaking second-generation American whose grandfather had emigrated from England. They are addressed to Mr. F. B., an Englishman who allegedly had spent five weeks on James Hector St. John's Pennsylvania farm and, upon returning to London, requested Farmer James to write him more about the spirit and fact of British-American life than the brief visit had revealed. In general, *Letters from an American Farmer* expressed satisfaction with Britain's imperial policies in North America and the way of life in the British colonies.

Influenced though he was by French and English literary models, Crèvecoeur seemed oblivious to the potential loss American culture would incur by immigrant abandonment of language and other ancestral patterns. Indeed, he was convinced that Europeans were carriers to America of "that great mass of arts, sciences, vigour, and industry which began long since in the east . . . . "[4] One can only conclude that he did not consider literature an art or else failed to comprehend the centrality of language as the medium of literature. Only when we assume that Crèvecoeur felt content with the domineering presence of English literature in the colonies does his insouciance become explicable. Perhaps the best explanation of his acultural attitude is the fact that *Letters from an American Farmer*, despite its genuine idealism, basically is a work in the genre of promotional tracts designed to stimulate emigration to North America since its initial European discovery. An artful addition to the genre, enlightened and universalistic, Crèvecoeur's work foreshadows the Americanization syndrome of later centuries.

There is nothing surprising or intrinsically more sinister about the British orientation of the thirteen coastal colonies which rebelled against Great Britain than there is about the French orientation of the Louisiana Territory. Conflicting political claims stemming from initial exploration and settlement of the coastal regions by Dutch, Swedes, and other nationalities had been resolved by the rise to power of the English. The latter were numerically predominant in the colonies, despite the co-existence of a heterogeneous population including Dutch, French, Scottish, Irish, Spanish, Jewish, German, and other ethnic elements. Ethnic conflict existed, minimal in the main, but sometimes serious enough to create social turbulence on a local level.

By 1776, however, ethnic rivalries became less significant than unified economic-political dissatisfaction with Great Britain's colonial hegemony. Leadership in the political struggle against Britain was assumed by those of English ancestry, and thus stimulated belief in the idea of cultural homogeneity. It led quite naturally to the assertion in the second *Federalist* paper that Americans in 1787 were "a people descended from the same ancestors, speaking the same language, professing the same religion, attached to the same principles of government, very similar in their manners and customs . . . . "[5]

The author of the second *Federalist* paper must have known that his assertion of total homogeneity was unwarranted. A native of New York, John Jay was active in its political and commercial life. As such, he could not have been unaware of the European, Black, and Native American elements who inhabited the province and the city in addition to those of British ancestry. Furthermore, he needed to look no further than nearby New Jersey and Pennsylvania to know that his generalizations of common ancestry, language, religion, and behavior were inaccurate. 16.6% of New Jersey's population in 1790 was of Dutch extraction; in Pennsylvania, Germans comprised 33.3% of the population, almost as great in numbers as the 35.3% who were of English origins.[6] South of Pennsylvania—in the tier of states stretching from Maryland through Georgia—Blacks were sufficiently numerous to constitute "somewhere between one-third and one-half of the population" by 1750.[7]

Now, two centuries after promulgation of the Declaration of Independence, we are not as ready as so many influential contemporaries of John Jay were to agree that his description of sociocultural uniformity was valid. Though it would have been unpatriotic in 1787 to have rejected Jay's declaration of uniformity, public policy in this year of the 200th anniversary of the American Revolution acknowledges and even fosters cultural diversity without apprehension that it will lead to national ruin. It is as if the federal principle that a national government properly may co-exist with state governments has been extended to legitimate the co-existence of a national culture with ethnic subcultures.

Having begun with a hypothetical anecdote about a Pennsylvania German farmer in 1776, I will now introduce a second and final hypothetical situation. Suppose that a congress of literary scholars such as this one had convened in 1776 in Philadelphia to consider the nature of American literature. The heat of the streets is seeping in and the sounds of political combat can be heard. National unity is a desideratum, but not yet the compulsive goad it will become in the 1780's and later. All about us in the city, and in our meeting hall as well, there is a babel of tongues, English but one of them. In proceeding, I shall, like Crèvecoeur, ask some questions and answer them as best I can. Unlike Crèvecoeur, I have the advantage of hindsight.

When did our American literature begin? Virtually all our authoritative histories, handbooks, and textbooks innocently mislead us with dates in the sixteenth or seventeenth centuries, when European explorers started writing about the American continent or European settlers encroached upon the land. American literature began with the oral literature of Native Americans whose arrival date from Asia antedates the first European's sight of the North American continent. This rich literature was created prior to European exploration and subsequently as well.

In declaring that Native American literature is properly a part of the totality of American literature, I have been guided by a simple geo-historical test. Specifically, were Native Americans inhabitants of that portion of the North American continent now comprising the United States of America? They were and still are. Should we, however, extend our range of inclusion to the literatures of peoples in areas not physically joined to the United States, yet politically a part of the nation? At the risk of seeming to be influenced by mere political factors, one must affirm that the literatures of Alaska and Hawaii are parts of the national literature. Similarly, solely by virtue of having been created within the United Stated and in territories joined to it in pre- or post-colonial times, the literature of any ethnic groups which fall within the scope of this category must be admitted to the canon of American literature.

The addition of a great body of writing to American literature, much of it written or otherwise created prior to 1776, is of considerable impor-tance to scholars concerned with literature in the colonial period. Not so long ago, colonialists were a rarity in American literary scholarship and concentration in the field looked upon as an eccentricity fit only for minds parochial in outlook or insensitive to belles-lettres. A brilliant his-torian such as Perry Miller demonstrated the profound intellectual depth and quality of New England Puritanism, its contribution to the develop-ment of Transcendentalism, and its relevancy to an America beset by crises in the 1930's and 1940's.

Unfortunately, Miller discounted the aesthetic component of Puritan-ism and its expression in Puritan literature. Fellow scholars reared in the midst of the twentieth-century revolt against nineteenth-century tradition-alism were quick to write off most colonial American literature as patheti-cally imitative of English literary traditions. The real American litera-ture, it was said, only began about the 1830's, after critics and writers had struggled for decades with the problem of developing an indigenous Ameri-can language as well as forms and themes equally indigenous. On the whole, significantly enough, the focus was upon English-language litera-ture.

The negation of early American literature was countered by the discov-ery and presentation of neglected and unknown colonial writers whose literary merits and productivity were noteworthy. Thomas H. Johnson issued the first edition of Edward Taylor's poetry in 1939 and soon there-after, in 1943, there appeared Harold S. Jantz's "The First Century of New England Verse," a monumental study, collection, and bibliography.[8] These had been preceded by an 1867 edition of the writing of Anne

Bradstreet[9] and some later editions of lesser New England poets, but it was the contribution of Johnson and Jantz which vivified colonialists. The momentum created led to the further recognition that early American prose writers, some of them not even Puritans, had written commendably in such relatively low-caste forms as biography, autobiography, history, epistle, and polemic.[10]

The experience of resurrecting English-language colonial literature, involving as it did radically new knowledge of aesthetic reality in the seventeenth and eighteenth centuries, indicates that recovery, publication, and evaluation of non-English colonial literature will be relatively more difficult and time-consuming. It was at least possible for Americanists to appreciate Edward Taylor because he reminded them of seventeenth-century English metaphysical poets, but how many Americanists can link minister-poet Henricus Selijns (1636-1701) of New York to his Dutch literary heritage? And what about the literary backgrounds and general cultures of the Swedes, Spaniards, Portuguese, French, Welsh, Irish, Scots, etc.? When one adds to this mélange the Polynesians of Hawaii, as well as the several hundred Native American languages and cultures which abounded in pre-1776 Alaska and continental North America, any Americanist possessed of but a single lifetime might well conclude that his field was being engulfed in linguistic and cultural chaos from which it could not possibly be extricated.

One reasonable way of re-establishing psychic equilibrium in the ranks of Americanists would be to assure them unequivocally that scholarly investigation of non-English colonial American literature is not animated by hostility to Anglo-American literature and its heritage. On the contrary, neglect and misrepresentation of that literature was reprehensible, and the procedures and values which led to proper knowledge and judgment of that literature provide admirable operational guides for those who now believe that it is necessary to plunge deeper into the colonial literary world. Because scholars courageously sought out unpublished materials in unlikely places and did not limit their conception of literary form by excluding all but poetry, fiction, and drama, we learned that the literary mind of colonial American Puritans was sensuous and passionate, steeped in European humanism, variable in direction and substance, all despite a supposedly anti-aesthetic theological superstructure. Writers of other ethnic groups which resided in colonial America may have had similarly complex literary lives which need to be concretized.[11]

Scholars who begin working with non-English ethnic literatures must expect to encounter linguistic and cultural problems. They are not insuperable, however, and not even unique when one recalls that critical editions of such colonial Anglo-American writers as Nathaniel Ward and Edward

Taylor contain glosses of obsolete and dialectal words present in the texts.[12] The archaeolinguists who recorded Native American poetry and prose for us mastered the complicated languages in which that oral literature had been preserved. Americanists can do likewise and, furthermore, should undertake collaborative research with specialists in the languages, literatures, and cultures of non-English ethnic groups. Since translations do not adequately convey many connotative nuances, critical bilingual editions of unpublished and newly translated literature ought to be projected.

How can a scholar interested in the pre-1776 literature of an ethnic group become familiar with the location, availability, and nature of that literature? As every scholar knows, no bibliography designed by another scholar ever is wholly adequate for one's own particular research project. This is especially the case in the fields of colonial American studies and ethnic studies. Bibliographical scholarship in both fields has not kept pace with scholarly needs, may be idiosyncratic or irresponsible, and—as is so often true of bibliographical scholarship—conforms less to general rules than to ad hoc decisions based on expediency, cost, predilection, and the like.

The ad hoc determinants are sometimes beyond the control of a bibliographer and sometimes even beneficial, particularly when they encourage depth or completion of a bibliographical project. I do not mean to be invidious, therefore, in citing the following passage of special relevance from one of the most valuable colonial bibliographies available, namely, J. A. Leo Lemay's *A Calendar of American Poetry in the Colonial Newspapers and Magazines and in the Major English Magazines Through 1765.*[13] In discussing his methodology, Professor Lemay declares: "Poems in foreign language are also frequently excluded; I began the calendar purely for my own purposes, omitting foreign language poetry unless it was of particular interest or unless it was part of a literary exchange."[14] A few poems in French have been cited, but obviously this bibliography is not helpful for our purposes.[15]

The scholar interested in a single ethnic literature or in the whole body of multi-ethnic literature written before 1776 soon discovers that he must serve as his own bibliographer before he can hope to function as a student. No general bibliography of all pre-1776 ethnic literature exists. A number of separate guides to individual ethnic-group literatures have been compiled, frequently by ethnic scholars or cultural institutions, but most tend to emphasize the formal genres of poetry, fiction, and drama and, of these, works created during the nineteenth and twentieth century. They are worth examining, but the scholar must count upon foraging for himself in bibliographies devoted to American literature and, since belletristic limitations in those bibliographies limit possibilities, in bibliographies of American history, anthropology, journalism, autobiographies, diaries, sociology, and folklore. Only time and imagination can limit the extent of the bibliographical hunting. Since most of the scholarship dealing with non-English literature—other than Native American—has been developed by modern language specialists not in the field of English, the ethnic literature scholar's preliminary bibliographical inquiries must include scrutiny of guides to books, articles, dissertations, and other resources dealing with European, Asian, and African languages.

The bibliographical literature involved is so vast that my comments here of necessity must be limited selectively to some of the most important works in the fields of literature and history. The starting point for general investigation of ethnic literature in the colonial period is Charles H. Nilon's *Bibliography of Bibliographies in American Literature*.[16] Annotated and also vastly more comprehensive is the interdisciplinary *Literary History of the United States: Bibliography*, edited by Robert E. Spiller and others.[17] The only general bibliography of early American literature issued in recent years is Richard Beale Davis's *American Literature Through Bryant, 1585-1830*.[18]

Historians at their best have valued historical writing as an art and all writing as potentially artful. Samuel Eliot Morison in *The Intellectual Life of Colonial New England*[19] displayed more perceptive literary judgment of Puritan poetry and prose than most of his compeers in American literary studies. Appropriately, Morison's "History as a Literary Art" occupies the opening pages of Frank Freidel's extensive, interdisciplinary *Harvard Guide to American History*.[20] The *Harvard Guide* is an indispensable complement to the bibliography volume of the *Literary History of the United States*. Even when historians were insensitive to literary values, they persisted in collecting, preserving, and translating colonial writings. Both of these major bibliographies offer many leads to the locations and types of rare materials, many as yet unstudied, in various American and foreign repositories.

Historians of ethnic groups in colonial America frequently provide highly useful footnotes and extensive bibliographical essays. An excellent example is W. J. Eccles' *France in America*.[21] Histories of ethnic groups in colonial America, as well as related aspects of colonial life, are listed in three bibliographies published by Appleton-Century-Crofts of New York: Alden T. Vaughan's *The American Colonies in the Seventeenth Century* (1971); Jack P. Greene's *The American Colonies in the Eighteenth Century, 1680-1763* (1969); and Gerald N. Grob's *American Social History Before 1860* (1970).

Brom Weber, guest speaker and Wolodymyr T. Zyla discuss the symposium program. (Photographed by Debbie Elkins)

Within the past few years, much effort has gone into the preparation of ethnic bibliographical guides. Some of those published have been exploitative, slapdash works and others have been or are being compiled by reliable scholars who responsibly classify and annotate their citations. An outstanding example of the latter type is Priscilla Oaks's *Minority Studies: A Selective Annotated Bibliography*,[22] which includes one section on general works and four separate sections on Native, Spanish, Black, and Asian Americans respectively. The bibliography is unusually valuable because it contains subsections which list literature by and about each of the ethnic groups. Those using the bibliography should be aware that some literary works, other than those cited under the category of "Literature," may be found in other categories such as "Culture."

In addition to published bibliographical resources, scholars should become familiar with the many resource centers in the United States which may be able to answer special inquiries or provide printed materials on ethnic matters. A listing of such resource centers appeared in the newsletter of the Society for the Study of the Multi-Ethnic Literature of the United States.[23] The cultural attachés of embassies in the United States may also prove helpful to scholars eager to learn about the availability of materials relating to colonial America in the archives and libraries of foreign nations.

Scholarly activity in the field of ethnic early American literature may not be to everyone's taste, but it is essential nonetheless. Without it, our literary histories will continue to lack the authority which stems from a comprehensive knowledge of all colonial literary activity; our anthologies will continue to be models of selectivity hamstrung by ignorance. How much longer will American literary scholars neglect the German religious poets of the early eighteenth century, even if only to dismiss them? When will the Dutch poetry of colonial New York be adequately translated and made available for criticism? Questions such as these merely scratch the surface of early American literary diversity. Its full character will be delineated only after the answers to similar questions about immigrants and their descendants, who wrote in English as well as in their first languages, are provided by dedicated scholars.[24]

University of California, Davis

NOTES

[1] The details of Crèvecoeur's life are derived from Thomas Philbrick, *St. John de Crèvecoeur* (New York: Twayne, 1970), pp. 11-12.

[2] J. Hector St. John de Crèvecoeur, *Letters from an American Farmer* (New York: Dutton, 1957), p. 39.

[3] Ibid., pp. 52, 54.

[4] Ibid., p. 39.

[5] Roy P. Fairfield, Ed., *The Federalist Papers: A Collection of Essays Written in Support of the Constitution of the United States* (Garden City, N.Y.: Anchor/Doubleday, 1961), p. 6.

[6] American Council of Learned Societies, "Report of Committee on Linguistic and National Stocks in the Population of the United States," *Annual Report of the American Historical Association for the Year 1931* (Washington, D.C.: GPO, 1932), I, 124.

[7] Robert V. Wells, *The Population of the British Colonies in America Before 1776: A Survey of Census Data* (Princeton: Princeton Univ. Press, 1975), p. 226.

[8] *The Poetical Works of Edward Taylor* (New York: Rockland); *Proceedings of the American Antiquarian Association*, LIII (1943), 219-523.

[9] John Harvard Ellis, ed., *The Works of Anne Bradstreet in Prose and Verse* (New York: A. E. Cutter, 1867).

[10] See, for example, the selected bibliography in Sacvan Bercovitch, ed., *The American Puritan Imagination: Essays in Revaluation* (New York: Cambridge Univ. Press, 1974), pp. 240-58, and the reviews, since 1963, of scholarship dealing with American literature to 1800 in James L. Woodress, ed., *American Literary Scholarship: An Annual* (Durham, N.C.: Duke Univ. Press, 1965-   ).

[11] An example is DeElla Victoria Toms, "The Intellectual and Literary Background of Francis Daniel Pastorius," Diss. Northwestern 1953. Pastorius was born in Germany in 1651, emigrated to Pennsylvania in 1683, and died there in 1720. He wrote prose and poetry in Latin, Greek, English, French, and Dutch, as well as German.

[12] Nathaniel Ward, *The Simple Cobler of Aggawam in America*, ed. P. M. Zall (Lincoln: Univ. of Nebraska Press, 1969); Donald E. Stanford, ed., *The Poems of Edward Taylor* (New Haven: Yale Univ. Press, 1960).

[13] J. A. Leo Lemay, *A Calendar of American Poetry in the Colonial Newspapers and Magazines and in the Major English Magazines Through 1765* (Worcester, Mass.: American Antiquarian Society, 1972).

[14] Ibid., p. xii.

[15] The compilation of an annotated bibliography of American non-fiction prose to 1820 has been announced as in progress by Professors Donald Yanella and John Roch of Glassboro State College, New Jersey.

[16] Charles H. Nilon, *Bibliography of Bibliographies in American Literature* (New York: Bowker, 1970).

[17] Robert E. Spiller, ed., *Literary History of the United States: Bibliography*, 4th ed., rev., II (New York: Macmillan, 1974).

[18] Richard Beale Davis, *American Literature Through Bryant, 1585-1830* (New York: Appleton-Century-Crofts, 1969).

[19] Samuel Eliot Morison, *The Intellectual Life of Colonial New England* (New York: New York Univ. Press, 1956).

[20] Frank Freidel, *Harvard Guide to American History*, rev. ed., 2 vols. (Cambridge: Belknap/Harvard Univ. Press, 1974).

[21] W. J. Eccles, *France in America* (New York: Harper & Row, 1972).

[22] Priscilla Oaks, *Minority Studies: A Selective Annotated Bibliography* (Boston: G. K. Hall, 1975).

[23] *MELUS*, 2, No. 2 (June 1975), 16-19.

[24] Wayne Charles Miller et al., *A Comprehensive Bibliography for the Study of American Minorities*, 2 vols. (New York: New York Univ. Press, 1976) appeared after this paper was written. The massive compilation cites references to English-language

works by and about Native Americans and virtually every immigrant group that came to colonial America, though the Dutch, Scots, and English are not included. Many sections are devoted to listings of fiction, poetry, drama, literary criticism, autobiography, and other genres. Annotations regrettably are minimal, frequently missing, apparently because of the vast size of the bibliography. The bibliographical works and approaches discussed in this paper remain relevant, but obviously scholars concerned with ethnic American literature written before 1776 should begin their research with *A Comprehensive Bibliography for the Study of American Minorities*.

Armenian Ethnic Literature in the United States

Nona Balakian

ABSTRACT

Despite substantial use of ethnic material in their work, Armenian-American writers have generally produced works that can only be described in the universal terms of contemporary fiction. Starting with William Saroyan in 1934, the Armenian milieu in this country has yielded at least a dozen writers of fiction who have been recognized for their literary quality and, among these, several have also been widely acclaimed by the American reading public. (The record is not quite so high in poetry or drama.) William Saroyan's exceptional place in American letters remains unpre-empted so far, although Michael J. Arlen's nonfictional book, *Passage to Ararat*, was accorded the distinction of a National Book Award in 1976. Saroyan's ever insistent humanistic concern (in stories, novels and plays) for the survival of the individual in a mass society and his unequivocal affirmation of man's spiritual being are the loftiest of the Armenian-American writers' purposes, which include a scrupulous search for self-identity and inner truth, reconciliation of opposing claims on the self, and the redemptive power of love. This paper's challenge has been to connect these supra-ethnic concerns with the national habits and ideals Armenians bring from their ancient heritage of more than twenty centuries. Their arduous pilgrimage through history has had the support of transcendent aspirations, and these have also been their mainstay since coming to this country in large numbers from 1895 to 1924, as a result of two attempted genocides to which they were subjected. Although a younger generation of Armenian Americans is increasingly becoming assimilated into the larger American scene, a strong sense of the Armenian "presence" still permeates the prose and poetry of Armenian-American writers. In recent years the Armenian community has accorded great encouragement to literary artists in its midst. A special focus of interest is the literary quarterly, *Ararat*, now in its seventeenth year, where many new writers try out their talents. Aside from Saroyan and Arlen, other writers treated in this article are Leon Surmelian, Richard Hagopian, Peter Sourian, Marjorie Housepian, Peter Najarian, and, more briefly, Katchig Minasian, Leon Srabian Herald, Harold Bond and Diana Der Hovanessian. (NB)

It must be said at the outset of this paper that the ethnic experience of Armenians in this country has been in many respects untypical. Though they came to these shores from distant lands (mainly the Near East), out of a past misted by legend, a little known people displaced and dispersed by two attempts of genocide, the Armenians suffered no great period of trial as immigrants. As individuals, if not as a group, they have sought, beyond acceptance, recognition for their talents in this adopted country. And, in proportion to their number (presently 500,000), they have had a conspicuous amount of it, particularly within the past fifty years.

Since the first Armenian landed in Virginia in 1618[1] historical records show that Armenians neither resisted assimilation in the new culture nor rushed to embrace it. Pride in a rich and ancient heritage which can be traced to the end of the seventh century B.C. has partly compensated for feelings of inferiority in the lack of an independent country of their own. And a tradition of close family ties and community life has helped ward off feelings of displacement while bolstering their natural gift for enjoying the simple things in life. Thus, as a group, they have conformed neither to Oscar Handlin's image of the immigrant as the alienated "uprooted"[2] nor to Louis Adamic's romanticized amalgam of Old World and New.[3] Rather, as evinced in the work of Armenian-American writers from William Saroyan to Michael J. Arlen, the Armenians have delved into their background for those values and attributes linking the human family which lie outside national bounds.

Thus, Michael Arlen writes in his recent book, *Passage to Ararat*: "Perhaps in the end the message of the Armenians is more particular than mere persistence. Perhaps, if there exists a deeper possibility in the psyche of this ancient, sturdy, and minor race, it is this: the capacity of a people for proceeding *beyond* nationhood" (p. 291).

One might label this a defensive attitude not without its practical application to a people which has been without independent rule for the past 600 years and presently numbers a mere five million people. But it is also, as I hope to show in this paper, the ingrained response to transcendence of a much persecuted people, surrounded throughout their history by hostile nations of superior strength and number. Having been among the earliest Crusaders,[4] the Armenians have a long tradition of according priority to the ideal over the real, the larger truth over the immediate, accommodating fact. Thus they have died to preserve their religious freedom, while at the same time holding on to those imperishable traces of culture which are immune to force and even transplantation.

Until recently, scarcely any extensive study had been made on Armenian immigration. The statistics through 1880 could not easily be determined for lack of compilation on the basis of ethnic groups. Thus Armenians coming from Turkey were labeled "Turkish," and so on, according to the region from which they came. There are bits and pieces of evidence that individual Armenian adventurers came to the British colony, to Georgia and to Massachusetts in the seventeenth century.[5] But the significant (and recorded) periods of immigration took place in the nineteenth and early twentieth centuries. According to one classic source, James Tashjian's *The Armenians of the United States and Canada* (p. 26), the following were the largest periods of Armenian immigration to this country: 1834-1894 (5,000); 1895-1914 (70,982) and 1920-1931 (26,146).

Students figured prominently in the first migration as a result of the educational opportunities which the American mission schools opened to Armenians in Turkey. In addition, business people and professionals came seeking their fortunes. These ambitious, well-educated pioneers made remarkable careers and provided leadership for later waves of immigrants. A third group of impoverished Armenians came from the interior of Turkey, many of them settling on farmlands in Fresno and in New England mill towns. Finally, from 1895 and up to 1924, came the major cause of Armenian immigration: the displacement of thousands of Armenians in Turkey through massacre and deportation.

Located at the crossroads of East and West, Armenia from the days of its kingdom has looked West more than East.[6] The lure of America was inevitable. And when Armenians immigrated, they generally tended to stay.[7] This was especially true of those who came to complete their education here. They came knowing their true roots—their Church, their art and literature, their family traditions, their food and their songs—were portable and would find here new fertile soil.

Though the earliest settlers in Massachusetts, Fresno and Detroit became factory workers and farmers, by the early part of the twentieth century the socio-economic status of Armenians had risen sharply.[8] In addition, after the massacres of 1915, large numbers of intellectuals immigrated to the large cities and their children subsequently took up academic studies and entered the arts.

In the introduction to their book, *Beyond the Melting Pot*, Nathan Glazer and Daniel Patrick Moynihan point out the divergences within each ethnic group which make generalizations difficult if not impossible, particularly where immigration is continuous. It would be misleading to suggest that Armenians have always adjusted easily to their new surroundings and have, in turn, readily been accepted by the American communities in which they settled. For many Armenian Americans, as for other ethnic groups, the transition from the old to the new created traumas which can be detected in their literature. In the 1920's and 1930's, when the theory of the melting-pot was still widely held, many of the more ambitious Armenians disguised their origin by changing their names. But as new and larger ethnic groups came along (Blacks and Puerto Ricans) and new concepts of ethnicity developed, fewer Armenians became evasive about their background.

From the older generation of patriot-refugees came a new burst of affirmation of the ancient glory of Armenia. The survivors of the holocaust dreamed now of an independent Armenia; here in a safe, free land they would await its realization. Though an independent Armenia came—and went—like a flash within scarcely a year (1920-1921), to this day the dream of independence still vaguely persists.[9]

Starting in the late 1890's the Armenian language press proved a major force in sustaining, indeed encouraging ethnic consciousness in the older generation. Since the Armenians were divided into political factions, their newspapers were party organs at first, but later became less politically oriented, printing, besides news, articles, poems and stories. Since the mid 1930's English-language newspapers and magazines (*Hairenik Weekly*, *The Armenian Mirror-Spectator*, *The Armenian Review* and *Ararat* are among the most professionally produced) have conscientiously served the cultural and literary needs of the Armenian-American community, both encouraging new talents and keeping the ancient heritage alive through new translations.

Native Armenian literature is too vast a subject to be summarized in a brief essay, but some reference to it cannot be avoided. Unlike European literatures, Armenian literature found its inspiration all but completely cut off when it was transplanted to the New World. Armenian immigrant writers in the late nineteenth century had no ready audience in this country, and it was impractical to expect publication abroad. Thus publishing in the Armenian language virtually ceased, except in the magazines and newspapers. As for those large numbers of Armenians who never mastered the written language,[10] they remained generally unacquainted with Armenian literature, translations not being available for a long time. What the second generation of Armenian Americans (even much of the first) knew of its literature was largely what it picked up from their elders or through excerpts in the English-language press. They knew about but never read the epics and songs of antiquity; knew about but never savoured the masterpieces of the Golden Age of Armenian writing (fifth century), among them the two-volume history of Moses of Khoren, and later, the mystic poems of St. Gregory Naregatzi and the work of Catholicos Nerses IV Shnorhali. To this day Armenians are unacquainted with the troubadour songs of Sayat Nova and other poet-singers of the sixteenth century. And even though many of the poets, novelists and playwrights of the eighteenth and nineteenth centuries have by now been translated in part, these works are not readily available.[11]

Unable to absorb their native literary tradition directly and still insecure in the new, Armenians of the second generation were slow in emerging as writers. Long before they began considering literary careers, they achieved prominence in business, agriculture, the performing arts, medicine, law and scholarship. But the literary gift was there and it would eventually declare itself. History had assigned the role of wanderer and adventurer to the Armenians, and they naturally had stories to tell, endless recollections that by repetition in the family circle took on the aura of fable and legend.

It is not without significance that the first American-born Armenian writer to achieve world-wide fame is one of the leading storytellers of our day—William Saroyan. In the forty-two years since he soared to instant fame with his first book, *The Daring Young Man on the Flying Trapeze and Other Stories*, William Saroyan has never ceased his relaxed, almost effortless "swinging," and by his fortunate example has attracted dozens of writers of Armenian descent into the literary stratosphere, where the going can be rough. In this short span of time, dozens of books by Armenian-American writers have appeared and won substantial critical attention. Some have also won top prizes (among them the Pulitzer Prize and National Book Award), some have become best-sellers and others scholarly successes. Inevitably, alongside Saroyan's genius, his extraordinary versatility, scope and productivity, the other writers' achievements appear greatly dwarfed. Indeed, Saroyan's vast library of stories, essays, plays and autobiographical writings[12] has become part of American literature, with some of his works being taught as contemporary classics in schools and colleges.

One looks for clues to Saroyan's unique achievement as the son of an earlier group of immigrants. Born in 1908 in Fresno, placed in an orphanage at age three when his father died, he was brought up after his seventh year by a mother who worked to provide for a family of four. As anyone might surmise who has read Saroyan's early stories, the writer spent his early years in a rural community largely made up of his extended family and other earthy compatriots. Interestingly, it is estimated that 90% of the students at Emerson School which he attended (and immortalized in *My Name is Aram*) were Armenian.[13] This did not, however, mean that ethnic friction was absent in the Fresno community. Records show that discrimination against Armenians in Fresno persisted well into the 1930's. But the largeness of the Armenian group must have had its supportive influence. To Saroyan's advantage as an aspiring writer, also, was his total lack of intellectual and social pretension (his education ended with high school)—*advantage* because it meant he was at home with "the common man," and found instant rapport with him on an emotional level. "The truth of art is the truth of emotion," he stated pointedly in the preface of a short play, *Opera, Opera* (1942).[14] On these terms, no ethnic barrier could come between him and his sense of elemental kinship with *all* humanity. This found its best expression in deceptively simple parable-like stories.

In the only extended study of Saroyan I know, Howard R. Floan[15] draws attention at some length to the melancholy undertone of Saroyan's early stories (in *Inhale, Exhale* and *Little Children*) without, it seems to me, adequately explaining its chief source: an ingrained, inner rebellion against restraints and injustices everywhere which even the author's irrepressible humor and gentle, lyric responses cannot hide. One has to understand this to appreciate the way in which Saroyan reconciles, indeed integrates the disparate elements of his national heritage and American environment; how even without using Armenian subjects (as has been the case in more recent years) he is able to declare his "Armenianness" to the extent that it has made him what he is.

One needs no systematic survey to conclude that, unlike the literature of many minority groups, the best Armenian-American writing does not hold a brief for the Old World, for another way of life. There is nothing in it to match the sad nostalgia of the Slovenian-American writer, Louis Adamic. In Saroyan's 1939 play, *My Heart's in the Highlands*, about an impoverished Scottish itinerant musician in Fresno, the "highlands" is a metaphor for the loss not of a *place* but of an ideal of beauty and freedom. And some years later when Leon Z. Surmelian speaks in defense of the Armenian cause in his autobiographical *I Ask You, Ladies and Gentlemen*, he speaks not just for one small nation's cause but for the universal cause of humanity. "I cannot resist the temptation to mock any law which is designed to hamper the spirit of man," writes Saroyan in an early story.[16] Indeed throughout his career Saroyan has affirmed that his mission as a writer is that of protecting the spirit of man (what renders him human) from the corrupting influences of society. And from this reverence for man's spiritual being comes the writer's love of life itself.

Though Saroyan's originality as a writer was promptly recognized in the mid-thirties, and his popularity with readers soared with each succeeding volume of stories, the critics of his day generally failed to accord him serious treatment. (To this day there is no comprehensive study of his work and no uniform edition.) Coming on the literary scene at a time when American fiction was weighed down with Naturalism and polemical writing, Saroyan's freewheeling, non-realistic approach, together with his boundless faith in "the beautiful people" (a phrase he coined to mean people with innate grace and goodness), was inevitably misunderstood and belittled. Moreover, his rare humor, his poetic insights into the most ordinary aspects of life, his complete delight in living and his felicitous ability to shift from mood to mood eluded the social-conscious critics of the period.

On the other hand, Saroyan's very personality created a fresh atmosphere. His natural Western brashness, augmented by sudden fame, his complete unconventionality as a writer and person, his gratitude for the simplest things in life—these in themselves were novel and attractive, and the press naturally played them up. Saroyan himself was not averse to drawing attention to himself, and his early stories set forth his fundamental beliefs.

The informal, ruminative tone of his early story, "Seventy Thousand Assyrians" is typical of all his work. In what begins as a low-keyed, light-hearted story, the narrator is a writer who, while talking to his barber (Badal), stumbles on the plight of the Assyrians, once a great people, now a vanishing race: "I am an Armenian, I say . . . I have no idea what it is like to be an Armenian or what it's like to be an Englishman or a Japanese or anything else. I have a faint idea what it's like to be alive. That's the only thing that interests me greatly." In a sudden flash of recognition of his fellowship with the barber, he tells him that he not only does not believe in races or governments but distrusts even languages: "We isolate ourselves in the language we know. If I want to do anything, I want to speak a more universal language, the heart of man, the unwritten part of man, that which is eternal and common to all races."[17]

These pronouncements of universality and fraternity—subsequently set forth with greater artistic eloquence in his two plays, *My Heart's in the Highlands* (1939) and *The Time of Your Life* (1939) and in his novel, *The Human Comedy* (1943)—do not diminish the ethnic dimension in Saroyan; indeed they encourage and enhance it. Through some magic of empathy, he draws his special Fresno-Armenians into the larger scheme of human action. Thus, even as we chuckle and exclaim over the wacky uncles and cousins, with their lovable foolishness and old country philosophy, we feel their kinship as "members of the human race," to use a term Saroyan has made his own.

And here one must point to another fortunate aspect of Saroyan's art. Paradoxical though it may seem, no influence has done more to reinforce Saroyan's claim as an *American* writer than his Armenian background. (I speak here of an earlier American style, not the contemporary, which has absorbed so many foreign influences.) Saroyan's childhood experiences among his uninhibited Fresno-Armenians have left a significant impact not only on his character but on his style, his manner of storytelling. I refer to that often long-winded, indirect manner of the Eastern *masal*, always at its best when it reflects the idiosyncrasy of the teller's personality. If, in

Saroyan, this does not stand out as a foreignism, it is because he manages somehow to blend it with a tradition familiar to Americans—the Western-American oral tradition so effectively used by Mark Twain and Ring Lardner which Saroyan absorbed through his reading and his environment. One need hardly give a representative quote here since nearly all of Saroyan's work is essentially of a piece in this respect.

Similarly to the benefit of his work, the American and Armenian influences cross as well on a moral plane. In his constant search for a universal statement of man's tenacity and resilience nothing proved more inspiring than the heroic story of his own Armenians. Their suffering and endurance through the centuries fused in his mind with the agony of America's impending involvement in World War II and the deep gloom of the depression years. The period in which he was emerging as a writer was a time of levelling off; white-collar workers, laborers, professionals mingled in a common pursuit for subsistence. Economic pressure drew people closer together as they sought solace in friendship, relief in humor and hope in love. Having been brought up to cherish these things, Saroyan sought from the first to bring a more mystical apprehension to the American Dream: "I want to restore man to himself," he wrote . . . "to lift him from the nightmare of history to the calm dream of his soul."[18]

In story after story, he shows the basic goodness of people when they are motivated by love—whether they inhabit a barroom (a favorite Saroyan setting), a barbershop or find themselves engaged in some clumsy sort of business, like one of his uncles who tries raising pomegranates on weedy soil because it is the most beautiful of fruits with its evocations of the old country. Of particular interest in terms of this paper are the stories in *My Name is Aram* (1940) in which Saroyan reveals with poignant force his relation to his ethnic background. It is a continuously affectionate response, flowing from his recognition of his people's moral strength, their often pathetic but also shining childlike faith. Because he sees with the eye of a poet, the reality of the immigrant's life is softened if not wholly evaded. Their problem, he sees, is not one of alienation (they are too clannish for that) but stems rather from the need to hold on to their dreams. Sixteen years later, Saroyan writes:

> What was the human race I discovered in Fresno? It was my family, my neighbors, my friends, the teachers at school, the classmates, the strangers in the streets, and myself; most of all myself, and the strangers who were not strangers . . . . Were the strangers any good at all? Was it possible to believe in them at all? They *were* good; good and hopeless and that is why I discovered art, for I did not want them to be hopeless. If they were hopeless, then of course so was I and I didn't want to be hopeless.[19]

As a novelist in the postwar years, Saroyan's work was less noteworthy. One wonders if the diminishing presence of the ethnic background contributed to his sense of dislocation; life in the Army, in New York and in Hollywood created a new order of frictions, disappointments, disenchantments. Though his mock-heroic war novel, *The Adventures of Wesley Jackson* (1944) and *Rock Wagram* (1951) have some fine passages, of his novels, only *The Human Comedy* (originally a screen play) would seem to have permanent value.[20] On the other hand, his dramatic work has been widely acclaimed and involves him to this day.

Offhand, one would not think that Saroyan could succeed as a playwright. His approach seems too informal, his view of life too detached from personal dramatic conflict. But the theatre has not always concerned itself with the study of motivation and social manners. The earliest English plays centered on allegorical abstractions and pageantry. In its indifference to logical, realistic action, Saroyan's theatre is akin to the English morality play, with characters representing aspects of humanity and actions representing inner, emotional truths. This is not the place for a critical estimate of Saroyan's contribution to the American theatre, which, I for one, find to be considerable.[21] It is enough to point out that in the drama he has been an important innovator. Though Eugene O'Neill and Thornton Wilder (in *Our Town*) had broken through some of the Naturalistic barriers of the American theatre, nothing quite so informal and spontaneous had happened on the American stage before Saroyan came along. Using himself only in bits and pieces through his various creations, he found it easier in the theatre to achieve the detachment that art requires. In such plays as *The Beautiful People* (1941), *Jim Dandy: Fat Man in a Famine* (1947) and *The Cave Dwellers* (1957), Saroyan's stage became a place where a man or woman could shed the false roles life had assigned them in order to play whatever roles they chose themselves. The non-realistic theatre in which Saroyan made his mark would eventually embrace the existentialist work of Sartre, the metaphysical plays of Beckett and Ionesco's Theatre of the Absurd.

I think it speaks for the classic dimensions of *The Time of Your Life*, Saroyan's first play (which won him the Pulitzer Prize in 1940), that two generations since it was written it is still being revived by reportory companies along with Chekhov and Ibsen. Because it is a play that forcefully captures an image of America which Saroyan holds in reverence, it is especially appropriate for discussion in this paper. Set in "an American place," as he calls it, "a honky-tonk bar" in San Francisco, it is a play of contradictions that denies human conditioning. Each of his characters, like performers in a variety show, appears in quickly recognizable guise: the quasi-cynical bartender, the lonely prostitute, the young gambler, the lover, the cowboy, the failed comedian, the bored, passive drunk. Life has fixed them all into molds, though not too finally; the true self, the soul— Saroyan shows—keeps surfacing, refusing to be stamped out. Though he is dealing here with a period of America in crisis—the depression years and the totalitarian threat—the overall theme is of America as a place of continuing promise, where if dreams are shattered they are also easily realized, where the individual remains important, his spirit protected when attacked.

A positive voice in a time of despair, Saroyan's plays have generally been faulted for their false optimism and lack of form. In the preface to *Don't Go Away Mad* (1949) Saroyan admits that his characters and events "turn out better than they appear to have a right to do." But, on the other hand, "despair is never by itself *all* of the story, whether in an individual or in an entire people" (p. 7). It is illuminating to compare this play with Samuel Beckett's *Waiting for Godot* (which postdates Saroyan's play by four years), for Saroyan's is also a "waiting" play. It is ostensibly about a miscellaneous group of men in a hospital ward waiting to die. But, unlike Beckett's pathetic tramps, Didi and Gogo, whose lives have been reduced to boring routines, Saroyan's crew finds itself with a heightened sense of life. Their awareness of the goodness of life and its infinite possibilities to the very end dissipates their fear of death. Keeping ever before him a fixed vision of the human potential, Saroyan in this play, as in so many other works, places before us fragments of what he has called "a world which can be inhabited,"[22] whether or not it conforms exactly to the more commonplace truth.

The Armenian writers who succeeded Saroyan have been nowhere as productive as he, but a number of them have merited serious critical attention. Leon Z. Surmelian is an outstanding example of a latecomer to this country who made his mark both as a creative writer and as a scholar-essayist.[23] Born and raised in the ancient Armenian city of Trebizond, he arrived in America at age seventeen, an orphan of war and protégé of the Armenian poet, Vahan Tekeyan. Instead of pursuing a career in Armenian literature, he studied agriculture at Kansas State, and later turned to journalism in Los Angeles. His first book, *I Ask You, Ladies and Gentlemen* (1945), is an eloquent document of the Armenian massacres that combines realistic detail with personal adventures filtered through a poet's imagination.

For four years after the Turks massacred his people and devasted their land, Surmelian had been a homeless waif. But never had he been so lonely as in his first few weeks in Kansas. In evocative prose that mingles lively incidents with philosophical insights, the young adventurer succeeds in disengaging the inner self from the sordidness around him. One cannot fail to note in this legendlike tale the absence of the conventional portrait of the villainous Turk. Surmelian's indignation, obliquely expressed, is directed not against any particular persons but against the outrages committed by a whole nation. In one of the most affecting and revealing passages he tells how he overcame his feelings of hatred and revenge.

One is astonished to find in a book that tells of so much sorrow the same divine joy in living which we observe in Saroyan. Both writers are idealists. But Surmelian, more directly aware of the suffering which men endure, tries to relate the ideal world to the world as it is, a place where man's courage is constantly tried. He vows at the end of the book: "Not to take my life for granted but always remembering death, experience mortality for all it's worth, as I did once as a child" (p. 314).

In a novel whose subject matter was innovative in 1950, *98.6*, Surmelian continued his philosophical concern with death and survival. Realistic in detail but symbolic in effect, this first novel tells of a young man's bout with tuberculosis at a time when it was still a possibly fatal disease. Though disease has been widely treated in fiction, it has rarely been made the subject of a whole novel. Writing with astounding authority about both the medical aspects of the subject and the everyday life in a TB sanatorium, Surmelian centers his search on the inter-relatedness of body, mind and soul which the illness reveals. Like his orphan-hero, Daniel Moore has faced death and survived; like him, he has "transcended his ego . . . felt he had finally come of age and become his true self and in his true, his present impersonal self, he was unconquerable" (p. 310).

Among the many Armenian-American short story writers who appear sporadically in annual anthologies, none has left a stronger impression than Richard Hagopian, whose first book of stories appeared in 1944. At a time when it was still fashionable to imitate Saroyan, Hagopian in *The Dove Brings Peace* not only ignored the master but seemed to contradict him. There were no gaily philosophical Armenians here, and one character even dared to say: "I'm sick and tired of life. Isn't laughter a luxury in Armenian life?"

Born in Revere, Massachusetts in 1914 (a place he often uses for the setting of his fiction), Hagopian suggests a certain New England austerity in his work. A serious student of music, he taught religion for a while and became a protégé of Robert Tristam Coffin. His stories are somewhat allegorical, with a strain of deep melancholy and moral concern. Unlike Saroyan's happy-go-lucky children, his young narrator, Levon, is almost painfully introspective; he is at best a spectator, awed by what he only half understands. One of the best stories in the volume tells of a friendship broken by unkind words, and the regret—symbolized by a dead dove— which drives one of the friends to his death and the other near to it.

Dealing more directly with immigrant life, Hagopian's first novel, *Faraway the Spring* (1952) tells the story of Setrak, a weak-willed, unlucky factory-worker whose redeeming quality is a deep love for his family.

Setrak has guilt feelings toward his son, a cripple, for he has indirectly been responsible for his accident. The atmosphere of gloom is heavy when the boy is around, but Setrak is cheered by a daughter who reads Shakespeare with passion. One of the poignant scenes in the book tells how Setrak (who has promised his little girl an Easter bonnet but in the meantime lost his money gambling) steals a hat from a department store, and the humiliation he suffers when his wife later makes him return the stolen goods.

In Hagopian's second novel, *Wine for the Living* (1956), the overtones of guilt, poisoned love and hidden resentment are still more pronounced. The plot hovers about the searing effect of a mother's negativism on her youngest son. The psychologically maimed mother, like the morally confused Setrak, is shown as a victim of displacement, which in turn leads to the chasm between the generations. Aside from a Balzacian gift for creating atmosphere that lives and breathes, Hagopian is most successful in this novel in his portrayal of a totally unlovable woman, conveyed with acute perception into the meaning of good and evil, love and hate.

The psychological dimension, only dimly suggested in Hagopian's work, becomes much more pronounced in the fiction of Peter Sourian. At twenty-three, Sourian, a New Yorker and graduate of Harvard, came to critical attention with his first novel, *Miri*, in 1957. A deliberately constructed novel in which all the pieces fall into place, it was praised for its precocity. But Sourian's concern with form, apparent as well in two subsequent novels, does not detract from his major thematic preoccupation: the psychological strains and defenses which an ethnic background can create. Though his work is highly charged with passions and emotions, he inclines toward a sophisticated and deliberate view of the shaping force of the ethnic element. There is no suggestion of man's one-ness in Sourian; quite the contrary—as he indicates by writing not only of Armenians but Greeks and Catholic-Irish-Americans. The surface trappings aside, each group responds in a highly individual way to the dislocation of values, conflicts of purpose and ambiguity of identity with which the hyphenated individual must contend.

In *Miri*, a young Greek refugee student becomes emotionally involved, first with an American, Josh, then with her Americanized cousin, Lexy. To show how differently each responds to the first experience of love, Sourian repeats the story three times, through their separate visions and conditionings. What looms as the greatest barrier, he shows, is the self-created fear of confrontation with oneself. Lexy, who unconsciously draws upon his vital Greek heritage, has an edge over the others in facing reality; devoid of illusions about himself, he is eager, like Surmelian, to experience "mortality for all it's worth," while at the same time he is aware he must "live uneasily ever after instead of happily ever after" (p. 218).

In his second, less successful novel, *The Best and Worst of Times* (1961), Sourian tells another story of self-discovery through love. But because he introduces social status as an additional factor, the novel's inherent point is somewhat blurred. Yet in individual scenes he brings new insights into the problem of conflicting ethnic values on a relationship and the transformations which a stronger set of values can have when it touches the deepest layers of the psyche.

Though less complex in the telling, Sourian's third novel, *The Gate* (1967), deals with a more complex enmeshment of separate lives. This time the separation is created by emotional distortions and dislocations which suppressed and festering pain and humiliation can bring about. Unlike Surmelian's self-transcendent orphan-adventurer, Sourian's first-generation immigrants are possessed of an inner rage for which no appropriate outlet remains. There is no retribution for the Armenian as a national being, and so his rage has become diffuse and is expressed as anxieties and ambivalent feelings toward those closest to him.

The character that Sourian is best able to understand in these terms is Sarkis, who wants to free himself of an oppressive past while at the same time defying assimilation into a society emotionally antithetical to him. Sourian's eye is quick to detect the fraudulent and cynical aspects of immigrant life. Sourian suggests that aspirations of an independent Armenia are no longer even a vague dream and that politics in Armenian life becomes self-seeking and, together with the lure of wealth, a path to power. *The Gate* unfortunately has too many threads of plot and a melodramatic ending that destroys the earnestness of its psychological probing. But there are moments when it touches a nerve of truth and we gain insights into the trauma of loss: "Armenia, what was Armenia," one character remarks, "How could one grasp it? It is everything, yet it was not in the air, not in the room, like a chair, or a table . . ." (p. 204).

The Armenians about whom Marjorie Housepian writes in a wise and engaging memoir-like novel, *A Houseful of Love* (1957) are often as deluded as Peter Sourian's, but they are scarcely aware of it. Living in close quarters (in a modest little brownstone off Lexington Avenue), they not only share each other's problems but bolster each other's often impossible aspirations. Though their English is poor, their prospects modest, these colorful characters want variously to lecture, paint, philosophize, even prophesy. In this "houseful of love" and laughter, the narrator, a teen-age girl of wide-eyed curiosity and precocious sophistication, provides a link between two worlds. The fact that her immigrant family (which includes uncles and distant relatives) has come out of a cultivated background (the ancient Greek-Armenian city of Smyrna) and that she herself is emotionally secure as the daughter of a doctor prominent in the community may account for the relative ease with which she alternates between the two ways of life. She can both empathize with them and view them with bemused irony as wise-foolish misfits. An innate tolerance for quirky individuals makes her seem at first Saroyanesque. But Miss Housepian's charity has its limits and she is unsparing, indeed hilarious, in her caricatures when the situation demands it. At the same time, she is drawn to their "craziness," which she contrasts effectively with the blandness of her "American" surroundings.

What Miss Housepian has caught so well is this eccentric group's rebellion against nothing in particular, or rather against whatever is momentarily an irritant to the spirit. Irrepressible optimists when it comes to the big things in life, these Armenians tend to be pessimists only toward the smaller things that stand in their way. They believe firmly that they will succeed, and they are sure they can overcome all obstacles. Unimpressed by wealth, they look down on the one member who has abandoned the clan to make his fortune. What each of them strives for is self-respect, or rather each other's declared admiration.

A paragraph at the opening of the book bears quoting as a characteristic scene of Armenian life with its accompanying sense of pathos:

> They came usually at dinner time . . . and they sat around the large oval table in our living room—a table that seated twelve comfortably, but if you drew in your elbows and let the silver overlap a bit you could manage sixteen. Our living room was cluttered and noisy and bright, with blue plush chairs (that itched) and three paintings of Mount Ararat . . . done by Uncle Boghos, who had never seen the mountain in his life but who had a vast collection of postcards. It was not until I visited the lady next door one day that I realized how bleak and dark our room really was, for hers, like ours, looked out on a brick wall two feet away. But she lived alone, with her cat and two canaries. (p. 18)

Miss Housepian has not only observed but understood, not only seen and felt but traced a pattern which gives it all meaning in larger human terms. Parenthetically here I must refer the reader to her subsequent book, *The Smyrna Affair*, which took her ethnic interest a step further—to historical documentation.[24] The book was acclaimed as a work of original research.

In Peter Najarian's 1971 novel, *Voyages*, the tug of cultures is complicated by the sudden rift in American life between the established values and those values a new Hippie generation sought to impose on the country. The impressionable hero, Aram, has had a traumatic childhood caught between the oppressive recollections of aged Armenian immigrants and his own observation of his parents' struggles in the drab world of Hoboken, New Jersey where their dreams have led them. His rage against

America for having failed his parents is compounded by his scorn for the "split-level Waspland" to which he is expected to conform as he graduates from college. Aram despises the "success" his brother has found in a mindless, secure, snug world. His shame is not in being Armenian but in being "American" in this period of history. "More, I want more of something. Beauty. Something to make me feel good . . . I want something more than what you have," Aram tells his brother. In a lyric, impressionistic prose style, Najarian suggests an estrangement from America which is partly of the American literary tradition, partly of the Beat Generation, but also partly of the transcendent needs of the Armenian soul.

Though many other Armenian-American writers of fiction are deserving of mention in this article,[25] their work is perhaps less relevant to the subject of this paper than the literary nonfiction of Michael J. Arlen. His recently acclaimed *Passage to Ararat* (winner of a National Book Award in 1976) caps a career which began in 1969 with the publication of an original work about the effect of television on our understanding of historic events, *The Living Room War*. The following year, in a memoir of great sensitivity he sorted out facts from legends about his parents (his father was the British-Armenian novelist, Michael Arlen of *The Green Hat* fame). In *An American Verdict* (1973) he wrote an anatomy of urban violence seen through the trial of the Black Panthers in Chicago. Though this book contained powerful and dramatic ethnic material, it was not until *Passage to Ararat* that Arlen grappled personally with ethnicity.

In a sense Michael Arlen's experience as an Armenian in this country is entirely untypical. Coming to America in his early teens, from a background that had severed all contact with Armenian life, Arlen could "sense something slightly dangerous or second-rate in being Armenian" (p. 7). It was not until he turned forty that, at the prodding of his intelligent American wife, his intellectual curiosity about Armenians was aroused. Many second-generation Armenian Americans can identify with the anxiety he lived through when he suddenly confronted his ethnic origin. "I realized," he writes, "that although for so many years I had gone without my Armenian background . . . at the same time its very vagueness in my life had been a form of protection; the remote familiarity of a dream" (p. 56). What was different for Arlen was that he came to his "education" totally unprepared for what he might find.

Writing with exquisite precision, in a style that consistently involves both mind and heart, Arlen suggests just what it means to be a committed Armenian and the extent to which true awareness of one's origin can alter one's life. Though the book encompasses Armenian history from earliest times to the present, *Passage to Ararat* is much more than a book about Armenians. It is the Armenian theme that draws attention first, because the story has an epic quality and is charged with larger human connotations. If, however, one reads the book with close attention, one sees that Arlen's search for his national roots is part of a larger search for fuller consciousness of the self, for the Truth. This quality of mind—so wary of its own deceptions—is characteristic of all Arlen's writings, including his TV criticism in *The New Yorker*. In this modern, scrupulous stance Arlen poses a challenge to the romantic, dreamy tendency of the Armenian.

In combining his search for the Armenian past with a search for a truer understanding of his famous father, Arlen is suggesting the inter-relatedness of the two quests, both important stages in the journey to the interior of the self where truth and honesty have their beginning. We are made aware throughout the book (though some reviewers missed this) that while Arlen comes to acknowledge and accept his Armenian roots, his commitment remains incomplete—and not simply because it takes time to grow a new skin. The task of assimilating the Armenian experience is complicated by a further fact: Armenia is both ancient and new. Perhaps that is true of many nations since past and present do not always merge; but the historical-political situation of the Armenians has taken them farther away than most from the original center of their cultural past. Looking down from their plane, Arlen sees Armenia as "utterly wild and empty of life . . . a tiny island in the ocean of the Soviet Union . . . squeezed into this rock-strewn, harshly beautiful, relatively infertile northern sector of the old Urartian perimeter" (p. 263). Wryly, he comments: " . . . the Armenians had certainly not reached their present geographical or political situation as a result of any *Armenian* grand design" (p. 264). Later, in America, he realizes: "The texture of my life is American," and while Armenians seem sometimes like brothers, other times they are like "distant cousins" (p. 290). What speaks most directly to his heart and mind is the abstract, collective "presence" of an immortal Armenia and the message that the totality of its experience suggests:

> . . . the capacity of a people for proceeding beyond nationhood. . . . To be an Armenian has meant that one has been compelled by circumstances to rise above or fall below—or anyway to skirt—these so-called imperatives of nation-hood and property and thus has been free to attempt the struggle of an ordinary life, and to dream more modest dreams, and to try to deal with one's dreams as best one could. (p. 292)

A very similar sense of an ideal Armenian "presence" can be felt in the work of many Armenian-American poets. In his introduction to a recent anthology, *Armenian North American Poets*, Lorne Shirinian writes: "It is unrealistic to expect that the Armenian culture our fathers lived and brought with them should remain static in a new land. The variety of subject matter of the voices in this book . . . attest to a change. Yet many of the poets remember. Doing this book I came to realize how strong the roots are" (p. 2).

The form which this remembering takes is never concrete and reportorial; it is always second-hand, most often intangible and abstract, like some melancholy, tender tune heard from a great distance. Thus, Leon Srabian Herald (who died this year at the age of eighty-three) writes in "Ballad," a bitter-sweet statement of his immigrant life, that he still carries "about my neck / my father's gift of long ago / a rosary."[26] Herald, who was born in Turkey, educated in Cairo and came to this country in 1912, learned English while working in a factory, and after serving briefly in the U.S. Army and attending the University of Wisconsin for two years, began writing poetry for publication. While living in Greenwich Village, he published a volume of poems, *The Waking Hour* (1925), and his poems appeared in various literary magazines and newspapers, among them the prestigious *Dial*, which also carried his autobiography in seven installments. With his growing involvement in the political movements of the 1930's, Herald turned from poetry to political and philosophical journalism, publishing mainly in the Armenian press. Vaughn Koumjian, who interviewed Herald in the Spring 1974 issue of *Ararat*, refers to Herald's poetry as "traditional . . . subjective feelings, nostalgia, the conflict of the prosaic and the exalted" (p. 6).

Publishing over a longer span of time, Khatchig (Archie) Minasian has had but a single contact with the publishing world: his cousin and contemporary, William Saroyan. Like Saroyan, born in Fresno, but educated at Fresno State College, Minasian has supported himself and his large family as a housepainter while writing poetry mainly for Armenian publications. Author of four small volumes of poetry, among them *A World of Questions and Things* (1950), Minasian achieves, as Saroyan puts it, "poetic laughter." The questions he asks are earthy-philosophical ones; the end he pursues "the inner joys" (the title of one of his recent poems).[27] Aware of the precariousness of "joy," he writes in a lyric, "On Expecting Friends":

> I must be ready
> to prepare my leap-of-joy
> at the slightest disturbance
> by the arbor bush
> and take my chances
> that the sly East Wind
> is not about again[28]

Among the younger poets, one would like to single out Harold Bond, Diana Der Hovanessian, Aram Saroyan, David Kherdian, Aram Boyajian, Michael Casey and Vaughn Koumjian. Their poems appear frequently in Armenian publications (chiefly *Ararat*) as well as in anthologies of American poetry and national magazines. Most of them have published at least one volume of poems.

Now in his thirties, Harold Bond writes low-keyed, carefully wrought blank verse, often metaphysical dissections of personal experiences which combine past and present contrapuntally. Like Sourian and Arlen, he is wary of the confusion between the true and the token feeling. In a recent poem, "Postscript: Marash," he broaches the Armenian subject with an irony that apposition of past and present invites:

> Now the old
> are so old they have
> grown wrinkles over
> their scars. They picket
> the UN Building
> in memory of the
> massacre. They demand
> justice for the one
> million dead.[29]

Also a New Englander, Diana Der Hovanessian combines her original work with translations from Armenian poetry. Her poetry evokes the Dickinsonian restraint of a very private person. Like Bond, she can be haunted by the Armenian past but feels diminished in contrast to the richness of the Armenians' experience. There is worshipful pride and respect in her recollection of her father:

> My father, a transcendental
> Armenian I can never hope to equal
> in imagery, escaped a holocaust
> of Turks and carved his initials
> in the belly of the Caucasus.[30]

And David Kherdian brings the same kind of reverence to his memory of his father in "On the Death of My Father": "His circling fading time / hovers over my head / his life my own to lose or live again."[31]

Since the writers I have discussed have not yet been writing long enough to have received extensive critical attention, I have had to rely chiefly on my own subjective responses. In certain regards these responses will no doubt be contested in some future time, but in certain essential points they seem to me authentic. It is surely incontestable that the Armenian-American writer, whether writing in prose or poetry, almost always centers his interest in the inner world of man, his inner needs and aspirations. It is significant that Saroyan achieved fame at a time when the Naturalistic novel depicted life in unqualified, brutal terms. Saroyan's plays and stories, with their emphasis on generous human impulses, were in contradiction to the work of his contemporaries. To this day, he continues to write against the current of his time, in the "universal language of the heart."

Since Saroyan, the Armenian-American writer has in general kept alive a tradition in American writing which holds to a fluid and flexible view of human nature. There is a generous acceptance of human weakness and a deep compassion, at times verging on the sentimental, at times almost mystical. A strong moral imagination supports his sense of good and evil. He can be gloomy and solemn, but a certain resilience in his outlook also makes humor possible, and his sense of irony, turned on himself, never embitters him hopelessly toward life.

Though a younger generation of Armenian-Americans is increasingly becoming assimilated into the larger American scene, the sensitive writer— most recently, Michael Arlen—still appears to retain a strong sense of the unique "presence" of the Armenian heritage. Within the community (in the larger cities) an appreciation of Armenian culture is kept alive through the efforts of the Armenian Church and various cultural organizations. In addition, the study of Armenian language and literature is now made possible through the establishment of Chairs in Armenian Studies (at Harvard, UCLA and Berkeley). Nor are the currents of ethnicity from abroad fully spent. On the one hand, there is an astonishing literary renaissance in the Armenian capital, Erivan;[32] on the other, there are additional centers perpetuating Armenian culture in Istanbul, Beirut, Cairo and Teheran, as well as in the monastaries of the Mekhitarist Fathers in St. Lazare and Vienna. Here in America, publication programs of translations and original works are presently under way, spurred by the lively creative focus of the quarterly *Ararat*.[33] Most important for the future of this ethnic group is the fact that it has established standards of literary professionalism. In Saroyan's words, it remains dedicated to "the English tongue, the American soil and the Armenian spirit."[34]

The New York Times Book Review

NOTES

[1] James H. Tashjian, *The Armenians of the United States and Canada*, 2nd ed. (Boston: Hairenik Press, 1947), pp. 2-3. "Martin the Armenian" is mentioned in several papers of the Colonial Records of Virginia.

[2] Oscar Handlin, *The Uprooted*, 2nd ed. (Boston: Atlantic/Little, Brown, 1973), pp. 4-6.

[3] Louis Adamic, *From Many Lands* (New York: Harper & Brothers, 1940). Adamic writes that "the strands of our complicated ethnic past [are] not yet interlaced into anything that gives pattern and texture to our life as individuals and as a people," p. 1.

[4] Christianity reached the southern borders of Armenia as early as the first century. In 301 A.D. Armenia became the first nation to accept Christianity as a state religion. The first translation of the Bible into Armenian was made by Catholicos Sahak in 434 A.D.

[5] Cf. Edward Minasian, "The First Armenians in America," *Ararat*, 9, No. 2 (Spring 1968), 9-10.

[6] Tigranes the Great, King of Armenia (c. 96 B.C.-55 B.C.) welcomed Hellenic scholars at the Armenian court. His son was the author of works in Greek. The last Armenian king, Leo V (1374-1375) was of French extraction, descendant of the French Lugisnan family; he is buried with other French royalty in the basilica of St.

Denis. It is noteworthy, too, that Armenian writers in the nineteenth century in Istanbul, looked to European literature, especially French, for their models and ideals.

[7] Robert Mirak, "Armenian Emigration to the United States to 1915, (I): Leaving the Old Country," *Journal of Armenian Studies*, 1, No. 1 (Autumn 1975), describes in detail how and why many young Armenian students failed to return to Turkey, p. 7 ff.

[8] According to Mirak (p. 22), close to 40% of the employed Armenians admitted during the period of mass migration were of the skilled professional or business classes.

[9] After the Russo-Turkish Treaty of 1921, Armenia became a Republic of the U.S.S.R. As such, it shrank greatly in size and for a long time seemed dormant. Presently it is one of the most flourishing of the republics, with nearly three million inhabitants.

[10] Armenian is an independent branch of the Indo-European family of languages. After the adoption of Christianity in Armenia, a special alphabet was drawn of 36 letters. The ancient literary language is preserved to this day in the ritual of the Armenian Church and it was used by Armenian scholars up to the nineteenth century.

[11] Especially noteworthy and partially translated Armenian writers include the lyric poets, Bedros Tourian (1851-1872), Daniel Varoushan (1884-1915), Vahan Tekeyan (1877-1944); the novelists, Hagop Baronian (1842-1891), Ervard Otian (1869-1926); the short story writer Grigor Zohrab (1861-1915), and the playwright Gabriel Sundukian (1825-1912).

[12] Saroyan's books to date include, besides collections of his writing, eleven short story volumes, eight novels, six autobiographical works and fourteen volumes of plays. His most recent book, "Sons Come and Go, Mothers Hang in Forever" (autobiography) was published in August 1976.

[13] Herbert Phillips, "The Armenians of Fresno County," *Ararat*, 3, No. 4 (Autumn 1962), 41.

[14] Cf. William Saroyan, *Razzle-Dazzle* (New York: Harcourt Brace, 1942), p. 125.

[15] Howard R. Floan, *William Saroyan*, Twayne's United States Authors Series (New York: Twayne Publishers, 1966). Although mainly centered on Saroyan's pre-World War II work, this is the only published book on the writer which approaches him as a conscious artist.

[16] Cf. William Saroyan, *The Daring Young Man on the Flying Trapeze and Other Stories* (New York: Modern Library, 1934), p. 58.

[17] Ibid., pp. 32-34.

[18] Ibid., p. 54.

[19] William Saroyan, "The Home of the Human Race," in his volume, *The Whole Voyald* (New York: Atlantic/Little Brown, 1956), pp. 15, 16.

[20] Saroyan's other novels include *Tracy's Tiger* (1951), *The Laughing Matter* (1953), *Mama I Love You* (1956), *Papa You're Crazy* (1957) and *Boys and Girls Together* (1963).

[21] His best known plays, beside those mentioned in this paper, are: *Hello Out There* (1941), *Get Away Old Man* (1943), *Across the Board on Tomorrow Morning* (1942), *Sam Ego's House* (1949) and *Sweeney in the Trees* (1949). His most recent produced plays include *Armenians* (1974), produced by the Armenian Church Diocese, and *The Rebirth Celebration at Archie Zabalas's Off Broadway Theatre.* (1975), produced by The Shirtsleeve Theatre in New York.

[22] Cf. preface, *The Great American Goof*, in *Razzle-Dazzle*: The entire sentence reads, "The job of art, I say, is to make a world which can be inhabited" (p. 64).

[23] Surmelian's *Daredevils of Sassoun* (1964) is a scholarly-creative retelling of the legendary Armenian epic of oral literature. He is Professor of English at California State College in Los Angeles.

[24] Marjorie Housepian, *The Smyrna Affair* (New York: Harcourt Brace Jovanovich, 1971). This work was the first comprehensive account of the burning of the city and the expulsion of the Christians from Turkey in 1922.

[25] The most interesting among these writers are (in alphabetical order) Harry Barba (short stories, one novel); I.A. Bezzerides (three novels); Fred Levon and Kenneth Flagg (Ayvazian) (three novels); Artin Shalian (one novel, translation of David of Sassoun); Charles Tekeyan (one short story volume, one novel); Emmanuel Varandyan (two novels) and Vartanig Vartan (two novels).

[26] *Ararat*, 15, No. 2 (Spring 1974), 9.

[27] Lorne Shirinian, ed., *Armenian North American poets* (Quebec: Manna Publishing Co., 1974), p. 5.

[28] Ibid., p. 6.

[29] Ibid., p. 56.

[30] Ibid., p. 81.

[31] Ibid., p. 19.

[32] Since 1970 publishing houses in Erivan have been producing some 1,100 books (over 800 in Armenian) with a total of almost 10 million copies a year, according to an article in the Fifteenth Edition of the *Encyclopedia Britannica* (Macropaedia, Vol. II, p. 27). This same article reports that there are today more than a thousand public libraries in Erivan, ninety-five magazines (seventy-one in Armenian), with a circulation of over half a million, and eighty-one Armenian language newspapers, with a circulation of one million.

[33] First published in 1959, *Ararat* is a quarterly chiefly subsidized by the Armenian General Benevolent Union in New York and has a circulation of about 1,000. Its first editor was Jack Antreassian (for ten years), a highly articulate member of the community and himself an essayist. The present editor is Leo Hamalian, critic, essayist and editor of several books of contemporary literature and presently on the English faculty of CCNY.

[34] Saroyan's dedication for *Inhale, Exhale*.

Introductory Remarks about the Black Literary Tradition in the United States of America

Darwin T. Turner

ABSTRACT

In order to understand the literature by Black Americans, one must perceive it as part of the tradition of American literature and also as a part of the tradition of Black Americans. It is American literature in the sense that it has been created by persons influenced by American culture. But it is also Black American in the sense that it emerges from the culture of Afro-Americans, who, aware of the restrictions placed upon them because of race, reflect psychological attitudes and degrees of concern not characteristic of most other American writers. The failure to recognize this duality results from two causes. On one side, Black American literature is separated from American literature by those who cannot perceive universal metaphors in the Black experience or by those who consider Black writers incapable of expanding American literary tradition. On the other side, discontinuities in publication history and forced comparisons with white American authors obscure the qualities which distinguish it from American literature created by non-Blacks. In order that this misreading may be corrected, there must be a willingness to recognize the human condition of Black American subjects and the creative capacities of Afro-American writers. There also must be a more rigorous analysis of Black American literature to identify distinctive qualities. In particular, more attention needs to be given to distinctive purposes, predilection for particular literary forms, identifiable literary movements or periods, a predominance of particular themes, a delineation of particular character types, and distinctive qualities of styles, especially in language and tone. (DTT)

In 1773 Phillis Wheatley, a teen-aged Senegalese, who had been sold into slavery in Boston, published a collection of poems.[1] Her volume was the first by an African living in the American colonies. Thus, it is the first book in the canon of Black American literature. Three years later the Congress of the American colonies published a document declaring those colonies independent from Great Britain. It is strange that, at a time during which the United States of America is celebrating its two-hundred-

71

year-old tradition, there are still many Americans who question whether a tradition can be discerned in Black American literature, which is three years older than the Declaration of Independence. In an effort to dispose of this issue so that scholars of Afro-American literature may move to the important task of analyzing that tradition, I wish to examine three aspects of the problem: (1) definitions and issues fundamental to the question, (2) possible reasons for previous failures to identify a Black American tradition, and (3) elements which scholars need to analyze as they try to describe the common characteristics of that tradition.

The first problem is the definition of Black literature. In his Introduction to *Understanding the New Black Poetry*, Stephen Henderson has proposed five possible definitions of Black poetry (these might apply as easily to all of Black literature).

> . . . we may logically say that Black poetry is chiefly:
>
> 1. Any poetry by any person or group of persons of known Black African ancestry, whether the poetry is designated Black or not.
> 2. Poetry which is somehow *structurally* Black, irrespective of authorship.
> 3. Poetry by any person or group of *known* (italics mine) Black African ancestry, which is also *identifiably* Black, in terms of structure, theme, or other characteristics.
> 4. Poetry by any identifiably Black person who can be classed as a "poet" by Black people. Judgment may or may not coincide with judgments of whites.
> 5. Poetry by any identifiably Black person whose ideological stance vis-à-vis the history and the aspirations of his people since slavery is adjudged by them to be "correct."[2]

If these definitions are considered mutually exclusive, it is possible, by rejecting the first definition, to conclude that literature by a Black American is not Black American literature. If the second definition is supported, then literature by some white Americans is Black American literature even if literature by some Black Americans is not. Rather than engage in this kind of verbal sport, I will define Black American literature for this paper as any literature created by a person of African ancestry who has been reared in the United States or who has lived here sufficiently long to be identified with Black culture. (It is not unjust to exclude white Americans who have written about Black Americans. Shakespeare is not considered part of the Roman literary tradition even though he wrote about Romans, and William Thackeray is not considered a part of the American literary tradition even though he once wrote in English about people living in America.)

The confusion in terminology is not prompted merely by those who wish to designate any work written about Black Americans as Black American literature; it is caused also by those who insist that Black literature must be unique from any literature written by people of other ancestries.

In America, such absolute distinctiveness is impossible. Even though Black American writers undoubtedly have been influenced to varying degrees by African cultures, just as all American writers have been influenced by European culture, Black American writers have been shaped also by the American culture in which they have been reared and educated. Whether one accepts or rejects the standards and the values verbalized as the American tradition, anyone educated in the schools of this nation has been exposed to that tradition and, consequently, affected by it. A conclusion derives logically from this premise: however much of their work may seem to differ from most writings by white Americans, Black Americans are creating American literature and are part of the American literary tradition, even though some editors of anthologies seem ignorant of the fact. (For example, two poems by Le Roi Jones constitute the only Black presence in the third edition of *The American Tradition in Literature*, edited by Bradley, Beatty, and Long.)[3]

If I thus identify "Black American" as part of the American literary tradition, I must be able to justify the concept of such a subdivision. Later in this paper, I will specify elements which I consider distinctive in most literary products by Black American writers. For the moment, however, let me point out that scholars use the term "tradition" so freely that it becomes absurd to believe in a need to justify the application of that rubric. Regularly, scholars identify as a tradition anything that they want to call a tradition.

Broad differences distinguish William Wordsworth from Lord Byron even though both are customarily named as part of the Romantic movement or tradition in English poetry of the first quarter of the nineteenth century. Undaunted by the difficulty of squeezing into a single tradition two contemporaries of the same nationality, scholars boldly dare more. They write about authors in the Romantic tradition of American literature or the Romantic tradition of Western literature. Scholars assert that the literary tradition of Western Civilization extends from the Greeks through T. S. Eliot to whoever is your favorite today. Undoubtedly correspondences exist: during the more than two thousand years of written literature in the West, writers periodically have patterned style and substance after the work of earlier generations. Thus, the English literary tradition is traced back to the Greeks and Romans because Ben Jonson articulated principles of Classicism, because a group of eighteenth-century authors called themselves "Augustans" and "Neoclassists," because Matthew Arnold praised that creativity which emphasizes the totality of the work rather than its individual parts—a principle which he insisted that he derived from the Greeks, and so on. Each of these revivals of "Classicism," however, was a reaction against a period in which there was an apparent absence of Classicism. Therefore, Western literary tradition includes both Classicism and practices opposed to Classicism. Sometimes, scholars rationalize these contrary elements within the same tradition. But all the rationalizations are based on one assumption—that all European and British authors are part of the literary tradition of Western Civilization; therefore, they are part of the tradition which stretches back to the Greeks. It is this kind of reasoning which locks Plato, Sappho, Jonathan Swift, and Charles Lamb into a single literary tradition. Surely, if the conventional concept of "tradition" is defined so loosely for European authors, I have no difficulty insisting that all Black American writers are part of the Black American literary tradition as well as the American literary tradition.

Of interest also in this game of defining traditions is that scholars seem able to begin a distinctive subdivision whenever they desire, despite the heterogeneity of the new materials. Thus, a division of the Western tradition is the English tradition, which includes literature of the Angles, the Saxons, the Normans, the Irish, the Scotch, sonnets from the Italians, derivations from the Greeks and Romans, countless cyclic borrowings from the French, and who knows what else. Other subdivisions of the English tradition are Scotch literature and Irish literature. On the other hand, even though it is written in English, American literature is identified as a distinct tradition, which, according to Bradley, Beatty, and Long, can include such mutually antagonistic souls as Cotton Mather, H. L. Mencken, Ezra Pound, T. S. Eliot, and Mark Twain, but not Richard Wright or Gwendolyn Brooks. Some Americans write of a New England tradition, a Southern tradition, a Western or Southwestern or Midwestern tradition, a Jewish tradition—all as subdivisions of the American literary tradition. Holding in mind the vision of such arbitrary identifications of literary tradition, I often wonder how anyone can dare to reject the concept of a Black American literary tradition.

I believe, however, that serious motives have caused some individuals to disavow a Black American literary tradition. Some repudiators have been conscientious people dedicated to integrating Blacks into the promise of America; consequently, they have challenged any idea, whether chauvinistic or derogatory, that Blacks differ from other Americans in any respect except skin color, hair texture, and such inconsequential physical features. Other decriers of a Black American tradition may be motivated by a racist desire to ignore any evidence which would refute their allegations that Blacks are mentally inferior to whites. Some skeptics of a Black American tradition, however, *would* be willing to acknowledge one if they could discover evidence of a continuity. For this group, I wish to propose possible reasons for the inability to package the Black American tradition neatly.

In order to win respect from the American literary public, many Black writers actually have chosen to prove their skill in the artistic patterns approved by that public. Thus, Phillis Wheatley, to gain a reputation in the eighteenth century, adopted the Neoclassical principles for which John Milton and Alexander Pope were praised by Phillis' contemporaries. Paul Laurence Dunbar and Countee Cullen of the early twentieth century chose as models the nineteenth-century English lyricists whom Dunbar and Cullen had studied in school. In the 1940's, Zora Neale Hurston, in *Moses, Man of the Mountain*, satirically debunked a legend in the manner of her contemporary, John Erskine. Margaret Walker (Alexander) has admitted her early indebtedness to Walt Whitman and Carl Sandburg, whose works she studied and taught. Melvin Tolson, a contemporary of Margaret Walker, patterned after Hart Crane, T. S. Eliot, and Ezra Pound. Frank Yerby, in his first published novel, *The Foxes of Harrow*, borrowed characters and subject-matter from *Gone with the Wind*, the best-seller sensation of the previous decade.

The practice has continued even among Black Americans of the 1960's. James Baldwin's short story "The Man Child" reminds one of D. H. Lawrence. William M. Kelley's first novel, *A Different Drummer*, bears unmistakable resemblances to William Faulkner's work. Le Roi Jones has roots in Dante and in Kafka. Many of Ed Bullins' dramatic devices can be paralleled with Expressionistic/Nonrepresentational experiments of some Europeans and Americans. Adrienne Kennedy, briefly a pupil of dramatist Edward Albee, writes Absurdist drama.

But, even while attempting to rival or imitate the practices of respected white writers, these Blacks have blackened the models. For example, Tolson's *Harlem Gallery* is Black, as the work of Eliot or Pound could never be. By adapting their models, these Blacks transcend any allegation of copy-book imitation; instead, they have expanded Black American literature. Consequently, the mere fact that they have utilized styles and forms of European and British tradition should not imply that these writers are significantly different from their Black American contemporaries and predecessors.

Such an assumption has been created partly by literary historians, critics, and even publishers who have forced comparisons with white writers. Sometimes the literary historians or literary critics may have stumbled into this trap innocently. That is, assuming that white readers would be unfamiliar with examples of Black American literature, historians sometimes have tried to explain the Black writers by drawing comparisons with well-known white writers. Let me use my own sins as an example. Writing about Langston Hughes as a dramatist, I have compared him with whites despite the fact that he is as distinctively and innovatively Black American as any dramatist before 1965.[4] In fact, his dramas are more similar to others in the Black American tradition than they are to those in the dramatic tradition of most white Americans. As another example, in an effort to win recognition for Jessie Fauset, William Stanley Braithwaite identified her as a Jane Austen even though her work could have been compared as validly with that of Pauline Hopkins, an Afro-American whose work preceded Fauset's by a quarter of a century. Such innocent comparisons inevitably distract attention from the continuity of a Black American tradition.

In other instances, the forcing of the resemblance may be deliberate and may suggest the white critic's contempt for the originality and creativity of Blacks. There is, for example, the tale of Roosevelt Smith by Frank Marshall Davis, a Black poet of the 1930's and 1940's, who was an associate of Richard Wright, Frank Yerby, Theodore Ward, and Margaret Walker. The poem reads:

You ask what happened to Roosevelt Smith

Well . . .

Conscience and the critics got him

Roosevelt Smith was the only dusky child born and bred in the village of Pine City, Nebraska

At college they worshipped the novelty of a black poet and predicted fame

At twenty-three he published his first book . . . the critics said he imitated Carl Sandburg, Edgar Lee Masters and Vachel Lindsay . . . they raved about a wealth of racial material and the charm of darky dialect

So for two years Roosevelt worked and observed in Dixie

At twenty-five a second book . . . Negroes complained about plantation scenes and said he dragged Aframerica's good name in the mire for gold . . . "Europe," they said, "honors Dunbar for his 'Ships That Pass in the Night' and not for his dialect which they don't understand"

For another two years Roosevelt strove for a different medium of expression

At twenty-seven a third book . . . the critics said the density of Gertrude Stein or T. S. Eliot hardly fitted the simple material to which a Negro had access

For another two years Roosevelt worked

At twenty-nine his fourth book . . . the critics said a Negro had no business imitating the classic forms of Keats, Browning and Shakespeare . . . "Roosevelt Smith," they announced, "has nothing original and is merely a blackface white. His African heritage is a rich source should he use it"

So for another two years Roosevelt went into the interior of Africa

> At thirty-one his fifth book ... interesting enough, the critics said, but since it followed nothing done by any white poet it was probably just a new kind of prose
>
> Day after the reviews came out Roosevelt traded conscience and critics for the leather pouch and bunions of a mail carrier and read in the papers until his death how little the American Negro had contributed to his nation's literature.[5]

Smith's first books are said to be an imitation of Sandburg, Masters, Lindsay, Stein, Eliot, Keats, Shakespeare, Browning. Those authors represent such a wide range of poetic style and substance that it might be difficult for any poet to avoid resembling at least one; yet Black Roosevelt Smith is accused of imitation and denounced for it.

If we turn from Davis' poetic statement to actuality, we can note similar criticism of Black Americans. Even though William Dean Howells judged Dunbar's dialect poetry to be a significant contribution to American literature,[6] one of my own teachers castigated Dunbar as an inferior poet capable only of bad imitations of James Whitcomb Riley. One wonders about Robert Bone's assertion that Charles Chesnutt would never have conceived of *The Conjure Tales* if Joel Chandler Harris had not written the Uncle Remus stories.

Bone, in fact, outdistances most contemporary critics in finding unsuspected white sources for Black literature. Some of his contentions would be amusing if they were not infuriatingly condescending. For example, in a recent book, Bone tries to explain the concept of an oral tradition (which identifies a literature passed from generation to generation by word of mouth). Immediately afterwards Bone reveals his own inability to understand the concept of an oral tradition; for he insists that, if Joel Chandler Harris had not collected Black folktales, these tales would no longer exist —even though some of them had been transmitted from generation to generation by Blacks for centuries before Harris was born. Soon, Bone exceeds the extreme in his effort to find a white author in the woodpile of every Black. Because Ralph Ellison, in *Invisible Man*, once identifies the narrator as Bruh Rabbit, Bone suggests that Ellison could not have created this image, and could not have written *Invisible Man*, if Harris had not collected Black folktales.

Even Black literary historians have forced these comparisons—on a milder scale, of course: W. E. B. DuBois blamed Carl van Vechten's influence for Claude McKay's *Home to Harlem*, despite McKay's protests that he had written the work before *Nigger Heaven* was published.

If one considers once more the tale of Roosevelt Smith, one notices that when Smith draws from a Black tradition, his work is dismissed as non-artistic because no white person has created a previous model. Such a critical approach might have eliminated respect for Langston Hughes' blues and bop poetry if Hughes had not forced critics to search in Black music for the patterns appropriate to his rhythms.

The tendency to prefer forms and attitudes familiar to white readers may have interrupted the appearance of a Black American tradition by preventing the publication of some works. Ever since Phillis Wheatley, most Black American writers have been forced to publish their books through white firms. It is impossible to know how many books continuing a Black American tradition have been rejected because prospective publishers were unfamiliar with the form or style.

Furthermore, how many Black American works have been rejected because publishers suspected that an excess of Afro-American books on the market that season would limit sales or because publishers feared alienating the white market? Certainly there is evidence of the former in Langston Hughes' complaint that publishers told him that they wanted only one or two Negro books during a year. Evidence of restrictions based upon publisher's fears of alienating a public can be found in the difficulty Charles Chesnutt experienced when he tried to publish *The House Behind the Cedars*, his first completed book.[7] Undoubtedly, in the early 1890's publishers trembled at the thought of possible reactions to a story in which fair-skinned Blacks successfully and happily pass for white, a story in which a white southern aristocrat proposes to marry a beautiful fair-skinned acquaintance—until he discovers her African ancestry. Even though Chesnutt had a completed manuscript, his publishers offered instead to produce a collection of his folktales if he would write more. That collection, *The Conjure Woman and Other Tales*, was deemed a less dangerous book because the framework of those tales resembled the framework of Harris' Uncle Remus tales. Next, Chesnutt's publishers accepted *The Wife of His Youth*, a collection of stories satirizing and defending Blacks. Finally, they risked *The House Behind the Cedars*.

Frank Yerby's first completed novel was a so-called "protest" story, an example of the kind of literature created by such contemporaries as Wright, Chester Himes, Ann Petry, Melvin Tolson, and Margaret Walker (Alexander) in the late Thirties and early Forties. When publishers made clear that they did not want a protest novel, Yerby turned to the historical romance popularized by Margaret Mitchell and other contemporaries. After his first best-seller, Yerby almost mockingly continued on the best-seller list by adapting, to his own purposes, models provided by Shakespeare, Sinclair Lewis, and other white authors.

On the surface, poetry might seem less restricted by white publishers, for the lower costs of producing short books of poetry may permit authors to publish their own. But it is difficult to verify the presence or absence of a continuous tradition when proof depends upon "vanity" books. On one hand, because most privately printed books have limited distribution, one may wonder about the actual influence of such books on subsequent writers. For example, Fenton Johnson, at the beginning of the twentieth century, Frank Davis in the 1930's, and Don L. Lee in the 1960's are within the same poetic tradition. But did Davis and Lee know the work of the earlier writers, or did Davis and Lee presume that they were original? On the other hand, literary historians must hesitate before discounting the possible influence of such vanity works. Literature unknown to scholars who depend upon the Library of Congress may be familiar to Black authors who have secured privately printed books through Black churches and bookstores, or who have heard the stories from Black teachers or other narrators in the Black American community. Consider, then, the problem of the literary historian who wishes to argue for a continuing tradition in Black American poetry. Many readers today know the poetry of Langston Hughes, who began his career in the 1920's, and Don L. Lee, of the 1960's. Fewer have read the work of the previously mentioned Johnson and Davis or Sterling Brown in the Thirties. If one knows only the work of Hughes and Lee, one may surmise erroneously either that Lee is different from other Black American writers or that he was preceded only by Langston Hughes. If, however, Brown, Davis, and others are revealed, suddenly one sees a fifty-year line of Black American poets who, in Black idiom, rhythm, and style, wrote proudly, bitterly, and satirically about the masses of Black American people—the so called "common" folk.

Despite the difficulty of documenting a Black American literary tradition, I maintain that one can be postulated and that it is possible to identify some elements which scholars and historians must search for as they try to define the common characteristics of that tradition. Once more let me remind you that I do not imply that these distinctive elements cause the works to fall outside the canon of American literature. But I do believe that they are distinctive/different from the approaches used by white Americans, so different at times as to justify the concept of a Black American aesthetic—that is, a Black American perspective for examining and creating literature.

Any contemporary student of literature by Black Americans knows that the term "Black Aesthetic" has provoked far more controversy than has the concept of a Black American literary tradition. I do not propose to analyze that issue, which is more often discussed politically than artistically or philosophically. Nor do I pretend that all proponents of a Black Aesthetic have been persuasive, either in theory or in practice.

But, if the concept of an aesthetic includes appreciation of ideas and institutions as well as art works, I consider it absurd to presume that a group restricted because of its appearance or ancestry should not favor some ideas dramatically opposed to those of the majority of nonrestricted citizens. For example, Richard Wright's fiction of the 1930's and 1940's is predicated upon the assumption that Black Americans live in a society in which they are continuously encompassed by violence, which may engulf them at unpredictable times. Certainly this attitude, shared by many Blacks, contrasts with the philosophy evidenced in most literature by white Americans of Wright's time.

In the interests of brevity, I have designed my list of distinctive elements to be suggestive rather than all-inclusive. I will even omit such frequently discussed matters as uses of and derivations from folksong, folktale, folklore. For a thorough discussion of such qualities in Black poetry, I refer you once more to Stephen Henderson's Introduction.

First, most Black American writers have had a distinctive purpose. Although some have desired merely to entertain, to create art, or to earn money, most have used their work for educational purposes. Desiring to be part of the American dream and believing that educated Blacks must prepare the way for their fellow Blacks, one group has sought to educate white America to understand the condition and psychology of Black Americans. Simultaneously these writers have wanted to demonstrate their proficiency in the styles most respected by white American literary critics. This group of writers has practiced in all genres for more than two hundred years: it includes, in fiction, writers from William Wells Brown (*Clotel*) before the Civil War to Ernest Gaines (*The Autobiography of Miss Jane Pittman*) today; in autobiography, those from Frederick Douglass' *Narrative*, written as a fugitive slave, to Claude Brown's *Manchild* of the 1960's; in essays, from Richard Allen, defending Blacks against allegations of cowardice during a plague in Philadelphia in the eighteenth century, to James Baldwin, John Killens, and Eldridge Cleaver, attempting to explain Black psychology to white Americans of the present generation; in poetry, from Phillis Wheatley, proving in the eighteenth century that an "Afric" could be moral and literate, to Michael Harper today.

These writers did not prepare tracts focused on the theme of Black need. Often the education was tendered subtly, as in their assumption that their own excellence would educate readers to discern the artistic potential of Black Americans in general. But, whether education was direct or implicit, the purpose always underscored their work.

This large group of writers—far too numerous to be named—includes many of the best-known, a rather probable condition since they wanted their work to be distributed among and known by the white community. A representative list, in addition to those already named, includes Frances Harper, a nineteenth-century poet who promoted abolition, temperance and women's rights; Charles Chesnutt, who, at the turn of the century, depicted the culture and "Americanness" of educated Blacks; W. E. B. DuBois, who, in the essays of *The Souls of Black Folk* (1903), explained the Black American psychology, culture, and condition in words meaningful for our own time; James Weldon Johnson, who in the second and third decades of the twentieth century, praised Black musical contributions in his fiction and demonstrated the beauty and dignity of Black sermons in his poetry; Georgia D. Johnson, who at the time of World War I, poetically bared the heart of a Black woman. In the 1920's, Jean Toomer sketched the conflicts between Black people and middle-class mores. Countee Cullen received praise in the 1920's for his lyric resemblance to A. E. Housman, Edna St. Vincent Millay, and others; and in the 1930's Cullen tried to counteract Carl van Vechten's *Nigger Heaven* by depicting the lives of ordinary, "decent" folk of Harlem. Melvin Tolson, in the Forties, evoked admiration from Karl Shapiro and Allen Tate for his verbal facility in poetry in which he commemorated Black American heroes and legends. Gwendolyn Brooks, in the Forties, won a Pulitzer Prize for poetry about Black people on the Southside of Chicago; and her contemporary Robert Hayden, winner of the Poetry Award at the First Festival of Black and African Arts in 1965, recreated Black history. James Baldwin and Eldridge Cleaver, carelessly grouped as political militants of the 1960's, wrote essays to explain Black American thought; Ernest Gaines delineated the Black reaction to America of the past hundred years through Miss Jane Pittman, a former slave.

But there is a parallel group of Black Americans, also within the Black American tradition: those who consciously have written to educated *Black* audiences to their needs and their condition.

An abbreviated list includes the murdered David Walker, who, in 1828, wrote essays attacking white American oppression and urging Blacks to educate themselves and to rebel against slavery; Martin Delaney, who advocated Black rebellion in his fiction and Black emigration in his nonfiction; Sutton Griggs who proposed a separate Black state in his fiction at the turn of the century; Monroe Trotter, who, in his newspaper—*The Guardian*, vitriolically opposed the policies of Booker T. Washington. The list would include Fenton Johnson, Hughes, and Frank Marshall Davis. It would include Oscar Micheaux, who wrote books to advocate Black capitalism, published them at his expense, and traveled from city to city to sell them in Black churches. And, in the past decade, the list would include such Black Arts writers as poets Amiri Baraka, Don Lee, Sonia Sanchez, Sarah Fabio, and dramatists Ed Bullins, Charles Russell, and Joseph Walker.

Whether in the first or second classification, the writers are part of a tradition which has a purpose distinctive from that of white Americans—

either to educate white America to the conditions of Blacks or to educate Black Americans themselves.

Many scholars and critics profess to find the most obvious tradition of Black American literature in the repetition of particular themes or subjects. Sometimes, however, scholars' fascination with exciting or significant themes has caused them to misconstrue the total picture. For example, sometimes the works of James Baldwin, Ed Bullins, and many Black Arts poets are cited as examples of the theme of violence in Black literature. A more perceptive analysis of these writings reveals the authors' strong emphasis on the need for love. The tendency of certain scholars to perceive only selected Black themes can be further evidenced by the miasma of Robert Bone. In his first book, Bone insisted that all Black fiction writers emphasized assimilation or nationalism. In his second book, although he examines the same writers who were the subject of his earlier work, Bone insists that the fiction of Black writers reveals either their acceptance of a heritage of Black folk culture or their repudiations of that folk heritage. Such willful simplifications look good on the vitae of academicians but interfere with attempts to analyze the *actual* correspondences in Black American literature.

Despite such misleading analyses of Black themes, a few patterns can be perceived. First, some themes, though familiar in the works of all Americans, have appeared with a higher frequency in the literature of Blacks than in the literature of whites. For example, "liberation" has been a theme of writers of all nations, but Stephen Henderson identifies it as the predominant theme of Black poets. Similarly "survival against oppression" is a frequent theme in literature, but it is especially familiar in Black literature, where it rivals (or is synonymous with) "liberation" in popularity.

Second, many themes recur in more than one generation of Black Americans. For example, themes link the poetry of the Harlem Renaissance (which some scholars unfortunately recall primarily as a period of exoticism) and Black Arts poetry (which some scholars erroneously describe only as poetry and drama of hatred, violence, and militancy). In the works of these writers of the 1920's and the 1960's and 1970's, more perceptive readers discover such emphases as liberation, alienation, reaction against oppression, satiric portrayals of foolish Blacks, and pride in Black people generally. "Black is beautiful" is a theme which extends from David Walker's *Appeal* (1829) to Black Arts today.

Third, a few themes seem distinctively Black American rather than white American. For example, few whites have emphasized the following which Sterling Brown identified as themes of the Renaissance:

> A discovery of Africa as a source for race pride, a use of Negro heroes and heroic episodes from American History . . . a treatment of the Negro masses

frequently of the folk, less often of the workers' with more understanding and less apology.[8]

There seems to be a distinctiveness in Black American treatment of such a theme as color-consciousness, which generated Brown's *Clotel*, Chesnutt's *The House Behind the Cedars*, James Weldon Johnson's *The Autobiography of an Ex-Coloured Man*, Wallace Thurman's *The Blacker the Berry*, George Schuyler's *Black No More*, Jessie Fauset's *Comedy American-Style*, Himes' *The Third Generation*, and others. White American authors who have explored the theme of color-consciousness most often have limited themselves to such obvious issues as "passing" or the internal tension of mulattoes who want to be accepted by white society. Perceptively, Black writers have found more varied conflicts. Fauset and Himes show the interfamilial tensions caused by a mother who favors her children according to the degree with which they resemble Caucasians. Thurman describes a dark-skinned Black American woman frustrated by the fact that, even though she is restricted by her Negroid appearance, she favors the same color standards that are used against her.

Moreover, even when Blacks do not use color-consciousness as a theme, they frequently "saturate" their works with awareness of color. Dunbar's villains are yellow-skinned, McKay revels in descriptions of varied colors in *Home to Harlem*, Himes picturesquely emphasizes the color of his characters, and so on.

This matter of saturation, as Henderson suggests, may be more important to a concept of a Black American tradition than any overt consideration of common themes or subjects. For example, except for William Stanley Braithwaite, who deliberately chose to write poetry which would not disclose his heritage, it is difficult to think of any Black writer whose composite work does not reveal either an awareness of the meaning of being Black in America or a pride in his or her identity as a Black.

Saturation, as Henderson has admitted, is difficult to define. It is not merely a matter of conscious allusion in order to educate white audiences to an awareness of the Black past. Nor is it merely a conscious use of Black idiom, in the manner of Zora Neale Hurston, who wanted to reveal the metaphorical quality of Black speech.

Saturation is more incidental and more pervasive. It is the Black American writer's sensitivity to the probable reaction of a Black character to a particular act of oppression; many sympathetic white authors will describe a reaction which Black readers judge to be overstated or understated. Saturation is an almost intuitive dependence upon allusions to and use of Black tradition, customs, heroes, heroic legend, folklore, and language or unique rhetorical devices.

For example, one often needs to explain to white audiences such rhetorical devices as "signifiying" and "the dozens"; yet one finds Black

84

writers using them (often in sanitized form) as a natural part of the dialogue of their characters. The call-and-response, a common feature of the service of some Black churches, is used almost casually by such a writer as Ellison in "Mr. Toussan," a short story in which two Black youths alternate in roles as caller and responder to create a myth about the history of Toussaint l'Ouverture, liberator of Haiti.

A similar quality of saturation may be a distinctive tone, sometimes identified as the "blues tone," an unusual mixture of humor and pathos which runs through the work of even the most serious and elegant (if you will) Black writers. In Ellison's *Invisible Man*, for example, there is the incident in the paint factory when the protagonist, in the midst of a fight, thinks that he has been stabbed but discovers that he has fallen on his opponent's false teeth, which had dropped on the floor. I do not find such mixtures of pathos and ironic humor in most white American literature.

Saturation may be evidenced perhaps by the manner in which particular aspects of Black culture affect all elements of Black writing. For example, the importance of the church in Black American life is unmistakably evidenced in Black American writing. It has constituted subject and setting, as in Baldwin's *Go Tell It on the Mountain* and *The Amen Corner* and Langston Hughes's *Tambourines to Glory*. It has provided theme and motivation, as in Baldwin's *Blues for Mr. Charlie* or Cullen's *One Way to Heaven*. It has provided archetypal characters, such as the religious gossip or signifier, who appears not only as a participant in the church setting of *The Amen Corner* but even as the narrator of Paul Laurence Dunbar's *The Party*. James Weldon Johnson's use of Black sermons as subjects in *God's Trombones* is well-known. Less often considered is the fact that a significant number of seemingly dissimilar Black writers all have written Black sermons in their poetry or fiction, almost as if the sermon were an essential creative element: Dunbar, Countee Cullen, Zora Neale Hurston, Richard Wright ("The Man Who Lived Underground"), Ralph Ellison, and James Baldwin all have consciously imitated Black sermons in works which vary widely in themes and purpose. It is even possible that Black sermons have influenced the style and form of writers who customarily would not be identified as religious. For instance, I wrote in an earlier paper:

> ... How many works by Afro-Americans derive their form (or imagery and rhetoric) from the author's unconscious echo of sermons? When they are judged according to the literary prescriptions of Henry James, W. E. B. DuBois's novels seem to be a chaotic mixture of fantasy and social realism: Does the mixture merely demonstrate DuBois's ineptness, his failure to blend the regional romance popular at the end of the nineteenth century with the social criticism which became popular in the early years of the twentieth; or does the mixture reveal DuBois's unconscious echo of a black preacher's characteristic use of allegorical romance as a device to vivify the social message in his sermon?[9]

As I have stated, my discussion of the distinguishing elements of a Black American tradition is suggestive rather than exhaustive. Scholars who propose to describe the tradition thoroughly must search for such distinctive Black characters as an archetypal image of a grandmother. White authors frequently suggest that all Black women past forty are fat; they are jovial Mammies. In contrast, many Black writers create elderly women who are wiry rather than obese, and who are both wise in thought and childlike in action. Examples are the grandmothers in Kristin Hunter's *God Bless the Child*, in Joseph Walker's *The River Niger*, and in Louis Peterson's *Take a Giant Step*; the aunt in Cullen's *One Way to Heaven*; and even Miss Jane Pittman.

Scholars need to look at literary periods during which a significant number of writers were following corresponding routes. I am not referring merely to the number of now-unknown poets who used "Black" dialect in the decade following Dunbar's first popularity, the numbers who participated in the "coon" shows of the late nineteenth century, or those who paraded the supposed exoticism of the literature of the 1920's. Instead, I am pointing to the fact that the best-known Black writers from 1890-1910—Chesnutt, Dunbar, Dubois, Hopkins, Griggs—were all trying, in different ways, to demonstrate to white Americans that Blacks should be respected for their virtues. In the 1940's and 1950's Black novelists moved from overt criticism of the treatment of Blacks, to attention to white protagonists and emphasis upon the similarity of Blacks to whites, to exploration of Black identity.

Scholars must also examine possible distinctions in form: Dunbar's earliest stories in *Folks from Dixie* are criticized for structural weaknesses. Since Dunbar handles narratives well in poetry, is it possible that in prose he was influenced by the rambling quality of the folktale?

I would even suggest the possibility of a distinctive kind of novel, which, following the pattern of slave narratives, structures itself according to (1) description of the conditions of oppression, (2) explanation of the source of the desire to free oneself from oppression, (3) description of the manner of escape from oppression, and (4) consideration of whether the new freedom corresponds with the ideal of freedom. This pattern can be considered in analysis of the structure not only of such well-known novels as *Native Son*, *The Outsider*, and *Invisible Man*, but also of less well-known novels, such as Kristin Hunter's *God Bless the Child*.

Even if Black Americans have not created totally new forms, they have shown predilections for particular types. For example, the pageant has been more important in twentieth-century Black American drama than in white American drama, which has minimized community theatre in its emphasis on commercial production. Black American drama has emphasized a pageantry extending from Willis Richardson, May Miller, W. E. B.

DuBois, and Langston Hughes (*Don't You Want to Be Free?*) to Amiri Baraka (*Slave Ship*) and some of the ritualistic drama of the Black Arts movement in Barbara Ann Teer's theater, the Kuumba Players of Val Ward in Chicago, and the New Lafayette Theater.

In poetry, the blues form might be considered distinctive. While it may not be considered "form" as such, declamatory poetry has been the style of major Black American poets far more than it has been the style of major white American poets. Dunbar, J. W. Johnson, Hughes, Sterling Brown, and the Black Arts poets are merely a few who have written declamatory poetry, perhaps in continuation of the oral tradition of African and Afro-American culture.

How should I conclude? Let me merely restate that there is a Black American literary tradition. It is Black. And it is American. Instead of spending time debating the question of its existence, let scholars follow the practice of that artist who, seeing his first elephant, drew what he saw without worrying about whether what he saw was real. Let Black writers follow Alain Locke's admonition to derive substance and style from their cultural heritage, but let them also have the freedom to borrow where they wish, with the knowledge that, doing so, they expand the Black American literary tradition rather than diminish it.

The University of Iowa

NOTES

[1] For publications by Phillis Wheatley, see *A Dictionary of Books Relating to America: From Its Discovery to the Present Time*, XXVIII, 168-73.

[2] Stephen Henderson, *Understanding the New Black Poetry* (New York: William Morrow & Co., Inc., 1973), p. 7.

[3] Sculley Bradley, Richmond Croom Beatty and E. Hudson Long, eds., *The American Tradition in Literature*, 3rd ed. (New York: W. W. Norton & Co., Inc., 1967), II, 1721-23.

[4] Darwin T. Turner, "Langston Hughes as Playwright," *CLA Journal*, 11 (June 1968), 297-309.

[5] Frank Marshall Davis, "Roosevelt Smith," in *Understanding the New Black Poetry*, pp. 146-47.

[6] William Dean Howells, "Introduction," *Lyrics of Lowly Life* (New York: Dodd, Mean & Co., 1896), p. xix.

[7] Darwin T. Turner, "Introduction," *The House Behind the Cedars*, by Charles W. Chesnutt (New York: Collier, 1969), pp. xiv-xv, xvii.

[8] Sterling A. Brown, *American Negro Poetry and Drama, and the Negro in American Fiction* (New York: Atheneum, 1969), p. 61.

[9] Darwin T. Turner, "Notes in Chaos: Issues in Interpreting and Evaluating Literature by Afro-Americans," unpublished lecture.

The Chicanos:
An Overview

Edmundo García-Girón

ABSTRACT

The origin of the term "Chicano" reflects the pronunciation of the grapheme X in Spanish. In Old Spanish the sign X denoted the palatal sibilant sound $š$ (English *sh*). The Spaniards used this grapheme to transcribe the Nahuatl $š$ in *Mexica* (Meshica), as the Aztecs called themselves. But by the middle of the seventeenth century the sound of X had changed to the palatal affricate $č$ (English *ch*, as in church): *México* and *mexicano* sounded like *Méchico* and *mechicano*. *Chicano*, then is an aphaeresis of *mechicano*. Chicano literature, as such, begins in 1848, but its roots, forms and themes go back to the era of the migrations of the Chicano's ancestors, the Mexicas, south from a mythical land called Aztlán, to Tenochtitlán, modern Mexico City. The literature of the Chicano is written in Spanish, Spanish-English, Pachucano, and in combinations of Spanish-English-Pachucano. It is above all a literature of protest, the protest and lament of the vanquished, the colonized and humiliated "Strangers in Their Own Land." History, the novel and short story, poetry and the theater are best represented by the works of Rodolfo Acuña, Tomás Rivera, "Corky" Gonzales, Raúl Salinas and Luis Valdez. (EG-G)

"My work consists of two parts: the one presented here plus all that I have *not* written. And it is precisely this second part which is the important one."[1]

". . . words say nothing . . . . There are no words for the deepest experience . . . . Of course, not everything is unsayable in words, only the living truth."[2]

The above quotations, I suppose, are another way of expressing my uncertainty, a feeling of insufficiency, maybe even unworthiness—my suspicion that a Chicano is not the ideal person to speak for, or even *about*, the Chicanos. Only if I were the Homeric singer, Pindar, an Attic tragedian, or the Psalmist, could I hope "to find shaped expression for primary human impulses of love and hatred, of civic and religious feeling."[3] For where shall I find the novel metaphor and simile with which to

87

reveal the sad, the moving, the living truth which is the Chicano's? But since I did agree to present this paper over eighteen months ago, I must now put aside my diffidence.

The story of the Chicano begins right here in Texas rather than in any other part of Aztlán ("el país del color blanco, junto a las garzas"), from which is derived "Aztecas, la gente de Aztlán,"[4] for, although Juan de Oñate led an expedition north from Mexico and founded San Gabriel de los Españoles (today called Chamita, a village near Santa Fe) in 1598, he first had to pass a point on the Rio Grande called Nuestra Señora del Pilar del Paso del Río del Norte (present-day Ciudad Juárez, across the river from El Paso, Texas).[5]

Thus, the forebears of the Chicano were here nine years before the English settled Jamestown (1607), and twenty-two years before the Pilgrims founded Plymouth (1620). For all we know they may have been here even earlier in the sixteenth century, since Cabeza de Vaca, Fray Marcos de Niza, Coronado and de Soto, all explored the Southwest before 1550—and they did not bring Spanish wives . . . .

* * *

The origin of the term "Chicano" has to do with the pronunciation of the grapheme X in Spanish. In Old Spanish and throughout the sixteenth century the sign X denoted the palatal sibilant sound $\check{s}$ (i.e., approximately, English *sh*).[6] The Spaniards used this grapheme to transcribe the Nahuatl $\check{s}$[7] in *Mexica*, as the Aztecs called themselves (from a tribal god "Mexitli," perhaps identical with Huitzilopochtli, the chief god of the Aztec pantheon).[8] But by the middle of the seventeenth century the sound of X had changed to the palatal affricate $\hat{c}$ (i.e., approximately, English *ch*).[9]

Thus *México*, the name the Spaniards gave to Tenochtitlán, the Aztec capital, sounded like "Méshico" to Cortés and Charles V at the time of the Conquest, but like "Méchico" to Philip IV in 1665. And the adjective *mexicano*, similarly, changed from *meshicano* to *mechicano*. *Chicano*, then, is an aphaeresis of *mechicano*. (The X, by the way, went on to develop into the modern Spanish *j*, *ks*, and *s* sounds. So the *x* spelling in *México* and *mexicano* is purely traditional and sentimental on the part of Mexico and the Mexicans—the *j* pronunciation is universal. However, the X has never lost its attraction for some. Valle-Inclán, when asked why he like Mexico so much, replied: "Porque México se escribe con x." And Alfonso Reyes has a fine essay titled *La X en la frente*).[10]

Chicano, as an aphetic form of *mechicano*, is fine as far as etymology goes. But the term may have a folk etymology after all. What happened to the *me* in *mechicano*? I do not know and I do not think anyone else does either. Besides, what about the *Chicanas*? *Chicano* is not in the dictionary, but *chicana* is. It means chicanery. *Chicanear* means to use trickery, to be cunning. And a *chicanero* is one who is tricky, crafty. These words may not have any connection with *Chicano*, but for my taste they are just a trifle too close for comfort.

Besides, not everyone is or wants to be a Chicano. There are those who call themselves "Americans of Mexican Descent" or "Mexican-Americans." Fernando Peñalosa characterizes a person from the first group— "Americans of Mexican Descent"—as acknowledging that he is a descendant of Mexican forebears, but attaches neither a positive nor negative value to the fact, because it plays an unimportant role in his life—or self concept.[11] The hyphenated "Mexican-American," on the other hand, is constantly aware of his Mexican lineage and this ancestry is an important aspect of his self-awareness. His Mexican ancestry can constitute a positive or negative value or, perhaps more generally, an ambiguous combination of both. The Chicano, finally, is not only acutely conscious of his Mexican identity and ancestry, but is also *engagé*, committed, involved in the defense of subcultural Mexican values and in an effort to work actively for the betterment of *La Raza*, his people.

As for myself, I prefer the term Chicano. Not because I am an activist, or militant, or young. I prefer it for aesthetic and linguistic reasons. Chicano is neater. It cannot be confused with Hispano, Latino, Mexicano, or the hyphenations. Hyphenation of compound words in Spanish is rare, unnatural. Chicano is a label chosen by *La Raza*, not one foisted on us by Anglo historians or demographers. Chicano, like Black, stands out. Chicano is very much in keeping with the paroxytonic stress so prevalent in Spanish—Chi-CA-no—just as monosyllabic Black (vs. Ni-gra) is linguistically Anglo-Saxon. Sergio Elizondo, a Chicano poet, has expressed the point much more eloquently in his work entitled "Chicanos":

> Yo, señor, pues soy Chicano,
> porque así me puse yo.
> Nadie me ha dado ese nombre,
> yo lo oí y lo tengo,
> es que ya no soy niño: soy hombre.
> Méxicoamericano porque hablando nací
> lengua de la Raza.
> Americano por estas otras costumbres
> de esta gente.
> Tengo dos palabras, español e inglés
> a veces bien, a veces mal,
> pero dos, ay se va, pues.
> Latinoamericano era hace treinta años,
> cuando me daba vergüenza mi cara
> negando ser lo que era,
> pero ya ve, viejo,

uno cambia, pasa el tiempo, piensa.
Americano de ascendencia española,
¿qué es eso, mano?
¡Qué largo y vacío suena,
pero me cubre la cara! [12]

Porfirio Díaz, a Mexican president who held power for thirty-two years, coined the expression: "¡Pobre México, tan lejos del cielo—tan cerca de los Estados Unidos! " Mexico, alas, has ever been plagued by religion, distance, the white man and the north. Long before the arrival of the Spaniards, tribes from the north—Toltecs, Chichimecs and Aztecs— invaded Anáhuac, the valley and central plains of Mexico and set up empires of varying duration. Notable architects, these tribes founded great cities and built vast ceremonial centers at Teotihuacán, Tula and Tenochtitlán:[13] their astronomers developed an almost perfect calendar and their linguists invented a language of hieroglyphs. In the third century A.D., according to Toltec myth and history, there appeared the legendary Quetzalcóatl, a man with white skin, long hair and a beard, a man who was wise and virtuous, who preached a pure religion and taught the Toltecs, by word and deed, the path to virtue, respect for the law and how to cultivate the soil. But Quetzalcóatl, represented in Toltec iconography as a plumed serpent, Bringer of Civilization, the God of Good—or his surrogate—was driven from his capital at Tula by a rival faction headed by Tezcatlipoca, the Aztec Eagle God representing the Sun, who observed the deeds of men on earth in a Smoky Mirror and, like another tribal diety in another time and place—Jehovah—demanded the sacrifice of flesh—this time human—in his honor.[14] Before embarking on a raft of serpents and returning whence he came, Quetzalcóatl prophesied that other men, white and bearded like him, would one day come by water from the East to conquer the country and destroy its idols.

Finally the Aztecs came. Natives of Axtlán or Aztatlán, a mysterious region somewhere in the north, located in Nayarit, or perhaps Jalisco,[15] the Aztecs, also as a result of a prophecy by their War God, Huitzilopochtli, had embarked on an immense journey south sometime in the seventh century of our era, a migration which ended in 1325 on the shores of Lake Texcoco. It was there, on a spot which is now the center of the "Zócalo" in Mexico City, they saw the sign prophesied: an eagle perched on a *nopalli*, the prickly pear cactus (*Opuntia ficus-indica*), with a serpent in its claws. . . .

Two hundred years later, in 1519, Quetzalcóatl's prophecy was fulfilled. Toward the end of April an armada of ten caravels under the command of Hernán Cortés, an army captain from Extremadura, landed on the small island of San Juan de Ulúa, now the fortress at the entrance of the port of Veracruz, with 400 soldiers, nineteen sailors and artisans, nineteen horses, ten cannon, four falconets (smaller cannon) and several hunting dogs.[16]

The rest is history. The incredible epic of the Conquest can be read, like a novel, in Bernal Díaz del Castillo and in Prescott. The only character in this drama that is of interest for my purpose is a slave, a young and beautiful Aztec maiden (among several given to Cortés by a chieftain). Her name was Malitzin or Malinche. She was bilingual (in Maya and Náhuatl) and later learned Spanish. She is the mother of Martín Cortés, the first Mexican, a mestizo bastard, remote ancestor of the Chicano.

This Malinche, or Doña Marina, as the Spaniards called her,[17] is also of interest because although she was given as a slave, she was a *cacica*, mistress of towns and vassals in Quetzalcoalcos, a matriarchy where women were the rulers.[18]

Here then is the Mexican (Chicano), product of a triple rape: rape of the land, rape of the mother, rape of the culture—by the white man. In short, an *hijo de la chingada.*[19] And *muy, muy macho*, but whose *madre* is *la Jefa, la Jefita*. This *hijo* is generally born and raised a Catholic, but, even when he is an agnostic or atheist, he will swear: "Juro por la Santísima Virgen de Guadalupe que Dios no existe."

Religion and the Indian Virgin figure again in the second main event in the history of Mexico. In 1810, on the night of 15 September, at a small village called Dolores, in Guanajuato, the parish priest, Don Miguel Hidalgo y Costilla and a handful of Indians raised the famous "Grito de Dolores": " ¡Viva la religión, viva nuestra madre santísima de Guadalupe, viva Fernando VII, viva la América y muera el mal gobierno! " Undoubtedly because it mentioned a *gachupín* monarch, this cry was immediately shortened to " ¡Viva Nuestra Señora de Guadalupe y mueran los gachupines! "

Capitalizing on the abuses and corruption of the Crown, not only in Mexico but in all the Spanish colonies during the short reign of Carlos IV, inept son of an enlightened monarch (Carlos III), Padre Hidalgo managed to stir his parishioners of Dolores and Indians from nearby villages to join the war against the hated *gachupines*. Hidalgo, born in 1753 of a *criollo* family in Valladolid (today's Morelia, Michoacán), was educated for the priesthood, taught theology and later became rector of the Colegio de San Nicolás in Valladolid. After two years as an administrator, he stepped down and became a parish priest in western and northern Mexico. Some said that he gave up the rectorship because of financial irregularities in the college, others that he was ousted because of his fondness for gambling and his fall from celibacy. He was quite human, it seems, and indeed sired several illegitimate children. But his personal life seems to have caused little comment in the lax ecclesiastical society of late eighteenth-century

Mexico. According to Robert Quirk, "The inquisitorial court investigated Father Hidalgo twice, not for personal licentiousness or theological heterodoxy, but on account of his political views. He was said to have been 'afrancesado'—corrupted by the dangerous ideas of the French Enlightenment:"[20]

Hidalgo indeed was more interested in the economic and social conditions of his people than in their spiritual needs. And he was a man of great courage, but unfortunately his courage was not matched by the necessary military talent to resist the Spanish regular troops. At first his hordes "destroyed haciendas, looted cities and towns, and killed Spaniards. Celaya, Guanajuato, Valladolid and Guadalajara fell before the terrible onslaught."[21] But Hidalgo had "alienated the responsible creole citizens" and "though his armies won a last victory near Mexico City, he failed to move on the capital. . . . Thereupon, his movement began to disintegrate." Less than a year after the "Grito de Dolores," "Hidalgo, Allende and other leaders of the insurrection had fled north" and been "captured by the Spanish authorities." Tried for treason, they were all executed in Chihuahua in 1811.[22] And although another priest, José María Morelos, took over after Hidalgo's death, and declared Mexico's independence in 1813, it was not until 1821 that independence was achieved—not by libertarian patriots, but by a young creole aristocrat, Agustín de Iturbide, the leaders of the Church and the conservative elements of the country, who succeeded in maintaining Mexico's colonial structure for another 100 years— until the Revolution of 1910.

The year 1821 marks not only the beginning of Mexico as an independent nation (as a federal republic modeled and named just like the young republic to the north), it also marks the beginning of a series of events that were to lead inevitably to war and the loss of over half of Mexico's territory (the best half, incidentally, "the one with all the paved roads," as Cantinflas put it).

In 1821 The Transcontinental Treaty with Spain, by which the United States acquired Florida, was ratified. Spain drew the boundary of the United States in such a way that it excluded Texas, then a part of Coahuila, a state of the independent Republic of Mexico. Anglo-Americans started making forays into Texas, similar to those they had made into Florida. For example, "in 1819, James Long led an abortive invasion of the province with the aim of creating the 'Republic of Texas.' "[23] For "Long, like many Anglos, believed that Texas belonged to the United States and the 'Congress had no right or power to sell, exchange, or relinquish an "American possession." ' "[24]

Nevertheless, "for a time Anglo filibustering activity in Texas was dormant, and Mexican authorities offered free land to groups of settlers.

Moses Austin was given permission to establish a settlement in Texas," under conditions set by the Mexican government: "that all immigrants must be Catholics and that they must take an oath of allegiance to Mexico." Moses Austin did not live to carry out his plan. "In December, 1821, Stephen Austin [son of Moses] founded the settlement of San Felipe de Austin. Soon Anglos were settling in Texas in great numbers; by 1830 there were about 20,000 settlers, along with about 2,000 slaves."[25]

The majority of these settlers came from the South, the Redneck and Cracker South. They brought their views of white superiority and black inferiority with them. Naturally, what they felt for the brown "Meskins" of Texas was not admiration. And "it was soon apparent that the Anglo-Texans had no intention of obeying Mexican law." Acuña explains that "Mexico became increasingly alarmed at the continuing flood of immigrants, most of whom retained their Protestant religion." Acuña also says that "many settlers considered Mexicans to be the intruders of the Texas territory," and that they "encroached upon lands belonging to native Mexicans." When Mexico nullified the grant of one of these encroachers, Hayden Edwards, and "ordered him out of the territory," Edwards "and his followers seized the town of Nacogdoches" and proclaimed the "Republic of Fredonia."[26] Another example: "When, like most progressive nations, Mexico abolished slavery on September 15, 1829," how did the Texans react? Acuña says that, according to the University of Texas historian Eugene C. Barker, they "evaded the law by 'freeing' their slaves and then signing them to lifelong contracts as indentured servants."[27]

The Chicano historian, Rodolfo Acuña, quoting from Anglo and Mexican sources, spells out a story of wanton agression, naked racism and outright theft even before "the antipathies of the Texans escalated into a full scale rebellion . . . . on September 19, 1835." Acuña also tries to set the record straight about the Alamo, or at least correct some "dramatic half-truths that have been accepted as history."[28] Since I do not recall seeing any of this information in standard textbooks used in Texas public schools I attended in my salad days, it might be illuminating to some of you—and besides give the historians in the house a chance to react—if I quote from Acuña's book, *Occupied America, The Chicano's Struggle Toward Liberation*, specifically from the first chapter, "Legacy of Hate: The Conquest of the Southwest," the section entitled "The Texas Revolt":

> Barker draws a parallel between the Texas revolt and the American Revolution, stating: "In each, the general cause of revolt was the same—a sudden effort to extend imperial authority at the expense of local privilege." In fact, in both instances the central governments were attempting to enforce existing laws that conflicted with illegal activities of some very articulate men. Barker further attempts to justify the Anglo-Texans' action by observing: "At the

close of summer in 1835 the Texans saw themselves in danger of becoming the alien subjects of a people to whom they deliberately believed themselves morally, intellectually, and politically superior. The racial feeling, indeed, underlay and colored Texan-Mexican relations from the establishment of the first Anglo-American colony in 1821." Therefore, the conflict, according to Barker, was inevitable and, consequently, justified.

It is difficult to pin the Texas apologists down. They admit that racism played a leading role in the causes for revolt; that smugglers were upset with Mexico's enforcement of her import laws; that Texans were upset about emancipation laws; and that an increasing number of the new arrivals from the United States actively agitated for independence. But despite these admissions, historians like Barker refuse to assign guilt to their countrymen.

. . . .

Too many historians have portrayed Mexico's attempt to suffocate the insurrection as an invasion and the Texas victory that followed as a victory of a small band of patriots against the "Huns" from the south. Dr. Félix D. Almaraz, a member of the history department of the University of Texas at Austin, underscores this, writing: "All too often, Texan specialists have interpreted the war as the defeat of a culturally inferior people by a culturally superior class of Anglo frontiersmen . . . ."

In reality, the Anglo-Americans enjoyed very real advantages. As mentioned, they had a sizeable population; they were "defending" terrain with which they were familiar; and although most of the 5000-or-so Mexicans living in the territory did not join them, the Anglos themselves were united. In contrast, the Mexican nation was divided, and the centers of power were thousands of miles away from Texas. From the interior of Mexico, Santa Anna led an army of about 6000 conscripts, many of whom had been forced into the army and were then marched hundreds of miles over hot, arid desert land. In addition, many were Mayan and did not speak Spanish. In February 1836, the majority arrived in San Antonio, Texas, sick and ill-prepared to fight. Although the Mexican Army outnumbered the Anglo contingent, the latter were much better armed and enjoyed the position of being the defenders . . . . Santa Anna, on the other hand, had overextended his supply lines and was many miles from his base of power.

The 187 men who were defending San Antonio refused to surrender to Santa Anna's forces and took refuge in a former mission, the Alamo. In the ten days of fighting that followed, the Texans inflicted heavy casualties on the Mexican forces, but eventually the Mexicans' sheer superiority in numbers won out . . . . Within the broad framework of what actually happened . . . there has been much distortion. Walter Lord, in an article entitled "Myths and Realities of the Alamo," sets much of the record straight. Since the myth has provided Anglo-Americans with a major justification for their historical and psychological subjugation of the Chicano, the story of the Alamo demands a brief retelling.

Texas mythology portrays the Alamo heroes as freedom-loving defenders of their homes; they were supposedly all good Texans. Actually, two-thirds of the defenders were recent arrivals from the United States, and only a half dozen had been in Texas for more than six years. Moreover, the character of the defenders is questionable. A work that is admittedly biased, but that nevertheless casts considerable light on the Alamo and its defenders, is Rafael Trujillo Herrera's *Olvídate de El Alamo*. . . . According to Trujillo, the men in the Alamo were adventurers and not virtuous idealists as they frequently are portrayed by Texas historians. Trujillo reveals that William Barret Travis was a murderer; he killed a man who had made advances to his wife. Rather than confess, Travis allowed a slave to be tried and convicted for his crime, and he fled to Texas, abandoning his wife and two children. James Bowie was an infamous brawler who had made a fortune running slaves and had wandered into Texas searching for lost mines and more money. And then there was the fading Davy Crockett, a legend in his own time, who fought for the sake of fighting. Many others in the Alamo were men who had come to Texas for riches and glory; a minority were men who had responded to Austin's call to arms. These defenders were not the sort of men who could be classified as peaceful settlers fighting for their homes.

. . . .

The facts are that the Alamo had little strategic value, the men fully expected help, and the Alamo was the best fortified fort west of the Mississippi. While the defenders only numbered about 180, they had twenty-one cannons to the Mexicans' eight or ten. The Anglo-Americans were expert marksmen and had rifles with a range of 200 yards; in contrast, the Mexicans were poorly equipped, inadequately trained, and were armed with smooth-bore muskets with a range of only 70 yards. In addition, the walls of the Alamo were thick, concealing the defenders, while the latter had clear shots. In short, ill-prepared, ill-equipped, and ill-fed Mexicans attacked well-armed and professional soldiers. . . .

Probably the most widely circulated story was that of the alleged heroism and last stand of the aging Davy Crockett who, when the end came, fell "fighting like a tiger," killing Mexicans with his bare hands. This is a myth; seven of the defenders surrendered, and Crockett was among them. They were executed.

The importance of these myths about the Alamo is that they falsely build up the valor of the Anglo-Texans at the expense of the Mexicans, who have been portrayed as treacherous, ruthless killers. This stereotyping conditioned Anglo attitudes about the Mexicans, and it served as a rationalization for later aggression against Mexico and the Anglo's mistreatment of Chicanos. It is also significant that the Spanish-surnamed "defenders" within the Alamo conspicuously have been omitted from the roll call of the Texas heroes.

. . . .

Many historians have dwelt upon the violence and cruelty of the Mexicans in Texas, especially in relation to the victory at Goliad. It is true that Santa Anna gave no quarter in his encounters with Texans, but the issue of Anglo-American violence usually has been evaded. The battle at San Jacinto was literally a slaughter of the Mexican forces. Few prisoners were taken. Instead, those who surrendered "were clubbed and stabbed, some on their knees. The slaughter . . . became methodical: the Texan riflemen knelt and poured a steady fire into the packed, jostling ranks . . . ." They shot the "Meskins" down as they fled. The final count showed 630 Mexicans dead versus two Texans.[29]

The conclusion of this account brings us to the Mexican-American War and the Treaty of Guadalupe Hidalgo.

On 2 March 1836, a convention of fifty-nine Anglo and Mexican delegates declared complete independence from Mexico, elected David Burnett as provisional president and Lorenzo de Zavala, an exiled Mexican liberal, as vice-president of the Republic of Texas. (Some of my students and colleagues seem to be surprised, shocked, even dismayed, to learn than any Mexican before Henry B. González ever held high public office in Texas— Zavala's name is not to be found in the textbooks.)[30]

After the massacre of the Alamo, where 187 Texans (including, incidentally, Mexican Texans under the leadership of Captain Juan Seguín and fighting, if you please, under a Mexican flag) were wiped out, and, after a month later at Goliad, Santa Anna slaughtered 450 Texas rebels, we get to 21 April 1836 and the Battle of San Jacinto, where Sam Houston routed the Mexican Army, captured Santa Anna and forced him (by the Treaty of Velasco) to agree to Texas independence in exchange for his freedom.[31] Mexico, of course, repudiated the agreement, but there was no way the Texans could be forced to resubmit. By 1840 the Republic of Texas had obtained recognition from the United States, France and Great Britain.

De facto independence—now the Texans wanted annexation to the United States (some non-Texas Anglos suspected it might be the other way around). But annexation proved to be a problem, for it threatened to upset the balance between slave and free states. The abolitionists, however, seem to have had stronger support at the time, so the Texans turned their attention and energies to other matters. They began doing a little annexing of their own: Texans claimed over half the territory of New Mexico—on the pretext that the Rio Grande was the "natural" boundary of the Republic. They even sent an expedition, in June, 1841, to Santa Fe to try to persuade the *nuevo mexicanos* to separate from Mexico. Five military companies and twenty-one wagons with about $200,000 worth of trade goods (the Texans, you see, were willing to share in the lucrative Santa Fe trade, in case the New Mexicans declined to become part of Texas) ran into some unpleasantness: hostile Indians, raging prairie fires, blistering heat, and they also lost their way. They were eventually captured, and at Santa Fe some of the Texans were executed while others were sent on foot on a long death march to prison in Mexico City.[32] Anyway, this unsuccessful attempt to annex New Mexico and the uncharitable treatment of the prisoners did not quite lead to friendly neighborliness between Texans and New Mexicans. To this day, in New Mexico, we say "Pobre Nuevo México, tan lejos del cielo, tan cerca de Tejas."

The Rio Grande was also claimed as the natural boundary of the Republic in that most fertile Mesopotamia between the Nueces and the Rio Grande. And it was in this area, in this disputed triangle, that war was to break out in May, 1846, after Texas had finally been annexed and President James K. Polk had deliberately provoked a clash between American and Mexican troops, had quickly declared war against Mexico, ordered

General Zachary Taylor to cross the Rio Grande, and General Winfield Scott to carry the war right into the "halls of Montezuma," in order thus to expand the territory of America from sea to shining sea, as Destiny had clearly made Manifest, and as God had so clearly revealed to his other chosen people of the New World, the Puritans,[33] and, in His infinite wisdom, also to President James Monroe.

The results are known. My friend and colleague, the revisionist Chicano historian, Ramón Eduardo Ruiz sums it up in one neat paragraph:

> No war waged by the United States has won more striking victories than the Mexican War of 1846-1848. After an unbroken string of military triumphs from Buena Vista to Chapultepec and the occupation of their first foreign capital, Americans added the sprawling territories of New Mexico and California to their domain. The United States had also fulfilled its Manifest Destiny, that belief of American expansionists that Providence had willed them a moral mission to occupy all adjacent lands. No American can deny that war had proved profitable.[34]

But what probably is not known or has been forgotten, as Ray Ruiz points out, is something the Mexican knows and does not forget (and neither does the Chicano): "The war is one of the tragedies of history. Unlike the Americans who have relegated the conflict to the past, Mexicans have not forgotten. Mexico emerged from the war bereft of half of its territory, a beaten, discouraged, and divided people."[35]

But why should the Chicano not forget—or forgive? He was not involved in the war. He cannot forgive or forget because of the Treaty of Guadalupe Hidalgo (before the treaty there were no Chicanos). Furthermore, he cannot forgive or forget because after that treaty the Chicanos, too, like the Mexicans before them, began slowly, sometimes legally (by American code of law, and, of course, in legal proceedings conducted in English)—but more often completely outside the law and in spite of the provisions of the treaty—to lose not only their land, their houses and belongings, but sometimes their lives as well.

The Treaty of Guadalupe Hidalgo[36] is so called because it was signed in the former city of that name in the State of Mexico (now called Gustavo A. Madero city), on 2 February 1848 and ratified on 4 July 1848—which, by the way, is the reason Chicanos celebrate or do not celebrate the Fourth of July. This treaty specifically provided, in article VIII, that "Mexicans now established in territories previously belonging to Mexico, . . . shall be free to continue where they now reside, . . . retaining the property which they possess . . . , or disposing thereof, . . . without their being subjected, on this account, to any contribution tax, or charge whatever."[37]

Article VIII also provided that Mexicans "who shall prefer to remain in the said territories may either retain the title and rights of Mexican citizens, or acquire those of citizens of the United States . . . ," by either making their election within one year from ratification or automatically, by remaining in the said territories after the expiration of that year, "without having declared their intention to retain the character of Mexicans, shall be considered to have elected to become citizens of the United States."[38]

And, so that there might be no mistake, the final paragraph of article VIII clearly emphasized the inviolability of the property rights of Mexicans—and Chicanos: "In the said territories, property of every kind now belonging to Mexicans not established there, shall be inviolably respected. The present owners, the heirs of these, and all Mexicans who may hereafter acquire said property by contract, shall enjoy with respect to it guarantees equally ample as if the same belonged to citizens of the United States."[39]

Article IX, which together with article VIII constitute the heart of the treaty, is short and to the point regarding the citizenship of the Chicanos: "The Mexicans who . . . shall not preserve the character of citizens of the Mexican Republic . . . shall be incorporated into the Union of the United States, and be admitted at the proper time . . . to the enjoyment of all the rights of citizens of the United States, according to the principles of the Constitution; and in the mean time, shall be maintained and protected in the free enjoyment of their liberty and property, and secured in the free exercise of their religion without restriction."[40]

The terms of this treaty are crystal clear. So what were Juan Nepomuceno Cortina, Joaquín Murieta, Élfego Baca and other folk-heroes "Frito Banditos" of yesteryear, or, in our own day, Reies López Tijerina, José Angel Gutiérrez, Rodolfo "Corky" Gonzales and César Chávez arguing about? Could it be because, as Anatole France once said (somewhere in *The Red Lily*), "The law, in its majestic impartiality, forbids the rich and the poor alike from stealing bread, begging in the streets and, sleeping under bridges"? Or maybe because an old African saying applies here: "In the beginning, we had the land and the white man had the Bible. Then we had the Bible and the white man had the land."[41]

By the way, it is interesting to speculate on the real reasons behind the suppression of article X. Article X dealt with the grants of lands made by Mexico in the territories ceded to the United States. Lamb points out that "Article X, as signed, was wholly stricken from the treaty, without substitution of new matter."[42] The Protocol of Querétaro, signed 26 May 1848, states that "The American Government by suppressing the Xth article of the Treaty of Guadalupe did not in any way intend to annul the grants of lands made by Mexico in the ceded territories," and that "These grants, notwithstanding the suppression of the article . . . , preserve the legal value which they may possess, and the guarantees may cause their legitimate titles to be acknowledged before the American tribunals."[43] Nevertheless, "After a great exchange of diplomatic correspondence, both governments finally agreed that the Protocol of Querétaro was not in any legal sense part of the treaty or obligatory as an international act."[44] And that was that.

Carey McWilliams explains an irony involved in the signing of the treaty: "Not only did Mexico forfeit an empire to the United States, but, ironically, none of the signers of the Treaty of Guadalupe Hidalgo realized that, nine days before the treaty was signed, gold had been discovered in California. That they had unknowingly ceded to the United States territories unbelievably rich in gold and silver—the hope of finding which had lured Coronado and De Oñate into the Southwest—must have added to the Mexicans' sense of bitterness and defeat."[45]

Furthèrmore, Carey McWilliams says,

> Nothing was more galling to the Mexican officials who negotiated the treaty than the fact that they were compelled to assign, as it were, a large number of their countrymen to the Yankees. With great bitterness they protested that it was "not permissible to sell, as a flock of sheep, those deserving Mexicans." For many years after 1846, the Spanish-Americans left in the United States were known in Mexico as "our brothers who were sold." As late as 1943 maps were still used in Mexican schools which designated the old Spanish borderlands as "territory temporarily in the hands of the United States." It is to the great credit of the Mexican negotiators that the treaty contained the most explicit guarantees to protect the rights of these people, provisions for which they were more deeply concerned than they were over boundaries or indemnities. *It should never be forgotten that, with the exception of the Indians, Mexicans are the only minority in the United States who were annexed by conquest; the only minority, Indians again excepted, whose rights were specifically safeguarded by treaty provision.*"[46]

* * *

Before talking about Chicano literature and examining representative samples thereof, I want to discuss, briefly, the phenomenon of Chicano speech itself. Why does the Chicano minority, unlike many other ethnic minorities which make up these United States (Blacks, Italians, Poles, Germans, Orientals, Jews, etc.) so strongly and persistently resist the constant pressure to become Americanized, linguistically acculturated? This pressure, incidentally, is not only social, economic, educational, etc., but sometimes official. For instance, President Theodore Roosevelt, in a letter read at the All American Festival in New York City, 5 January 1919, said: "We have room but for one language here, and that is the English language, for we intend to see that the crucible turns our people out as Americans and not as dwellers in a polyglot boarding house."[47]

I do not think that physical contiguity with Mexico is alone sufficient to explain Chicano speech, although cultural continuity with our mother country is certainly evident in Chicano literature. (In Canada there is a similar phenomenon with the *Québecois*, and yet physical and cultural contact between Quebec and France has been practically non-existent since the British took the province in 1759.)

What I mean by Chicano speech is not "standard" language, for in that case the Chicano would speak and write standard Spanish or standard English. Rather what I mean is what is hinted at in the following quotation: "Separate languages can exist side by side for centuries without touching each other, maintaining their integrity with the vigor of incompatible tissues. At other times, two languages may come together, fuse, replicate, and give rise to nests of new tongues."[48] In other words, the speech of the Chicano is just such a new tongue, and as such it is one of many forms of his protest. Without the influence of, and reaction against, English, much of the Chicano *caló*, *pocho*, *pachuco*, *pachucano*, *Tex-Mex* would not exist.

But there may still be another reason for the Chicano's hold on his native language. You may recall that in connection with his *machismo* I mentioned that, in spite of it, he venerates his *madre—la Jefa, la Jefita*. Sure, somewhere in the Chicano's lineage there must have been a man, a Spaniard—hence his language and his religion—one sperm. But what is that compared to the mother's blood and milk? "La lengua se mama." Language is suckled at the mother's breast.

The Chicano's speech, like his character and psyche, is hybrid—neither a complete fusion or replication of English and Spanish, but rather something new, an amalgamation of English and Spanish, but with a bonding agent which is neither: in short, an alloy, like bronze, the idiom of *la raza de bronce*.

A significant majority of the Chicanos are bilingual, a factor which in this country, perhaps out of ethnic or monolingual perversity, is not considered an asset. Some of us are polyglots—we have a pretty good command of English (standard and Texas), Spanish (Latin American dialect), and Barrio or Chicano Spanish, plus a smattering of several other European languages. Unfortunately, not every Chicano is biliterate—for which I do not think he is entirely to blame.[49] Yet, even when the Chicano is completely bilingual and biliterate, he is not accepted. There seems to be a catch or two: his name and his pigmentation. (I once deliberately asked a captious question of one of my graduate students: "What do you think of me as a Mexican?" "Well, for a Mexican," he replied, a little too quickly, "I think you are very articulate and well-read." "Only as a Mexican?" I continued. "Oh, I see what you mean . . . "). Still, when the Chicano wants to express himself intimately, confidentially, to another Chicano, he will almost invariably switch to Spanish, even though the conversation may have been going on in English. And when a Chicano asks another, "What are you?" the answer is usually quite simply, "mexicano."[50] I wonder why?

* * *

In a strictly political sense, Chicano literature begins in 1848. Nevertheless, it does not spring full blown overnight, even though all Mexicans here who did not elect to retain Mexican citizenship woke up on the morning of 5 July 1848 to discover that they had become American citizens by a stroke of the pen. No, in a larger sense we can say that the historical beginning of Chicano literature is more logically 1836, the year of the secession of Texas.[51]

Prior to 1848 and indeed, until around the decade 1910-1921 (the Mexican Revolution), Chicano writers elaborate on Mexican themes, borrow and maintain Mexican forms, as is evident in the anonymous and often oral folklore tradition of *corridos*, *décimas* and *coplas*. But from 1848 on Chicano literature begins to reflect the changed situation and we can detect a new expression. Old themes are treated in new ways, and themes not found in the Mexican heritage begin to appear: dislocation, migration, exploitation by the white conqueror, the barrio, the struggle for identity and self-definition in what Rudy Acuña calls "Occupied America." Indeed, probably the main characteristic of Chicano literature is "that it is rooted in human experience within two cultures, that of Mexico and that of the United States."[52] It is a literature of protest.

Another aspect of Chicano literature is that, like the Chicano himself, it is "the best kept secret in America."[53] Or it was, at least, until fairly recently. Although from 1971-1972 there has been a flood of Chicano publication, I had the honor or distinction of being the editor of the first anthology of Chicano literature published by an American publisher of national reputation.[54] Honesty compels me, however, to admit that I did not seek out the compilers; they brought the project to me—because I was the only Chicano language editor of a major commercial publishing house in the whole United States.

The change in the publication picture is of course welcome, even if it has been brought about mainly by the familiar profit motive, and even if a lot of trash is currently being published in the sudden vogue of anything labeled "Chicano." But it was not always so. In the first edition of the anthology I published, *Literatura chicana: texto y contexto*, the compilers lamented:

> These being the general characteristics of Chicano literature, why is there such a dearth of published literary representations of this experience? Why

are Chicano authors not included in anthologies of North American literature
used in junior and senior high schools and colleges throughout the country?
Why, when the above antecedents go back ten centuries in two cultures, is
Chicano literature so unavailable?

. . . .

It is impossible to separate the fulfillment of a people's artistic and esthetic
sensibility from the question of their access to power in economic and political terms, as well as to education and social justice. The scarcity of Chicano
literature is primarily the result of an exclusionist and intolerant American
society that has maintained a purist and static view of literature. The basis for
what is literarily valid and thereby publishable has been the degree of conformity to pre-established literary, ideological and linguistic norms—norms
which reflected the interests of the groups in power.

It has been the nature of these oppressive socio-political and educational
structures, impeding publication of non-English works, that in effect discouraged literary expression which may have portrayed a negative image of the
United States. The movement of Anglo-Saxons into the Southwest and the
subsequent establishment of Anglo institutions that sought to exclude Chicanos from participation in the new order, in effect suppressed much of the
publication and the dissemination, although not the growth of Chicano literature.[55]

How about the Chicano's written expression? Like his spoken language, it is a melange, and its most evident characteristic is experimenta-
tion with language: "In a fluid, complex, and expressive manner, Chicano
authors write in Spanish, in English, in combinations of Spanish-English, in
Pachucano, and in combinations of Pachucano-Spanish-English. This process involves the forging of new vocabulary and new images of reality.
Often a single piece of writing will contain several variations of these
linguistic modes, creating multiple levels of meaning and emotional response."[56]

The multilingual approach is nothing new: "Bilingual and multilingual
poetry [or literature] . . . goes back at least to the Middle Ages and to
contrapunctal uses of Latin and the vulgate."[57] I must say, however, that
the combination of languages, to be effective, must not be capricious or
arbitrary. In the hands of a good poet, like Alurista, it produces remarkable effects. His poem, "Must be the Season of the Witch," creates a
chilling picture of suffering and loss of identity. This poem is a double
lament; *la llorona* as ever cries for her lost children, but now they are in
the grip of modern civilization and can no longer draw strength and suste-
nance from her as a cultural symbol:

> Must be the season of the witch
> la bruja
> la llorona
> she lost her children
> and she cries
> en las barrancas of industry
> her children

        devoured by computers
            and the gears
    Must be the season of the witch
        I hear huesos crack
    in pain
            y lloros
    la bruja pangs
            sus hijos han olvidado
    la magia de Durango
            y la de Moctezuma
            –el Huiclamina
    Must be the season of the witch
    La bruja llora
    sus hijos sufren; sin ella[58]

Who are the Chicano authors? They are students, teachers, migrant workers, prisoners in penitentiaries, newspapermen, theater directors, actors, folk singers, union organizers, lawyers, politicians, veterans, housewives and college professors (in departments of Chicano Studies, mainly, but not exclusively).[59] What do they write? Poems—lots of poems, plays, short stories, novels, newspapers,[60] newsletters, magazines, journals, bulletins, essays, articles and studies in psychology, sociology, political science, economics, linguistics, history, bibliography, masters theses, doctoral dissertations—and graffiti on any available blank wall. Ray Padilla, in his article "Documentación chicana," estimates that there were 513 Chicano bibliographies as of 1972! [61]

I will now present a small sampling of recent Chicano literature. A poem by a Chicano student, Richard Olivas, should be of special interest to historians:

        I'm sitting in my history class,
        The instructor commences rapping,
        I'm in my U.S. History class,
        And I'm on the verge of napping.

        The Mayflower landed on Plymouth Rock.
        Tell me more! Tell me more!
        Thirteen colonies were settled.
        I've heard it all before.

        What did he say?
        Dare I ask him to reiterate?
        Oh why bother
        It sounded like he said,
        George Washington's my father.

        I'm reluctant to believe it,
        I suddenly raise my mano.
        If George Washington's my father,
        Why wasn't he Chicano? [62]

104

Undoubtedly the best-known, although in my estimation not the best written, Chicano poem is Rodolfo "Corky" Gonzales' epic poem "I am Joaquín." Here is a fragment:

                ... Here I stand
                        before the Court of Justice
                            Guilty
        for all the glory of my Raza
                to be sentenced to despair.
        Here I stand
            Poor in money
            Arrogant with pride
                Bold with machismo
                Rich in courage
                    and
                Wealthy in spirit and faith.
        My knees are caked with mud.
        My hands calloused from the hoe.
        I have made the Anglo rich
                        yet
            Equality is but a word,
            the Treaty of Hidalgo has been broken
            and is but another treacherous promise.
        My land is lost
                and stolen,
        My culture has been raped,
            I lengthen
            the line at the welfare door
        and fill the jails with crime.
            These then
        are the rewards
                this society has

        for sons of Chiefs
                and Kings
                and bloody Revolutionists.
        Who
        gave a foreign people
            all their skills and ingenuity
        to pave the way with Brains and Blood
        for
        those hordes of Gold starved
                            Strangers
        Who
        changed our language
        and plagiarized our deeds
                        as feats of valor
                        of their own.
        They frowned upon our way of life
        and took what they could use.
            Our Art
            Our Literature
            Our music, they ignored

so they left the real things of value
and grabbed at their own destruction
            by their Greed and Avarice
They overlooked that cleansing fountain of
            nature and brotherhood
Which is Joaquín.
        We start to MOVE.
    La Raza!
Mejicano!
  Español!
    Latino!
      Hispano!
        Chicano!
or whatever I call myself,
        I look the same
        I feel the same
        I cry
            and
        Sing the same

I am the masses of my people and
I refuse to be absorbed.
        I am Joaquín
The odds are great
but my spirit is strong
            My faith unbreakable
            My blood is pure
I am Aztec Prince and Christian Christ
        I SHALL ENDURE!
        I WILL ENDURE! [63]

In prose fiction Tomás Rivera's "... *y no se lo tragó la tierra*"[64] is a literary masterpiece. It is also "a social revolutionary attack against superstition (*religiosidad*) and outmoded traditions and thus constitutes the greatest advance in the *alma chicana* (sensibility)."[65] It deservedly won the first annual Quinto Sol literary award for 1970 and was published in a bilingual edition in August, 1971. The English translation of the Spanish original is by Herminio Ríos (who also wrote the introduction), in collaboration with the author, with assistance by Octavio Romano. Rivera is a native-born Texas Chicano (Crystal City) and a Professor of Spanish and Associate Dean of the College of Multidisciplinary Studies at the University of Texas at San Antonio.

"... *y no se lo tragó la tierra*" has an unusual structure. It is made of fourteen selections. Of these, thirteen are preceded by a short anecdote, six to fifteen lines at most. The first selection or story, "El año perdido," sets the tone and introduces the fictional narrator: "That year was lost to him," it starts. "He would hear someone call him by name.... he could never find out who it was calling him, nor the reason," until "once he stopped himself before completely making the turn [to see who was calling], and he became afraid. He found out that he had been calling himself. That was the way the lost year began" (p. 3).

"The Lost Year," which is only twenty-four lines long, ends with this sentence: "But before falling asleep he would see and hear many things . . ." (p. 3). So the stories that follow are the things that the narrator saw and heard, in the course of one year. These twelve stories, one for each month of the year, are grouped around the title story, ". . . y no se lo tragó la tierra," in which the protagonist curses God, and yet, ". . . the earth did not part." The last story, "Debajo de la casa," is a recapitulation and a synthesis of the thirteen anecdotes and stories, and this story, according to the translator, "provides a unifying effect on the total work" (p. xvi). So, in a sense ". . . y no se lo tragó la tierra" is an ingenious novel or a collection of short stories, as you wish. It (or they) deals with suffering, superstitious fear of punishment, self-deception, oppression, commercial exploitation, and the existential discovery that the Chicano (i.e., Everyman) is alone in the universe. Yet this discovery, rather than leading to anguish and despair, leads to hope and happiness—this is the final paragraph of the last story:

> Smiling he went through the street full of mudholes that led to his house. Suddenly he felt very happy because, when he thought about what the lady had said [she said, in the previous paragraph, " 'Poor family. First the mother, and now him. Maybe he is going crazy, I think he is losing his mind. He has lost his sense of time. He's lost track of the years.' "], he realized that he hadn't lost anything. He had discovered something. To discover and to rediscover and synthesize. To relate this entity with that entity, and that entity with still another, and finally relating everything with everything else. That was what he had to do, that was all. And he became even happier. Later, when he arrived home, he went to the tree that was in the yard. He climbed it. On the horizon he saw a palm tree and imagined that someone was on top looking at him. He even raised his arm and waved it back and forth so that the other person could see that he knew that he was there. (p. 177)

Here are portions of the central title story ". . . and the Earth Did Not Part." They illustrate how low key and yet how intensive and effective, for that very reason, is the outrage and the protest. First I quote the anecdote which precedes the story:

> One afternoon a minister from one of the Protestant churches in town came to the farm and notified them that someone was coming to teach them manual skills so that they would no longer have to work only in the fields. Almost all the men were excited. He was to teach them carpentry. Two weeks later the young fellow came in a pickup truck and a house trailer. He brought with him the minister's wife. She was to be his assistant as an interpreter. But they never taught them anything. They spent day after day inside the trailer. A week later they both left without having said a word. Later the men found out that he had run off with the minister's wife. (p. 73)

Now from the story, Rivera says:

The first time he felt hate and anger was when he saw his mother cry for his uncle and his aunt. They had both gotten tuberculosis and each of them had been sent to different sanatoriums. The children had been parceled out among their aunts and uncles and they had taken care of them as best they could. His aunt had later died and shortly afterward his uncle had been brought home from the sanatorium, but he was already spitting blood every time he coughed. It was then that he saw his mother crying all the time.

. . . .

Then he thought about whether his father was going to die from the sunstroke. From time to time he would hear his father pray and ask God for help. At first he had hoped that he would get well soon but the following day he felt his anger increase. . . . And their father's moans had awakened them that night and also at dawn and their mother had gotten up and had taken off his scapularies from around his neck and washed them for him. She had then lighted some small candles. But to no avail. It was the same as with his uncle and his aunt.

. . . .

"There you are. See? And my uncle and my aunt? You tell me. And now their poor children not knowing their parents. Why did He have to take them? So you see, God doesn't give a damn about us poor people. Look, why do we have to live under these conditions? Are we hurting anybody? You are such a good person and yet you have to suffer so much. Can't you see? Tell me! "

"Oh, son, don't talk like that. Don't question the will of God. The ground might open up and devour you for talking like that. One must resign oneself to the will of God. Please don't talk like that, son. You frighten me. It seems that already the devil is in your very blood."

. . . .

Each step that he took toward the house brought forth the echo of the question "why? " Half way down the road he became furious and then he started to cry out of despair. His other brothers and sisters didn't know what to do and they also started to cry, but out of fear. He then began to swear. And he didn't know when, but what he said he had been wanting so say for a long time. He cursed God. Upon doing it he felt the fear instilled in him by time and by his parents. For a split second he saw the earth open up to devour him. But, although he didn't look down, he then felt himself walking on very solid ground; *it was harder than he had ever felt it.* Anger swelled up in him again and he released it by cursing God. Then he noticed that his little brother no longer appeared so ill. He didn't know if his other little brothers and sisters realized how serious his curse had been.

That evening he didn't go to sleep until very late. He was experiencing a peace that he had never known before. . . . Time after time he felt surprised at what he had done the previous afternoon. He had cursed God and the earth had not parted. He was going to tell his mother but he decided to keep it a secret. He only told her that the earth didn't devour anyone, and that the sun didn't destroy anyone either.

He left for work and he was faced with a very cool morning. There were clouds and for the first time he felt himself capable of doing and undoing

A moment between symposium lectures permits an exchange of ideas among symposium guest speaker Tomás Rivera and Glenn E. Barnett, Executive Vice President, Texas Tech University. (Photographed by Paul Tittle)

Symposium registration: Professor Jules Renard receives symposium folder and badge. In the background are from left to right Wendell M. Aycock and Victor Terras, guest speaker. (Photographed by Paul Tittle)

whatever he chose. He looked toward the ground and he kicked it and said to it,

"Not yet, you can't eat me yet. Some day. But I won't know." (pp. 74-79)

I wish we had more time to devote to Tomás Rivera and his novel. Some of the stories in it are absolutely marvelous, perfect jewels. It will endure. It will prevail. I strongly recommend that you read it for yourself.

Another Chicano genre that is perhaps even more exciting and vital than the novel, the short story, or poetry, is the theater. And in this genre the outstanding playwright is Luis Valdez, founder of *El Teatro Campesino*, a bilingual theater company created in 1965 to teach and organize Chicano farm workers.

Actually, although Chicano theater-Teatro Campesino is very new, its roots go back to medieval church plays, after the rituals and ceremonies of the Church were moved outdoors, transformed into public fiestas and in effect became a people's theater. And in the New World, "Chicano theatrical history is one of the oldest in the continent, with roots which date back to the pre-hispanic indigenous dramas like the *Rabinal Achí*."[66] Here in our country, Juan de Oñate and the settlers from Mexico performed the first drama of La Raza on Ascension Day, 1598 on the banks of the Rio Grande, a symbolic play to bless their journey.[67]

What is Chicano theater? Here is Luis Valdez's answer:

> What is Chicano theater? It is theater as beautiful, rascuachi, human, cosmic, broad, deep, tragic, comic, as the life of La Raza itself. At its high point Chicano theater is religion—the huelguistas de Delano praying at the shrine of the Virgen de Guadalupe, located in the rear of an old station wagon parked across the road from DiGiorgios' camp 4; at its low point, it is a cuento or a chiste told somewhere in the recesses of the barrio, puro pedo.[68]

Most of the plays are called "Actos," perhaps an allusion to their source, the old Spanish *Auto Sacramental*:

> We developed what we call "actos": one-acts or skits, though skit is too light a word, dealing with the strike, the union, and the problems of the farm worker. Humor is our major asset and our best weapon: not only satire, but comedy, which is a much healthier child of the theater than tragedy or realism. Our use of comedy originally stemmed from necessity—the necessity of lifting the strikers' morale. We found we could make social points not in spite of the comedy, but through it. Slapstick can bring us very close to the underlying tragedy—the fact that human beings have been wasted for generations.[69]

For a look at one of the classics in the repertoire of *El Teatro Campesino*, here are selections from an acto called "Las dos caras del patroncito," by Luis Valdez, 1965:

A FARM WORKER ENTERS, CARRYING A PAIR OF PRUNING SHEARS

Farmworker: (TO AUDIENCE) Buenos días! This is the ranch of my patroncito, and I come here to prune grape vines. My patrón bring me all the way from México here to California—the land of sun and money! More sun than money. But I better get to jalar now because my patroncito he don't like to see me talking to strangers. (THERE IS A ROAR BACK-STAGE) Ay, here he comes in his big car! I better get to work. (HE PRUNES)

THE PATRONCITO ENTERS, WEARING A YELLOW PIG FACE MASK. HE IS DRIVING AN IMAGINARY LIMOUSINE, MAKING THE ROARING SOUND OF THE MOTOR.

Patroncito: Good morning boy!

Farmworker: Buenos días, patroncito. (HIS HAT IN HIS HANDS)

Patroncito: You working hard, boy?

Farmworker: Oh, sí, patrón! Muy Hard! (HE STARTS WORKING FURI-OUSLY)

Patroncito: Oh, you can work harder than that, boy (HE WORKS HARDER) Harder! (HE WORKS HARDER) Harder! (HE WORKS STILL HARDER) Harder!

Farmworker: Ay, that's too hard, patrón!

. . . .

Patroncito: Ain't you scared of me, boy? (FARMWORKER NODS) Huh, boy? (FARMWORKER NODS AND MAKES A GRUNT SIGNIFYING YES) What, boy? You don't have to be scared of me! I love my Mexicans. You're one of the new ones, huh? Come in from. . .

Farmworker: México, señor.

Patroncito: Did you like the truck ride, boy? (FARMWORKER SHAKES HEAD INDICATING NO) What? !

Farmworker: I loved it, señor!

Patroncito: Of course you did. All my Mexicans love to ride in trucks! Just the sight of them barreling down the freeway makes my heart feel good; hands on their sombreros, hair flying in the wind, bouncing along happy as babies. Yes sirree, I sure love my Mexicans, boy!

Farmworker: (PUTS HIS ARM AROUND PATRONCITO) Oh, patrón.

Patroncito: (PUSHING HIM AWAY) I love 'em about ten feet away from me boy. Why, there ain't another grower in this whole damn valley that treats you like I do. Some growers got Filipinos, others got Arabs, me I prefer Mexicans. That's why I come down here to visit you, here in the field. I'm an important man, boy! Bank of America, University of California, Safeway Stores—I got a hand in all of 'em. But look, I don't even have my shoes shined.

Farmworker: Oh, patrón, I'll shine your shoes! (HE GETS DOWN TO SHINE HIS SHOES) . . . . Come on, stop it. STOP IT!

CHARLIE "LA JURA" OR "RENT-A-FUZZ" ENTERS LIKE AN APE. HE IMMEDIATELY LUNGES FOR THE FARMWORKER.

Patroncito: Charlie! Charlie! No! It's okay, boy. This is one of MY Mexicans! He was trying to shine my shoes.

Charlie: You sure?

Patroncito: Of course! Now you go back to the road and watch for union organizers.

Charlie: Okay.

CHARLIE EXITS LIKE AN APE. THE FARMWORKER IS OFF TO ONE SIDE TREMBLING WITH FEAR.

Patroncito: (TO FARMWORKER) Scared you, huh, boy? Well lemme tell you, you don't have to be afraid of him, AS LONG AS YOU'RE WITH

ME, comprende? I got him around to keep an eye on them huelguistas. You ever heard of them, son? Ever heard of Huelga? Or Cesar Ch'vez?

Farmworker: Oh sí, patrón!

Patroncito: What?

Farmworker: Oh, no señor! Es comunista! Y la huelga es puro pedo. Bola de colorados, arrastrados, huevones! No trabajan porque no quieren!

Patroncito: That's right, son. Sic 'em, Sic 'em, boy!

Farmworker: (REALLY GETTING INTO IT) Comunistas! Desgraciados! Méndigos huevones!

Patroncito: Good boy! (FARMWORKER FALLS TO HIS KNEES, HANDS IN FRONT OF HIS CHEST LIKE A DOCILE DOG; HIS TONGUE HANGS OUT. PATRONCITO PATS HIM ON THE HEAD) Good boy! THE PATRONCITO STEPS TO ONE SIDE AND LEANS OVER: FARM-WORKER KISSES HIS ASS. PATRONCITO SNAPS UP TRIUMPHANTLY.

Patroncito: Atta baby! You're OK, Pancho.

Farmworker: (SMILING) Pedro.[70]

Patroncito explains to the *Farmworker* how well off he, the *Farmworker*, is: he has no housing problems, for the *Farmworker* lives in the *Patroncito's* labor camp in "nice, rent-free cabins, air-conditioned . . . almost like camping out, boy. A free vacation" (p. 49). No transportation problems. "Don't I let you ride free in my trucks? To and from the fields? " (p. 49). But the *Patroncito* says "boy I got problems" (p. 49). His Lincoln Continental cost $12,000 cash, and his "LBJ Ranch Style house, together with the hill which I built, how much you think a house like that costs? $350,000! " (p. 49). And his wife, "You see her coming out of the house, onto the patio by the pool? The blonde with the mink bikini? " *Farmworker* says "What bikini? " to which *Patroncito* responds "Well, it's small, but it's there. I oughta know—it cost me $5,000! And every weekend she wants to take trips—trips to L.A., San Francisco, Chicago, New York. . . . It all costs money! You don't have problems like that, muchacho—that's why you're so lucky. . ." (p. 50). In fact, the *Patroncito*, sometimes, sits in his office there, brooding, "I'm going to let you in on a little secret. . . . I wish I was a Mexican" (p. 50). So he decides to trade places with the *Farmworker* for one day. The play continues:

PATRONCITO REMOVES HIS MASK WITH A BIG GRUNT. FARM-WORKER LOOKS UP CAUTIOUSLY, SEES THE PATRON'S REAL FACE AND CRACKS UP LAUGHING.

Farmworker: Patrón, you look like me!

Patroncito: You mean . . . I . . . look like a Mexican?

Farmworker: Sí, señor!

FARMWORKER TURNS TO PUT ON THE MASK, AND PATRONCITO STARTS PICKING UP FARMWORKER'S HAT, SIGN, ETC. AND PUTTING THEM ON.

Patroncito: I'm going to be one of my own, boys.

FARMWORKER, WHO HAS HIS BACK TO THE AUDIENCE, JERKS SUDDENLY AS HE PUTS ON PATRONCITO MASK. HE STANDS TALL AND TURNS SLOWLY, NOW LOOKING VERY MUCH LIKE A PATRON.

Patroncito: (SUDDENLY FEARFUL, BUT PLAYING ALONG) Oh, that's good! That's . . . great.

Farmworker: (BOOMING, BRUSQUE, PATRON-LIKE) Shut up and get to work, boy!

Patroncito: Hey, now that's more like it!

Farmworker: I said get to work! (HE KICKS PATRONCITO)

Patroncito: Hey, why did you do that for?

Farmworker: Because I felt like it, boy! You hear me, boy! I like your name, boy! I think I'll call you boy, boy!

Patroncito: You sure learn fast, boy.

Farmworker: I said SHUT UP!

Patroncito: What an actor. (TO AUDIENCE) He's good, isn't he?

Farmworker: Come 'ere boy.

Patroncito: (HIS IDEA OF A MEXICAN) Sí señor, I theeenk.

Farmworker: I don't pay you to think, son. I pay you to work. Now look here—see that car? It's mine.

Patroncito: My Lincoln Conti—Oh you're acting. Sure.

Farmworker: And that LBJ Ranch Style house with the hill? That's mine too.

Patroncito: The house too?

Farmworker: All mine.

Patroncito: (MORE & MORE UNEASY) What a joker.

Farmworker: Oh, wait a minute. Respect, boy! (HE PULLS OFF PATRON-CITO'S FARMWORKER HAT) Do you see her? Coming out of *my* house, onto *my* patio by *my* pool? The blonde in the bikini? Well, she's mine too!

Patroncito: But that's my wife!

Farmworker: Tough luck, son. You see this land, all these vines? They're mine.

Patroncito: Just a damn minute here. The land, the car, the house, hill, and the cherry on top too? You're crazy! Where am I going to live?

Farmworker: I got a nice, air-conditioned cabin down in the labor camp. Free housing, free transportation—

Patroncito: You're nuts! I can't live in those shacks! They got rats, crock-roaches [sic]. And those trucks are unsafe. You want me to get killed?

Farmworker: Then buy a car.

Patroncito: With what? How much you paying me here anyway?

Farmworker: Eighty five cents an hour.

Patroncito: I was paying you a buck twenty five!

Farmworker: I got problems, boy! Go on welfare!

Patroncito: Oh no, this is too much. You've gone too far, boy. I think you better gimme back my things. (HE TAKES OFF FARMWORKER SIGN AND HAT, THROWS DOWN SHEARS, AND TELLS THE AUDIENCE) You know that damn César Chávez is right? You can't do this work for less than two dollars an hour. No, boy, I think we've played enough. Give me back—

Farmworker: GIT YOUR HANDS OFFA ME, SPIC!

Patroncito: Now stop it, boy!

Farmworker: Get away from me, greaseball! (PATRONCITO TRIES TO GRAB MASK) Charlie! Charlie!

CHARLIE THE RENT-A-FUZZ COMES BOUNCING IN. PATRONCITO
TRIES TO TALK TO HIM.

Patroncito: Now listen, Charlie, I—

Charlie: (PUSHING HIM ASIDE) Out of my way, Mex! (HE GOES OVER
TO FARMWORKER) Yeah, boss?

Farmworker: This union commie bastard is giving me trouble. He's trying to
steal my car, my land, my ranch, and he even tried to rape my wife!

Charlie: (TURNING AROUND, AN INFURIATED APE) You touched a
white woman, boy?

Patroncito: Charlie, you idiot, it's me! Your boss!

Charlie: Shut up!

Patroncito: Charlie! It's me!

Charlie: I'm gonna whup you good, boy! (HE GRABS HIM)

Patroncito: (CHARLIE STARTS DRAGGIN HIM OUT) Charlie! Stop it!
Somebody help me! Help! Where's those damn union organizers?
Where's César Chávez? Help! Huelga! HUELGAAAAA!

CHARLIE DRAGS OUT THE PATRONCITO. THE FARMWORKER TAKES
OFF THE PIG MASK AND TURNS TOWARD THE AUDIENCE.

Farmworker: Bueno, so much for the patrón. I got his house, his land, his
car—only I'm not going to keep 'em. He can have them. But I'm taking
the cigar. Ay los watcho. (EXIT) (pp. 51-53)

I should like to end this overview of the Chicano and his literature,
to demonstrate that you can take the Chicano out of the Barrio, but you
can not take the Barrio out of the Chicano, by reading a poem, the best, in
my estimation, of all Chicano poems: "A Trip Through the Mind Jail," by
Raúl Salinas. Raúl Salinas was in prison—probably for possession of some
grass, but I do know that after he completed his sentence at Leavenworth
he was to be returned to Texas and start serving another sentence. Joseph
Sommers, then at the University of Washington at Seattle, appealed to me
and to other "influential" professionals to write to the Texas Board of
Pardons and plead for a parole. Evidently our appeal was successful. Raúl
Salinas was paroled to Sommers and the University of Washington in 1973,
where he joined a writers' conference. To my knowledge, he is still
there.[71] Salinas' poem reads:

for ELDRIDGE

["A Trip Through the Mind Jail" is dedicated by a Chicano poet, raúlsalinas, from his little room at Leavenworth, to his camarada wherever he is, El
Eldridge (Leroy) Cleaver de Rose Hill, barrio de Con Safos]

la loma
Neighborhood of my youth
        demolished, erased forever from
        the universe.
        You live on, captive, in the lonely
        cellblocks of my mind.
Neighborhood of endless hills
        muddied streets—all chuckhole lined—
        that never drank of asphalt.

Kids barefoot/snotty-nosed
playing marbles, munching on bean tacos
(the kind you'll never find in a café)
2 peaceful generations removed from
their *abuelos'* revolution.
Neighborhood of dilapidated community hall
. . . Salón Cinco de Mayo . . .
yearly (May 5/Sept. 16) gathering
of the familias. Re-asserting pride
on those two significant days.
Speeches by the elders
patriarchs with evidence of oppression
distinctly etched upon *mestizo* faces.
"Sons of the Independence."
Emphasis on allegiance to the *tri-color*
obscure names: Juárez & Hidalgo
their heroic deeds. Nostalgic tales of war
years under Villa's command. No one listened,
no one seemed to really care.
Afterwards, the dance. Modest Mexican
maidens dancing polkas together
across splintered wooden floor.
They never deigned to dance with boys!
The careful scrutiny by curbstone sex-perts
8 & 9 years old. "Minga's bow-legged,
so we know she's done it, huh? "
Neighborhood of Sunday night *jamaicas*
at Guadalupe Church.
Fiestas for any occasion
holidays holy days happy days
'round and 'round the promenada
eating snow-cones . . . raspas . . . & tamales
the games—bingo   cake walk   spin the wheel
making eyes at girls from cleaner neighborhoods
the unobtainables
who responded all giggles and excitement.
Neighborhood of forays down to Buena Vista—
Santa Rita Courts—Los projects—friendly neighborhood
cops n' robbers on the rooftops, sneaking peaks
in people's private night-time bedrooms
bearing gifts of Juicy Fruit gum for
the Projects girls/chasing them in adolescent heat
causing skinned knees & being run off for the night
disenchanted walking home affections spurned
stopping stay-out-late chicks in search of
Modern Romance lovers, who always stood them up
unable to leave their world in the magazines pages.
Angry fingers grabbing, squeezing, feeling,
french kisses imposed; close bodily contact, thigh &
belly rubbings under shadows of Cristo Rey Church.

Neighborhood that never saw a school-bus
  the cross-town walks were much more fun
  embarrassed when acquaintances or friends or relatives
  were sent home excused from class
  for having cooties in their hair!
  Did only Mexicans have cooties in their hair?
   Qué gacho!
Neighborhood of Zaragoza Park
  where scary stories interspersed with
  inherited superstitions were exchanged
  waiting for midnight and the haunting
  lament of La Llorona . . . the weeping lady
  of our myths & folklore . . . who wept nightly,
  along the banks of Boggy Creek,
  for the children she'd lost or drowned
  in the river (depending on the version)
  i think i heard her once
  and cried
  out of sadness and fear
  running all the way home nape hairs at attention
  swallow a pinch of table salt and
  make the sign of the cross
  sure cure for frightened Mexican boys.
Neighborhood of Spanish town Café
  first grown-up (13) hangout
  Andrés,
  tolerant manager, proprietor, cook
  victim of bungling baby burglars
  your loss: Fritos n' Pepsi-Colas . . . was our gain
  you put up with us and still survived!
  You too, are granted immortality.
Neighborhood of groups and clusters
  sniffing gas, drinking muscatel
  solidarity cement hardening
  the clan the family the neighborhood the gang
   Nomás!
  Restless innocents tattoo'd crosses on their hands
  "just doing things different"
  "From now on, all troublemaking mex kids will
  be sent to Gatesville for 9 months."
  Henry home from *la corre*
  khakis worn too low . . . below the waist
  the stomps, the *greña* with ducktail
       —Pachuco Yo—
Neighborhood of could-be artists
  who plied their talents on the pool's
  bath-house walls/intricately adorned
  with esoteric symbols of their cult:
  the art form of our slums
  more meaningful & significant
  than Egypt's finest hieroglyphics.

Neighborhood where purple clouds of *Yesca*
    smoke one day descended & embraced us all.
    Skulls uncapped—Rhythm n' Blues
      Chalie's 7th. St. Club
    loud funky music—wine spodee-odees—barbecue—grass
    our very own connection man: big black Johnny B . . . . .
Neighborhood of Reyes' Bar
    where Lalo shotgunned
    Pete Evans to death because of
    an unintentional stare,
    and because he was *escuadra*,
    only to end his life neatly sliced
    by a prison barber's razor.
    Durán's grocery & gas station
    Guero drunkenly stabbed Julio
    arguing over who'd drive home
    and got 55 years for his crime.
    Ratón: 20 years for a matchbox of weed. Is that cold?
    No lawyer no jury no trial i'm guilty.
      Aren't we all guilty?
    Indian mothers, too, so unaware
    of courtroom tragi-comedies
    folded arms across their bosoms
    saying, "*Sea por Dios.*"
Neighborhood of my childhood
    neighborhood that no longer exists
    some died young—fortunate—some rot in prisons
    the rest drifted away to be conjured up
    in minds of others like them.
    For me: only the NOW of THIS journey is REAL!
Neighborhood of my adolescence
    neighborhood that is no more
    YOU ARE TORN PIECES OF MY FLESH! ! !
    Therefore; you ARE.
LA LOMA . . . AUSTIN . . . MI BARRIO . . .
    i bear you no grudge
    i needed you then . . . identity . . . a sense of belonging.
    i need you now.
    So essential to adult days of imprisonment,
    you keep me away from INSANITY'S hungry jaws;
      Smiling / Laughing / Crying
    i respect your having been:
    My Loma of Austin
    my Rose Hill of Los Angeles
    my West Side of San Anto
    my Quinto of Houston
    my Jackson of San Jo
    my Segundo of El Paso
    my Barelas of Alburque
    my Westside of Denver

Flats, Los Marcos, Maravilla, Calle Guadalupe, Magnolia, Buena
Vista, Mateo, La Seis, Chiquis, El Sur and all
  Chicano neighborhoods that now exist and once existed;
  somewhere . . . . . , someone remembers . . . . .

raúlsalinas
14, Sept.–'69[7] [2]

Texas Tech University

NOTES

[1] Ludwig Wittgenstein, Letter to Ludwig Ficker, October or November, 1919. Quoted in George Steiner, *After Babel* (New York: Oxford Univ. Press, 1975), p. 184.

[2] Entry in Eugène Ionesco's diary. Quoted in Steiner, p. 185.

[3] Steiner, p. 186.

[4] Walter Krickeberg, *Las antiguas culturas mexicanas* (México, D. F.: Fondo de Cultura Económica, 1973), p. 43.

[5] Matt S. Meier and Feliciano Rivera, *The Chicanos—A History of the Mexican Americans* (New York: Hill and Wang, 1972), pp. 13-14.

[6] J. D. M. Ford, *Old Spanish Readings* (1934; rpt. New York: Gordian Press, 1967), p. 310.

[7] W. J. Entwhistle, *The Spanish Language* (London: Faber and Faber, 1962), p. 269.

[8] Krickeberg, p. 44.

[9] Robert Kilburn Spaulding, *How Spanish Grew* (1934; rpt. Berkeley: Univ. of California Press, 1962), p. 161.

[10] Alfonso Reyes, *La X en la frente* (México, D. F.: Porrúa, 1952).

[11] Gilberto López y Rivas, *Los chicanos. Una minoría nacional explotada*, Apéndice I (México, D. F.: Editorial Nuestro Tiempo, 1971), p. 114.

[12] Sergio Elizondo, *Perros y antiperros* (Berkeley: Quinto Sol Publications, Inc., 1972), p. 24.

[13] Robert Quirk, *Mexico*, The Modern Nations in Historical Perspective (Englewood Cliffs, N. J.: Prentice-Hall, Inc., 1971), pp. 8, 21.

[14] Ignacio Bernal, *Mexico Before Cortez* (Garden City, N. Y.: Doubleday and Co., Dolphin Books, 1963), p. 133.

[15] Ibid., p. 125.

[16] Bernal Díaz del Castillo, *Historia verdadera de la conquista de la Nueva España* (México, D.F.: Fondo de Cultura Económica, 1955), p. 23.

[17] Ibid., p. 75.

[18] Hernán Cortés, *Cartas de Relación de la Conquista de Méjico*, 4a. carta, quoted in Aniceto Aramoni, *Psicoanálisis de la dinámica de un pueblo* (México, D. F.: B. Costa-Amic, 1965), p. 82.

[19] Octavio Paz, *The Labyrinth of Solitude* (London: Allen Lane, The Penguin Press, 1967), pp. 70-71.

[20] Quirk, p. 44.

[21] Ibid., p. 45.

[22] Ibid.

[23] Rodolfo Acuña, *Occupied America: The Chicano's Struggle Toward Liberation* (San Francisco: Canfield Press, 1972), p. 11.

[24] Ibid.

118

[25] Ibid.

[26] Ibid.

[27] Ibid., p. 12.

[28] Ibid., p. 17.

[29] Ibid., pp. 15-18.

[30] For a short but good treatment of Chicano history as it is not taught in public schools, see Julián Nava, "Educational Challenges," specifically the sections titled "Mexican American Assertions," and "Re-viewing our History," in *Mexican-Americans Tomorrow*, Gus Tyler, ed. (Albuquerque: Univ. of New Mexico Press, 1975), pp. 120-22.

[31] Meier and Rivera, pp. 60-61.

[32] Ibid., p. 62.

[33] Acuña, p. 21.

[34] Ramón Eduardo Ruiz, *The Mexican War: Was It Manifest Destiny?* (New York: Holt, Rinehart and Winston, 1963), p. 1.

[35] Ibid.

[36] The texts of the Treaty of Guadalupe Hidalgo are reprinted in English and Spanish in Ruth S. Lamb, *Mexican Americans: Sons of the Southwest* (Claremont, California: Ocelot Press, 1970), pp. 62-79.

[37] Ibid., p. 68.

[38] Ibid.

[39] Ibid.

[40] Ibid., p. 69.

[41] John W. Gardner and Francesca Gardner Reese, *Know or Listen to Those Who Know: A Book of Quotations* (New York: W. W. Norton and Co., Inc., 1975), p. 95.

[42] Lamb, p. 56.

[43] Ibid., p. 80.

[44] Ibid., p. 81.

[45] Carey McWilliams, *North from Mexico*, 2nd ed. (New York: Monthly Review Press, 1961), p. 102.

[46] Ibid., p. 103. Italics mine.

[47] John Bartlett, *Familiar Quotations*, 12th ed. enlarged (Boston: Little, Brown, and Co., 1951), p. 734.

[48] Lewis Thomas, "Social Talk," *The Lives of a Cell—Notes of a Biology Watcher* (New York: Viking Press, 1974), p. 90.

[49] See an excellent article on comparative Spanish-Chicano speech by Rosaura Sánchez, "Nuestra circunstancia lingüística," *Voices: Readings from El Grito*, 2nd. rev. ed. (Berkeley: Quinto Sol Publications, 1973), pp. 420-29.

[50] See Richard L. Nostrand, " 'Mexican American' and 'Chicano': Emerging Terms for a People Coming of Age," *The Chicano*, Norris Hundley, Jr., ed. (Santa Barbara: Clio Books, 1975), p. 143.

[51] Ray Padilla, "Apuntes para la documentación de la cultura chicana," *El Grito*, Vol. V., No. 2 (Winter 1971-72), reprinted in *Voices*, p. 118.

[52] Antonia Castañeda Shular, Tomás Ybarra-Frausto and Joseph Sommers, *Literatura chicana: texto y contexto* (Englewood Cliffs, N.J.: Prentice-Hall, Inc., 1972), p. xxiv.

[53] Carey McWilliams, "Once a Well-Kept Secret," *The Chicano*, p. 50.

[54] Castañeda Shular et al., *Literatura chicana: texto y contexto*.

[55] Ibid., pp. xxv-xxvii.

[56] Ibid., p. xxv.

[57] Steiner, p. 188.

[58] Castañeda Shular et al., pp. 104-05.

[59] Julián Nava, pp. 129-30.

[60] Guillermo Rojas, "Chicano/Raza Newspapers and Periodical Serials Listings," *Hispania*, 55, No. 4 (December 1975), pp. 851-63, lists 188 newspapers, newsletters, journals and bulletins in the Southwest, except Colorado and Utah, and also does not include holdings of UCLA.

[61] Padilla, p. 157. At the Texas Tech Library, the holdings on Chicano literature of all types number close to 700 titles. (One of our panelists, Adam F. González, and I have compiled a Chicano bibliography which we hope to publish soon.) And we have been rather late starters here, so you can imagine what the Chicano holdings are at Berkeley, Austin, Los Angeles, San Diego, Tucson.

[62] Frontispiece, *El Espejo-The Mirror*, 5th Printing (Berkeley: Quinto Sol Publications, Inc., 1969-1972).

[63] Castañeda et al., p. 89-90.

[64] Tomás Rivera, " . . . *y no se lo tragó la tierra*" " . . . *and the earth did not part*" (Berkeley: Quinto Sol Publications, 1971).

[65] Juan Rodríguez, rev. of novel, *Explicación de Textos Literarios* (Sacramento, California, 1974-1975), III-2, pp. 201-02.

[66] Tomás Ybarra-Frausto, "Teatro Chicano: Punto de partida," in Castañeda Shular et al., p. 44.

[67] Luis Valdez and Stan Steiner, *Aztlán: An Anthology of Mexican American Literature* (New York: Alfred A. Knopf-Vintage Books, 1972), pp. 353-54.

[68] "Notes on the Chicano Theater," in Valdez and Steiner, *Aztlán*, p. 354.

[69] Luis Valdez, "El Teatro campesino," ibid., pp. 360-61.

[70] Castañeda Shular et al., pp. 46-48.

[71] See Glauco Cambón: "raúlsalinas: a new voice in american poetry," *Entrelíneas*, 4, No. 1-2 (Spring-Summer 1975), 11-13.

[72] Castañeda Shular et al., pp. 182-86.

In Memoriam

As this edition of the Proceedings was in press, we were notified of the untimely death of Dr. David Hsin-Fu Wand, poet, editor, teacher, and scholar. His tragic death on April 8, 1977 was not only an unfortunate loss to scholarship in the fields of multi-ethnic literature in the United States and comparative literature, but also a deeply felt personal loss to his friends and colleagues throughout the world.

The Chinese-American Literary Scene: A Galaxy of Poets and a Lone Playwright*

David Hsin-Fu Wand

ABSTRACT

Differing in their subjects and in the degree of their Third World consciousness, the leading Chinese-American writers nevertheless share a deep awareness of their dual heritage, their Chinese ancestral background and their immediate American environment. In their free verse, the poets Diana Chang, Stephen S. N. Liu, Wing Tek Lum, David Rafael Wang, and Mei Berssenbrugge combine a Chinese sensitivity with the American idiom. This sensitivity is characterized by their recognition of the heritage of their ancestors as well as by an attempt to synthesize their unique Asian-American experience with the English that is spoken around them. The duality of the Asian-American cultural heritage is reflected in individual poems and plays, with emotional reactions ranging from sangfroid and humor in Chang, Liu, and Lum to snarls and rage in Frank Chin, the lone playwright. On the whole, the poets are more Asian: they are willing to accept their dual Asian and American heritage with the equanimity and syncretism of the Chinese. The playwright, however, reflects the Chinese-Western dichotomy in projecting on the stage the conflicting voices of his Chinese and American identities. (DHW)

Ask the average man in the street if he has ever read a book by a Chinese-American writer and his answer might be "I never heard of a Chinaman writing a book!" That particular answer is a line taken from Frank Chin's play *The Chickencoop Chinaman*. The ignorance of Chinese-American literature characterizes not only non-Chinese readers but also the majority of Chinese living in the United States. Having been indoctrinated to think of literature as either Chinese or white by their Chinese ethnocentrism on the one hand and by their public American education on the other, few Chinese in this country have paid much attention to the

*I am indebted to Diana Chang and Stephen S. N. Liu for access to their unpublished manuscripts. All material cited in this essay without specific notes are previously unpublished poems quoted with the kind permission of Ms. Chang and Mr. Liu.

growth and maturity of Chinese-American literature in the years since the Second World War. With the possible exception of Frank Chin, whose plays *The Chickencoop Chinaman* and *The Year of the Dragon* have appeared at the American Place Theater on New York's Broadway, virtually no Chinese-American authors have been properly examined by literary critics. In fact, Frank Chin's plays are not even available in print. Only the first act of *The Chickencoop Chinaman* has been published in the anthology *Aiiieeee!*, and *The Year of the Dragon* was videotaped only after a TV production of the play.

Why is Chinese-American literature so neglected in the United States? The answer is more psychological than literary. The average Chinese in the United States assumes that "Chinese" literature is written in Chinese and printed in China. In his mind, a Chinese is not expected to write in English, which is "no real language of my own to make sense with."[1] On the other hand, he associates American literature with literature written by white American authors, those who are the literary heirs of Hawthorne, Melville, Emerson, Thoreau, Poe, Longfellow, Mark Twain, and Henry James, etc. It seldom occurs to him that a Chinese would write in English, the language usually associated with white men. Educated in the public school system, the Chinese in the United States have often been indoctrinated to equate American literature with white-American literature. The failure of standard American literary anthologies to include Chinese-American literature contributes to the neglect and ignorance of this literature in the U.S. and in the world.

The bulk of Chinese-American literature is written in English, or specifically American-English. For a Chinese-American writing in Chinese, there is always the question of an audience. Unless he expects to be published in China, Hong Kong, or Taiwan, he cannot find a sizable reading public in the United States to warrant the sales of his book. According to official statistics, Chinese immigration between the years of 1820 and 1974 totalled 0.48 of a million (as contrasted to 6.95 and 5.26 million respectively for Germans and Italians). Even today the Asian-Americans (including people of Chinese, Japanese, Korean, and Filipino origin) constitute less than 1% of the entire U.S. population. Therefore, if a Chinese-American expects to be read in the U.S., he has a better chance being read in English than in Chinese. Furthermore, the younger generations of Chinese born in the United States, far removed from their ancestral homeland and educated in American public schools, are more at ease reading and thinking in English than in Chinese.

That the bulk of Chinese-American literature is written in American-English does not refute the fact that there was literature written in Chinese by early Chinese immigrants who settled in the United States. But the literary quality of these early poems and biographies, written in classical rather than vernacular Chinese, has not been properly assessed. Most of them were printed in Chinese-language newspapers and periodicals on the West Coast, but unfortunately all are out of print and hardly accessible. It remains a task for a team of Sinologists to unearth these old publications and winnow out the best poems and prose for posterity.

There are many Chinese-Americans writing today in the United States, and they generally fall into two categories: (1) those born in China but educated in the U.S., and (2) those born and educated in the U.S. The first category includes poets Stephen S. N. Liu, David Rafael Wang, and Mei Berssenbrugge. The second category includes poets Diana Chang and Wing Tek Lum and playwright Frank Chin. Both Diana Chang and Mei Berssenbrugge are Eurasian in origin, the former having a Chinese father and a Eurasian mother and the latter a Dutch-American father and a Chinese mother. Whereas Diana Chang was born in New York City and brought back to China to be educated in American schools until the end of the Second World War, Mei Berssenbrugge was born in Peking and brought to the United States when she was nine months old. In the cases of Stephen S. N. Liu and David Rafael Wang, both were born in China, but came to the U.S. in their teens and received all of their post-high school education here. On the other hand, Frank Chin and Wing Tek Lum were respectively born in California and Hawaii and received their education through the American public school system. All of these Chinese-American authors, especially Mei Berssenbrugge, Diana Chang, Frank Chin, and Wing Tek Lum, converse more readily in English than in Chinese. Although both Stephen S. N. Liu and David Rafael Wang are bilingual in Chinese and English, they have chosen to communicate in their second language rather than their mother tongue. In this respect, they have chosen to be international writers rather than exclusively Chinese writers.

Probably because the psychological novel is a genre alien to the Chinese imagination, few Chinese, including Chinese-Americans, excel in writing it. The Chinese-American novels written in the last thirty years, including Jade Snow Wong's *Fifth Chinese Daughter* and Virginia Lee's *The House that Tai Ming Built*, tend to be biographical in nature and have little style to recommend them. More interesting are Diana Chang's *Frontiers of Love* (1956), which deals with the conflict of a Eurasian, and Frank Chin's unfinished novel, which is a spoof on Charlie Chan. But both Chang and Chin have other abilities to merit critical attention. Diana Chang, whose poetry has appeared in numerous little magazines, stands on solid ground as a poet in her humorous comment on her Asian-American identity:

"Are you Chinese?"
"Are you American?"

124

I am fascinated
but other

anywhere

so it follows
(laconically)

I
must
be
     Jewish

Leading to an eye-opener:
real Chinese in China,
not feeling other,
    not international,
    not cosmopolitan

are gentiles, no less

no wonder
I felt the way I did
in the crowd

my Israel
not there

not here[2]

Nowhere in Diana Chang's poetry are hyperboles and exaggeration. The best of her lines are characterized by understatement and tonal control, as in:

My Chinese body
out of its American head,

Yet
I have no talent for insanity

Instead,
we speak
English
reasonably . . . .

Reflecting on her "Appearance of Being Chinese," which is the title of this poem, she comments wryly that "I look more Chinese here/and pretend too." In referring to "here," she is suggesting that she looks more Chinese in the United States than she would in China. She is also pondering the thin demarcation between reality and illusion (or appearance) as in such lines:

My grandparents are dead
and I never properly introduced
I've always been
In search of a body
not quite Chinese
to call their own . . . .

and

> The Hindus achieve a Self which is not a self.
> There's no earthly call
> for being real . . . .

A scintillating wit and a keen eye for observing the paradoxical make her create "Saying Yes," "Otherness," and "Second Nature," all poems reflecting her Asian-American identity. This wit and love for the paradoxical can also be found in such lines as "Again young,/old departures begin" from the poem entitled "Arrivals."

Although Diana Chang writes in free verse, she uses a subtle rhyme scheme in some of her poems. She surprises the reader by rhyming "twenty" with "sobriety" in "Filiae" and uses off-rhyme skillfully in the first three lines of "Second Nature":

> How do I feel
> Fine wrist to small feet?
> I cough Chinese[3]

The ring of "feel," "feet," and "Chinese" catches and stays in the ear of the reader.

In addition to her wit and her ear for unexpected rhymes, Diana Chang has a painter's eye for details. Her love for art is obvious. One of her poems is entitled "What Matisse Is After." Other poems by her refer to Cezanne, Picasso, Hokusai, and "a Sung painter." In a poem entitled "Rhythms," she combines both the eye of a landscape artist and the subtle rhythm of a lyricist:

> The landscape comes apart
> in birds
>
> A horse
> detaches himself
>
> from a fence
> A criminal of love
>
> breaks away
> The child drops out of a tree
>
> A ship uncouples
> from the street
>
> The canal, unhinged,
> proceeds
>
> Cars are pieces of the world
> tearing away
>
> But the crows
> collect
>
> in heaps
> And stone

and sky
poised with being

grow steep
before

they faint
into the wind

and things
fly

again[4]

The publication of a volume of her poems is an event we should wait for.

In contrast to Diana Chang's prosody, Stephen S. N. Liu writes in more traditional meters. Even some of the titles of his poem, such as "I Lie on the Chilled Stone of the Great Wall," fall into the iambic pentameter pattern of English poetry. Lines such as "No form, no taste, no knowledge, no beauty, no sense" from the poem "On Modern Poetry" and "It happened after the jet plane had cast me" from "Visitors at the Peking Inn" are again in iambics. Many of his poems, including "Old School," "The Wild Horse Star," and "Chung Shin," are nostalgic about his childhood in China. As recollections of his past in a China before the communist takeover, they are poems distinguished by "the quality of affection" (to borrow a phrase from Ezra Pound). "Chung Shin," the poem mourning the death of his youngest brother, is restrained in its grief:

Chung Shin, my little brother, left us
after he had seen nine springs.
It was morning, a sunny day,
the fields outside the window
were green and full of joyful sparrows.

Then came the black-robe priests,
with ancient instruments of music.
Days and night they stood before a row
of haunting candle flames and sang
their scriptures with never changing
sleepy tune, as if they were soliciting
favors for my brother from gods in heaven.

After Chung Shin's soul was saved by
the holy scriptures and by
the blood of the red-ear cocks,
my father brought from the village
a paper carriage and horse,
with a paper lantern and paper driver,
and burned them in the graveyard,
in order that my little brother
might find his way home in the night.
We burned, too, a thousand paper dollars,

so that he might have something to spend.
Lastly my mother burned a paper kite,
for Chung Shin's favorite sport
was to fly a kite in the spring wind.

I saw my mother dry her eyes and face
with a white handkerchief.

Despite the seriousness of tone in many of his China-based poems, Stephen Liu can be sardonically humorous as in a poem entitled "On a 1970 T. V. Singer":

I had thought those icy-shield
rocky mountains would shelter me
from a nation-wide-permeating infection,
but when this creature of Ying or Yang,
more shaggy than my Persian cat,
or this mister-mademoiselle minion,
far, far from Jonny's New York desk
thrusting and hurling a basketful of
blood-red kisses at me, along with
a delirious Christmas song, love song,
immediately I begin to choke, sneeze,
quiver, shiver, and thus and thus . . .
Dear girls, dear boys, just like you,
I'm sick, I'm dying,
and I've too caught this Hong Kong flu:
Christ God, have mercy upon us![5]

Here his allusion to "Jonny's New York desk" should strike a responsive chord in American TV viewers.

After his recent visit to the People's Republic of China, Stephen Liu turned out at least a half dozen memorable poems, most of which are compounded of nostalgia for the old and thrill of seeing a different but revitalized China. In a poem such as "Visitors at the Peking Inn," Liu turns to confront modern Peking after facing the ghosts of the past, such as Kubla Khan, Emperor Chun Tseng of the Ming Dynasty, and the Empress Dowager. After telling the Empress that "these banks [of the Summer Palace] are mine, / these orange groves, these water buffalos, these / homeward villagers floating into the sunset . . . ," Liu finds himself thus:

I was only a few green acres from my Szechuan, too
close to my bed made of cool bamboo bars. I have
a hundred faces to see, a hundred graves to visit.
Could I go back to sleep in this increasing daylight?

Liu concludes his poem with a reference to the cyclical nature of the seasons and with a realization that he is in a new but perennial China:

Summer has lapsed into Autumn. Wu Tung leaves will fall.
Peking is now awakening in the cries of the crows.

In "Window View from a Shanghai Hotel," another poem grown out of his experience of revisiting China, Liu opens the window of a Shanghai hotel only to recall an old love:

> Twenty seven summers distant: her pleading audible,
> her teeth crushing litchis against my mouth,
> her tendril fingers entangling with these of mine,
> and in the gasping of the evening wind, her tears
> invincible, strong as death, still burning in my face.

But the most memorable of his poems dated after his return from the People's Republic of China is, to my mind, the one entitled "I Lie on the Chilled Stones of the Great Wall":

> A north wind dies half way to the Gobi Desert
> as I lie on the chilled stones of the Wall:
> watch towers dangling above me like steel helmets,
> sunlight of Chin dynasty cooling away into a lamp
> at farm windows: unknown seasons falling in rocks,
> white-headed mothers lamenting over the snow:
> Emperor Chin must have one hundred mountains removed.
> My naked arms gluing to the ancient fort,
> my ears listening to the far-off bugles . . .
> I see Su Wu moving with his herd, by the North Sea,
> 19-year captivity, tears freezing in his old face.
> "Nay, you may not return," the savage Chief says;
> "unless your male sheep have become pregnant . . ."
> I see Chao Chun's sedan in a blizzard, her beauty
> once shining through Ch'ang An streets, her heart
> forever longing for a home, her Pi Pa and her singing
> saddening the air at the foreign court; and before the
> skies of West Han turning dark, over the sand ridges
> more barbarian arrows shooting out like locusts,
> but the Mid-Kingdom's banners stand: riders marching on,
> lances clashing, shields colliding: kill! kill! kill!
> invaders wince, scampering about like frightening mice;
> battle cries of Li Ling's braves shaking the earth,
> their bright swords smashing a thousand warriors of Fu,
> and the clouds over my head amassing in wild beasts:
>
> I find myself staggering among the fallen chariots,
> bumping into the manes and breath of dying horses;
> in the struggle I've been wrestling with something
> grizzly, whose eyes are fleeting like fires, whose furry
> feet dancing like a devil, whose icy paws sinking deep
> into my flesh: I endure the pain, and with my scimitar I
> cut his swinish mouth open: the taste of blood wakes
> myself to the noisy tourists:
> the 1975 midsummer sun shines on me like an illusion,
> two thousand years swirling through my bones at once.

Here the past, as represented by Emperor Chin, Su Wu, Chao Chun, and Li Ling, all of whose lives were inextricably linked with the Great Wall of

China, and the present, as represented by the "1975 midsummer sun" merge as "two thousand years [are] swirling through my bones at once."

All the names Liu alludes to in the poem are familiar to readers of Chinese history. Emperor Chin, as even non-Chinese know, was the builder of the Great Wall, a ruthless tyrant who also burnt books and buried scholars alive. Su Wu and Li Ling were both Han poets and courtiers; the former refused to surrender to the Tartars despite 19 years of captivity by the northern tribe and the latter surrendered only after he heard that his family had been put to the sword by the Han court. Chao Chun was a beauty sent by the Han court to appease the Tartar Khan, who had repeatedly invaded the territory of the Middle Kingdom. As the Great Wall was supposedly built to keep the barbarians out, entrances to and exits from China proper must pass through its gates. Su Wu, Li Ling, and Chao Chin were three who were fated to spend some time outside of the Great Wall of China.

No reference to China itself can be found in the poems of Wing Tek Lum, although he is presently living in Hong Kong. Born in Honolulu and educated in New England and New York, Lum does not believe in biographical notes, because he claims to have "an aversion/reaction to the traditional Chinese emphasis on a person's reputation/status in society, at the expense of, and often clouding, the quality of his work."[6] Whereas Stephen Liu's poetry is often written in blank verse or in iambics, Wing Tek Lum often prefers short staccato lines as in his "Minority Poem":

> Why
> we're just as American
> as apple pie—
> that is, if you count
> the leftover peelings
> lying on the kitchen counter
> which the cook has forgotten about
> or doesn't know
> quite what to do with
> except hope that the maid
> when she cleans off the chopping block
> will chuck them away
> into a garbage can she'll take out
> on leaving for the night.[7]

Here we also find a wry, ironic humor which is characteristic of much of his poetry. For instance, in "Blessings" Wing Tek Lum uses dramatic irony to confess to his audience:

> My muse is quite jealous,
> If I ever found another true love
> There'd be poems to pay in hell.[8]

This is the equivalent of an "aside" in the theater, since the muse which is "quite jealous" is presumed not present to hear this confession.

But probably the most humorous of Lum's poems is one entitled "Upon Hearing About the 1971 Fourth Coming of Charlie Chan":

> So sorry. I dislike
> watching black and white television
> so I never heard of it
> till now. I know what I would do
> though:
>   Late at night
> I'd steal a ladder, climb all the way
> up to the marquee
> of Grauman's Chinese Theater.
> During the next day, I'd gorge
> myself full of bananas,
> waiting.
>   I'd watch
> as, little by little, the crowd
> would form, then the sudden
> applause—
>   Ross Martin in his tuxedo
> with no shoes, coming
> down the walk to be cemented.
>
> Just as he passes below me,
> I'd whip out my Yellow Peril
> and drench him.
>   You see,
> I know from experience:
> no matter how many bananas
> I eat, my piss
> always keeps coming out yellow.[9]

Charlie Chan is, of course, a stage Chinaman who has always been portrayed in Hollywood movies by white actors made up to look Oriental and speak a false Chinesey accent. The reference to "Yellow Peril" is a reminder of the anti-Chinese and anti-Japanese mentality of the 1800's when the "inscrutable Orientals" were regarded with suspicion and danger. "Banana" in the parlance of young, radical Asian-Americans means any Oriental who is yellow on the outside, but white inside. The combined use of "Charlie Chan," "Yellow Peril," and "banana" shows Lum's keen sense of irony. Drenching Charlie Chan, as portrayed by Ross Martin, with yellow piss would be an irreverent act, but it would be the most serious comment an Asian-American can make about Hollywood's version of the Honolulu detective chief.

In Lum's poetry, line-breaks are determined by breath-units and muscular tensions. For example, this section is from a long poem entitled "Silences":

Often writing
is like a forced vomit.
After disgorging
all you have, there's still
the dry heaves:
the arrogant excess.
As penance, you walk around for
days on end, wearing
the wasted look.[10]

In this respect, his poetry has the open form of projective verse.

Third World consciousness, marked by his sympathy for the down-trodden and the oppressed and revulsion at social injustice, characterizes such Lum poems as "To Li Po" and "On George Jackson." In the former, he reminds the poet Li Po, who got drunk on elegant wine, that "They [the masses] were illiterate, you knew. /Better than words,/cheap liquor was solace for them."[11] In the latter, he pays his tribute to George Jackson, the black revolutionary who died in Soledad Prison. Lum uses verbal irony to castigate the hypocrisy of the establishment who "have them [the revolutionaries] put away" and then declare "it's humane."[12]

David Rafael Wang, the most widely published of Chinese-American poets, has appeared in more than 70 U.S., Canadian, English, and Australian magazines and has three books of poetry to his credit. *The Goblet Moon*, a limited edition of his early poems, appeared in 1955, about the time of his graduation from Dartmouth College, where he was Class Poet. *The Intercourse*, which celebrates the intercourse, both verbal and physical, between and among the sexes, was released in 1975 by the Greenfield Review Press. A third volume, *River on Fire*, is scheduled for release by the Basilisk Press in 1977. He has been called a "fine poet" by poets as different as Clarence Major and Alvaro Cardona-Hine, a "good poet" by Gary Snyder, and "an expert in the art [of poetry]" by William Carlos Williams.[13] His poetry and translation have also been discussed in articles by Dante Thomas, William Bly, and Hugh Witemeyer in the United States, and mentioned in Yu Suwa's Japanese journal.[14] As the relationship between this author and David Rafael Wang is a symbiotic one much as that existing between Dr. Haggard and Mr. Jive, I will leave him to the critical scrutiny of someone other than myself. I shall take the liberty of quoting from an essay entitled "The Poetry of David Rafael Wang" written by Hugh Witemeyer, who has been considered a noted Pound critic ever since the publication of his book, *The Poetry of Ezra Pound: Forms and Renewal 1908-1920* (Univ. of California Press), in 1969.

According to Hugh Witemeyer, "David Rafael Wang is a Chinese-American poet in a very literal sense of the term." After stating the fact that Wang came to the United States in 1949, Witemeyer makes the following claim:

Because the immigration took place in Wang's own lifetime rather than that of his parents or ancestors, the dialectic between Chinese and American elements in his poetry is particularly vivid and interesting to follow. The term "dialectic" is appropriate because there is a definite pattern of thesis, antithesis, and synthesis in the three volumes of poetry that Wang has published in the United States.

Witemeyer calls *The Goblet Moon* (1955) Wang's "apprentice work." He finds that the poems in the volume "are traditional in form—two are Shakespearean sonnets—and more than half of them have either Chinese subjects or a distinctively Chinese tone." He further notes that "the English is correct but cautious and conservative."

Witemeyer observes that "twenty years . . . passed" between *The Goblet Moon* and "the publication of Wang's second book, *The Intercourse*" in 1975. He points out that during those years Wang met Ezra Pound, William Carlos Williams, and Gary Snyder and "began to write in open form and in a distinctively American idiom." He finds *The Intercourse* "the antithesis of *The Goblet Moon*," because the poems in Wang's second volume are "all in free verse" and only two of them have "Chinese subjects or tone." To Witemeyer, the poems in *The Intercourse* are "squarely in the Williams/Olson tradition of projective verse," and the following poem, "The Rub," is one he uses to support his point:

> Watching you wash him,
> a small
> washcloth held tight,
> your hands going up
> and down, rubbing Balmain
> over his sweat
> from armpits past navel
> to his back, I see you
> both on fire/the bodies
> in the concentration
> of your mind/the act
> cuts thru the grease, the smudge
> as the muscle
> beneath his skin
> extends & gathers light.[15]

After quoting "The Rub," Witemeyer remarks that "mind is merged into the rhythms and wisdom of the body in *The Intercourse*," and he hails the book as " 'naked poetry' in theme as well as form." In using the term "naked poetry," Witemeyer is referring to a recent anthology of American poetry edited by Stephen Berg and Robert Mezey, who claim in their Foreword that much of the best American poetry of recent years are written in "Open forms," which means that the poems "don't rhyme (usually) and don't move on feet of more or less equal duration (usually)."[16]

Witemeyer discovers that the poems in *The Intercourse* fall into two categories: (1) "lyric celebrations of physical and sexual activity" and (2) "wry epigrams on the same themes." As a Pound scholar, Witemeyer states that "the division between lyrics and satires" in Wang's book "is reminiscent of Ezra Pound's *Lustra*" and that the following poem (entitled "Intaglio") "could have appeared in any Imagist anthology":

> The crocus
> that thrusts its
> stamen up in the air
> has not a more independent stance
> than when she bends to rub
> lotion over his sunburnt legs
> his hardness waking
> to the caress of her hand.[17]

Claiming that "Wang's satirical epigrams are aimed at contemporary *mores*, but use that timeless tactics that have sustained such poems since the days of Martial and Catullus," Witemeyer quotes the following poem (a section from "Out in Hollywood") to illustrate his thesis:

> At ten he admired
> Tarzan's physique.
>
> At fifteen he worked—
> out like Steve Reeves.
>
> Now in his twenties he sells
> his buns all week.[18]

He further calls the above poem "a section from . . . a caustic, funny sequence about the midnight cowboys of Los Angeles." Witemeyer's overall assessment of the book is this:

> *The Intercourse* displays an impressive command of diction and tone, from the street slang of "Out in Hollywood" to the snatches of black dialect in "The Ash-Hauler" to the formal eloquence of the more intense lyrics.

He concludes his evaluation of *The Intercourse* by quoting "The Stake," another poem from the volume:

> Stay cool
> baby
> stay cool/he says
> a boy of 18 or
> 19/if over a day
> It's all your mind/control
> —that's where I'm ahead/the only thing
> real is his/not
> the Beatle haircut or
> blond locks of hair/the
>
> white T-shirt or levi
> also
> other boys wear/but

134

```
      the flesh
          skin
             outthrusts
                   the plain wear
   declares:
          In my physique
                 you see
                      the mind
   reigns.¹⁹
```

What Hugh Witemeyer has to say about Wang's third book, *Rivers on Fire*, can only be properly presented by quoting it *in toto*:

American speech and Chinese experience come together in Wang's next book of poems, *Rivers on Fire*, published in 1977. "Should I consent to the union of opposites/ Or face the clashing of America and Asia?" asked the speaker of an amusing poem about East/West marriages. In *Rivers on Fire*, Wang has consented to a union of opposites in his own work. This third book of his is a synthesis of the different directions taken by the first two. The marriage is especially fruitful in a sequence of fifteen poems entitled *The Grandfather Cycle*, to my mind Wang's most impressive poetic achievement to date. The poems are part of a long family epic in progress which, when finished, is to contain 101 cantos. The "Cycle" is dedicated to William Carlos Williams, whose strong sense of family and locality may have been an inspiration to Wang. The "Cycle" has the "sequence" structure characteristic of many modern American long poems such as Williams's *Paterson* and Pound's *Cantos*. The central figure in the sequence is "His Excellency F. K. Wang, my grandfather,/ the sire of some twenty bastards,/ the heater of virgins' coverlets,/ a classic Chinese scholar,/ an impeccable mandarin official." The poem celebrates both the culture and "the epic fornications" of this great man. The speaker, his grandson, envies him both activities and thinks of him with nostalgia:

```
   In Shanghai
          by the Yangtze
   Where I watched
             the ships
   Coming in going out
          of the harbor
   And the tiny sampans
             tremulous on the waves,
   I used to sit
          beneath the peach blossoms
   Near the Lunghwa Tower,
          with swallows
   Dipping over my head
          and sandcrabs
   Scurrying near my feet
          And think about
   The epic fornications
                   of my
   Fabulous
          Grandfather.
```

Great Man!
        He sired
Eight sons
        and some
Twenty bastards
        by
                Three wives
        and
Four dozen
        Concubines,
In an age
        when virginity
Was the eunuch's lot
        and polygamy
        the strong man's goal.

His offspring
        Multiplied,
Spread from
        Hangchow to
London,
        Paris to
Mukden—
        Some begotten
On ships,
        Some made
in sampans;
        All different:
Blonde hair,
        Grey eyes,
Widow's peak,
        Curly beard,
Till even
        Tao Kwan &
T'ung Tse
        the emperors,
Became envious of
        him,
        the plucker of peaches &
        apple blossoms.

Strong though the Chinese sensibility is in these poems, they are entirely American in their language. A poem like "The Bamboo Drippings" builds off Pound's thirteenth canto, and moves with complete assurance and independence in the linguistic area that Pound calls "logopoeia," language employed with a consciousness of its ordinary social usages, "the dance of the intellect among words."

Wang lived without moderation,
    Dedicated to deflowering virgins.
His specialty:
        "unnatural positions";

The result: still
             pregnant women.
For 60 years he dogged
             the path of peach blossoms
And at 72 contracted
             the willow ailment,
Impolitely called V.D.
                   in the Occident.
Seldom a lady he met
             escaped his blessings;
All engaged his attention
             except the ungainly,
Who violated his code
             of aesthetic honor,
Irrevocable as
             the Confucian canons.

His triumph was one of will,
                   not of instrument,
For nature did not endow him
                   with unusual proportions.
In the company of nymphs
             he practiced abstinence;
But confronted with a shy virgin he was
                   compromising.
His moral: kindness above
             sex relations,
With a bed and a pasture
             as intermittent dispensations.

"Young man, do not copulate
             with wolves:
They might bite off
             your testicles
—especially those who have
             a taste for them."
Such was his advice to me, his grandson.

These are the tones of a mature American poet dealing with a family experience that is entirely different from the American norm. This union of contemporary American language with a profoundly Chinese sensibility is what makes *The Grandfather Cycle* so exciting. Here David Rafael Wang is breaking new ground, and writing a kind of poetry that is not like anything I have seen before.

As early as 1963, Gary Snyder has observed in a letter dated 7 June to David Rafael Wang that "You are developing a new style . . . *con cojones* & deep breathing." In a letter dated 27 October 1975, Stephen Liu reacts to the poems in *The Intercourse* by saying:

Your diction is always fresh, much better than that of some of our poets who write modernist poems. Your structural ambiguity is also very intriguing. I admire your courage to have done away with the manacles of the traditional

English poetry. . . . After reading through your book I wish you would write more stuff like "In the City," "The Break," "Dynamo," "The Untamed," "The Rite," "The Intercourse," "Cool Cat," and "The Stake." In these poems your wit and your imagery burn more bright than others. And I still think that "Quartet for Gary Snyder" is one of your most original poems, and that "Cool Cat" is your best imagistic poem. I suggest you write your Chinese poems like Bly and Pound: paraphrasing instead of translating. Certainly you can do a better job than most of these American poets. They simply can't preserve that Chinese flavor from a translation. Your Yueh Fei poem and "Poems of Separation" are good, but you may try a volume of paraphrased Chinese poetry: nobody has done such work besides Pound.

The observations of both Gary Snyder and Stephen Liu seem to concur with those of Hugh Witemeyer. Both Liu and Witemeyer have noted that Wang's poetry is in the Imagist tradition, while Snyder and Witemeyer have pointed out the physicality of Wang's poetry.

Like David Rafael Wang, Mei Berssenbrugge has written about the family in her poetry. In a poem entitled "Chronicles: Number One and Two," she devoted her first stanza to her Dutch-American father, but her second stanza to her Chinese grandfather. Here Mei Berssenbrugge and David Rafael Wang share something in common: they both show an affection for their respective grandfathers. Whereas Wang's grandfather came to the U.S. as a diplomat and was stationed for several years in Washington D.C., Berssenbrugge's grandfather came as a student and attended Harvard College. In her own words, she gives a very vivid sketch of the man:

> My Chinese grandfather
> survived a mule trek first-hand,
> a steam ship journey
> to Cambridge, Massachusetts
> in 1910;
> he wanted to do some
> mission work
> at Harvard College
> he roomed with a widow and three
> hoop-skirted daughters on Mount Auburn Street
> and went home
> with a taste for apple pie.[20]

What appeared as "Chronicle" in her book, *Summits Move with the Tide* (1974), reappeared later in an anthology, *Settling America* (1974), as "Chronicles: Number Three." This poem about her family is distinctly Chinese in its sensitivity and is worth quoting in its entirety:

> I was born the year of the loon
> in a great commotion. My mother—
> who used to pack $500 cash
> in the shoulders of her fur gambling coat,
> who had always considered herself
> the family's "First Son"—

took one look at me
and lit out again
for a vacation to Sumatra.
Her brother purchased my baby clothes;
I've seen them, little clown suits,
of silk and color.

Each day
my Chinese grandmother bathed me
with elaboration in an iron tub;
amahs waiting in lines
with sterilized water and towels
clucked and smiled
and rushed about the tall stone room
in tiny slippers.

After my grandfather
accustomed himself
to this betrayal by First Son,
he would take me in his arms,
walk with me
by the plum trees, cherries, persimmons;
he showed me the stiff robes
of my ancestors and their drafty hall,
the long beards of his learned old friends,
and his crickets.

Grandfather talked to me, taught me.
At two months, my mother tells me,
I could sniff for flowers,
stab my small hand upwards to moon.
Even today I get proud
when I remember
this all took place in Chinese.[2][1]

In stating that she "was born [in] the year of the loon," Mei Berssen-brugge is obviously being facetious, since there is no such sign in the twelve animal zodiac signs of the Chinese calendar. She is suggesting that she was born crazy as a loon (to use an American cliché). The line takes on additional meaning in the context of the rest of the stanza, because "My mother . . . took one look at me/and lit out again/for a vacation to Suma-tra." Here Mei Berssenbrugge is showing a self-deprecating humor, al-though she does not spell out for the reader what exactly made her mother leave for a trip in such a hurry. In stanza three, Mei further talks about "this betrayal by First Son." Much is left to the conjecture of the reader.

Mei Berssenbrugge is masterly at writing love poetry. The poems in the second section of *Summits Move with the Tide* are all about love. "Old Man Let's Go Fishing in the Yellow Reeds of the Bay," "Travelling through Your Country," and "Propeller Sleep" are three of the finest love poems in contemporary American poetry. "Propeller Sleep" is not only subtle but also witty:

I've learned to recognize angels
riding the city busses
in their white T shirts
by their utterly plain faces

Their flesh
which is human almost
shifts to air at its frontiers

Their shadows
are casual shapes their friends wear
the unfleshed dreams accompanying them
across the vapor lamps

Angels beat their wings
so we won't forget them
They grieve
at being born of men and not angels
Even if one stays by your side seven years
it is a parallel flight[22]

The last line about "a parallel flight" has enough wit to make any eye sparkle, since "parallel," which has the meaning of running side by side but not touching, suggests the relationship of these "angels" with their women.

The precision in her choice of words can be illustrated by her use of "rampant" in the last line of "Abortion," a poem she uses to end the second section of her book:

When we walked outside at sunset
a tenement was burning to the ground
water tore bricks from the walls
and ashes fell in my hair
I wore your big goosedown jacket
and hugged my sleeves watching
from behind a playground fence
the rampant light[23]

Here "rampant," which has the dictionary meaning of (1) unrestrained; wild and (2) standing on the hind legs; rearing like a quadruped, suggests a great deal about the man wearing the "big goosedown jacket" who is only seen in profile. Through subtlety and indirection, Mei evokes in one word what may take others many lines to describe.

A Taoist-like serenity, as characterized by man's harmonious blending with the universe, is achieved in such a poem as "In Bhaudanath":

If your eyes fall
let them
if the thigh bone
takes off and hollows out
it makes
a good flute

> if your shining
> amber skull
> fills with liquid
> you know
> it is clean
> water
> from the mountains.[24]

Here the attitude of the poet toward death reminds us of that of the philosopher Chuang Tzu, who believed that "not nature only but man's being has its seasons, its sequence of spring and autumn, summer and winter."[25]

Robert Creeley, the foremost Black Mountain poet, once wrote "Love is dead in us/if we forget/the virtues of an amulet/and quick surprise."[26] "Quick surprise" is an element often found in Mei's poetry—for instance, in the last two lines of this stanza of a poem entitled "Bog":

> Leaves rotting into each other
> nuclei falling away
> the great subterranean arms
> of trees and small skeletons embrace.[27]

The embrace of "trees" and "small skeletons" in a desolate scene is the last thing we expected. But it implies a continuity of life and death.

Sometimes Mei surprises us with surrealistic details such as "contaminated wanderers," "sour sunlight," and "vampires" in "Hudson Ice Floes":

> Ice breaks in the river
> between piers and ship prows
> inhaling and exhaling the current
> or it speeds free
> luminous heavy swans downstream
> Contaminated wanderers
> garbage falls on their mirrors
> with the sour sunlight
>
> Tugboats plow them under
> Vampires melt them with flicked ashes
> Blue dying whales who swallow them
> gag, toss out clean
> gunmetal blue bubbles
> that float away over us like music.[28]

She could also surprise us with far-flung metaphors as in the last stanza of a poem named "Blossom":

> Look
> at your fingertips
> The planets rising in your nails
> are beginning to orbit
> Those veins in your wrist, already
> a brave distance from the heart.[29]

Diana Chang, Stephen S. N. Liu, Wing Tek Lum, David Rafael Wang, and Mei Berssenbrugge are the most widely published Chinese-American poets writing today. But standard anthologies of American poetry, which have given some token recognition to black poets in recent years, have yet to open their pages to them. Although each of these five poets has a unique voice, which can easily be recognized by careful readers, they share three characteristics in common: (1) they all have a sense of humor, which is an ethnic heritage of the Chinese and is found in Chinese literature from the earliest satirical poems in *The Book of Poetry* (called by Ezra Pound *The Confucian Odes*) down to the bawdy Yuan and Ming novels such as *Water Margin* and *Chin Ping Mei*; (2) despite their occasional revulsion at social injustice in the U.S., they maintain an equanimity, which is characterized by understatement rather than frontal attack; and (3) they have a syncretism, as typified by their acceptance of the Yin-Yang duality and of ambiguities in the spectrum of life.[30] In these respects, all five poets are highly Chinese in their sensibility, despite their choice to write in English rather than Chinese.

Although Frank Chin has written prose-fiction and some occasional poems, he is first and foremost a dramatist. Like the protagonists (or heroes), Tam Lum in *The Chickencoop Chinaman* and Fred Eng in *The Year of the Dragon*, "his own 'normal' speech jumps between black and white rhythms and accents."[31] Sometimes, he probably feels like Tam Lum that he has "no real language of my own to make sense with, so out comes everybody else's trash that don't conceive."[32] The protagonists of his two plays are both in conflict, obsessed with the problem of identity. Tam (short for Tampax) Lum in *The Chickencoop Chinaman*, who has been victimized by the white world that surrounds him, is ambivalent toward the Chinese, as characterized by the following dialogue couched in irony:

> Robbie: You're Chinese aren't you? I like Chinese people.
> Tam: Me too. They're nice and quiet aren't they?[33]

This ambivalence is further shown by Tam Lum's acceptance of the Lone Ranger as a hero. In his list of characters, Frank Chin describes the Lone Ranger as follows:

> A legendary white racist with the funk of the West mouldering in his blood. In his senility, he still loves racistly, blesses racistly, shoots straight and is coocoo with the notion that white folks are not white folks but just plain folks.[34]

In the action of the play, the Lone Ranger not only gets away with shooting a silver bullet into Tam Lum's hand, but also lectures him, as he rides away:

> China boys, you be legendary obeyers of the law, legendary humble, legendary passive. Thank me now and I'll let you get back to Chinatown preservin your culture.[35]

He further insults Tam Lum by making him a "honorary white" and relegates him to the company of Pearl Buck, Charlie Chan, and Helen Keller. To Frank Chin, Helen Keller, who lacks a voice of her own, is the image of a passive Oriental. Early in *The Chickencoop Chinaman*, Tam Lum has remarked about Helen Keller ironically:

> Helen Keller overcame her handicaps without riot! She overcame handicaps without looting! She overcame handicaps without violence! And you Chinks and Japs can too.[36]

Not contented with being an "honorary white" or whitemen's pet Chinaman, Tam Lum tries to find a voice of his own to articulate his own consciousness. He lashes out at the synthetic Chinamen, "who are made, not born—out of junk imports, lies, railroad scrap iron, dirty jokes, broken bottles, cigar smoke, Cosquilla Indian blood, wino spit, and lots of milk of amnesia."[37] He articulates his own agony by shouting:

> [I was] no more born than nylon or acrylic. For I am a Chinaman! A miracle synthetic. Drip dry and machine washable.[38]

In *The Chickencoop Chinaman*, Tam Lum has only one close friend, Kenji, a Japanese-American "research dentist" who lives in the depth of Pittsburgh's black slum called "Oakland." Kenji, who gathers around him some bizarre characters living at his expense, shares with Tam Lum the problem of identity. Nicknamed "BlackJap Kenji," the dentist denies that he is a "copycat," that he is imitating black people:

> I know I live with 'em, I talk like 'em, I dress . . . maybe even eat what they eat and don't mess with, so what if I don't mess with other Orientals . . . Asians, whatever, blah, blah, blah . . .[39]

He also goes on to state:

> I'm not Japanese! Tam ain't no Chinese! And don't give me any of that "If-you-don't-have-that-Oriental-culture, -baby, -all-you've-got-is-the-color-of-your-skin," bullshit . . . .[40]

Living in a black ghetto and going to a school where the majority were black, Kenji had to adapt in order to survive:

> Schools was all blacks and Mexicans. We [Kenji and Tam Lum] were kids in school, and you either walked and talked right in the yard, or got the shit beat outa you every day, ya understand? But that Tam was always what you might say . . . "The Pacesetter." Whatever was happenin with hair, or the latest color, man—Sometimes he looked pretty exotic, you know, shades, high greasy hair, spitcurls, purple shiney shirt, with skull cufflinks and Frisko jeans worn like they was fallin off his ass. "BlackJap Kenji" I used to be called and hated yellow-people. You look around and see where I'm livin . . . and it looks like I still do, Pittsburgh ain't exactly famous for no Chinatown or Li'l Tokyo, you know.[41]

Here Kenji has given a brilliant explanation of his strange identity. Having lived as a minority in the heart of a black ghetto, he has adopted the values and *mores* of his immediate environment. From the psychological point of view, introjection is what made him more black than Japanese in behavior.

The plot of *The Chickencoop Chinaman* revolves around Tam Lum's coming to Pittsburgh to make a documentary film about a black boxer and to interview Charley Popcorn, whom the boxer has claimed to be his real father. But Charley Popcorn, who runs a pornographic movie house in Pittsburgh, denies that he is the father and claims that he was only the boxer's manager. Here we find another case of the problem of identity. Perhaps the boxer has chosen to live with the myth, just as Tam Lum, since his childhood, has chosen the Lone Ranger as his cultural hero and expected to find Chinese eyes behind his mask. The problem of identity is never resolved for either Tam Lum or Kenji in the course of the play, but in the last scene Tam Lum ends up in the kitchen, whetting his meat cleaver. This meat cleaver, like Frank Chin's own pen, may chop away much nonsense about white America's stereotyped images of the silent and docile Orientals.

As compared with *The Chickencoop Chinaman*, Chin's second play, *The Year of the Dragon*, has more recognizable Chinese characters, because all the conflicts and headaches take place in an old apartment located in San Francisco's Chinatown. Fred Eng, the protagonist of the play, shares with Tam Lum his eloquence and he uses it to "badmouth" tourists who come to gawk at Chinatown. Making his living as a Chinatown tour guide, he still lives at the Chinatown apartment of his parents. Although he is already in his forties, he cannot get away from his parents, partly because of the antiquated Chinese tradition of filial duty and partly because of self-doubts and internal conflicts. Fred finds his antagonist in his father, who rules the family with an iron hand. The family affair is further complicated by the arrival of "China Mama," the first wife Pa left behind in China in 1935. Ma Eng, American-born and raised, tries hard to be a peacemaker in the family, but it is a thankless task because there is a real conflict of three cultures. The three cultures are represented by the traditional Chinese ways of Pa Eng and "China Mama," the Chinese-American ways of herself and Fred, and the assimilated American ways of Sissy and Johnny, Fred's younger sister and brother. Sissy manages to escape from the problem of identity by marrying a white American and living away in Boston. But when she visits her parents in San Francisco, she finds herself caught in the storm of the conflict. Johnny, who can hardly speak a word of Chinese, has become a tough street kid, plagued by a sense of displacement. Fred Eng, born in China but raised in America, tries to help his younger brother and urges him to move away from home. Torn by filial piety for his parents on the one hand and hatred for the iron-clad Chinese tradition on the other, he lashes out at Pa Eng, the family patriarch, who retaliates by threatening to die. The generation gap or lack of communication between the generations may remind some Chinese readers of that in Pa Chin's novel, *Family* (1931).[42] The protagonist in *Family* tries to discover his identity and chart a new course for his own generation. He rejects the tradition of the past as irrelevant to his time.

As Bernard Shaw once said, "Without conflict there is no drama," Frank Chin has projected onto the stage his own internal conflicts in the two plays, *The Chickencoop Chinaman* and *The Year of the Dragon*. The voices of his characters in the plays are basically the conflicting voices of his Chinese and his American identities. Like the five Chinese-American poets, Frank Chin shows a sense of humor. His humor is shown through the dialogue and the characterization in his plays. But unlike the Chinese-American poets, he lacks their syncretism and equanimity. His humor is mordant and bitter. In this respect, he might be more American than Chinese, an heir of Mark Twain, who wrote such dark tales as "The Man that Corrupted Hadleyburg" and "The Mysterious Stranger," rather than a literary descendant of Chuang Tzu and the classical Chinese poet-drunkards. But his contribution to the stage is substantial: for the first time in the theater there is an authentic Chinese-American voice. He has demolished the stage Chinaman with his plays and succeeded in articulating his own consciousness. In a strange but different way, Frank Chin's work in the theater reminds us of the effort of that Irish genius, James Joyce, who tries to "forge in the smithy of my soul the uncreated conscience of my race,"[43] and, in Frank Chin's case, "the race" is neither the Chinese of the distant land nor the American of the white establishment, but the hitherto unheard and unsung world of the Chinese-Americans.

The University of Texas at Dallas

NOTES

[1] Frank Chin, *The Chickencoop Chinaman*, acting version (New York: American Place Theater, 1972), ACT I, 3.

[2] David Hsin-Fu Wand, ed., *Asian-American Heritage: An Anthology of Prose and Poetry* (New York: Pocket Books, 1974), pp. 135-36. The poem is entitled "Otherness."

[3] *Asian-American Heritage*, p. 137. Hereafter cited as *AAH*.

[4] Diana Chang, "Rhythms," *The Painted Bride Quarterly* (Winter 1975).

[5] *AAH*, p. 149.

[6] Quoted from a letter by Wing Tek Lum in *Asian-American Heritage*, p. 301.

[7] *AAH*, p. 152.

[8] *AAH*, p. 150.

[9] *AAH*, pp. 151-52.

[10] *AAH*, p. 154.

[11] *AAH*, p. 150.

[12] *AAH*, p. 151.

[13] See Clarence Major, "Editors (and Others) Write," *Trace*, No. 37 (May-June 1960), pp. 16-17; Alvaro Cardona-Hine, letter dated 29 May 1962; Gary Snyder, letter dated 28 June 1959; and William Carlos Williams, letter dated 14 December 1959.

[14] See Dante Thomas' "William Carlos Williams' Bridge to China" (*La Huerta*, 1, No. 2 [1972], n.p.), in which he discusses Wang's poetic association with Williams; William J. Bly's book review of *Asian-American Heritage* (*Arizona Quarterly*, 32, No. 1 [Spring 1976], 92-93); Hugh Witemeyer's "The Flame-style King" (*Paideuma*, 4, Nos. 2 and 3 [1975], 333-35), in which he discusses Wang's relationship with Ezra Pound, and Witemeyer's "The Poetry of David Rafael Wang," forthcoming in a book of collected essays on minority literatures to be edited by Walter J. Ong and released by the Modern Language Association. Yu Suwa's journal, whose title can be translated as *Avant-garde*, is issued only in Japanese and unavailable in the United States. But Vol. 2 of its 1960 issue discusses briefly Wang's poetry and his editorship of the "Li Po" issue of the *Galley Sail Review*, No. 5 (1959-1960).

[15] David Rafael Wang, *The Intercourse* (Greenfield Center, New York: Greenfield Review Press, 1975), p. 22.

[16] Stephen Berg and Robert Mezey, eds., *Naked Poetry: Recent American Poetry in Open Forms* (Indianapolis: Bobbs-Merrill, 1969), p. xi.

[17] Wang, p. 13.

[18] Wang, p. 30.

[19] Wang, p. 15.

[20] Mei Berssenbrugge, as quoted in *Settling America: The Ethnic Expression of 14 Contemporary Poets*, David Kheridan, ed. (New York: Macmillan, 1974), p. 2.

[21] Mei Berssenbrugge, *Summits Move With the Tide* (Greenfield Center, New York: Greenfield Review Press, 1974), pp. 42-43. See also *Settling America*, pp. 2-3.

[22] *Summits Move With the Tide*, p. 29. Hereafter cited as *SMT*.

[23] *SMT*, p. 36.

[24] *SMT*, p. 20.

[25] This translation comes from Cyril Birth, ed., *Anthology of Chinese Literature: From Early Times to the Fourteenth Century* (New York: Grove Press, 1965), p. 82. It was rendered by Arthur Waley.

[26] Robert Creeley, *For Love: Poems 1950-1960* (New York: Charles Scribner's Sons, 1962), p. 46. The poem is entitled "The Warning."

[27] *SMT*, p. 13.

[28] *SMT*, p. 47.

[29] *SMT*, p. 46.

[30] For a discussion of Chinese syncretism and Yin-Yang duality, see my article "To the Summit of Tai Shan: Ezra Pound's Use of Chinese Mythology," *Paideuma*, 3, No. 1 (Spring 1974), 3-12. See also William Theodore De Bary, Wing-tsit Chan, and Burton Watson, eds., *Sources of Chinese Tradition*, I (New York: Columbia Univ. Press, 1964), 239. In general, this syncretism entails the ability to reconcile contrary or opposite doctrines or beliefs. For Chinese-American poets particularly, it is the blending of Chinese sensibility and American speech in a fruitful Yin-Yang union.

[31] Frank Chin, *The Chickencoop Chinaman*, acting version (New York: American Place Theater, 1972) Act I, 3. Hereafter cited as Chin.

[32] Chin, Act I, 3.

[33] Chin, Act I, 19.

[34] Chin, "The Characters."

[35] Chin, Act I, 43.

146

[36] Chin, Act I, 7.

[37] Chin, Act I, 2-3.

[38] Chin, Act I, 4.

[39] Chin, Act I, 23.

[40] Chin, Act I, 23-24.

[41] Chin, Act I, 21.

[42] Available in English as Pa Chin, *Family*, Introd. by Olga Lang (New York: Doubleday Anchor, 1972).

[43] James Joyce, *Portrait of the Artist as a Young Man* (New York: Viking/ Compass, 1956), p. 253.

Croatian-American Literature

Branimir Anzulovic

ABSTRACT

The principal purpose of this paper is to describe and analyze the literary activity of Croatian Americans from its beginning until the present. This activity started toward the end of the nineteenth century, when the large number of recently arrived Croatian immigrants created a market for newspapers, magazines, and books in their native language. Most of the early immigrants were peasants who had little or no formal education but who were familiar with folk poems and tales. They wrote poems in that traditional style to chronicle current events of interest, and this type of poetry constituted the largest part of the early Croatian ethnic literary production. The most interesting creation of that period was the legendary figure of Joe Magarac, the steel hero, developed anonymously by Croatian steel workers in the Pittsburgh area. World War I interrupted an intense literary activity of that kind, and until the end of World War II there was a relative stagnation caused by the drastically curtailed influx of new immigrants and by progressive assimilation of older ones. However, the assimilation led to the appearance of literary works in English. World War II ushered in the third period of Croation-American literature, which is characterized by a much higher degree of sophistication and quality of literary production. This improvement is not the result of the development of a Croatian literary tradition in America but of the fact that the postwar emigration from Croatia brought to this country a large number of highly educated people, some of whom are professional writers. (BA)

The beginning of literary activity of Croatian immigrants in the United States is directly linked with the emergence of a Croatian press in this country. Newspapers provided the first opportunity to have literary works printed in that language and distributed to the readers.

Croats started to arrive in America very early. This is not surprising since they are a maritime people who have been actively engaged in shipping for many centuries. The ships of the free republic of Dubrovnik, chartered by Spain, sailed regularly between the Iberian peninsula and her colonies soon after the discovery of the New World. Some Croats also came to America as missionaries and explorers. But it was only after they started arriving in the United States in large numbers around 1880 that their communities became extensive enough to sustain publishing.

Some newspaper publishers soon expanded their activities with the publication of magazines, almanacs, and calendars. These were even more important than the newspapers themselves as the vehicles for literary activity. They published both works of writers in the home country and works written by immigrants. The first Croatian-American almanac (*Hrvatsko-amerikanska Danica*) appeared in 1895. The mid-1890's, therefore, marked the beginning of Croatian ethnic literature in this country.

At first, immigrant literary activity found its outlet in periodicals only. Then, in the first decade of this century, poetry and fiction began to appear in book form, and until the mid-1910's their number steadily increased. In fact, as far as the number of published volumes is concerned, the years 1910 to 1914 have never been surpassed.

I will limit myself here mostly to works published in book form; otherwise the scope would be too wide. Moreover, many periodicals, especially from the early period, have been completely lost. (But some of the books can no longer be found either, and it is highly probable that there have been titles of which we do not even know.)

According to George J. Prpić, who has compiled a bibliography of Croatian emigré literature and who has on several occasions written about the history of Croat immigration in America,[1] the first Croatian volume of fiction was published in this country in 1904. It was a novel *Zapisci* (Notes) by Medo Krašić,[2] whose theme is the unfortunate life of a poor Croatian immigrant girl. Seven years later, S. R. Danevski published a collection of short stories, *Pripovijesti*[3] some of which also deal with the life of immigrants, both in the United States and upon their return to the native country, while others are based on purely American themes. This book was favorably reviewed in Croatia and regarded as the beginning of a Croatian literary tradition in America.[4]

But with these two works we have practically exhausted the volumes of prose written in the first period of Croatian literary activity in this country, that is, the period until 1918. The dominant vehicle of literary expression in that period was poetry. This may at first sound surprising if we take into account that the great majority of immigrants at that time were not sophisticated people but peasants, many of them from the poorest and most backward areas of Croatia. Illiteracy among these immigrants was much higher than the average in their country. Yet, although these people had little or no schooling, they did have their cultural heritage. This consisted, among other things, of folk songs, poems, and tales. It was poetry written in this popular tradition which dominated the literary scene of Croatian immigrants at the beginning of this century.

One important traditional function of folk poetry in the home country was the chronicling of both past and current events. The folk style poetry that the immigrants wrote in their new country fulfilled the same role. There were poems describing the voyage from the native village to America;[5] at that time such a voyage was not only long but also full of all kinds of experiences, especially for those who had left the narrow circle of their village for the first time. Other poems had wars as their theme: Russo-Turkish, Russo-Japanese, Chinese Revolution, Balkan, and First World War.[6] There were also poems dealing with themes from immigrants' everyday life and family problems, as well as a poem about the sinking of the Titanic.[7]

All of these poems were written in the traditional style of Croatian folk poetry. The only poet at the time who departed from that pattern was Matija Šojat, a newspaper publisher in Calumet, Michigan; he wrote a large number of sonnets.[8]

The literary activity of Croatian immigrants had little contact with the literary life in the home country and was very different from it. By the beginning of the twentieth century folk or folk-style poetry was cultivated only in the villages, whereas the publishing world in the cities was concerned mostly with works written by intellectuals and professional writers who participated in international literary currents prevalent in European and American culture. The education and taste of Croatian immigrants in America created a different literary market. It was, in a way, like going backwards in literary history.

The artistic value of these works is varied and usually not very high. The decasyllabic verse, mostly trochaic, with a caesura after the fourth syllable is readily constructed in Serbo-Croatian, and this easiness attracted dilettantes. But there were also individuals who combined a rich diction and sensitivity for variations in meter and rhythm with an intense experience. Such a poet was Grgo Turkalj, who was a young *guslar*—a singer of folk tales accompanying himself on a one-string fiddle—before coming to the United States. He crossed the ocean several times and had the misfortune of visiting his home in 1914, when he was drawn into World War I. He came out of the war alive, minus one leg. He dedicated his first book, *Hrvatske narodne ratne pjesme* (Croatian Popular War Poems), to his fellow Croats "so that they may read and see what hell it was that not only the author experienced but all our nation and with them almost all mankind."[9] This 220-page-long poem has still retained its freshness and the power to convey to the reader the brutality of the war and the suffering caused by it.

It is interesting that what can be termed without vacillation the most original and most valuable contribution of Croatian immigrants to the culture of their new country was a cluster of stories created anonymously in the oral tradition by steel-mill workers in the Pittsburgh area, many of whom were illiterate. These are stories about Joe Magarac, the giant hero built of steel, a legendary character similar to the lumberman Paul Bunyan. And the stories, which were created around the turn of the century, were almost completely lost. They have survived only through the version written down by Owen Francis, a steel-man who ventured into writing. He listened to several oral renditions and published his transcription in 1931.[10] The saga—as Francis called it—of Joe Magarac was subsequently reprinted several times in collections of American folklore. Yet the readers of his text will not know that it was the Croatian steel-mill workers who created the legend. In his effort to make the text as colorful as possible, he imitated the broken English of the tellers of the stories and referred to them as "Hunkies," a derogatory term which is a derivation from the word "Hungarian," but which was applied around Pittsburgh to Slavs and other nationalities from Central and Eastern Europe, especially those from the Austro-Hungarian empire.

The Croatian word *magarac* means donkey, jackass. It is a very important animal in the coastal area of Croatia. Frequently the owner develops a feeling of tenderness for that stubborn, hard-working animal who is satisfied with little food and water. Francis noticed that when his fellow workers called each other by that name, there was no offensiveness in the tone and manner in which it was used. One worker defined the term like this: "Magarac! Dat is mans who is joost the same lak jackass donkey. Dat is man what joost lek eatit and workit, dats all" ("The Saga of Joe Magarac: Steelman," p. 505). In other words, those steel workers used the donkey as a symbol for their own existence. Yet that definition does not quite fit Joe Magarac. He has no need for food; his outstanding characteristic is his extraordinary strength. He is dedicated to his work and is generous, as the following synopsis of Francis's story demonstrates.

Steve Mestrovich, a steel worker, wanted his daughter Mary to marry the strongest young man in the community. Therefore, one Sunday he gave a big party and asked the guests to lift three big dolly bars, one weighing 350 pounds, another 500 pounds, and the third more than the other two put together. The description of the contest has many humorous incidents of teasing, bragging, and rivalry between men from different towns or steel-mills, but only three young men managed to lift the second dolly bar. One of the three, Pete, was Mary's sweetheart. Yet neither Pete nor the other two could lift the heaviest bar. Then a stranger appeared; nobody had seen him before: "he have back bigger as door, hands bigger as Pete nor Eli together, neck lak big bulls, and arm bigger as somebodys round waist. I betscha my life he was more as seven feets tall. Oh, he was prettiest mans whatever anybody ever see" ("The Saga of Joe Magarac: Steelman," p. 508). He was the strongest one, too: he lifted the bars with only one hand. Then the stranger introduced himself as Joe Magarac, showing his body made of steel and explaining that he was born inside an ore mountain many years ago. He refused, however, to accept the beautiful Mary as his wife. She was not for him; he lived only for his work. But he noticed that Mary liked Pete and suggested that they should get married. The suggestion was followed, and all ended very happily.

The story of the end of Joe is more fantastic. One day at the steel mill, when they were making extra good steel for use in the construction of a new mill, Joe jumped into the furnace and melted, his body merging with the rest of the steel. That day they made the best steel ever, and Joe Magarac continued his life embodied in a new plant. This incident is, to some degree, symbolic of the workers' own lives, which were sacrificed to the voracious steel mills.

Another article, which touches on the figure of Joe Magarac only very briefly and superficially, gives another version of his end: Joe retired to a cave in the Allegheny mountains, where he is still sleeping, his spirit roaming among the steel workers.[11]

Croatian steel workers who created these stories must have been proud of their work. The feeling of identification with their work is so prominent in these stories that it is almost surprising, since the lot of a steel worker was not easy, especially at the time when these stories were conceived. There was no concern with the safety of the workers and hardly any protection for them in case of injury or disease. But in the native country there was no work for them, and here they earned money and were engaged in a useful productive activity. Moreover, there is something in the process of pouring iron or steel that stimulates the creation of a legend. For, as an observer has said, "the gushing out of fiery metal from a great wheel-like container seems like the beginning of Creation."[12]

Yet Joe's story also seems to reflect a sense of powerlessness. Legendary heroes of the south Slavic folklore, like Prince Mark, King Matijaš, or Veli Jože (The Big Joe), are projections of the people's longing for power at a time when they had none. Similarly, the strength and endurance of Joe Magarac can be a subconscious psychological compensation for the precariousness of existence of the people who invented that figure. Thus the story of Joe Magarac resulted from the meeting of a tradition of storytelling with the peculiar circumstances of the life of a group of Croatian immigrants in America.

Pittsburgh area steel mills are also very much present in a story by Gabro Karabin that won the first prize in a contest of *Scribner's Maga-*

zine in 1937. It is titled "An Honorable Escape." But instead of glorifying steel and its production, the story tells of people who were swallowed by steel in a less glorious way than Joe Magarac—of "a man stumbling back from his job against a hot pipe that seared his legs off in a screaming fraction of time—hoarse bellowing from the blooming mill where a drowsy assistant had been sucked into the rollers and mashed to a pulp" (*Scribner's Magazine*, p. 42). Such events and the steel-mill deaths of his father and brother are not the main subject of this factual, autobiographical story; they provide only the background for the author's reflection on his escape from this pattern of existence.

The story is so well written that the editor's enthusiasm over it was by no means exaggerated: "All the work that all of us put into the contest fades into the background, we feel, before the discovery of a story such as Gabro Karabin's. To be the first to see the work of a man, who, in our judgment, has the qualities of a great artist, is worth slaving many days for" (*Scribner's Magazine*, p. 6).

Originally the author himself worked in a steel mill, but later he got a clerical position. Yet he felt somewhat guilty for accepting the new employment, fearing that it might alienate him from the community in which he was raised. He was not sure whether his escape was quite honorable, but he thought that it offered him "a better chance of making Croat and Slavish art and literature and customs more than mere mill energy" (*Scribner's Magazine*, p. 7). Unfortunately, Karabin, twenty-five years old when his story was published, never appeared in print again.

Croatian immigrants wrote no English prose or poetry in the first period of their literary activity, that is, in the period before 1917. Most early immigrants had jobs that did not require a good command of English, and life in ethnic neighborhoods and boarding-houses did not stimulate the learning of the new language. In addition, there were not many second-generation Croats with American education.

One justification for taking the years 1917-1918 as the borderline between two periods of literary activity of Croatian Americans is that, during the years of American participation in World War I, the intense publishing activity of the preceding years completely ceased, and, when it was resumed after the war, several changes could be noted. In the first place, publishing activity was much less intense. The two most important publishing houses, Marohnic in Pittsburgh and Sikocan in St. Louis, no longer existed. By then, most immigrants had improved their command of English; service in the army and the desire to follow daily news on the radio and in the press stimulated the learning of the language, and this led to a diminished interest in Croatian publications. Moreover, in 1914 the influx of new immigrants stopped and was never resumed on a large scale.

Thus the market for Croatian literature had shrunk. It is also important to keep in mind that the rise of isolationist sentiment after the war did not favor ethnic activities.

But while the number of books written in Croatian drastically diminished, there appeared literary works written by Croatian immigrants in English. Between 1925 and 1938, three such works appeared, all of them autobiographical. Anton Mazzanovich, who came to this country as a child, published in 1926 a book entitled *Trailing Geronimo.*[13] Mazzanovich was a restless character who loved adventure and frequently changed professions; he was a musician, saloon owner, soldier, cowboy, and ranger. In his book he describes his childhood and youth and gives a detailed account of the campaign against the Apache Indians in 1881, in which he participated and met Geronimo.

Victor G. Vecki was a well-known physician in Croatia and Austria when he emigrated to the United States. He settled in California and had a very successful career. Besides books on medicine he also published a novel, *Threatening Shadows.*[14] The novel relates the love affairs of the protagonist, Dr. Ivan Nemir, from his student days through his middle age. Like the author, the hero is a physician with a Slavic name who lives in San Francisco, yet the work is not an autobiography but a venture into the writing of fiction, an endeavor in which the author was not as successful as in medicine.

The third work in English consists of the memoirs of a Croatian Lutheran minister, Louis Sanjek, titled *In Silence.*[15] The title alludes to the fact that the author lost the power of speech. This disability made it impossible for him to continue his pastoral work—which he had practiced for twenty years, mostly among Slovak Lutherans—and prompted him to write this book. Sanjek did not limit himself to describing his life and work but offered the reader a lot of information about his beloved native country.

A phenomenon present since the beginning of Croatian literary activity in America has been the participation of newspaper publishers and editors. One of them was Stjepan Brozović, who, among other literary works, published around 1919 a collection of stories about immigrants' life in America, *Sabrane pripovijesti iz američkog hrvatskog života.*[16] He dedicated his book to American Croatians, speaking of it as the first collection of stories printed in the U.S. in their language. He evidently did not know that Danevski had published such a collection in 1911. I regard this detail as highly significant, because it is not an isolated, accidental instance of oversight. Literary works of immigrants, frequently sold and published by the authors themselves, are not widely distributed. They do not enter public libraries, receive few or no critical reviews, and become all too easily forgotten. In the same period (i.e., between the two world wars), there appeared still another collection of short stories and two volumes of poetry.[17]

The Second World War had an even deeper influence on Croatian-American literature than the first one. To begin with, its paralyzing influence lasted longer: from 1939 to 1946, not a single work was published. And when books started to appear again, at a faster pace than in the previous period, there were some notable differences, for that brutal war and its consequences led to the exodus of highly educated people from Eastern and Central Europe. As a result, the majority of Croatian authors in this third period had a university education. Some of them were well known authors before leaving their native countries. As for the folk-style poetry, it completely disappeared, the same as it had in the villages of Croatia, where television gave it the last mortal blow. And while the earliest immigrant writers wrote mainly for their compatriots living in ethnic communities, now that such neighborhoods had all but disappeared, the writers addressed themselves to the Croatian diaspora all over the world. The main vehicle for this communication was and still is the literary and cultural magazine and publishing house, *Hrvatska revija*, now in its twenty-sixth year, which was founded in South America but has since moved to Europe.

Antun Nizeteo is a fine example of these new trends. Presently a librarian at Cornell University, he began a promising career in his native country. From 1935 to 1939, he published two well-received collections of poems and one of short stories, edited an anthology of Italian lyrics, and wrote a number of reviews and critical articles. This intense activity stands in marked contrast to his low output during the many years he has lived in the United States. Although he has published some interesting poems and critical articles in emigré periodicals, the only book he has published since his arrival in America is the collection of short stories *Bez povratka* (No Return).[18] However, not even all of these stories were written in this country; only those that have immigrants as protagonists were produced here. This slowing down of Nizeteo's literary output is certainly not a sign of a decline of his creative power; his newer stories are superior to the earlier ones. The reason for his diminished output probably is the lack of a direct contact with his native language, fellow writers, critics, and readers.

The title of the collection, "No Return," must not be taken literally as meaning that the hope of returning to the native country has been lost. Some of Nizeteo's characters do go back, but the places and people they find are not the same as when they left them. It is in this sense that there is no return, no escape from time, no way of erasing the years of loneliness and suffering caused by separation.

It is significant that, in the last story, which has the same title as the collection, the main character, an immigrant who has just returned to his home town after twenty years in America, is not compelled by economic need to emigrate; he belongs to one of the wealthiest families in town. This fact partly explains why his wife does not react with joy to his return. The mood of resignation that filled her during those twenty years she spent caring for the house, working in the fields, and raising children without male help and company is not changed by the husband's return. Nor does she respond to the sexual desire awakened in the husband by his still attractive wife. There is no return to the love and passion of the years before the separation when they were a young, recently married couple. In the story "Andriana," it is the wife who crosses the ocean to join her husband, but here, too, there is no return to their original relationship.

Nizeteo shows a deep understanding for the suffering of women who were left behind. There were actually tens of thousands of such wives, and he must have met some of them before he left his native Dalmatia. Many husbands never returned, because they might have been killed in industrial accidents or felt ashamed at not having succeeded in America. Often they came back crippled or diseased, only to die at home. The author possesses a fine sense for the shades the feeling of frustration can take, and not only in women. His story "Na prolasku" (Passing Through) tells of a prosperous emigrant, a man who succeeded abroad as an artist. During a visit to his native city, on the eve of his return to America, he meets a former schoolmate whom he has not seen for more than twenty-five years. The latter also had artistic talent and ambitions, but these ambitions were victims of the struggle to survive and feed his family. It is a melancholy meeting. The success of the artist reminds the other man of his own failure; but the artist, a divorced man, notices in his friend things that he lacks: wife, children, and contact with the soil of his youth and his ancestors.

Nizeteo's stories are ethnic literature in the strict sense of the word because in them he deals with the impact of emigration to America on his fellow countrymen. Some of the stories, like "U luci" (In the Harbor), are based on his personal acquaintance with the world of working-class immigrants. Yet the situation described in several of the stories is more typical of the first half of this century than of the present. Nor are the stories quite contemporary stylistically. Though written without sentimentality, with economy and reserve, they are narrated in the traditional omniscient point of view, without any major stylistic innovations. Still, they are the best stories written by a Croatian writer in America.

Another excellently written collection of stories is the work of a world-famous Croatian artist who came to the United States in 1947, after he had already passed the zenith of his creative power as a sculptor. Ivan Meštrović wrote the stories contained in the volume titled *Ludi Mile* (The Crazy Mile) in his seventies, when he was resident sculptor at Syracuse University and at the University of Notre Dame. He had already published a book of memoirs and one of historico-political reflections, but this collection was his major venture in fiction writing. It seems that he was prompted into writing these stories primarily because of an intense need for a contact with the world of his childhood and youth—the rocky hills of the Dalmatian hinterland. In this search for the past, he created a masterful evocation of life in that area—of village fools, courtships, weddings, quarrels, births, and deaths. The diction of immigrant writers is sometimes not very rich because of their separation from the source of their language, but Meštrović displays an unusually rich vocabulary, both in the literary language and in the local dialect. The stories also show that their author was primarily a visual artist; they abound in elaborate descriptions that show a fine gift of observation but slow down the action. However, Meštrović was not interested in fast action and suspense; his stories are inspired by the genre of poetry that he learned in his youth—the folk poetry of the *guslars*—which is also characterized by slow pace and elaborate details. This slow pace is appropriate to the theme of these stories—the traditional way of life as it had gone on for centuries.

These stories were not published in the United States but in Zagreb, the capital of Croatia. The place of publication seems quite appropriate, since they have nothing to do with the life in the U.S., and they will find many more readers in Yugoslavia. However, the bio-bibliographical notice contained in the book should have given the information about where and when the stories were written.

Karakteristika by Hrvoje Lorković[19] is also based on experiences, including literary experiences, which the author brought with him when he entered this country. Subtitled "Study-Novel-Chronicle," it is one of the best literary works written by a Croatian American, although the author is not a writer by profession but a professor of biology at the University of Iowa. In the introductory note, he states that this is his "only" book. Like most such books, it is autobiographical. It is based on the diary the author kept as a high-school boy in Zagreb in the years immediately following World War II. The title of Lorković's book refers to one aspect of life in Yugoslavia at the time: the "characteristic" was a secret document which contained the description of an individual's political views, character traits, and other data of interest to the regime that could open or close the possibility of getting a job or enrolling at the university. *Karakteristika* is a very interesting chronicle of those years, whose atmosphere it successfully evokes, but it is written as a novel, with a plot, vivid characters, and lively dialog. All the episodes are skillfully integrated through the experience of the protagonist-narrator.

Croatian fiction written in the United States during the last twenty years has attained a much higher artistic value than any written before, but it also includes a number of works that do not deserve to have been published. In normal circumstances, when the writer lives in his native country, editors and critics will point out his deficiencies and prompt him to improve his writing or else refuse to publish it. Of course, one can always finance the publication himself, but to do so is tantamount to branding the work as inferior, and it also keeps the work outside the literary market. For immigrant writers who write in their native tongue, however, self-publication is a usual and accepted practice, which eliminates the screening function of editors and makes the literary world of immigrants open to dilettantism. Even when a work is published by an immigrant publishing house, the editors do not always possess sufficient literary culture to judge the quality of a submitted work. Especially if the work is full of patriotism, it will find sympathizers. But, of course, it is not patriotic to write, or to publish, substandard literature.

As far as fiction in English is concerned, it is unfortunate that the most prolific and successful Croatian-born American novelist, George J. Hitrec, did not write about his native country or about his life in the United States. All of his novels and stories[20] deal with India. Several Americans of Croatian descent, like Philip M. Basvic and Thomas Raste, have also published novels,[21] but there is not much in them that can be called ethnic.

The difference from previous periods is particularly noticeable in the case of modern poetry, for this branch of literary activity was previously very much neglected. The anthology of Croatian emigré poetry in the period from 1945 to 1955, *Pod tudjim nebom* (Under Foreign Skies), edited by Vinko Nikolić and published by Hrvatska revija in Buenos Aires in 1957, was an evidence of significant poetic achievements of the postwar emigrants. The anthology included authors living in the United States: Ivan Meštrović, Antun Bonifačić, Antun Nizeteo, Nada Kesterčanek, Stjepan Hrastovec, and Jure Prpić.

Foremost among these poets is Antun Bonifačić, who came to this country in 1954 as a mature artist, having already published several novels, as well as collections of poems and essays. He has an excellent knowledge of French poets and especially of Paul Valéry. In 1974, he published his American poems in the volume of his collected poems, *Sabrane pjesme*. Although, like Nizeteo, he has not been very productive in his exile, he has retained all his poetic power and affirmed himself as the leading Croatian poet in America.

One characteristic of Bonifačić's poetry is its variety—variety of themes, tone, and verse forms. Yet it is not difficult to notice that he prefers a formal structure to free verse and that he does not let himself be dominated by emotions. Unlike many lesser immigrant poets, he does not cry for his native country or for his native island of Krk. The reader is aware of Bonifačić's rootedness in the landscape of his childhood and youth, especially through the recurrent mention of sails, vessels, waves, and sea, but the poet usually associates these images with the general condition of man's voyage through life. There is an occasional outburst of nostalgia, but the dominant feeling is that of vitality and affirmation of life.

Nada Kesterčanek-Vujica was one of the more prolific emigré writers. She started her literary career in her native country, and, during her life in the United States, she published a volume of poetic prose, one of short stories, and one of poems in prose and verse.[22] All of her works are dominated by an intense lyricism which gives them a dreamlike atmosphere. In his Foreword to her first American volume, Nizeteo has pointed out the author's gift of observation and a certain easiness of narration, but he also wonders whether she would expand the scope of her experiences. However, Kesterčanek always remained limited to the same themes and mood.

Zlata Ivezić, who published her first collection of poems *Srebrne suze* (Silver Tears) in Chicago in 1974, also shows feminine qualities in her verse. The themes of her small volume are love, family, and, above all, her native province of Slavonia. It is an intimate, personal poetry written in free verse. But her nostalgia and lyricism are controlled by a sense of measure, and her expression is enriched with vivid images and original suggestive metaphors.

There are a number of other poets who have so far published their poems only in periodicals. Especially worth mentioning are Fr. Hrvoslav Ban, Božo Cokljat, and Vid Mak. It is also interesting to mention that the Croatian Franciscan Press in Chicago published in 1958 Rev. Vjenceslav Vukonić's translation of Longfellow's *Evangeline.*

I will conclude my review of the history of Croatian-American literature by stating that there is, in fact, no such history. What I mean is that any particular writer in this category does not continue the work of his American predecessors nor does his work represent a stepping stone for those who follow. Instead, most immigrant writers who write in their mother tongue have developed their literary taste and style before crossing the ocean. Therefore we cannot expect a self-sustained growth of Croatian-American literature. Its future development will depend mainly on the influx of fresh talent from the old country.

Indiana University

NOTES

[1] George J. Prpić, "The Croatian Immigrants in the United States of America," in *Croatia: Land, People, Culture*, ed. Francis H. Eterovich and Christopher Spalatin, II (Toronto: Univ. of Toronto Press, 1970), 394-478. George J. Prpić, *The Croatian Immigrants in America* (New York: The Philosophical Library, 1971). With co-author Hilda Prpić, he wrote *Croatian Books and Booklets Written in Exile* (Cleveland: Authors in Cooperation with ISEES, John Carroll Univ., 1973). Without Prpić's valuable pioneer works on Croatian immigration in America it would have been much more difficult to handle the theme of the paper. My information on the works of Brozović, Danevski, Krašić, and Mazzanovich is derived from Prpić's writings.

[2] Medo Krašić, *Zapisci* (New York: Croatian Printing Co., 1904).

[3] S. R. Danevski, *Pripovijesti* (Chicago: The Author, 1911).

[4] A. Milčinović, "Hrvatska Pripovijetka i roman," *Kolo Matice hrvatske* (Zagreb, 1912), pp. 487-88.

[5] Šime Sinovcić and Josip Mikečin, *Od Novigrada do Amerike* (St. Louis: Sikocan, 1914).

[6] Josip Marohnić, *O bojevima na Plevni* and *Rat rusko-japanski* (both of these books were published in Pittsburgh in 1913 by the author's own publishing house); Ciril Pavelin, *Rat u Kini* (Chicago: Strmic, n.d.); Milan Gnjatović, *Krvave pjesme balkanskoga rata* (Pittsburgh: Marohnic, 1913); Stjepko Brozović, *Ratne pjesme o ratovanju i junačtvu Hrvata i hrvatskih regimenta u krvavom svjetskom ratu* (New York: Narodni list, 1915).

[7] S. Čulibrk, *Odbjeglica ili posljedica nevjere u braku* (St. Louis: Sikocan, 1916); Milan Gnjatović, "Potonuće broda Titanica," *Narodna američka pjesmarica* (St. Louis: Sikocan, 1913).

[8] "Sonetni vienac," *Narodni list*, 6-10 Oct. 1903; *Sto uzdisaja* (Calumet, Mich.: The Author, 1910).

[9] Grgo Turkalj, *Hrvatske narodne ratne pjesme* (New York: Hrvatski list and Danica hrvatska, 1925), p. 6.

[10] "The Saga of Joe Magarac: Steelman," *Scribner's Magazine*, 90 (1931), 505-11.

[11] "The Phantom Men of Republic Steel," *Cleveland Plain Dealer Pictorial Magazine* (9 Nov. 1952), p. 16.

[12] Mary Heaton Verse, *Men and Steel* (1920), p. 20. Quoted in B. A. Botkin, *A Treasury of American Folklore* (New York: Crown, 1944), p. 189. Botkin's book also contains the reprint of Francis's "Saga of Joe Magarac" (pp. 246-54).

[13] Anton Mazzanovich, *Trailing Geronimo* (Los Angeles: Gem. Publ. Co., 1926).

[14] Victor G. Vecki, *Threatening Shadows* (Boston: Stratford, 1931).

[15] Louis Sanjek, *In Silence* (New York: Fortuny's, 1938).

[16] Stjepan Brozović, *Sabrane pripovijesti iz američkog hrvatskog života* (New York: Croatian Printing and Publishing Co., n.d.).

[17] Luka M. Pejović, *Prikazi naših iseljenika* (Chicago: The Author, 1939); Viktor Vojvodić, *Sabrane pjesme* (San Jose, Calif.: Sokol, n.d.); Nikola Kekić, *Pjesma iseljenikova* (Whiting, Ind.: The Author, 1936). Vojvodić's collected poems are, according to Prpić, among the best written by that time (ca. 1920). Kekić's poems are extremely dilettantish and lack any artistry.

[18] Antun Nizeteo, *Bez povratka* (Buenos Aires: Hrvatska revija, 1957).

[19] Hrvoje Lorković (pseud. Rok Remetić), *Karakteristika* (Hills, Iowa: The Author, n.d. [1972]).

[20] George J. Hitrec, *Ruler's Morning and Other Stories* (New York: Harper, 1946); *Son of the Moon* (New York: Harper, 1948); *Angel of Gaiety* (New York: Harper, 1951).

[21] Philip M. Basvic (pseud. Barton Michael Phillips), *And the Angels Won't Blame Him* (Dallas: The Story Book Press, 1955); Thomas Raste, *The Destroyers* (New York: Vintage, 1968).

[22] Nada Kesterčanek-Vujica, *Tragovi* (Buenos Aires: The Author, 1959); *Short Stories* (Wilkes-Barre, Pa.: The Author, 1959); *Koluti vremena* (Wilkes-Barre, Pa.: The Author, 1969).

Czech Literature in America

Rudolf Sturm

ABSTRACT

Since the 1860's, when the Czech immigrants started their first newspaper and brought out their first book, an astonishing quantity of periodical publications and book titles have appeared in the United States. Most of these periodicals, usually written in obsolete Czech, are American both in spirit and in content and deal with literature only marginally. Most of the books are translations or adaptations from English or reprints of works published previously in the mother country. The original production, be it prose fiction or verse, has little aesthetic value, with the exception of a handful of writers who received acclaim both here and in Czechoslovakia. Towering among the nineteenth century literati is Josef Václav Sládek (1845-1912), author of nineteen volumes of poetry and a prolific translator from American and English literature. During his sojourn here in 1868-1870, he wrote eighteen poems expressing his sympathy for the Indians, his compassion for the Czech immigrants, his own *Weltschmerz*, his yearning for faraway Bohemia, and his longing for his mother and fiancée. While in America he also translated Longfellow and other American and British poets. Sládek's stay here also inspired him to write thirty-two short stories, essays, and travelogues on life in the United States. From among several scores of contemporary or nearly contemporary writers in the Czech-American community, novelist Egon Hostovský (1908-1973) and literary critic René Wellek (1903-) are acclaimed as the most important in their respective fields. (RS)

Can American literature with Czech, Polish, or German ethnic themes, regardless of the author's nationality, be considered part of that particular ethnic literature? I am inclined to say no. But even if the answer were yes, the limited space allotted to this study would not allow me to give more than a page or two to the numerous American writers whose novels or poems deal with Czech subjects. No meaningful analysis and only a partial enumeration of those many works would be possible here, and I do not intend to do that injustice to this intriguing and important topic. Just think of the good king Wenceslas; the medieval Prague Jewish legend of the Golem; the events of the Thirty Years' War taking place in Bohemia and Moravia; the Czech immigrants in the United States; Lidice and other Czech-German encounters during World War II; the Communist take-over in 1948 and the death of Jan Masaryk; the Czech-Russian involvement in the Prague Spring of 1968. All these and many other Czech themes found their way into hundreds of American stories, poems, dramas, films, and even opera and operetta libretti. (I do not speak of the works of non-fiction here. Just consider that the Prague Spring alone is the subject of close to 200 book-length studies in English.)[1]

My article, then, will deal with Czech belles-lettres created in the United States by immigrants or émigrés, if this distinction is necessary, and written for the immigrant consumption. A few paragraphs about the beginnings and development of Czech immigration seems, therefore, in order. The immigrants started to come as early as the first third of the seventeenth century. During the Thirty Years' War some 300 came from Bohemia and Moravia. The first known to land here was Augustin Heřman, a Protestant refugee who came to New Amsterdam (New York) in 1633. He was in the employ of the West India Company as a surveyor. After having played an important role in the business and political circles in New Amsterdam, Heřman settled in Maryland where Lord Baltimore commissioned him to make the first map of Maryland and Virginia. The mapping project was a difficult task, since Heřman had to explore the then wild and uninhabited parts of those provinces. His map, however, was such an excellent work that Lord Baltimore rewarded him with a deed for some twenty thousand acres of land, partly in Maryland and partly in Delaware, later known as Bohemian Manor. Another of Heřman's estates was called Little Bohemia and still another, Three Bohemian Sisters, being designed for Heřman's three daughters. The rivers on which the estates are situated are still called Big Bohemia River and Little Bohemia River. Heřman was proud of his Czech origin, as can be seen not only by the names of his estates, but also by the way in which he signed the famous map and even his testament: "Augustine Herrmann, Bohemian."[2]

A contemporary of Heřman was Bedřich Filip (or Frederick Philips), also a native of Bohemia, who came to America in 1658. He became one of the wealthiest men here and was called by the colonists "the Bohemian merchant prince." Philipse Manor, a town north of New York City, by its name still bears witness to his activities.[3] One of Filip's descendants, Marie Phillips, was so intelligent, witty, and attractive that George Washington, then a twenty-four-year old colonel of the Virginia Volunteers, fell in love with her, but she did not marry him. Marie Phillips is the heroine of James Fenimore Cooper's novel *The Spy*.

In the eighteenth century the only known immigrants from Bohemia and Moravia coming to America were the descendants of the Czech Brethren who, after the battle of the White Mountain in 1620, fled to Germany. More than a hundred years later some of their families, calling themselves Moravian Brethren or *Unitas Fratrum*, and being Germanized, moved to America. Their ties with the Czech homeland were weakened, if not broken, during their long stay in Saxony and Prussia, and after settling in the New World they were neither capable nor eager to renew them.[4]

The most colorful among the Czech immigrants who came in the early nineteenth century was without doubt Anthony Michael Dignowity, a native of Kutná Hora, Bohemia. We know of his wanderings and exploits from the autobiography which he published in English at the time when he was already—or still—an important physician and wealthy businessman in San Antonio, Texas.[5] In 1830, at the age of twenty, Dignowity joined the Polish Revolutionary Army to fight against the "tyrannic czar." After the supression of the uprising he fled with other members of the defeated Polish Army to Hamburg, and from there he sailed in 1832 for the United States. He lived in ten different States of the Union and wandered through sixteen others, trying his hand at various jobs. Later he studied medicine in Cincinnati. As a doctor, real estate broker, and owner of mines he played an important part in the public affairs of Texas. As the conflict between the South and the North approached, Dignowity's misfortunes began, as we can learn from a very informative book by Hudson and Maresh on early Czech settlers in Texas.[6] He was an ardent Unionist and opponent of slavery and was against the withdrawal of his State from the Union. He left Texas in 1861, only a few hours before he was to be hanged at the Plaza of San Antonio, and traveled alone on horseback to Washington, D.C., where he obtained employment with the Federal Government. In the meantime his property in Texas was confiscated. Two of his sons were drafted into the Confederate Army, but while on a furlough they swam across the Rio Grande, made their escape through Mexico, and joined the Union forces. After the Civil War Dignowity, sick and poor, returned to Texas to die there in 1875.

The sporadic Czech immigration assumed large proportions only after 1848. In the mid-1860's, the number of Czech-born people and their American-born children was estimated at 120,000. Just before World War I, the number was about 500,000 and in the 1920's, approximately 700,000. Today there are some 300,000 persons of Czech stock here, including the new wave of refugees who left Czechoslovakia in the aftermath of the Soviet invasion of 1968.[7] The potential readership of Czech literature in the United States was, therefore, and still is considerable.

The first Czech-born writer to publish in America was, as we have seen, the Texan Dignowity. But he wrote in English. The first material printed here in Czech was the weekly *Slowan Amerikánský*, which started publication in Racine, Wisconsin, on 1 January 1860. A few weeks later, a second Czech weekly, *Národní Noviny*, appeared in St. Louis, Missouri. Both these periodicals were named after Karel Havlíček's *Slovan* and *Národní noviny*, published a decade earlier in Bohemia and eventually suppressed by the Hapsburg Government. By 1910, no less than 326 periodicals in Czech came into existence in America. Most of them, to be sure, ceased publication or fused with others in a short time, often within months of their inception. In the early 1920's, some eighty-five periodicals were regularly published, including four daily newspapers in Chicago, two in New York, two in Cleveland, and one in Omaha. At present, given the unfavorable economic situation, only one daily newspaper survives, *Denní Hlasatel* in Chicago, and about thirty weeklies, monthlies, and quarterlies. Some are bi-lingual (Czech-English) and a few even tri-lingual (Czech-Slovak-English), to keep the dwindling readership, particularly the second and third generations, interested.[8]

The Czech journals in America have traditionally represented many shades of public opinion, from conservative Roman Catholic to anarchist and agnostic. The division along religious lines prevailed especially in the nineteenth century, but is maintained by some even today. A majority of them have supported the Democratic Party. The circulation has ranged from a few hundred to 30,000, if we can take the circulation departments at their word. The editors, as a rule, have been Czech-born, but their language in daily contact with English has suffered, becoming obsolete and ridden with Americanisms or at best clumsy translations from English. The spirit of the writing is American, not Czech, as the interests of the readership turn from things Czech to American matters. During World Wars I and II all these periodicals supported the claim of the Czech nation for independence from Austria-Hungary and Nazi Germany, respectively. After the Communist take-over only one or two expressed their preference for the new regime; one journal remained neutral. All the others joined the cold war campaign against the Soviet Union and the Prague Government, some of them with deep conviction and great gusto.

Purely literary interests of the Czech American press have been only peripheral. Occasionally the papers do print a poem or a short story, or they serialize a novel, but these are usually works published previously in Czechoslovakia. I know of only two journals consistently publishing belles-lettres. One is *The Bohemian Voice*, sponsored by the Bohemian-American National Committee, a group of immigrants interested in literature. It was published in Omaha from 1892 to 1894. The other is *Proměny*, a quarterly issued in New York since 1964 by the Czechoslovak Society of Arts and Sciences in America. The forty-nine issues of *Proměny* published so far (each issue contains up to 128 pages of text) offer an extensive survey of original poetry, essays, short stories, and even chapters from novels written by two scores or more exile writers. Some of them, e.g., Antonín Cekota, Egon Hostovský, Antonín J. Liehm, František Listopad, Milada Součková, Milan Schulz, Josef Škvorecký, Ivan Sviták, came into exile as accomplished writers, and there they simply continued to write. Many other contributors, too numerous to be mentioned, began their literary careers here. *Proměny* was edited from 1964 to 1970 by Ladislav Radimský (essayist Petr Den) and since then by poet Pavel Javor (the pen name of Jiří Škvor).

No statistics exist on the number of Czech books published in America, but estimates place their number at between two and three thousand titles. At one time or another there were five publishing houses in New York, three in Chicago, and one each in Cleveland, Milwaukee, and Omaha, bringing out Czech books in editions called usually *Knihovna* ("Library") or *Matice* ("Foundation"). In addition, nearly each journal and newspaper occasionally published books, and some of them still do. The Czechoslovak Society of Arts and Sciences in America (New York) and the Czechoslovak National Council of America (Chicago) also have modest book publishing departments. Most of the book production, probably ninety per cent, are works of non-fiction. The subjects vary greatly. There are books on history, politics, religion, anti-clericalism and freethinking, farming, gymnastics, parliamentary rules, the U.S. Constitution, several editions of the Bible, catechisms, and cookbooks. Many a title has been devoted to advising the housewife, the sick, those in love, the public speaker, the letter-writer, and so on. There are a number of textbooks and bi-lingual dictionaries designed to teach the immigrants English, and other textbooks and readers to teach their children Czech. Translations and adaptations from English, German, and French (in this order) abound, as do reprints of titles published originally in the mother country. The first book in Czech was published in 1861 by the weekly *Slavie* in Racine, Wisconsin. It was a brief survey of American history entitled *Amerika*, with no author listed.

Most of the Czech-American fiction deals, as can be expected, with the life of Czech immigrants and reminiscences of the old country. It is not of high quality. Its literary merits are usually surpassed by local interests and color, be it those of a group of Czech farms in Texas, a parish in Nebraska, a factory in Cleveland, or the life of small shopkeepers in Chicago. The leading genre is the short story, but there is a surprising amount of poetry, mostly meditative and patriotic. Novels are rare, and there is hardly a handful of dramas.

Only occasionally have the Czech-American writings been published, or reprinted, in the mother country. Pavel Albieri (the pen name of Jan

Mucek, 1861-1901), who for ten years lived in Chicago, California, and Texas where he died in a train accident, published in Prague several volumes of short stories about the life of Czech immigrants. Jan Havlasa (the pen name of Jan Klecanda, Jr., 1883-) came to the United States in 1904 and stayed until 1914. He wrote here and later published in Prague a number of short stories with locale in California and Chicago. The mood of both Albieri's and Havlasa's tales is pessimistic. More often than not they write about unhappy immigrants who are frustrated in their expectations, meet with failures in private life as well as in their occupations, and are left with a life-long yearning for their homeland to which they are unable to return. Neither Albieri nor Havlasa is an important writer. Their stories are conventional, at times even trivial, and only in a few of Havlasa's narratives do we find pages with the description of nature or psychological analyses that rise above the average.[9]

By far the most important writer of the older period of Czech-American lettres is Josef Václav Sládek (1845-1912). His place in the mainstream of Czech intellectual life is somewhat ambiguous. Czech literature and the cultural life in general since the middle of the nineteenth century have been dominated by two contrary trends, nationalism versus cosmopolitanism. The conflict between these two opposing ideologies reached its climax in the last three decades of the century. The national school, deriving its literary themes from the native soil and patriotic past, maintained the traditions established during the renaissance of the Czech nation at the beginning of the century; its most representative writer was Svatopluk Čech (1846-1908). Opposed to the nationalists were the "citizens of the world," whose leader was Jaroslav Vrchlický (1853-1912), the most prolific Czech writer and translator of all time. Sládek stood somewhere in the middle of these two tendencies, with sympathies for both sides. This "poet of the homeland," as he is called by his biographers, got his cosmopolitan coloring, his understanding of Western cultures, and his love for American and English literature while living in the United States, mostly in Wisconsin, Texas, and Illinois from 1868 through 1870. Only a small part of his huge literary production, to be sure, originated here and belongs to America.[10]

The ever-increasing emigration of Czechs to the United States, the mushrooming of their press here, the participation of many Czech soldiers in the Civil War[11] —these facts were well known in Prague in the eighteen-sixties and helped Sládek in his decision to travel to America. His attention was turned towards this country also by the influence of Vojta Náprstek, who, after spending the years 1848-1857 here, had returned to Bohemia and begun familiarizing his countrymen with the American way of life. Náprstek founded the Club of American Women in Prague and Sládek became its frequent visitor.[12] In 1867 a Czech merchant from Chicago, Karel Aleš Kadiš (Cadish) was visiting Bohemia, and Sládek taught his son the Czech language. From the Kadišes he learned many more things about life in America.[13] But all these were only contributing factors.

The main reason for leaving Bohemia was Sládek's psychological malaise, the "Lenauesque demon" of discontent and uneasiness which was getting hold of him.[14] He was unhappy about the Hapsburg rule over Bohemia and Moravia and the resulting physical and spiritual "slavery" of the Czech people, as his generation called it with some exaggeration. His unhappiness grew with the bitterness which crept into his relationship with his fiancée, for her wealthy parents wanted someone with a better social position for their son-in-law. Sládek's relationship with his parents, too, was rather tense. They still were not reconciled to his refusal to become a priest and his decision to study natural sciences instead. Zdeněk Němeček wrote an imaginary conversation between himself and Sládek, inquiring about the latter's reason for going abroad. To his questions Sládek supposedly replied: "Well, sir, the wide world with its sharp smell, that's the only remedy for my very complicated psychological state, for my grief which has no name."[15]

Such was Sládek's state of mind when in 1868, at the age of twenty-three, he received a letter from Chicago in which Kadiš invited and urged him to come to America. By then he had the reputation of one of the most talented young poets, having published a number of patriotic and political poems and edited a volume of "the poems of Czech youth" under the title *Ruch.*[16] The invitation from Kadiš gave a solid basis to his heretofore vague plans to travel abroad. He had no money, but it was not difficult for him to obtain loans from friends, a small travel grant from Svatobor, an association of Czech writers, and an advance from *Národní listy*, the leading Prague daily newspaper for which he promised to write articles from America.

His travels in the United States can be reconstructed quite accurately from the numerous letters that he sent to Jaromír Čelakovský, the son of the poet František Ladislav Čelakovský. He spent a few days in New York and then went to Chicago to visit the Kadišes. In October, in the desire to take a job on his own, and to earn money, he went to Wisconsin, where he accepted the position of a teacher of Czech children in the "Moravian village" in Caledonia County. Soon he gave up teaching and lived with a Czech farmer right in the forest, paying for his room and board with game that he hunted. He described his stay in Caledonia in two sketches, "Moravia" and "On the Farm" and in a humorous narrative "A Czech Opera in America."[17]

In February, 1869, Sládek left Wisconsin still covered with snow and set out for a trip south "towards the spring," as he called the journey in a travel sketch bearing the same title ("Jaru vstříc"). He went by train to Chicago and St. Louis and from there by boat on the Mississippi to the Gulf of Mexico and to Galveston. On this part of his journey "the charming, blossoming country side near Batton Rouge," as he misspelled its name, captivated him most. He spent the whole month of March wandering alone, with a rifle on his shoulder, from Houston to San Antonio. In San Antonio a young Polish priest, Wincenty Barzinski, offered him hospitality and later the position of sacristan, organist, and teacher of Polish children. Sládek stayed six months with Barzinski, whom he liked and esteemed. He later portrayed him with affection and described his own activities in the Polish settlement in the short stories "Polish Missionary," "Under the Black Cassock," "The Bishop," and "How We Baptized and Confirmed."[18]

He left the Polish parish for St. Louis, where he wanted to work for some time and earn enough money to pay his return trip home. He reached the city after some five weeks of wanderings in woods and prairies, some of which he later described in "On a Czech Farm in Texas." In St. Louis he became editor of the Czech weekly *Národní Noviny*, using the pen name of Josef S. Počátecký, after Počátky, the home town of his fiancée. In a short story entitled "My Boss," Sládek later drew a humorous picture of the magazine's publisher and described his own editorial troubles. When the publisher moved the periodical to Chicago, Sládek went with him and worked there until May, 1870. In his article "Chicago" he devoted affectionate words to the city, the "giant in work and crime." Upon the urging of his friends he then returned home, arriving in Bohemia in June, 1870.[19]

Except for a short trip to Scandinavia, which he made with Czech poet Julius Zeyer in 1878,[20] Sládek never went abroad again. When after a year of happy marriage his wife Emilie died in 1874, giving birth to a child who also died, "the world ceased to exist" for him; grief-stricken and distraught, he confided to Jaroslav Vrchlický that he wanted to go back to America. "He [Sládek] would like to return to America," wrote Vrchlický to his uncle in January, 1875, "but his mother does not want to let him go, so he wants to go at least to London and offered to take me along. I am learning English slowly from him."[21] The trip did not materialize, however. Years later Sládek still thought of living in the United States. In 1882 he wrote to Zeyer:

> You write about America. Somewhere in the south, in Texas, there in the mountains are charming places where one can live alone and almost for nothing. But I think that even there you would not stay long because of

nostalgia. I learned what it is. I spent weeks in the wilderness without seeing a human being, and everything is empty then. But if you can only find peace, it does not matter where. I myself, if I had enough money to buy land with, would go there for the sake of my health, if not for other reasons.[22]

Sládek's sojourn in America supplied him with subjects for thirty-two travelogues, essays, and short stories. I have mentioned some of them above. While in America, he published some articles (as well as poems) in *Slavie* (Racine) and *Pokrok* (Chicago and Racine).[23] In several of his stories he described the life of the Czech immigrants, praising some, especially the Forty-eighters, for their untiring devotion to the Czech cause, and castigating others for their indifference and negligence in Czech national matters. Another group of these prose writings is devoted to the American Indians, whom Sládek portrays with sympathy and understanding for their misfortune and sufferings. Very informative are his longer articles on Indian mythology and a study of the American constitution, public affairs, and literature "during the first century of the North American Republic." Although these essays and studies contain a few small mistakes and some of Sládek's conclusions would not be generally accepted today, on the whole they show how well he had mastered the subject.[24]

Being primarily a poet, Sládek's two-year stay in America left a marked imprint on his works in verse. In his first volume of poetry, published under the simple title *Poems*,[25] there were fourteen American pieces, just one-fourth of the whole contents. For his second collection of poetry, *The Sparks on the Sea*,[26] his oversea sojourn supplied only the title and one tardy American poem, "The Immigrants." Subsequently Sládek wrote seventeen more volumes of verse in which we find only occasionally an allusion to his American experience. These seventeen volumes are, for the most part, patriotic songs, meditative lyrics, love poems, and poems for children. For the definitive edition of Sládek's collected works, published in Prague in 1945-46, the editor, Albert Vyskočil, found three more American poems in the poet's unpublished writings, thus bringing the total to eighteen pieces.[27]

In these American poems Sládek writes mostly on the same two subjects that we find also in his short stories and essays: the unhappiness of the immigrants who are unable to find a real home in the new country and for the rest of their life think with nostalgia of their home back in the old country; and the poet's compassion and understanding for the Indians and his anger at the inhuman treatment they receive from the hands of white Americans. In several instances the poems' titles themselves are suggestive of these themes: "The Immigrants," "Yearning," "The Grave in the Forest," "On Indian Graves," "The Papoose," "An Indian's Tombstone." Through many of his poems runs a constant undertone of his own melancholy and *Weltschmerz*, an echo of the same "Lenauesque demon" that drove him from home. His hope that America will cure his malaise, his feeling of uneasiness, had failed him.

While living in America, Sládek translated Longfellow's *Hiawatha* and *Evangeline* and minor poems of other American and English poets.[28] This was the beginning of an extensive translating career that made Sládek, next to Vrchlický, the most prolific Czech translator. From American literature, in addition to Longfellow, he translated Bret Harte, Nathaniel Hawthorne, Edgar Allan Poe, Mark Twain, and others. He also translated from Spanish, Polish, and Russian. But he was at his best in translating from English. His masterpiece remains his rendering of thirty-three of Shakespeare's plays which he translated into Czech with great care and elegance.[29] And finally, let me mention one more undertaking of Sládek's which was due to his stay in America: his translations *into* English. It is unique in Czech literature to find a poet of Sládek's stature who is a prolific translator from English and who also translates into English, and his own poetry at that. He published these translations in *The Bohemian Voice* (Omaha), as a group under the collective title "A Handful of Bohemian Heather."[30] The series includes one lyric by Josef Kalus, a minor Czech poet, and five of Sládek's own poems. A few metrical imperfections and minor irregularities in diction do not detract from them much. Considering that they were made by a foreigner, they were done remarkably well. The following is the opening stanza of Sládek's poem "Těm, kteří truchlí" (To Those Who Mourn) which is my favorite. He translated it:

> Leaf after leaf falls from the trees
> And wintry blows the mountain breeze.
> The naked branches moan and moan,
> And thou complainest thou are left,
> Like yonder trees of leaves bereft
> So all alone.

As for contemporary or nearly contemporary Czech writers in America, I hesitate to make a catalogue of the good ones leaving out the others, for fear that any evaluation or omission will be pounced on, and probably rightly so. Scores of people from among those who came to this country from Czechoslovakia in the immigration waves of 1938-1939, 1948, and 1968, have published one, two, and even ten books. No exhaustive bibliography exists to cover these writings. Some of their books have been selling well, some not at all. A score of them have been translated into English and other languages. I doubt that any one person has read even one third of these books. I for one admit that I have read only a small part of this rich production, and to make any valid assessment I would have to rely on the judgment of others, which I do not intend to do. Hence my hesitation to enumerate and to judge. The works of two people, highly valued by thousands of readers in this country as well as in Europe, must, however, be cited. They are the pride of the Czech-American community. I speak of Egon Hostovský and René Wellek.

Hostovský (1908-1973), the author of three volumes of short stories, twenty novels, and one play, spent nearly one half of his life in New York and New Jersey, where he died. He wrote eleven of his books here, all of them published in Czech and English. His works written before and during World War II deal with alienation, loneliness, fear of life, and the inability of their heroes, many of them Jewish like Hostovský himself, to communicate. In his later writings, after 1948, he uses, in addition, political themes and espionage, possibly as a reflection of the cold war. His books were translated into twenty languages; two were made into movies. They are not works of optimism, are not peopled with positive heroes. Yet, in describing all the gloom, deception, and wickedness, Hostovský does not feel bitter, he does not despair. He does not deny the miracle of life and the salvation of man, but is offering us *the labyrinth of the world*—to use the Comenius title—rather than *a paradise of the heart*.[31]

René Wellek (1903-), whose main interest lies in literary criticism and aesthetics and who is a prolific writer in these fields, taught literature at the University of Iowa in 1939-46 and since then at Yale University until his retirement in 1973. Countless honors have been bestowed on him for his extraordinary achievements as a writer and educator. He received a dozen honorary doctorates from leading universities here and abroad, including Harvard, Yale, Columbia, Oxford, and Rome. He is the recipient of such prestigious awards as the prize for distinguished scholarship in the humanities from the American Council of Learned Societies and the Bollingen Foundation Award. Several academies of arts and sciences made him their member, including the Royal Netherlands Academy, Italian National Academy, American Academy of Arts and Sciences, and Bavarian Academy. From 1962 to 1966 he served as president of the Czechoslovak Society of Arts and Sciences in America.[32]

Egon Hostovský is known to a great many readers of serious literature in the United States, and René Wellek's name is quite familiar to persons who teach English or literature. Neither Hostovský nor Wellek ever hid his ethnic identity, and neither was afraid of the taint of the parochial or was ever accused of it. In America today we have a score of important literary figures who, in Czechoslovakia prior to 1968, had the reputation of being accomplished or highly promising authors. It is understandable that their books, published after their arrival here—and many of them are first class writings—have so far reflected more about their past Czech experience than any present American activities, let alone more universal impressions and feelings. Given their number and their talents, I have no doubt that American as well as universal themes will also, in due time, appear in their works, and thus make them true participants in the mainstream of American culture. The future of Czech-American lettres seems promising indeed.

Skidmore College

NOTES

[1] Some of these studies are listed in Michael Parrish, comp., *The 1968 Czechoslovak Crisis: A Bibliography, 1968-1970* (Santa Barbara, Calif.: American Bibliographical Center-Clio Press, 1971).

[2] Tomáš Čapek, "Augustin Heřman," *Památky českých emigrantů v Americe*, 2nd ed. (Omaha: Národní Tiskárna, 1907), pp. 17-61. Heřman is also the subject of a Czech novel by Jaroslav Koudelka, *Pán na České řece* (Prague: J. Salivar, 1946).

[3] Robert Bolton, *History of the County of Westchester* (New York: A. S. Gould, 1848), passim; also, Čapek, "Bedřich Filip," *Památky českých emigrantů*, pp. 63-79.

[4] A huge literature exists on the Moravians. One of the more authoritative sources is Edmund A. De Schweinitz, *The History of the Church Known as the Unitas Fratrum* (Bethlehem, Pa.: Moravian Publications Office, 1885).

[5] Anthony M. Dignowity, *Autobiography: Bohemia under Austrian Despotism* (New York: The Author, 1859).

[6] Estelle Hudson and Henry R. Maresh, *Czech Pioneers of the Southwest* (Dallas: Southwest Press, 1934), passim.

[7] Reliable figures are hard to come by; even the ethnic statistics of the U.S. Census Bureau are often deficient. The figures I am using here are based on the results of U.S. Censuses since 1870, adjusted by estimates of the following: Jar. E. Salaba Vojan, "Kolik je nás? ," *Česko-americké epištoly* (Chicago: Literární kroužek, 1911), pp. 57-70; Vratislav Bušek, "Statistics on the Czechs and Slovaks in the United States," *Panorama: A Historical Review of Czechs and Slovaks in the United States of America* (Cicero, Ill.: Czechoslovak National Council of America, 1970), pp. 13-14; and information gleaned from current Czech-American periodicals, passim.

[8] In addition to my own extensive file of Czech-American periodicals, I have consulted, or used information from, Tomáš Čapek, *Padesát Let Českého Tisku v Americe* (New York: Directors of the Bank of Europe, 1911) and Vojtěch N. Duben, *České a slovenské noviny a časopisy v zahraničí* (Washington and New York: Czechoslovak Society of Arts and Sciences in America, 1970).

[9] On Albieri, see Jan V. Novák and Arne Novák, *Přehledné dějiny literatury české od nejstarších dob až po naše dny* (Olomouc: R. Promberger, 1913), pp. 514-15. On Havlasa, see Rudolf Havel and Jiří Opelík, eds., *Slovník českých spisovatelů* (Prague: Čs. spisovatel, 1964), pp. 138-39.

[10] "Sládek in America" is the subject of a number of articles scattered in the Czech periodical press both in the United States and in Czechoslovakia. Two comprehensive studies dealing with the topic are Rudolf Sturm, "Sojourn of the Czech Poet Josef Václav Sládek in the United States and the American Influences in his Writings," Diss. Harvard 1956; and Josef Polák, *Americká cesta Josefa Václava Sládka* (Prague: SPN, 1966).

[11] Josef Čermák, *Dějiny občanské války. S připojením zkušeností českých vojínů* (Chicago: A. Geringer, 1889), passim.

[12] J. E. S. Vojan, *Nedělní New-Yorské Listy*, 10 June 1934.

¹³Ferdinand Strejček, *Josef Václav Sládek, jak žil, pracoval a trpěl*, 2nd ed. (Prague: J. Otto, 1948), p. 51.

¹⁴Josef Václav Sládek, *Americké obrázky a jiná próza*, Ferdinand Strejček, ed. (Prague: J. Otto, 1914), II, 269. He is referring to the German poet Nikolaus Lenau (1802-1850) who, too, went to America, because he was "tired of Europe," but soon came back disillusioned.

¹⁵Josef Václav Sládek, *Americké obrázky*, Bohumil Novák, ed., 2nd ed. (Prague: ELK, 1941), pp. 216-17.

¹⁶*Ruch: Básně české omladiny* (Prague: The Editor, 1868).

¹⁷"Morava," "Na farmě," and "Česká opera v Americe," *Americké obrázky*, I. See note 14, above.

¹⁸"Polský misionář," "Pod černou sutanou," "Pan biskup," and "Jak jsme křtili a biřmovali," ibid.

¹⁹"Na českém dvorci v Texasu," "Můj pan chef," and "Chicago," ibid.

²⁰Julius Zeyer in *Časopis Českého musea*, No. 75 (1902), p. 450.

²¹Strejček, *Sládek, jak žil*, p. 90.

²²Strejček, ibid., p. 98.

²³Sládek's poems and articles published in these periodicals are discussed in Josef Polák, "Sládkovy příspěvky v česko-amerických listech *Pokrok* a *Slavie*," *Česká literatura*, No. 6 (1958), pp. 91-107.

²⁴See Sturm, "Sojourn of the Czech Poet Josef Václav Sládek in the United States . . . ," pp. 123-59.

²⁵Josef Václav Sládek, *Básně* (Prague: Grégr a Dattel, 1875).

²⁶Josef Václav Sládek, *Jiskry na moři* (Prague: Militký a Novák, 1880).

²⁷It is a five-volume edition. In vol. I, *Píseň života*, Vyskočil placed ten American poems under the collective heading "In the Shadow of Death." The remaining eight poems he placed in vol. II, *Obrazy*, under the heading "From the New World."

²⁸Sládek, *Americké obrázky* II, 303-04.

²⁹All published in Prague, 1894-1912.

³⁰In the issue for 1 February 1892.

³¹For Hostovský, see Jiří Pistorius, ed., *Padesát let Egona Hostovského* (New York: Moravian Library, 1958) and Rudolf Sturm, ed., *Egon Hostovský: Vzpomínky, studie a dokumenty o jeho díle a osudu* (Toronto: Nakladatelství 68, 1974).

³²Wellek is listed in several editions of *Who's Who in America* and other directories.

American-Estonian Poets

Victor Terras

ABSTRACT

Estonian poetry is of two kinds: folk poetry, based on an ancient oral tradition, and written poetry, which emerged under German influence in the early nineteenth century. Poetry has been not only a mirror but also an active organ of national life throughout Estonia's history. With language and its most active form, poetry, the only inalienable national attributes, their cultivation has been more intensive than it sometimes is in nations secure in their national identity. Estonians in exile number less than 100,000, yet they support numerous periodicals, including two literary journals, *Mana* (in the U.S.A.) and *Tulimuld* (in Sweden), and among them there are hundreds of active poets and writers. For example, there are in the U.S. Ivar Ivask, Jyri Kork, Tiit Lehtmets, Ilmar Mikiver, Ants Oras, Liili-Anne Parlo, Aleksis Rannit, and Asta Willmann. Common denominators are found in these poets' keen interest in problems of poetic structure, especially prosodic, and in modern poetic forms; in a rivalry between nostalgic Estonian themes and a fascination with the world abroad, and between traditional and modern values. The leitmotif of this survey can be found in the conception of poetic creation not only as a substitute for a lost home, but also as a triumph of spiritual values over physical adversity. (VT)

The twentieth century has produced some moving appreciations of the gift of language by men who were reduced to a condition in which language is their only remaining asset: Osip Mandel'štam, Paul Celan, and Jorge Guillén, for example. More than in any earlier century, poets have been exiles, and exiles have become poets. "All poets are Jews!" Marina Cvetaeva once exclaimed. This paper deals with poets in exile, poets who have gratefully acknowledged that language is perhaps the one part of their national heritage which is still fully and inalienably theirs. One might almost speak of a cult of language. Certainly some of the most moving lines written by poets whom I shall discuss here are addressed to their

175

native language. Allow me to quote only two stanzas from two different poets; Ivar Ivask says:

> I live securely in my language,
> Where every word is my birthplace,
> My mind is often full of fear and anguish,
> And only in my language does this menace vanish.[1]

And Aleksis Rannit says:

> I shall forever but distort and break your purity,
> Tongue-tied and alien, our language!
> I shall forever cry for help in anguish, unceasingly,
> Like a helpless infant, our powerful language![2]

A poet in exile goes through an evolution which reflects his progress in the host country. I shall distinguish four stages in this progress, all of which are represented by American-Estonian poets to be discussed here. At first the poet is an exile, or refugee, who by the power of inertia continues to create more or less in the same vein as he did in his home country. Such, for example, is some of Asta Willmann's best poetry, her very fine, dramatic ballads in particular.[3] To take another example, Ants Oras, a great master of poetic translation, has continued to work as Professor of English at the University of Florida much as he probably would have, if he had continued as Professor of English at the University of Tartu, Estonia.

But there comes the time when the poet in exile begins to react to his new condition; his homeland is then a memory and new impressions begin to have an impact on him. Whenever he thinks of his homeland, his point of view suggests that he is an expatriate; for the moment, at least, there is no return. Poetry reflecting this stage is found in the works of almost all poets discussed here.

At the next stage the poet in exile has found a new home, even a new citizenship. Figuratively speaking, he is then a citizen of two countries. The civilization, as well as the literature and poetry of his host country may have a certain influence on him. While his point of view of the host country is still an estranged one, there may occur instances of reverse estrangement. Macaronistic verse may sometimes suggest the latter. Such is the condition of much of the poetry of Ivar Ivask, Tiit Lehtmets, and other American-Estonian poets.

Finally, the poet has come to terms with his condition, a condition which he now understands to be a permanent one. Fully at home in his host country (which sees him as an "ethnic" poet), he is fluent in the host language, often using it in his writing, or even poetically (Rannit, Ivask, and others). But he has also found a secure rationale for remaining true to his native language:

Why in heaven's name
don't you write your verse
in our major tongue
which you handle so well
think of the global audience
why on earth persist
in your crazy dialect?
Hold your horses Sir[4]

And here the poet proceeds in Estonian, explaining that he was born not with a fiddle in his hands, but an Estonian *kannel* ("–no no not a harp rather / like a zither but fewer strings / some wild Finn made it / even out of a pike's bone–"), and concludes the dialogue with three lines in traditional Estonian folk verse.

Aleksis Rannit has eloquently suggested that exile brings out certain qualities in a poet which life in his native land never would have brought out. Rannit's own indubitable growth as a poet while in exile stands by no means alone as a recent example of this phenomenon. Rimvydas Šilbajoris' book *Perfection in Exile* deals with several Lithuanian poets of whom the same is true.[5]

Viewing the question soberly and leaving difficult-to-assess emotional factors (such as the triggering effect of the shock of being suddenly deprived of one's homeland) out of the picture, one can make the following observations about *prima facie* effects of exile on a poet's creations.

The sounds and sound patterns, and the rhythms and cadences of a language are affected but little, at least in the short run,[6] by the speaker's being removed from his native environment. It is this, virtually inalienable, level of language that seems to be particularly dear to Estonian poets in exile; on the whole they seem to be more sound and rhythm-conscious than poets in Soviet-occupied Estonia. This is particularly true of Oras and Rannit.

The level of semantic units and their structures are certainly affected by exile, for the poet in exile is at least partly deprived of that source of constant rejuvenation, the living vernacular. He still possesses the resources of his own verbal creativity and, perhaps, the added stimulus of a foreign language or languages, but there definitely is a void, particularly for the lyric poet, whose language is often closer to the colloquial vernacular than to the language of literary prose. Estonian emigré poetry is on the whole linguistically rather "literary." There are some notable exceptions: Tiit Lehtmets has some refreshingly "earthy" poems.[7] But there are other ways to generate the necessary tension between poetry and prose. The structure and linguistic traditions of the Estonian language are extremely propitious to the creation of neologisms. In Rannit's poetry these are so prominent that some critics have spoken of his "Rannitisms." Neologisms certainly tend to make poetry even more "literary."

The real world (people and their social relationships, the landscape, the city and its peculiar character) poses problems. The emigré poet has the advantage of facing a new and exciting world, and the task of saying and describing in his language things that had never been said in it before. Estonian emigré poetry has responded to life all over the globe. If there is one trait that is characteristic of American-Estonian poets as a group it is that they are well-travelled.[8] But there are losses also. The landscapes of one's native land appear in vague, dreamlike shapes, rather than with vivid freshness, and the social aspect of life is inevitably impoverished. (I am assuming that the poet is not significantly relating to the society of the host country: certainly American society and its problems are not an important element in American-Estonian poetry.) In the long run, there is this question: can a "normal" national and social consciousness be replaced by a cosmopolitan, or dual (e.g., Estonian-American), or strictly individual consciousness? A glance at the "real world" (or "external frame of reference") of American-Estonian poetry shows a profile quite unlike that of a body of poetry originating from its native country.

The Estonian community in the United States has always been small. It developed a significant literary life only with the arrival of a wave of refugees who entered the country under the Displaced Persons Act in the late 1940's and early 1950's. The total number of Estonians who left their homeland during World War II to escape Soviet rule is estimated to have been about 75,000, of whom a full third went to Sweden, the remainder scattering all over the world. Today, the United States, Canada, Australia, and Germany are the principal host countries. The total Estonian population of any of these countries does not exceed that of a small city. Yet these small groups have been amazingly active culturally. According to Bernard Kangro, author of a periodically updated bibliographical summary, Estonian exile literature had produced, by 1971, 118 collections of verse, 276 volumes of fiction, 2 volumes of plays, 106 volumes of memoirs, about 20 volumes of literary criticism, plus a number of travel and children's books. In addition to these works, there is a very large volume of all genres of literature appearing in periodicals. For every poet who has brought out at least one volume of verse, there are several who have published some poems in various periodicals [9]

The small Estonian community in the United States has been able to support newspapers and journals, several Estonian clubs and societies, including the Estonian Learned Society in the United States which for many years has produced a yearbook of scholarly articles and a number of scholarly books, mostly in the humanities. Even more remarkable is the fact that this small group of people has produced a galaxy of poets several of whom have a distinct poetic individuality. A presentation of this extraordinary phenomenon requires some historical background, a summary of which I shall now submit.

Traditional Estonian folk poetry is in many ways quite different from anything we know in the poetry of Western nations or in Estonian literary poetry. Its rhythm is obtained through delicate interplay of a quantitative meter (basically a trochaic tetrameter) and shifting word boundaries. Its language is lexically and grammatically archaic, and quite distinct from spoken Estonian. Alliteration and assonance are integral parts of Estonian folk poetry, often becoming an aesthetic end in themselves. It has no end rhyme. Traditional Estonian folk poetry sees reality through a poetic prism, stylizes it, presents its harshness *con sordino*. Estonian literary poetry in general shows little continuity with traditional folk poetry. There are some notable exceptions, with the Estonian national epos *Kalevipoeg* (1857-1861), by F. R. Kreutzwald (1802-1882), the most important one. *Kalevipoeg* is a conglomerate of authentic folk verse recorded by Kreutzwald himself or by others, Estonian folk traditions versified by Kreutzwald, and Kreutzwald's own poetry, loosely adapted, both in style and in meter, to the Estonian folk song.

The origins of Estonian literary poetry are varied. There was a new type of folk song in existence, certainly as early as the eighteenth century, whose form and content was quite close to Western (German) songs. Local German burghers and clergyman wrote some Estonian *Gelegenheitsdichtung*, imitating German patterns, as early as the seventeenth century. Protestant song books were also created in the seventeenth century, again along German patterns, and finally, ever since K. J. Peterson (1801-1822), Estonians have sought to create a poetic idiom that would be on a par with that of any Western nation.

The beginnings of Estonian literary poetry in the mid-nineteenth century show it largely imitating German classical, romantic, and pseudoromantic poetry. Technically, such imitation suggests the mechanical transfer of German syllabotonic versification and rhyming rules into a poetry whose language is quantitative, has no phonemic stress, and is poor in rhymes (other than "grammatical"). It was thus the task of every "natural" Estonian poet to avoid mechanical, schematic application of the German versification system, and to amalgamate his poetry with the rhythms and cadences of spoken Estonian.

Juhan Liiv (1864-1913) started as a not very remarkable romantic epigone, but then around 1893 began to break the shackles of syllabotonic metrics and regular end rhyme, also replacing conventional literary imagery with nature images of great immediacy and symbolic depth. The rhythms of Liiv's best poems range from the meter of Estonian folk verse to free verse. Their effect depends on virtuosic use of vowel assonance and vowel modulation, a discriminating use of consonant alliteration, and a delicate feeling for quantity balance and sound symbolism.

The poems of Villem Ridala (1885-1942), a member of the *Noor Eesti* ("Young Estonia") group, quite deliberately overcame the constraints of foreign patterns. Ridala's nature poems tend to have a trochaic-dactylic rhythm, generated by the natural phrase contour of his lines rather than by any ideal metric patterns. Ridala's verses also have a much higher degree of acoustic organization (i.e., repetition and modulation) than would be tolerable in English (or German, or Russian) poetry. But this organization is consistent with the poetics of the Estonian folk song, and apparently, with the structure of the language itself. For example,

> Midagi helendab, helgib ja tuikab
> kaugete kinkude takka;
> kaugete metsade takka
> midagi kutsub ja hüüab ja huikab.[10]

The "Young Estonian" poets of the early 1900's, whose leader was Gustav Suits (1883-1956), were intellectuals of a strongly Western orientation. Their poetry shows a trend toward more formal and thematic variety, and it is also more precise in its imagery and versification. The poetry of Gustav Suits shows, along with a new intellectual dimension, a much closer, yet more sophisticated, adherence to syllabotonic versification rules and conventional rhyme theory than had been the case with his predecessors, such as Juhan Liiv. An eminently conscious artist, Suits shows that perfect rhymed and syllabotonic verse can be written in Estonian, provided one remains alert to possible clashes between the natural rhythm of the language and the ideal form of the poem. His poetry demonstrates that, in Estonian, both the rewards for a rhythm—conscious and discriminating—as well as the penalties for a merely mechanical use of meter and rhyme are greater than, for example, those in German syllabotonic verse.

The poets of the *Siuru* circle, among whom Marie Under (1883-   ) and Henrik Visnapuu (1890-1951) were the most prominent, put Estonian poetry fully abreast with twentieth-century experimental poetry. Ever since the teens of this century, Estonian poetry has been sure to respond, almost instantaneously, to whatever new trends have appeared in either East or West European poetry. Free verse, "inexact" rhymes, "prose poems," in short, any modern device known elsewhere, are as current in twentieth-century Estonian poetry as are such traditional forms as the sonnet (of which Marie Under is a great master) or the elegiac distich. Likewise such "modernist" trends or moods as expressionism, surrealism, primitivism, futurism, etc., are amply represented.

The formal and thematic searchings of Estonian poetry have been continued, with particular energy, by some American-Estonian poets. Ivar Ivask, a poet well familiar with the rhythms of all Western poetries, has created a great deal of interesting unrhymed free verse in which the tension between natural speech contour and poetic cadence (along with euphonic sound patterns) is responsible for the poetic effect. Aleksis Rannit has been one of the boldest innovators in both meter and rhyme. Rannit's more recent poetry is composed in lineary-quantitative meters, where only long or over-long syllables may stand in the strong part of a foot, and the number of syllables in a foot is constant (no spondees are allowed). As a result, a trochaic or dactylic rhythm of word boundaries accompanies the basic quantitative rhythm. Rhythmic variety is created by alternation of long and over-long ictuses, as well as by variations in positioning of word boundaries.[11] Rannit's rhymes consist of assonance of two or three vowels, plus alliteration between the rhyming words, where the final consonant is, however, not allowed to coincide: "liitumaks—liikuma," "meloodia—loodima," "keskel—orkester," "värvist—värsis," etc. Needless to say, these rhymes are a great deal more "difficult" than conventional perfect rhymes. In addition, Rannit's verses are saturated with patterns of sound repetition and modulation, to a degree which would appear "unnatural" in a Western language.

Next to the lack of freedom of expression, the most deleterious circumstance under which Estonian poetry in Soviet-occupied Estonia must suffer is the relative difficulty of exchange of ideas, moods, and techniques with the literatures of the West. It is in this area that literature in exile can do the national literature an inestimable service. The foreign themes, images, landscapes, ideas, and forms found in emigré poetry act as a bridge between world literature and the centripetal existence of a minor literature which is trying hard to maintain its national character in its forced association with the other nations of the Soviet Union. American-Estonian poetry is a poetry of world travellers and students of many different cultures of the world. Mediterranean, French, Latin motifs abound in the poetry of Ivask and Rannit. Lehtmets sailed the Seven Seas for ten years, and his poetry takes us to exotic places. American motifs occur quite frequently in Ivask's and Jyri Kork's poetry.

More important yet, the verses of these poets conquer for their language some areas of thought and culture which are inaccessible or forbidden to poetry in Soviet-occupied Estonia. Thus, a good deal of surrealist verse has been produced by Estonian poets in exile, and an American-Estonian poet, Ilmar Mikiver, is one of its principal representatives. Metaphysical, mythological, and mystical moods, frowned upon by Socialist Realism, flourish freely in emigré poetry. Only recently there appeared a

182

substantial collection of religious verse by Liili-Anne Parlo, an American-Estonian poet. The unabashed estheticism and cult of pure form professed by Aleksis Rannit would hardly be tolerated in the Estonian SSR. And, naturally enough, there is some eloquent political, anti-Soviet verse, from painful expression of sympathy with one's suffering brethren in that "great prison of nations" to outright invective.[12]

The greatest compliment I can pay to Estonian emigré poetry in general and American-Estonian poetry in particular is that it cannot be given a common denominator. It is represented by a number of creative individuals, each with his own style and *Weltanschauung*, and more or less blessed with talent and originality of vision. What is largely absent from American-Estonian poetry is the deadening uniformity of form, the monotonous repetition of themes, and ideological predictability which is found in much of Estonian poetry on the other side of the iron curtain, with noteworthy exceptions, to be sure. Therefore, rather than trying to give a digested synthesis, I shall now try to sketch the creative personalities of some American-Estonian poets.

I shall not discuss Henrik Visnapuu, although technically he may be called an American-Estonian poet. He spent the last years of his life in the United States and his last volume of verse, *Linnutee* (The Milky Way), appeared in New York in 1950. Some American themes appear in it. Regrettably, Visnapuu's American poems, like his Austrian and German poems, are of relatively minor significance. Visnapuu, of course, is a major poet and a brief discussion in the present context would not do him justice.

Ants Oras (1900-), one of the most remarkable figures of Estonian academic and cultural life, has been living in the United States for a quarter of a century (since 1949). Until his retirement, he was for many years professor of English literature at the University of Florida in Gainesville. A literary scholar of rarely paralleled scope and depth of erudition, and for fifty years one of Estonia's leading critics and theorists of literature, Oras is also an unbelievably fertile, versatile, and virtuosic translator of poetry from an almost unlimited number of languages into Estonian, as well as into English and German.[13] Oras' translations are invariably *Nachdichtungen*, authentic works of art, whose form arises organically from the structure of the language. Thus, for his masterful translations of Vergil, Oras has created an Estonian quantitative verse system which is close to the Latin hexameter, yet naturally develops from the phonology and prosody of Estonian. Amazingly, Oras has done equally well with syllabic (Molière, Baudelaire, and others) as well as syllabotonic and accentual meters (Shakespeare, Goethe, Puškin, Shelley, Keats, and many others)—a remarkable achievement in view of the fact that Estonian prosody features no phonemic stress, but rather a delicately balanced system of quantity and intonation patterns. Oras has also produced many excellent translations of Estonian poetry into German and English.[14] To suggest the quality of his skill, I should like to say that I believe Oras to be one of the two or three best translators of Russian poetry into English—and this is only a "side line" of his.

Aleksis Rannit (1914-   ), for many years Curator of Slavic and East European Studies at Yale University, is a man of similar versatility. An art critic of considerable eminence, he has written some authoritative pieces on the Estonian graphic artist Eduard Wiiralt and the Lithuanian painter M. K. Čiurlionis, among others. As a literary scholar, critic, and bibliographer, Rannit has successfully dealt with poets of the symbolist and post-symbolist period of many European literatures. Rannit's critical approach is characterized by broad comparative and synesthetic vistas, an intuitive sense of style and *Zeitgeist*, encompassing its manifestations in all art forms, and a deep sensitivity for nuances of form. Like Oras, Rannit is a fine essayist in several languages, besides Estonian. He is an equally fine translator, though not nearly as prolific. Lithuanian poetry is one of his specialities.

As a poet, Rannit published his first collection as early as 1937, but he definitely has done his best work since moving to the United States in 1953. Rannit has his very own place in Estonian poetry. His style and basic attitude are classical—a rarity in Estonian poetry—in that they feature voluntary subjection to very demanding formal rules and an extraordinarily high degree of formal structuredness and intellectual discipline. Rannit believes that every detail of acoustic and rhythmic formation is directly relevant to a poem's content, and hence matches his difficult rhythms and rhymes with a singularly high incidence of vowel and consonant modulation, assonance, and alliteration. His poems are phonetic and rhythmic compositions of considerable complexity.

A purely "lyric" poet, Rannit expresses, first and foremost, the most basic states of the human soul in simple elementary imagery.[15] Decidedly a poetic *aquarius*, Rannit is perhaps at his best expressing man's experience of the eternal sea; he does so, for example, in one of his finest poems, "The Sea." His beautiful cycle of poems, "Cliffs" (1969), begins with an aquarian's dreamlike landing on a rocky shore, whose jagged outlines are an alien and threatening sight. In contrast to the rhythmic swaying of the waves of the sea, the terra firma seems formless. After a brief and blissful encounter, on a flowering meadow, with an earth maiden, *aquarius* returns to the sea, but with a new vision of the rocky coast line: he now recognizes in its sternly geometric shapes a regularity that is kindred to his own aquarian rhythm. Inserted is a song "To a Skylark," in which the aquarian senses, for a fleeting moment, the joy of being airborne. A thunderstorm at sea provides some fire imagery, though in an aquarian context.

Whenever Rannit's poetry does not deal with these very basic and elementary cosmic experiences, its object is a synesthetic vision of world art, in which all art forms are represented. In a way, all of Rannit's many poems about music, painting, sculpture, and of course poetry itself are "definitions of art," or "definitions of poetry," and the whole is Rannit's *Ars poetica*. For example, in a poem entitled "Poetry," he writes:

> It is the tender embrace of my silence,
> drought of suffocating remoteness, without a ray of light,
>
> melancholy, reluctant to couple with rhythm,
> sadness, which lingers even in rhyme,
>
> a glance, languid from a simile's tenderness,
> lightning frozen in its tracks—a dithyrambic image,
>
> ashes, dusted off lacerated eyelids,
> the song of one who is in the grip of a waning radiance,
>
> a song of nirvana.[16]

Among Rannit's preoccupations as a poet there is the dichotomy of "line" and "color"—literally, and also as metaphors of "form" and "expression." Sensitive lyric poet that he is, his intuitive and immediate impulse points toward color, and he has in fact created some beautiful poetic conceits featuring color, with blue clearly a favorite; an example is "Medici Blue":

> Given but one colour to choose,
> I chose the blue, to keep our union
> and our words alive. Good, the paint still runs,
> colour floating on the palette ebbs and flows.
>
> For distances and depths the measure,
> colour marks your spirit and your ken—
> like the lucid ice of your recent passion,
> like the bluest shade of sound you have spoken.
>
> Mistaken, he who can sense
> only the breadth of cold in the blue tone—
> for you are the warmth of blue, the substance,
> glowing from light that flows from within.[17]

But Rannit's whole striving as a conscious, sophisticated artist is aimed at the pure simplicity of a line and of brilliant white light, the ideal image of which he finds in a cut diamond, a favorite conceit of his. Let me conclude my remarks on Rannit by citing his poem "Line":

> Love toward line,
> toward your all illuminating power,
> O all ennobling rune—
> line of the thunderbolt and not the thunder.

All binding and all bounding line,
accurate as the rhyme of death:
Phidias, Ingres, Wiiralt,
Bach and Valéry.

I have broken faith with color.
Now my verses measure for the line—
for you, line perfection engendered
in the ascetic square of the mind.[18]

Ivar Ivask (1927-   ), currently Professor of German literature at the University of Oklahoma and editor of *Books Abroad*, has much in common with Oras and Rannit. A polyglot and productive scholar, Ivask, who began his academic career as a Germanist, has more recently shown a great affinity for Spanish civilization and poetry, an affinity reflected in his scholarly work as well as in his poetry. Like Rannit, Ivask has a native knowledge of another Baltic language, Latvian in his case. Like Oras, he has mastered German and English verse. His collection of German verse, *Gespiegelte Erde* (1967), is no less remarkable than his several Estonian collections.[19] A significant trait of Ivask's poetic personality is his rediscovery of Finland, its landscape and its people. To Estonians, Finland has been for a long time not merely a neighboring fraternal nation, but an ideal as well, a country and a people in whom one's own way of life and one's own aspirations were realized in a higher degree. This feeling has run even higher since Estonia lost her independence while Finland retained hers. And so Ivask's many "finnish" poems are in a way a projection of an Estonian's nostalgia for his native land.

Ivask's poetic corpus is spectacularly polarized. On the one side, we see the intellectual panorama of a sophisticated world traveller and scholar, on the other an atavistic return to an earlier, simpler identity. The poet is himself intensely aware of this deep rift between existence in and outside history:

I do not notice you here, history,
because a sudden rise in the rustling of birch trees muffles
                                the sounds of gunfire,
blood turns to water, death approaches like an avalanche,
like a bear, who quietly lines up bones of various sizes,
like polished pebbles on a river bottom.
A pine's outstretched arms put earth under its roots,
the wind peels rocks of the spirit free of the flesh.[20]

Ivask's form reflects this polarity. On the one hand, he produces the most "modern" free verse, where the distinction between poetry and prose rests on the razor's edge of a critically placed pause, austerely spurning all other forms of poetic organization. On the other side, he lapses, almost inadvertently, it might seem, into the quantitative or accentual meters of

Estonian folk poetry. Accordingly, Ivask's poetic lines may be classically straightforward in their acoustic structure, or they can be saturated with sound patterns and sound symbolism, the latter, for example, in some recent verses which are patterned on magic incantations of Finnish and Estonian folklore. Similarly, while elegant intellectual conceits are found in some of Ivask's poems, other poems feature "primitive" verbal magic, etymologism, and "anthropological" imagery.

Ivask's themes range far and wide. Although at first glance his poetry would appear to be very different from Rannit's, closer scrutiny shows that these two poets have much in common. Like Rannit's, Ivask's nature poetry displays "cosmic" moods and a confluence of microcosm and macrocosm.[21] It also features a great deal of elementary imagery, and, much as in Rannit's poetry, water imagery clearly prevails. Ivask's nature poetry has, however, an extra "atavistic" or "anthropological" dimension.[22] Ivask is fond of imagery which reflects the mythic world view of a primeval Finnish fisherman: "Ichthyophile" is a term one might apply to some of Ivask's poetry, and the Finnish country sauna, very much a traditional part of this world, is a recurring image or setting.

Like Rannit, Ivask is a world traveller. The Ulysses motif occurs in both, and each has a cycle of poems tracing the stops of a voyage in the Aegean.[23] Like Rannit, Ivask greets a whole galaxy of great contemporary poets and writers in his poems (Guillén, Borges, Ungaretti, Doderer, and others), and world art and culture are a presence throughout. But there are also many things which Ivask does differently. His poetry has a much more subjective flavor than Rannit's austerely objective compositions. Much in it reads like pages from a poet's notebook. Some poems have a personal ring; for an example, there is a recent cycle, "Four Trees in Rõngu" (*Oktoober Oklahomas*, pp. 75-82). Furthermore, Ivask, who has after all lived over half of his life in the United States, has also shown himself capable of manifesting a warm and affectionate feeling for the American landscape.

A peculiarity of Ivask's poetry is his fondness for what I would call the metaphysical landscape. "Castilian Message" will suggest what I mean:

> This landscape is never subdued:
> Its hills are a single roll of drums
> Stonily telling you of death,
> Yet also dancing in the blaze of day
> To honor life. Then, night falls like a sword
> Into the congealed river of your dreams:
> One of its banks that which you were,
> The other that which you will never be.[24]

Here and elsewhere Ivask attunes his consciousness to the cosmic rhythm of time spans unlike those with which we deal in everyday life. In some of his poems we meet the aeons of geological time, in others a finely set biological clock.[25]

Another interesting dimension in Ivask's poetry is its occasional surrealism, which is particularly pronounced in the poet's third collection, *Ajaloo aiad* (Gardens of History). Ivask cultivates different patterns of dream "logic," prelogical thinking, "pure language," and such. For example, there is a poem, parenthetically called "Concise Estonian Phonology for Advanced Students" (*Ajaloo aiad*, p. 78), which performs the *tour de force* of telling a story of sorts through a string of interjections and onomatopoetic morphemes. There are whole poems based on the "logic" of etymologism, e.g., "Reactionaries," *Ajaloo aiad*, p. 79, and there are others which are the verbal equivalent of a painting by Chagall, or even Dali.[26]

Ivask is a versatile and prolific poet who keeps developing new forms. Thus his most recent collection, *October in Oklahoma* (1975), contains a number of novelties, most prominently a cycle of haikus, "A Summer in Haikus." Ivask, like Rannit, always abreast of every new development in world poetry, responds alertly to many different stimuli and is sure to produce many more interesting contributions to Estonian poetry.

There are other American-Estonian poets whose entire output was produced after they had arrived in this country. Time and space force me to treat them more summarily than Rannit and Ivask. The relative brevity of my account is justified by the smaller volume of their output, but implies no value judgment.

Jyri Kork's (1927-   ) collections , *Singers by the Sea of Glass* (1958) makes one regret that it has remained the poet's only one. Kork is a space engineer with NASA, and most of his publications are in his scientific speciality. Yet his poems are in no way dilettantish, but on the contrary show the polish and sophistication of a talented man of letters and are strongest precisely on their "professional" side: variety and skill of rhythm, rhyme, and phrasing; sure-handed control of sound patterns and poetic syntax, and ingenuity of poetic conceits. Kork's themes are varied: reminiscences of childhood and youth in Estonia, war poems gathered in a cycle, "Steel Helmets and Bayonets," poems from the notebook of a world traveler, sea poems, and poems about the poet and poetry (the cycles, "A Poet's Life and Death," and "Poetry's Metamorphoses"). The most interesting and original poem of the whole collection is, in my opinion, "The Sea Across the Horizon" (pp. 74-76). Written in vigorous free verse, the poem paints a fascinating expressionist vision of a friendly ocean beyond the forbidding shapes of blast furnaces at a mythical Steel Town, Pennsylvania, where

> liquid iron, blinding, cruel,
> flows like the blood of giants,
> the blood of legendary giants,
> once born of dragon teeth.

If I have to place Kork below Rannit and Ivask, it is because he has not developed a distinctive style, his own "voice," as it were. Every artist begins by trying out a variety of styles and forms made available to him by his predecessors, until he discovers, often by accident, his very own style. Ordinarily a poet has to write a great deal of poetry before this happens.[27]

Tiit Lehtmets (1927-   ) is another American-Estonian poet who has produced a single, yet rather remarkable collection of verse, *The Seagull in a Desert* (1966). Lehtmets was a sailor for many years before he settled in New York in 1954. Unlike most Estonian emigré poets, whose concepts and language are those of intellectuals, Lehtmets presents (or successfully affects) the sensibility and diction of a once rough-and-tough, once tearfully sentimental self-educated blue collar worker. His themes are again those of childhood and adolescence in Estonia, the war, sailing the Seven Seas. But the last cycle of his collection, "Graffiti on a Bar Counter," is refreshingly "different" in its robust cynicism, gallows humor, and unaffected vulgarity. The syncopated rhythms and crude rhymes of these pieces, usually quite short, are somewhat reminiscent of American Negro blues, as is the mood of many of them, for instance, "Waking up in Harlem" (p. 47).

Other American-Estonian poets who have published collections of their poetry are August Pihlak and Liili-Anne Parlo.[28] Both are considered by critics to be poetic *dilettanti* (I am using the Italian form of this word to avoid a deprecatory connotation), and use conventional forms. Liili-Anne Parlo's collection *I Seek Your Face* is remarkable on the thematic side; her verses are devoted to religious themes familiar from Lutheran hymnals, whose language and imagery they also display. But only a few of them have that musical quality which transforms an expression of sentiment into poetry. One such poem is "At Sunrise":

> When the Sun rises once more
> and scatters the gloom,
> turning the countryside bright
> and making it sparkle again,
>
> Then that very Sun
> that very moment
> scatters the gloom
> from my anguished soul.
>
> My faith comes back to me,
> and peace.
> In the birth of thy Light
> there is salvation.[29]

The American-Estonian literary journal *Mana*, which has been in existence since 1957, has published over the years poetry by many Estonian poets other than those already mentioned: Ivar Grünthal, Reet Hendrikson, Margus Jukkum, Toivo Kallas, Urve Karuks, Eduard Krants, Ilona Laaman, Silvia Luige-Kuriste, Aime-Liis Martinson, Ilmar Mikiver, Hannes Oja, Kaarel Saar, Vello Salo, Arved Viirlaid, and many others. Among them there are some young poets who left Estonia as children, or were actually born abroad. Mikiver's daughter, Triinu Mikiver, for example, is herself a poet. Most of these poets live in Sweden or in Canada, but some live in the United States. Among the latter there is at least one poet who has published enough poetry to have developed a distinctive poetic style. He is Ilmar Mikiver, a well-known newscaster and journalist. Mikiver, along with his friend, the remarkable formalist poet Ilmar Laaban (1921-   ), who lives in Sweden, represents the most radical "modernist" wing of Estonian poetry in exile. He has experimented with traditional meters (even sonnets and elegiac distichs) and rhymed verse, but likes free verse best. Mikiver's speciality is a kaleidoscopic stream of images, broken through the distortion prism of a fascinatingly estranged consciousness. Mikiver's surrealism is different from that of his fellow poets in that its images are often pointedly anti-poetic, its association patterns whimsical, and its metaphors boldly "metaphysical." The following example may suffice:

> Here he hangs, man,
> Hook of heaven in his throat,
> Weights of hell on his feet.
>
> His every fibre
> trembling in the wind of tenderness
> and a beautiful explosion circling slowly
> in his veins.
>
> He lives, he lives.
>
> Time smells, making his head turn,
> to him who stews in the oil of millennia,
> Time tastes like pure salt
> on his tongue, shredded by centuries.
>
> Time drives matchsticks of years
> under his fingernails . . .
> Not to mention hours and seconds.
> Time is a murderer,
> yet man lives.[30]

While many Estonian poets from Europe and Australia publish their verse in *Mana*, American-Estonian poets often publish theirs in *Tulimuld*, a literary quarterly which has been appearing in Sweden since 1949. Besides, a great deal of poetry has been and continues to be printed in Estonian newspapers in this country, in Canada, in Sweden, and elsewhere. A number of almanacs, yearbooks, Festschriften, etc. have also produced some poetry. Thus, my account is not nearly exhaustive.[31]

There remains the question of the future of Estonian poetry in exile. There was a time when Estonian literature in exile far outweighed Estonian literature at home. This is not quite so anymore, as several fine young poets are now active in Soviet-occupied Estonia and some poets of the older generation have been able to express themselves somewhat more freely. Nevertheless, the poetry and prose published in the free world are something without which Estonian literature would be poorer in many ways. In fact, its presence gives Estonian literature an unusual and exciting dimension. While it is true that for the past hundred years Estonian poets and writers have travelled and lived abroad, it is certainly new to have poets and writers some of whom have lived in their host country for a quarter century or more, while others have never seen their native land at all, or at least not as adults. It is to be expected that Estonian literature in exile will exist for at least another generation; there are enough writers and readers now middle-aged or younger to guarantee this. Unforeseen political developments may change things. Thus, new waves of emigrants have prolonged the life of the Russian literature in exile well into a third, or even fourth, generation.

Brown University

NOTES

[1] Ivar Ivask, "Faith in Language," in *Tähtede tähendus* (Lund: Eesti kirjanike kooperatiiv, 1964), p. 67. Other collections of poetry by Ivask: *Päev astub kukesammul* (1966), *Gespiegelte Erde* (1967), *Ajaloo aiad* (1970), *Oktoober Oklahomas* (1975). If not otherwise stated, translations are mine.

[2] Aleksis Rannit, "Language," in *Sõrmus* (Lund: Eesti kirjanike kooperatiiv, 1972), p. 41. Other collections of poetry by Rannit: *Akna raamistuses* (1937), *V okonnom pereplete*, trans. Igor' Severjanin (1938), *Via dolorosa*, trans. Igor' Severjanin (1940), *Käesurve* (1st ed., 1945; 2nd ed., 1946), *Suletud avarust* (1956), *Verse an Würalt und an das geklärte Gleichnis*, trans. Ants Oras (1960), *Kuiv hiilgus* (1963), *Meri* (1964), *Aleksio Rannito eilerašciai* (1964), *22 verse*, trans. György Alblàncy (1965), *Kaljud* (1969), *Line* (1970), *Sõrmus* (1972), *Donum estonicum*, trans. Cid Corman and H. W. Tjalsma (1976).

[3] Asta Willmann-Linnolt (1916-   ) has been active as a playwright, director, and drama teacher in Hartford, Connecticut for many years. In Estonian emigré literature she is known primarily as a prose writer of considerable accomplishment. Her only volume of verse, *Ihuüksi* (All Alone [Stockholm: Autori kirjastus, 1950]), is remarkable for the fluent form of its verses and the wit and originality of its imagery. But only in the several folk style ballads of this collection does she attain true originality and a "voice" all her own.

[4] Ivar Ivask, *Ajaloo aiad* (Lund: Eesti kirjanike kooperatiiv, 1970), p. 83.

[5] Rimvydas Silbajoris, *Perfection in Exile* (Norman, Oklahoma: Univ. of Oklahoma Press, 1970). In recent years two Russian-American poets, Jurij Ivask (with a

strong affinity to Estonia, his former home) and Igor' Činnov (a native of Latvia) have also shown an amazing capacity for growth and change.

[6] In the course of decades, the cadence of speech changes, of course. Today a Russian emigré poet of the old generation can be readily distinguished from a Soviet poet when they *recite* their verse. I have observed nothing similar in Estonian poetry so far.

[7] Ivar Ivask, who uses quite a few neologisms himself and is on the whole an intellectual poet, has made efforts to give some colloquial freshness to his poetic idiom.

[8] Rannit, Ivask, Kork, and Lehtmets all have whole cycles of poems dealing with their travels in various more or less exotic countries.

[9] For at least a partial catalogue, see Arvo Mägi, Karl Ristikivi, and Bernard Kangro, *Eesti kirjandus paguluses 1944-1972* (Lund: Eesti kirjanike kooperatiiv, 1973).

[10] "Kevade tunne" (1903), quoted from *Eesti luule antoloogia*, 2 vols., ed. E. Sõgel et al. (Tallinn: Eesti Riiklik Kirjastus, 1955), I, 341. The translation reads: "There's something shining, sparkling, and pulsating / beyond those far-off hillocks; / beyond those far-off forests, / something is calling, and shouting, and yelling" ("A Feeling of Spring").

[11] Ants Oras has demonstrated this most convincingly in his article "Silpidest ja luulest" (Of Syllables and Poetry), *Tulimuld*, 18 (1967), 131-136.

[12] Ivar Ivask, in a poem (*Ajaloo aiad*, p. 91) asks the question: What if I had to change places with a friend suffering in a Siberian, rather than American, exile? Tiit Lehtmets would like to kick the belly of that "Great Motherland of Socialism" ("A Song to Moscow," *Kajakas kõrbes*, p. 31).

[13] See in particular his *Acht estnische Dichter*, ausgewählt und übertragen von Ants Oras (Stockholm: Vaba Eesti, 1964).

[14] For a bibliography of Oras' works, see *Estonian Poetry and Language: Studies in Honor of Ants Oras*, ed. Viktor Kõressaar and Aleksis Rannit (Stockholm: Estonian Learned Society in America, 1965), pp. 13-24. The same volume contains a critical appreciation of Ants Oras by Aleksander Aspel, "Ants Oras au coeur de son temps," ibid., pp. 32-66.

[15] For more details see Victor Terras, *Aleksis Rannit* (Lund: Eesti kirjanike kooperatiiv, 1975), pp. 49-55 and passim.

[16] "Luule" (Poetry), *Sõrmus*, p. 17.

[17] "Medici Blue," trans. Henry Lyman, *Suletud avarust* (Lund: Eesti kirjanike kooperatiiv, 1956), p. 57.

[18] "Joon," trans. Henry Lyman *Suletud avarust*, p. 43. For a discussion of Rannit's poetics, see Victor Terras, "The Poetics of Aleksis Rannit: Observations on the Condition of the Emigré Poet," *Journal of Baltic Studies*, 5 (1974), 112-16.

[19] Like Rannit, Ivask writes most of his scholarly prose in English.

[20] "Ma ei pane sind siin tähele, ajalugu," *Ajaloo aiad*, p. 62.

[21] For instance: "Groves of fir, pine, alder, and birch trees / you stand around me, watchful and childish / yet even in you there is a trembling of cosmic terror / your tip still measures day when your roots plumb the depths of night" (*Ajaloo aiad*, p. 69).

[22] A master of this particular genre is Bernard Kangro (1910-   ), Estonian emigré poet and writer who lives in Sweden.

[23] See Rannit's cycle, "Via purgativa," *Kuiv kiilgus* (Lund: Eesti kirjanike kooperatiiv, 1963), pp. 31-57, and Ivask's cycle "Rändad, lendad" (You Travel, Fly),

Tähtede tähendus, pp. 39-40, or his poems, "Oliivipuu moondumisi" (Metamorphoses of an Olive Tree) and "Kreekalikku" (Grecian), *Päev astub kukesammul*, pp. 23-27.

[24] *Tähtede tähendus*, p. 36.

[25] See, e.g., a poem identified parenthetically as "Mammoth Hot Springs" (*Ajaloo aiad*, p. 55) or "Oma maa ja taevas" (My Own Land and Sky), *Päev astub kukesammul*, p. 45, where the Icarus motif (a recurring one in Ivask) combines with a cosmic perspective. The poem, "La Granja pargia" (At La Granja Park), *Päev astub kukesammul*, p. 13, likens the creative process to the thickening of a chestnut's seeds into a prickly ball: "They are still raw under their pale and swelling skin, / yet their fertility has strength and drive."

[26] "Who will you turn to without a timepiece / (a golden calf is lowing in the barn) / an azimuth plotted by rule of thumb / only leads you to the doghouse / where you tremble keeping a growling mutt company / Lazarus without timepiece without golden calf / shrouded like a dead man drunk with life / in the opening you discover to your surprise / the proximity of space to your naked body / (the mutt does not care at all) / but you begin to scream / a cuckoo lays his egg in someone else's nest / timepieces tumble from towers / in a surprise of resurrection" (*Ajaloo aiad*, p. 92).

[27] In this connection, Tiina Vedro (1919-   ) deserves to be mentioned. She has published very little, but her cycle of free-verse poems published in *Tulimuld*, No. 1, 1971, reveals a sensitive and discerning poetic consciousness. It takes more than a few interesting poems, however, to establish a poetic identity.

[28] For a bibliography of Pihlak's poetry, see *Eesti kirjandus paguluses 1944-1972*, p. 154. Parlo's collection is entitled *Su palet ma otsin* (I am Searching for Thy Face [Uppsala: Eesti vaimulik raamat, 1975]).

[29] *Su palet ma otsin*, p. 40.

[30] Ilmar Mikiver, "What a Swine, II," *Mana*, 1 (1970), 7.

[31] For more information see *Eesti kirjandus paguluses 1944-1972* which also contains a bibliography. Cf. also Ivar Ivask, "Baltic Literatures in Exile: Balance of a Quarter Century," *Journal of Baltic Studies*, 3 (1972), 1-17.

The Franco-American Literature of New England: A Brief Overview*

Armand B. Chartier

ABSTRACT

The Franco-American literature of New England chronicles the evolution of the ethny, the movement toward apparent or actual assimilation conflicting with attempts to preserve ethnic identity. One finds unique variations on universal literary themes as well as on themes common to all ethnic American literatures, especially in the novel. Albéric Archambault's *Mill Village* shows an immigrant family's adaptation to the American way of life as demonstrated by their upward socio-economic mobility. Gérard Robichaud, in *Papa Martel,* transcends the melancholy destiny of Franco-Americans by illustrating the harmony which can be achieved between preservation of the ethnic heritage and acceptance of a different cultural environment, while at the opposite end of the spectrum, Grace Metalious' *No Adam in Eden* exemplifies the disintegration of traditional values. The works of Jack Kerouac doubtless remain the best expression of the Franco-American collective unconscious in which profound discomfort is felt and is made manifest by a refusal to accept defeat, i.e., full cultural integration into the American mainstream. Most Franco-American poets of the past fifty years, by breaking with traditional themes and versification, have achieved a universality which is perhaps greater than that of the novelists. The rich diversity of their works is most striking, for example in the poetic prose "landscapes" of Henri D'Arles, the "mysticism" of Rosaire Dion-Lévesque, and the fusion of ancient and modern strains in the abundantly variegated poems of Paul-P. Chassé. It is argued by some that the future of Franco-American Literature is in serious jeopardy, yet the recent revival of interest in ethnicity suggests that to envision a partial eclipse might be more realistic than to state that we have witnessed the final sunset. (ABC)

To my parents and grand-
parents who kept brightly
lit the flame of ethnic
heritage.

193

Most Franco-Americans immigrated to the United States either from Québec, or from Acadie, a land even less familiar to Americans. While there are no accurate figures available on the precise number of Franco-Americans in New England, it is doubtful that they are much fewer than two million. For the most part, their literature has received scant attention even though it has been quite substantial and not unseemly despite highly unfavorable circumstances. For the existence of this literature, especially in its very beginnings, one must thank the journalists—men such as Philippe-Armand Lajoie, Wilfrid Beaulieu and Antoine Clément—who have energetically encouraged novelists, poets, historians and critics by seeking out their writings and by offering them a forum. Again recently, Monsieur Wilfrid Beaulieu has manifested his dedication in a very special way by devoting a full page of his newspaper to previously unpublished writings. To such men, we therefore owe a public tribute.

Early Franco-American literature has been studied by men such as Alexandre Bélisle[1] and competent scholars including Soeur Mary-Carmel Therriault,[2] and Paul-P. Chassé.[3] Without in any way implying that the last word has been said concerning this early literature, I have chosen to concentrate upon more recent Franco-American novels and poetry, relative to which precious little has been written and about which I hope a great deal more will someday be said. Nothing herein pretends to be exhaustive or definitive; it is simply my intention to share with you a few personal reactions to certain books read with admiration and enthusiasm by Franco-Americans—and others—whose judgment I have long respected.

A passing reference should be made to one of the works which links the early years to the contemporary period. *Mill Village*, published by Albéric Archambault in 1943,[4] is a documentary novel on the immigration of a French-Canadian family and on their settlement in New England shortly after the Civil War. The hesitations of a family about to emigrate, their arrival in Connecticut, the tedium of work in the mills, the exploitation and the prejudice they endured, their fondness for oral narratives and their efforts to preserve the best of their cultural heritage—all the familiar themes are developed. It is also to the credit of Albéric Archambault that he devotes a large part of his novel to the new wave of French-Canadian immigrants, those who came after the turn of the century. Less docile, better educated and eager for political involvement, many of them were elected to public office and strove to bring about legislative change designed to improve the lot of the mill workers. Their attitude is aptly summed up by the author in terms prophetic of President John Kennedy's Inaugural Address: " . . . they came to the States, not to see what this country had to offer them, but to show this country what they had to give."[5]

Jack Kerouac is not generally thought of as an ethnic author, so secure is his niche in the mainstream of American literature, and so myopic has been the majority of his readers. Yet the freight of his ethnic heritage is nothing short of overwhelming for an objective analyst striving to summarize it in a few short pages; such work should provide future researchers with an abundance of material, the richness of which will be merely adumbrated here.

Explicit references to his national origins abound in the author's works. In one of his more expansive moods, he referred to himself as a "French Canadian Iroquois American aristocrat Breton Cornish democrat."[6] In the "Author's Introduction" to *Lonesome Traveler* he states tersely: "Nationality: Franco-American," and declares that his people go back to "Breton France," adding further details about his forebears.[7] To probe more deeply into his ancestral past, he undertook a genealogical journey to France, of which *Satori in Paris* is the chronicle. It may appear paradoxical that the man whose life-style and works in many ways expressed the specific hopes and frustrations of American youth could feel at home outside this country, yet, referring to France, he tells us: "I'm home."[8]

Yes, to the extent that he could feel *home* at all on this planet, Jack Kerouac, the Dalai Lama of the Beat Generation, was *home* in France; he was *home* too in French Canada, "the illuminated Northern land"[9] where, as an "outsider American Genius Canuck" (ibid.), he could relate to his "brother French-Canadians" (*Dreams*, p. 117) to the point of not taking nonsense from any "non Frenchman of Canada" (*Dreams*, p. 118). But above all, he was *home* in the "Little Canada" of his native Lowell, Massachusetts, where his boyhood friends with names like Scotty Boldieu, Albert Lauzon and Zaza Vauriselle play hockey, the favorite French-Canadian sport, where "the poor Canucks my people of my God-gave-me-life"[10] frequent such places as Laurier Park, the Daumier Club, Destouches' store, Saint Jean-Baptiste church that "Rouault Gray Baroque Strasbourg Cathedral"[11] and Sainte Jeanne d'Arc church where in 1954 he will "see" "The *Beat*ific Generation" (*Dreams*, p. 159).

Kerouac's first novel, *The Town and the City*, published in 1950, is atypical from both a personal and an ethnic point of view. The author accomplished far more in it than do most writers in their first novels, too many of whom merely transcribe autobiographical experiences with no visible artistry. In the works of many hyphenated-American writers, the ethnic theme looms large and is clearly the major focus. *The Town and the City*, on the one hand, transcends fictionalized autobiography, whereas the Franco-American theme is kept in the background—"for personal reasons," the author stated to Rosaire Dion-Lévesque.[12] If one bears in mind that it was not fashionable to be Franco-American in the nineteen-forties (when the work was written), these "personal reasons" are not completely unfathomable. Yet *The Town and the City* develops many of the ethnic themes which occupy a central place within the entire Kerouac corpus.

The locus is Galloway, i.e., Lowell, Massachusetts, one of several Franco-American industrial cities and milltowns on the banks of the Merrimac River. The novel relates the coming-of-age of the Martin children, the eight sons and daughters of George and Marguerite (Courbet) Martin. In the size of this family lies the first and most obvious clue that we are here in the presence of a family which precisely by virtue of its sheer number is clearly not Anglo-American. It is very much as if Kerouac had found his own family—consisting of a brother who died at age nine when Kerouac was four and one sister—too small, too American, and had decided to create a more typically ethnic family group. In this respect as in others, *The Town and the City* is reminiscent of Gabrielle Roy's *Bonheur d'occasion* (*The Tin Flute*, a Book-of-the-Month Club Selection and hence very well known in the nineteen-forties), to the extent of warranting a comparative study.

The Martin family, representative of second and third-generation Americans undergoing the process of assimilation, is a closely-knit group capable of exceptional solidarity in times of disaster, but the children's need for closeness inevitably diminishes as they adapt to life in the American mainstream. This adaptation, however, is not an entirely smooth transition; it is marked by much questioning, self-doubt, a sense of not belonging, so painfully familiar to all ethnics in the United States. The young Francis Martin, for example, feels "like someone lost in a strange, hostile foreign country."[13]

It is difficult to dispute Kerouac's assertion that the Franco-American theme has been kept in the background of *The Town and the City*. It is less difficult to demonstrate the importance of Kerouac's ethnic heritage throughout the entire breadth of his work, and I would submit that one of the major influences on his thinking has been the Catholic religion in which he was born and bred. The full extent of this influence has yet to be equitably assessed and can be outlined here only in broad strokes. One of our first glimpses of this Catholicism reveals a young boy piously doing a novena—a well-known custom consisting of nine days of prayers petitioning God for some special favor (*Sax*, p. 176). Soon enough, however, Jack would terminate his formal observance of religious duties and adopt a more personal form of spiritual life, strongly marked, one must insist, by his native Catholicism. The predominant image in this personal spirituality is the Cross, a recurring symbol which spans a lifetime, first seen as a crucifix in a boyhood home, a "phosphorescent Christ in a black-lacquered

Cross" (*Sax*, p. 44). Four decades later, near the end of his short life, he writes: "Yet I saw the cross just then when I closed my eyes after writing all this. I can't escape its mysterious penetration into all this brutality. I just simply SEE it all the time, even the Greek cross sometimes. I hope it will turn out true."[14] The suffering and salvation perfectly symbolized by the Cross were obsessive preoccupations for Kerouac; explicit references to the need for suffering are numerous and one of the most eloquent is the following: "Then the boy looked up again at the altar manger and saw that he too must suffer and be crucified like the Child Jesus there, who was crucified for his sake, who pointed out his guiltiness that way but who also pointed out what was going to happen to him, for he too, Michael Martin, was a child with a holy mother, therefore he too would be drawn to Calvary and the wind would begin to screech and everything would get dark" (*Town*, p. 178). Suffering, then, inextricably linked to life's purpose, is multi-faceted, ineluctable, ubiquitous, yet only a means to an end which is personal salvation, i.e., sanctity. The first person in Kerouac's life to embody the ideal of sanctity was his brother Gerard, who taught him something about a reverence for life which Jack " . . . translated as meaning that life itself is the Holy Ghost—That we all wander thru flesh, while the dove cries for us, back to the Dove of Heaven" (*Angels*, p. 238). A later avatar of sanctity is Neal Cassidy, the Dean Moriarty of *On the Road*, "who had the tremendous energy of a new kind of American saint."[15] At least once, Jack disclaimed the designation "beat" to which he preferred another: "Am actually not 'beat' but strange solitary crazy Catholic mystic . . . " (*Traveler*, p. vi).

The path to sanctity, however, is strewn with obstacles, and foremost among these is lust. Here too the astute reader would find abundant material for a separate study, but the following points are of the essence. A short passage in *Big Sur* gives us a first clue, the passage where Jack refuses to undress before a group of people: " 'But it's very typical of me and Cody that we won't undress in this situation (we were both raised Catholics?)—Supposedly the big sex heroes of our generation . . . . ' "[16] Jack's comment indicates clearly enough his awareness of the gap between the private person and his public image; so great was his attempt at total sincerity in communicating his true self that one can easily infer that he was not particularly comfortable with this gap. But one must not transform him into a non-human anomaly having no sexual needs and never fulfilling those needs. The interpretation given by a friend of his is quite probing: " 'They [women] all wanta be loved, they're all human trembling souls scared of you because you glare at them because you're afraid of them' " (*Angels*, p. 261). Elsewhere, Jack does not repudiate the charge that he has been withholding his love even from women who loved him,[17] and he expresses views of sex hardly compatible with his persona, in images which Baudelaire himself would not have disavowed. Such an unorthodox, negative view of sex is not widespread, and, though extreme, it becomes vastly more comprehensible if placed within the context of the rigoristic Catholic teachings of the author's boyhood. Kerouac, in fact, goes beyond this position when he expresses his feeling that " . . . lust was the direct cause of birth which was the direct cause of suffering and death and I had really no lie come to a point where I regarded lust as offensive and even cruel. 'Pretty girls make graves' was my saying . . . . And the absence of active lust in me had also given me a new peaceful life that I was enjoying a great deal."[18] We all recognize that this highly negative view of sex is reminiscent of that set forth by Tolstoy in *The Kreutzer Sonata*, where lust is portrayed as a vile force detracting from the achievement of life's purpose—the attainment of moral perfection through service to humanity. The "new peaceful life" enjoyed for a time by Kerouac is analogous to the inner peace intensely sought after by Tolstoy, but with the significant difference that for Kerouac a peaceful life is a life in which one makes strides toward sanctity, toward a perfect union with God. Kerouac hoped that death would bring an end to the inner strife wrought by the temptations of the flesh and his aspirations to sanctity, and he phrased this hope with succinctness and eloquence: " 'I just wanta pass through, Lord, to you—I'd rather be in your arms than the arms of Cleopatra . . . till the night when those arms are the same' " (*Angels*, p. 213).

To discuss Kerouac's religion solely in terms of strife, sin and guilt would be to misrepresent it most unfairly, for it offered him a goal—sainthood—and various means of achieving it. One of these was the practice of kindness, in keeping with his "vow of kindness" (*Angels*, p. 269) in which it is easy to recognize the notion of "Agape" (Christian love); another means was "the preachment of universal kindness which hysterical critics have failed to notice beneath frenetic activity of my true-story novels about the 'beat' generation" (*Traveler*, p. vi). He also resorted to prayer as a means of communing with God; indeed, some of the most moving pages he wrote are those relating his kneeling in prayer beneath "a great tormented statue of Christ on the Cross" (*Traveler*, p. 33) in a Mexico City church; the prayers, reflections and vivid portrayal of the crucifixion scene are clearly the work of an inspired Catholic artist (*Traveler*, pp. 33-36). Finally, the case can easily be made that Kerouac's Franco-American Catholicism, personal as it may have been, not only justified his writing, helped determine its purpose and form, but also contributed significantly to shaping his destiny as a writer. He is quite explicit when he states that, "if I don't write what actually I see happening in this unhappy globe . . . I think I'll have been sent on earth by poor God for nothing" (*Sur*, p. 135). Writing, then, was a duty, a vocation, a sacred calling, and the purpose of literature was "to teach something religious, of religious reverence, about real life" (*Satori*, p. 10). The form of his writing, "spontaneous prose," also has religious origins according to the reference he makes to his frenzied "scribblings," " . . . all of it innocent go-ahead confession, the discipline of making the mind the slave of the tongue with no chance to lie or re-elaborate (in keeping not only with the dictums of Dichtung Warheit Goethe but those of the Catholic Church of my child-hood)" (*Angels*, p. 238). In short, these are some of the noteworthy ways in which Kerouac's Franco-American Catholicism contributed to his writing.

There is yet another nexus of themes inspired by the author's ethnic heritage, and these are related to the role of success in his life and to his self-image. In Peter Martin, of *The Town and the City*, who resembles the author more than does any other character, the sense of alienation is heightened by his unexpected success as a football player. His reactions to his new role as a local sports hero attest to something more complex than the ambivalence of success: "He [Peter] hurried on home, and gloated because no one noticed him. He wished suddenly that no one would ever notice him again and that he would walk through the rest of his life like this, wrapped in his own secret mysteries and glories, a prince disguised as a pauper, Orestes returned from distant heroisms and hiding within the land . . . " (*Town*, p. 82). This short passage gains plausibility if placed in a psycho-historical framework, the essentials of which can be reduced to what follows: after losing a decisive battle to the British two centuries ago, the North American French never once forgot that they were a conquered people; they became resigned to living under British domination and until very recently have viewed defeat as part of their manifest destiny; the state of defeat has become familiar, while victory—at almost any level—is a novel experience. Enter Jack Kerouac, shaped by a milieu—the "Little Canada" of Lowell, Massachusetts—which itself bore the deep scars of two hundred years of history. It is not surprising that he found even a personal victory an embarrassing betrayal of his ethnic group: victory had long been an Anglo-American phenomenon, and young Franco-Americans were ill-prepared to deal with it . . . yet in the collective subconscious distant memories persist of proud French rule on the North American continent; hence the allusion to "Orestes returned from distant heroisms" is particu-larly apt, followed as it is by the indicated plight of this new Orestes who is now "hiding within the land." Many other examples could be adduced, none so incisive, none so eloquent. One might see in Kerouac's quest for sanctity additional reasons for his obstinate reluctance to accept success.

When he states, for instance, that "to triumph was also to wreak havoc" (*Town*, p. 63), he recognizes at least implicitly that triumph as havoc violates a precious tenet of his personal ethics—reverence for life. The conflict between success and his striving for sanctity becomes even more acute if one bears in mind the importance of humility in the life of an aspiring saint. For pride is an ever-recurring temptation and there is no surer occasion for sins of pride than a victory witnessed and applauded by thousands. With victory, then, can come a feeling of betraying an ideal shared by his own humble people and compensation might be sought in a self-created Purgatory, in self-flagellation—excessive drinking, declaring oneself a failure (*Duluoz*, p. 78), or cultivating a negative self-image. This doctrine may cast a ray of light on the numerous self-deprecating remarks found throughout his works, remarks such as, "My life is a vast inconsequential epic . . . " (*Angels*, p. 33), or "This cowardly Breton (me) watered down by two centuries in Canada and America, nobody's fault but my own . . . " (*Satori*, p. 77). Yes, the man could be hard, exasperatingly, impossibly hard on himself; ultimately, he became convinced of his own worthlessness and concluded the last book published during his lifetime by being grossly unfair to himself: " . . . [I] did everything you're supposed to do in life. But nothing ever came of it" (*Duluoz*, p. 213). Nothing—except for a secure place in American literature and a permanent contribution to his ethnic group.

One of the more obvious traits of ethnic heritage, of course, is language, and again there are unmistakable marks of Franco-Americanism in the works of Jean-Louis Lebris de Kérouac. The boy who did not learn to speak English before age five made liberal use of the Franco-American dialect throughout his works; indeed, there are very few of his books in which one does not find many phrases and often entire paragraphs in French, usually followed by an English translation. He was acutely aware of the difference between his native dialect and the language spoken in Paris, all in arguing "my French *is* French" (*Satori*, p. 30). During his genealogical journey to France, he was rightfully proud of communicating with the people: "The amazing long sincere conversations in French with hundreds of people everywhere, was what I really liked, and did, and it was an accomplishment because they couldn't have replied to my detailed points if they hadn't understood every word I said. Finally I began being so cocky I didn't even bother with Parisian French and let loose blasts and *pataraffes* of *chalivarie* French that had them in stitches because they still understood . . . " (*Satori*, p. 46). Ever sensitive to the subtleties of language, he refers to his father's communicating to him in French and making clear "meanings that can never be recorded in the English language."[19] On at least one occasion he showed unusual insight into the psychology of language, when commenting on his mother's accent: "Why does it tear my heart out that she pronounced it 'pwaint'—that French Canadian way of using English to express its humility-meanings—no non-French Canadian knows this" (*Dreams*, p. 31). And when he questioned the dubious practice of Anglicizing foreign names, he demonstrated awareness of a very ethnic problem.

The foregoing should make it obvious that Jack Kerouac is clearly a Franco-American writer, but I have barely scratched the surface, for he also possessed other characteristics which typify not only Franco-Americans, but French-Canadians as well. In concluding this brief presentation of him, I should mention that anthropologists have identified two basic types of French-Canadian: the *habitant* or sedentary type, and the *coureur de bois* whose goal always lay beyond the next mountain range or across the next several lakes. That Jack Kerouac was a twentieth century *coureur de bois* is borne out by his endless transcontinental journeys. That he had a certain degree of the French-Canadian resignation to the less pleasant aspects of existence is evident, for he apparently took to heart the advice once proffered by his mother about taking the bad with the worse (*Sax*, p. 123). Further, if one keeps in mind that the motto of Québec is "Je me souviens" ("I Remember"), and that Allen Ginsberg referred to Jack as "The Great Rememberer," the psychological kinship is striking. Finally, he once proclaimed the wish that he were a Negro (*Road*, p. 148), thereby indicating the same negative self-image made public by the French-Canadian Pierre Vallières in his *White Niggers of America*, a book which has had a resounding success throughout French Canada.

Another Franco-American writer who has achieved international renown is Grace Metalious, whose maiden name was de Repentigny; while she is best known as the author of *Peyton Place*, her one truly ethnic novel, *No Adam in Eden*,[20] has been undeservedly neglected. For its vignettes of French-Canadian life, for its portrayal of immigrants from Québec, it ranks high in modern Franco-American literature.

Rural life in French Canada at the turn of the century was circumscribed by the village, the neighbors, the farm, and above all by one's large family. It was a rugged, demanding life in which fear was often met with derision; when a mother expresses concern over the safety of her son gone on a hunting excursion, the father comments: "Ah, you are like an American. . . . You are like one of those skinny sticks from the States with the look of ice on your face" (p. 7). It is a valid indication of the manner in which Americans were perceived by some of their neighbors to the north a century or so ago. But it was also a life in a conquered country where national identity could sometimes be obfuscated, leading even Francophones to make statements such as: "I am a Canadian, not a Frenchwoman" (p. 11). At the same time, something like a regional identity had been developed, so that French-Canadians could be annoyed by recent arrivals from Paris, people who spoke the so-called "true French" rather than the dialect of Québec (p. 31). Incidents such as these point up the distance—both geographical and historical—separating French-Canadians and Franco-Americans from France, the first mother country.

Despite the healthy, robust nature of life in French Canada, economic opportunity was lacking, and it became impossible for some men to live with dignity if they could no longer support their families. The trickle of emigration slowly became a stream, and the French-Canadians who had arrived in this country extended a warm hand of welcome to those who were compelled to migrate. In this regard, the letter written by Aristide Jolicoeur to his friend Toussaint Montambeault (a widower) is quite eloquent: "You must come to us with your three children . . . . Jacqueline and I have six of our own so three more will not make that much difference to us. You will stay with us until you secure a job and then I will help you find a place to live. Hurry, old friend. It has been too many years since I have seen you" (pp. 35-36).

French-Canadians by the tens of thousands came to work in the textile mills of New England. While the story of these workers still awaits its Balzac, Grace Metalious affords us precious insights: "Every single weekday, the company's million spindles spun out one mile of cloth every minute and in Boston the financiers and bankers sat on their bony behinds and counted the profits with their thin, dry fingers and congratulated one another through narrow, vinegary lips" (p. 45). The working day began at six-thirty, lasting until seven-thirty in the evening, and failure to report for work after the thirty-minute lunch break was grounds for immediate dismissal. There were also rules prescribed for those living in the Company's boarding houses, including a curfew at nine-thirty. The sordidness of life in the mills is heightened by a description of the 1918 influenza epidemic, a thoroughly lurid description despite its briefness. It is the reader's good fortune to be spared the sights and sounds of disease invading the mills; luckily, we are not forced to "feel the wet heat in those rooms," in the words of the local doctor who promises the manager a complete tour and concludes: "When we're finished I guarantee that you'll be able to hear influenza growing and spreading, spreading into every last corner of your mills" (p. 53).

The French-Canadians who came to this country had to survive more than economic exploitation, however; they had also to reckon with many facets of prejudice, including the prejudice against their own names. When young Bill Endicott begins frequenting Angélique Bergeron, the boy's mother reacts thus: "But whoever *heard* of such a name! . . . It sounds like one of those foreign names like those people who work in the mills. Andgaleek Burdgaron indeed! " (p. 156). Ethnic readers will readily feel the intensity of scorn with which such summary indictments are handed down and will feel it again when the boy's father—to whom the girl is completely unknown—self-righteously declares: "No son of mine has to fool around with some little Canuck tramp" (p. 159). This latter is followed by a more general and definitive *pronunciamento*: "The Endicott men don't marry Canucks" (p. 160).

In the person of Monique Bergeron, Grace Metalious has embodied a subversion of traditional French-Canadian values, an all-pervasive spirit of revolt tantamount to a negation of life. Looked at through her eyes, Franco-American life is seen through a glass most darkly: men must cleanse themselves daily of the grime produced by work, while the women, she adds, in addition to bearing and rearing children, must submit to the constant humiliation of sexual intercourse. Endowed with a different perspective than most, she does not recognize, however, that such modest beginnings are merely a prelude to a less unsavory existence. Frustrated in her attempts to seek refuge in a convent from what she perceives as ugliness, yet fortunate enough to escape from the mills, she nurtures a hatred of anything associated with her childhood: limited living space, dirt and, most of all, people. Almost miraculously, she does marry and gives birth to a daughter, Angélique, but she will hasten her husband's premature death by alcoholism. Self-absorbed almost to the point of solipsism, she continuously sublimates her most basic needs and desires, devoting all her energy to the maintenance of an antiseptic household and to the inculcation in her daughter of the notion that she (Angélique) is several notches above common mortals. One can easily visualize her carbolic smile as she makes, to her daughter, statements which illustrate her thoughts rather well: " 'You must not spoil your hands. A lady is always judged by her hands, I never want anyone to be able to say that I have not turned out a little lady' " (p. 78). Or she says " 'It is a sin to be dirty. The good Lord has made the body as the temple for the soul. Can you imagine a dirty church? No. Then it is the same with people. A person who is dirty is committing a sin against God' " (ibid.). A perpetual dissident, she condemns herself to be forever atypical and alone in the desert she has created, refusing to learn the English language, refusing to become an American citizen, unmindful even of the personal advantages which either of these might have brought her. As such, she can easily be seen as representing the ultimate resistance to assimilation, totally unresponsive to social pressures, striving ruthlessly to bury her past, ending up in an insane asylum.

Angélique Bergeron, the offspring of an alcoholic father and a psychotic mother, at first benefits, but eventually suffers from her parents' superiority complex and from their legacy of self-centeredness. She is the object of her father's ceaseless adulation, and he lavishes upon her the abundant affection he might have shared with numerous children, children his wife refused to bear: Angélique fills the enormous void created by his wife's acidulous nature and by his own religious indifference. Confronted with his worship of her and with his repeated designation of her as his "little angel," we know that we have gone beyond the love of a father for his child; we sense that we are dealing with a redirected spirituality. In addition, her father is the source of Angélique's "fancy" ideas, her "Yankee" ideas, i.e., those which appear extravagantly out of keeping with her modest origins (p. 118).

Of necessity, her relatives view her differently, deeply resenting her refusal to speak French—an act of treason against one's ethnic group which meant that one would be branded as Irish (p. 127). But to her acquaintances, "Angélique was the cleverest girl they had ever known. She had read books that none of them had ever even heard of and no one in Livingstone called *her* 'Frenchie.' Angélique's English had not a trace of an accent, not even when she used words with the horribly difficult *th* in them. . . . She could do anything just like an American" (p. 112). In this last remark one can detect something very much like the ultimate tribute an immigrant can expect; even today, only in exceptional circumstances will a person receive an homage for being a Latvian-American, a Greek-American, a French-American, etc. For Angélique, as for most of us, assimilation is a prerequisite for respect or homage.

Despite many differences and their apparently shocking subject matter, both Grace Metalious and Jack Kerouac share a deep spirituality inherited from a common Franco-American past. While Kerouac was more explicit in his quest for sanctity, in Metalious we find an implicit denunciation of evil, an inverted spirituality, for we see here much more than an anatomy of sin; we see something which might be termed satanism. This element of sin or satanism is the very antithesis of love and life; it is ultimate, total selfishness which causes wanton violation of trust and even murder; it is, in essence, the ultimate in destructiveness, a virulent, sado-masochistic, death-dealing force.

Quite other is the subject-matter of Gérard Robichaud who created one of the most appealing characters in Franco-American fiction and entitled his novel after him; the novel is *Papa Martel*, published in 1962.[21] The father of seven children, Louis Martel and his wife, Cécile, hold their family together by that most cohesive of forces, love, which consists largely of giving and sharing. Both Louis and Cécile Martel disagree just enough to make each one of them individualized and plausible human beings, but they agree on essentials: the birth of each child is awaited with gladness and he or she, too, is taught to give or share. The results are a solid upbringing, based on the Catholic faith and a Catholic education—acquired both at home and at school. The Martel home is proud of using the French language; it maintains certain Franco-American customs; it fosters solidarity amongst its members and the remembrance of a glorious French past; while retaining these, the Martels adapt quite well to American life.

The beginnings, however, were difficult. Lacking extensive formal education, Louis Martel became a free-lance carpenter earning just enough money to support a wife and a child, but he lacked neither confidence in himself nor faith in the future. Without a trace of self-pity, the Martels spent their first Christmas alone in a humble shack built by Louis' own hands during his free time, near Berlin, New Hampshire; it was an excellent opportunity to concentrate upon the true meaning of Christmas—which is love—and to develop this same attitude toward the world at large.

As Louis secured permanent employment, the family moved to the fictitious Franco-American community of Groveton, Maine, and here a routine evolved which would appear dullness incarnate to many, but which, in reality, exuded a true French "joie de vivre." This "joie de vivre" existed in the Martel home even before the birth of a child, for the parents shared the old French-Canadian belief that the expectant mother should entertain nothing but glad thoughts, not only to assure the physical and mental well-being of the new-born, but also to prevent it from fretting for a year and a day after birth (pp. 4, 129). Every new-born is welcomed with love and joy, for each one is a source of marvel and wonder, a reminder of the Eternity whence it came and to which it will someday return.

The Martel apartment, far from extravagant, proves adequate to the needs of a large brood. The parlor is a very special room used only for visits from the pastor or for serious courtship. The kitchen is the fulcrum of family life; significantly, all doors lead into it and it is roughly the equivalent of today's living room. It is the locus of "quiet time," the hours religiously set aside every evening for homework and for family reading. While the children were young, Madame Martel would do the reading herself—from the Groveton *Daily Herald*, to be sure, but from *Le Messager* as well, one of the better-known Franco-American dailies in Maine; but there were also biographies of historical personages—of the Church, of France, of Canada and of the United States, a wide enough range, attesting to the multifarious springs flowing into the Franco-American mainstream. "Quiet time" was also the occasion for oral history, the story of the courtship of Louis and Cécile, for example, a tale the children never wearied of hearing, especially with Louis himself embroidering the story, so that its variations made the re-telling ever more delightful.

Education, then, remained an ongoing concern and, in this endeavor, Madame Martel, more learned than Louis, became more involved than he. She insisted that her children be perfectly bilingual and, in an entirely constructive frame of mind, sensitive to the requirements of the American environment in which the children must grow up; she dared to be a non-conformist, and she dared to criticize the parish school. Risking ostracism, she withdrew her children from the school for a time, until the authorities recognized that she was unquestionably right and promptly restructured the curriculum, in order to make room for more English, History and Civics—in direct compliance with her demands. This quiet, persistent voice of the "esprit critique" inherited directly from the French, is a voice too often muffled in Franco-American literature.

Such a degree of dedication to her offspring brings with it substantial consolation and rewards. When Cécile Martel gives birth to her last born, a trying, painful birth, the children and the father not only keep a vigil, but their thoughts, prayers and short verbal exchanges are all centered about the outcome of *Maman*'s ordeal, the oldest daughter serving as a nurse, the other members of the family assisting in whatever capacities they can. And when, several years later, Cécile Martel lies dying from an incurable disease, her thoughts are selflessly directed to Louis—her wish being that he remarry—and to her children—her sole concern being for their total welfare.

There are several French-Canadian/Franco-American customs described at some length in the novel, and one of these is the old custom of the "veillée," the large, periodic family get-together, sparked by the merest pretext, just for the sheer joy of being together; the merriest of these reunions are those occasioned by the return of an older son, Emile, from the seminary he is attending near Montreal. (One might add parenthetically that this, too, is a custom and a privilege enjoyed by some Franco-American families, namely of having a son study for the priesthood, often enough somewhere in French Canada.) When Emile returns for a rare vacation, the clan gathers in joyous tumult, and the future priest is given the honors of a visiting statesman. As the years pass, his opinion on various moral matters will be eagerly sought after and freely given. Surely one of the high points in the novel is the late evening dialogue between father and son on the nature of the priesthood. Louis' advice in no way conflicts with seminary teachings but rather complements them, for Louis' conception of the priestly life is at once less rigoristic and more down-to-earth than that of his son's theology masters. He does indeed conceive of it as a sacred calling, requiring great courage, demanding far more than bookish learning or knowledge of the proper methods of castigating parishioners: " . . . it's to help people, all kinds of people, that they . . . will not be afraid . . . and there is . . . the great hunger of the flesh . . . " to be dealt with (p. 167). Such are the thoughts of a man, unscholarly but wise, and so obviously knowledgeable about the implications of a sacred vocation and the weakness of human beings.

Louis Martel is a man of courage and derring-do, vehemently opposed to cowardice and fear, as if he himself had struggled to overcome them and had succeeded brilliantly in doing so. He keeps insisting that French-Canadians or Franco-Americans don't know how to brag or to accept compliments (p. 102) and that the Martels should never be afraid (p. 101). He also invents a new commandment "thou shalt not fear! " (p. 52), and he demonstrates a sound psychological sense when he asserts that the fears of yesterday should be forgotten, in order to deal with those of today (p. 113).

In conclusion, throughout the novel, Louis' openness of mind is reflected in his teaching his children tolerance of other ethnic groups (pp. 78-79), in discouraging scrupulousness (pp. 86-88), and in taking his religion seriously, despite his bantering about its lighter aspects as in his reference to "a short-sermon church and a one-collection parish" (p. 109). His role in the successful raising of a large family amounts to an appreciable achievement, particularly if one considers that his formal education was minimal and that life did not spare him his share of hardships. The novel is obviously a labor of love, and one can understand that in his Foreword the author would single out for special mention his own father, Michel Robichaud.

Franco-American poets of the past fifty years have evolved with the literary times, finding new forms to express contemporary concerns; a few, following the prestigious example of Jules Supervielle, have shown that spontaneous forms can express the moods and feelings of the modern era.

Of these poets, one of the most captivating is Henri D'Arles,[22] a master of prose poetry, a prolific writer whose work is best described by the designation "poetic realism," for Henri D'Arles combines the sensitivity of a Chateaubriand with the penetrating visual perception of a Huysmans. Some of his finest cameos consist of descriptions of nature rich in the most delightful of pathetic fallacies. Whether he is evoking the tranquil laughter of serenity spread throughout a given landscape,[23] or suggesting that a scene is inebriated with life[24] or that the ocean is perpetually troubled and worried,[25] he ascribes to nature the most diversified of human emotions with felicitous results. Exceptionally sensitive to the most capricious moods of nature, he virtually captures landscapes with the precision of photography and transposes them into verbal art with the

208

melodiousness of a Mozart. For Henri D'Arles, nature was a constant and totally absorbing refuge from the prosaism of urban settings. Though little has been revealed about his personal life, one senses something of the dandy in his writings—the aloofness, the disdain, the viewing of life as a form of art—but, paradoxically enough, the dandyism here was cultivated in the solitary contemplation of nature rather than in some posh drawing-room. The net result was a profound awareness of nature's sublime artistry and of its transitory beauty, rendered with such refinement that, after the publication of his *Laudes*, the French Academy bestowed its laurels upon him.

To this day, Rosaire Dion-Lévesque is still considered the Franco-Americans' "national poet"—a mark of his stature, a sign of the esteem in which he is held for his poetic achievements. Throughout his life (1900-1974), moving constantly against the current, he succeeded despite overwhelming odds, succeeded in earning international recognition for his poetry and won various honors and awards including the highly-coveted designation of "Laureate of the French Academy." In addition to several collections of poetry, he has published a monumental biographical diction-ary of Franco-Americans[26] and a remarkable French translation of Walt Whitman.[27]

That he went beyond the poetic confines attained by earlier Franco-American poets is made manifest in one of his first published collections, *Les Oasis*, a work in which he establishes his mastery of the sonnet and of that elusive phenomenon called the mood poem. The first poem, "Liminaire,"[28] sets a tone of tranquil recollection, of quiet dream-like creativity, suggesting a world of reverie in which the poet can build the "blue minarets of [his] poems" (p. 11), many of which will have a religious theme. At times, the poet will evoke the beauty of a stained-glass window (pp. 50-51) or the atmosphere of a solitary church at eventide, with can-dles lit and a catafalque in the aisle (pp. 44-45). There are also poetic prayers of supplication formulated in sumptuous language (pp. 42-43) or tributes to Mary, "Mother of Sorrows" enshrining her image in his heart (pp. 112-13). There is, too, a most poetic statement about the quest for God outside oneself when, according to the poet, God is found within the self (pp. 114-15).

The path to spiritual perfection, however, is arduous, and one some-times seeks respite, in dreams of escape to magical Orients (pp. 26-27), in memories of youth (pp. 72-73), or in other memories, "la poussière du Temps s'agglomérant sur l'or . . . " (p. 46). But memory, too, is merely a snare, a digression about which the "I" of the poem must be lucid, for Memory

> ... nous montre à travers des rideaux de cristal,
> Ces spectacles perdus dorés par l'Idéal,
> Et dont nos yeux charmés retrouvent les mirages. (pp. 46-47)

Poetry will remain the most sensible escape, a proven way to lofty thoughts, including thoughts about other poets such as Poe or Baudelaire; in his homage poems to these masters, Dion-Lévesque captures the essence of each (pp. 78-81).

Nature, too, might be considered a form of momentary escape from one's "taedium vitae"—momentary because the inebriation caused by Spring's aromas and vibrations makes one oblivious to the beloved dead concealed within the bosom of the earth (pp. 38-39) and the sun itself can be viewed as a symbol of deceitful promised splendor (pp. 66-67). None of this keeps the poet from listening to the night (pp. 96-97) or from being entranced by the fanciful flight of glow-worms (pp. 98-99), and the reader himself can be somewhat bewitched by the beauty created by mood and imagery:

> C'est un soir débordant de clartés opalines,
> D'inquiétude étrange et de désirs passifs. (p. 100)

The collection which Rosaire Dion-Lévesque published in 1939 is appropriately entitled *Vita* and opens with an exuberant tribute to Walt Whitman.[29] It is a paean to a liberator, a spiritual forebear to whom the poet attributes his own regeneration, most notably in the new equality which can be established between body and soul and in the full acceptance of physical love. Gone at last is the dichotomy between Truth and Beauty: "Je vois encore le triomphe de ce qui fut longtemps dédaigné, renié: je vois le triomphe de . . . la Vérité et [de] la Beauté" (p. 18).

Truth and Beauty, for the poet, are found in part—and only for a time—in a woman, the marvel of whose existence is suggested by paradox and by a poetic questioning of a woman's specific nature in the lengthy sequence of sensual love poems entitled "Inamorata" (pp. 79-92):

> Dis-moi quel est ton but, vibrante Volupté
> Qui mêles tant de fiel à tes divins dictames?
> Quelle est donc ton essence, Eternelle Beauté,
> Qui de neige pétrie attise tant de flammes? (p. 79)

In detailing the physical charms of the woman, he reverts to the *blason*, the description of a person, so popular in sixteenth-century French literature. Loving moods, moments, dreams, sensations and settings are conjured up, but amidst these are interspersed disquieting reflections on the nature of love, that "frail happiness contested by the great void" (p. 84). He evokes love's ecstasy in luxuriant nature-imagery, as he shows us emeralds, jasmine, hollyhocks and "la toison verte des saules pensifs" (p.

80), but the great void of nothingness triumphs as he ceases to be loved. In an ironic use of the "flame-fanning" leitmotiv, he begs in vain for her love, and concludes on a note of utter desolation:

> Et j'ai la conscience amère,
> De notre amour ancré,
> Sur les sables mouvants, très chère,
> De nos coeurs séparés. (p. 92)

Sensual love need not exclude religious concerns, and the book is replete with expressions of these concerns. In addition to a sequence of short poems on the capital sins (pp. 20-21), there is also the denunciation of the somnambulist (p. 22), i.e., the person who is only half alive; the piece might be a poetic paraphrase of the Lord's condemnation of those lukewarm souls whom He promised to vomit from His mouth. *Vita* is truly a milestone in the evolution of Dion-Lévesque's religious thinking, if only because of the self-acceptance it reveals. In his "Magnificat" (pp. 23-25), he states unequivocally: " . . . je suis tel que Tu m'as voulu . . . pour ta gloire et ton agonie! " (p. 25).

Finally, *Vita* gives ample evidence of the poet's ongoing relationship with nature, particularly in his "Petite suite marine" (pp. 113-16), a short series of seascapes, with rhythms often imitative of ocean-rhythms. But the sea, much like the poet of "Inamorata," speaks ultimately of ended dreams, defunct love and stormy roadsteads (p. 116).

Quête ("Quest"), the last volume published during Dion-Lévesque's life-time,[30] takes up many of the familiar themes, but the poet develops them with a surer grasp of his art and the same is true of the newer themes. Despite its briefness, this collection of poems also has substantial variety. Here, the victory of ennui is openly avowed:

> L'ennui m'enveloppe comme un suaire humide
> Et je suis comme un dieu mort, hanté par sa croix! (p. 18)

But the poet's Catholicism remains intact, as he reaffirms his belief in life after death which is seen as an assurance of the solidarity between the living and the dead ("Le chapelet de la morte," p. 24). Indeed, there are several explicitly religious poems here[31] and, of particular interest, a sequence on the poet's native land, "Amor patriae" (pp. 43-47) in which he expresses his love for *his* city, *his* woods, *his* river, the "indolent Merri-mack" (p. 46). In concluding these few remarks, we might quote the last two stanzas of the final poem as a public tribute to Rosaire Dion Lévesque:

> Les bois sont mon refuge en toutes les saisons,
> Et le temple éternel où je fais ma prière,
> Tête nue, et debout, sans rimes ni façon.

Et me livrant encore à leur voix familière,
Au temps des lourds frimas et des maigres buissons,
De la survie j'apprends les amères leçons. (p. 47)

Paul-P. Chassé has written novels, social commentary and history, but we are concerned here with the poet. The number of poetic influences he has undergone and assimilated is quite remarkable, for he is obviously well acquainted with every "ism" in French poetry, from the classic through the romantic and the symbolist to the modern, but this is merely a small part of the total portrait, for the Greco-Roman tradition as well as the Old and New Testaments have also contributed much to this poetry. There are indubitably other influences at play, lying somewhere in a vast literary topography extending from the Bible to Saint-John Perse, to say nothing of the other arts; these might be detectable to the more erudite readers, but what matters is less the scope of influences than the use made of them by the poet. The poetry of Paul Chassé cannot be categorized; it has reminded some readers of Villon, others of Jules Laforgue and still others of Paul Valéry. In short, we are in the presence of a poet whose creativity and originality have not been stultified by prodigious reading and learning.

To date, he has allowed only two volumes of verse to appear, but the recent publication of "Le Schofar" from the collection "Poèmes de guerre" confirms one's suspicion that there are many other treasures left to be unearthed, and one hopes that this will occur soon. In any event, some of the most striking aspects of the poet's originality include sustained intensity—in defiance of Poe's dictum—and a spontaneity of emotion not unmindful of the requirements of poetic art.

The title of the first collection, *Et la mer efface* . . .[32] is taken from two lines by Jacques Prévert:

Et la mer efface
sur le sable les pas des amants désunis.

These lines provide the first clue to the volume's thematic content; nature here will be used not solely as a backdrop, it will be a frequent theme, and also the source of splendiferous imagery. The lovers alluded to in Prévert's poem will reappear again and again, leaving the reader with a sense of hopelessness, or the virtual impossibility of human love, despite repeated attempts. The title also suggests the presence, in Paul Chassé, of the "moraliste," a very French type of writer, concerned not only with mores, but with morality as well.

It would be inaccurate, however, to so limit the range of themes. Admittedly, the "I" in these poems has been haunted by passion and the violence of separation; yet such themes allow for variations without number, and they have been handled here with dexterity. In addition, even in the most violent poems, one often finds notes of tenderness, gentleness, affection and submission rather than revolt. Conversely, the predominance of a light, airy, delicate tone can be broken by a sudden, unexpected eruption of violence.[33]

Despite the disclaimer that the "I" of the poems is ready for silence and solitude,[34] the search for human warmth, for the fusion of two souls goes on. Most poems in this first collection record these vain attempts at meaningful, total communion. Whether the references are to particularized, individualized failings or to the human condition in general matters little, for the most part; the unequivocal message conveyed deals with the fundamental incommunicability of human beings. This message is borne out by poems such as "La brèche" (p. 14), "Souvenir tronqué" (p. 15) or "Dernier soir" (pp. 16-17). In "La brèche," the opening in the wall has merely widened despite protracted efforts to close the gap—an obvious image of two souls failing to reach one another. "Souvenir tronqué" evokes the death scene of a loved one, but attempts to remember the deceased yield only a "truncated memory," as the title indicates; again, love is lost, this time through death. "Dernier soir" is a melancholy meditation on the grief and solitude caused by death, symbolized by a sunset viewed through dead branches.

Apart from a tribute to Robert Frost ("Querelle d'amourex," p. 27), an occasional lighter poem, descriptive nature poems ("Du pont de l'hôtellerie," p. 21), the theme of love is equally important and as omnipresent as that of death; this theme is obvious in "Pourquoi avril? " (p. 20) where love is once more renounced and equated with death, and in the most solemn and majestic piece of the volume, "Saisie d'une vie" (pp. 31-37), an elegy on the death of President John Kennedy. Tragic irony abounds throughout the selection: e.g., evil sometimes proceeds from apparent good, for the sun shining on 22 November 1963 blinded the scene whence the fatal shots were fired; the waving hand was—unknowingly—waving farewell, as the President slumped over in agony upon his wife, the source of life for a daughter and son. Memories of classical tragedy and of other assassinations are interspersed with startling images in an attempt to speak the unspeakable: roses absorb his blood, the sea loses its salt; there is the granite nothingness of gaping lips; far more than paradox, the most apparent implausibilities are required to react to unutterable horror. Anguish is the sole possible response, anguish, silent weeping—and the genius of a poet capable of offering a significant tribute, formulating explicit questions on the future of life or love and the implicit question about the "Why? " of a seemingly senseless tragedy, mixing with this the pathos of well-chosen, realistic details, making the reader witness the lying-in-state, the caisson followed by the riderless horse and the eternal flame invoked thus:

rappelle-nous les ardeurs de nos héros, de nos pères
rallume en nous leurs soucis de paix et de survie. (p. 36)

The volume of verse published by Paul Chassé in 1968, *La Carafe enchantée* ("The Enchanted Decanter"),[35] shows a marked evolution toward a greater variety of forms and also toward a more concerted orchestration of themes. The collection contains instances of hermeticism ("Après-midi d'octobre," p. 9), versified games ("Mnémosyne," p. 15, and "Le Carrousel des carafes," pp. 55-56), modernism ("Soirée de jazz," p. 14) and a series of "Suites" culminating in the highly poignant "Suite espagnole" (pp. 42-46). Each of these "Suites" would warrant a lengthy explication, but space permits only a brief, general indication of their mood and content.

"L'été expire" (pp. 5-8) reveals the poet's continuing intimacy with nature as shown by his acute observation of summer's demise; but the season's passing also signals the passing of thwarted hopes for a meeting of souls. "Symphonie de Balcon" (pp. 17-20) evokes the pain and helplessness of a sagacious onlooker witnessing youth's momentary refuge in alcohol and loveless sex, raising questions such as "How many hearts have become desiccated tonight?" (p. 18). The quest for true love is recorded again in "Suite latine" (pp. 24-26): the lover has departed, as the "I" of the poem ponders the reasons for the broken relationship, and after expressing bitterness and a request for forgiveness, concludes on a note of resignation: "The long November nights are approaching" (p. 26). The "Suite Abbatiale" (pp. 27-30) records resignation to a feeling of utter futility as the poet makes masterful use of nature-imagery, revealing a profound sense of dark irony as well: the cry of stars is heard, the garden is deserted by flowers and birds, while even the deer covets its own solitude; the final section of the poem is a lament on "Douces séductions qui mènent à la tombe," and there emerge dark forebodings of death's imminence and finality everywhere in nature: death for every living being is inescapable, it is definitive. In the sequence ironically entitled "Suite de Noël 1966," there is a powerful fusion of two major obsessions:

quand l'amour me reviendra-t-il
sera-ce comme un voleur dans la nuit
comme la mort pour n'y plus revenir. (p. 31)

The sumptuous winter scene in "Suite du Nouvel An 1967" suggests a quasi-Manichean view of life, with the forces of good engaged in a cosmic struggle with the forces of evil. A calm winter night is depicted as sepulchral, the charm of every stone is "tomb-like" (p. 35) and existence takes on a futility so all-pervasive as to become a death-in-life. The "Suite" betrays an aching awareness of evil forces, and of their deviousness in particular. This is masterfully and succinctly stated:

214

> Et les joies nous menacent chaque nuit
> Quand la vie nous terrasse le matin. (p. 38)

For the moment, evil triumphs over good, as the poem ends with the sound of "laughing ashes" (p. 38), and triumphs again in the acidly ironic "Epiphanie." The theme of lost love is best developed, however, in "Suite espagnole" (p. 42-46), a majestic soliloquy in which the poet finds appropriate imagery to give voice to unutterable grief: "Car je t'aimai à incendier les neiges et tu m'as quitté" (p. 46).

About Paul Chassé's poetry it can be fairly stated that imagery, rhythm and harmony are combined with fierce intensity of emotion and, at least for this reader, it is analogous to that of Baudelaire, for Paul Chassé, too, has mastered the art of extracting beauty from evil—evil *not* necessarily defined as sin but rather as life's imponderable injustices.

* * *

In this article, I have merely reviewed some of the high points in the recent past of New England's Franco-American literature about which, I repeat, much more needs to be said. Further, with regard to the French-American literature of the United States, there are enormous areas as yet uncharted by literary historians, and I refer specifically to the body of works produced by French Americans in the Middle West and in Louisiana; one hopes that such lacunae will soon be filled.

To some, the future of Franco-American literature in New England is in serious jeopardy; whether it *has* a future will depend, of course, on exactly how "unmeltable" Franco-Americans will prove to be. For now, there is still quality writing being done by people such as Gabriel Crevier, Rodolphe-Louis Hébert, Claire Quintal, Robert L. Paris (who is combining poetry and music) and several others yet to be published. In concluding, I can only voice my most ardent hope that the torch passed on by our ancestors be kept brightly lit.

University of Rhode Island

NOTES

[1] Alexandre Bélisle, *Histoire de la presse franco-américaine et des Canadiens-Français aux Etats-Unis* (Worcester, Mass.: L'Opinion Publique, 1911).

[2] Soeur Mary-Carmel Therriault, *La littérature française de Nouvelle-Angleterre* (Montréal: Fides, 1946).

[3] Paul-P. Chassé, *Les poètes franco-américains de la Nouvelle-Angleterre* (Somersworth, New Hampshire: Abbaye de Thélème, 1968).

[4] Albéric Archambault, *Mill Village* (Boston: Bruce Humphries, 1943).

[5] Ibid., p. 118.

[6] Jack Kerouac, *Desolation Angels* (New York: Bantam, 1971), p. 340. First published in 1965. Hereafter cited in the text as *Angels*.

[7] Kerouac, *Lonesome Traveler* (New York: Grove Press, 1970), pp. iv-v. First published in 1960. Hereafter cited in the text as *Traveler*.

[8] Kerouac, *Satori in Paris* (New York: Grove Press, 1966), p. 59. Hereafter cited in the text as *Satori*.

[9] Kerouac, *Book of Dreams* (San Francisco: City Lights Books, 1973), p. 118. First published in 1961. Hereafter cited in the text as *Dreams*.

[10] Kerouac, *Doctor Sax* (New York: Grove Press, 1959), p. 6. Hereafter cited in the text as *Sax*.

[11] Ibid., p. 67. See also Jack Kerouac, *Maggie Cassidy* (New York: Avon Publications, 1959), p. 52.

[12] Rosaire Dion-Lévesque, *Silhouettes franco-américaines* (Manchester, New Hampshire: Association Canado-Américaine, 1957), p. 433.

[13] Jack Kerouac, *The Town and the City* (New York: Harcourt Brace Jovanovich, 1950), p. 191. Hereafter cited in the text as *Town*.

[14] Kerouac, *Vanity of Duluoz* (London: Quartet Books, 1973), p. 211. First published in 1967. Hereafter cited in the text as *Duluoz*.

[15] Kerouac, *On the Road* (New York: New American Library, 1960), p. 34. First published in 1957. Hereafter cited in the text as *Road*.

[16] Kerouac, *Big Sur* (New York: Bantam Books, 1962), p. 86. Hereafter cited in the text as *Sur*.

[17] See *Big Sur*, p. 137.

[18] Jack Kerouac, *The Dharma Bums* (New York: Viking, 1971), p. 29. First published in 1958.

[19] *Maggie Cassity*, p. 95.

[20] Grace Metalious, *No Adam in Eden* (New York: Pocket Books, 1967). First published in 1963. Hereafter cited in the text.

[21] Gérard Robichaud, *Papa Martel* (New York: All Saints Press, 1962). First published in 1961. Hereafter cited in the text.

[22] For much of my information on Henri D'Arles, I am gratefully indebted to Paul-P. Chassé.

[23] Henri D'Arles, *Miscellanées* (Montréal: Editions du Mercure, 1926), p. 178.

[24] Henri D'Arles, *Horizons* (Montréal: Librairie d'Action Canadienne-Française, 1929), p. 167.

[25] Henri D'Arles, *Laudes* (Paris: Paul Lefebvre, 1925), p. 138.

[26] Rosaire Dion-Lévesque, *Silhouettes franco-américaines*.

[27] Dion-Lévesque, *Walt Whitman* (Montréal: Les Elzévirs, 1933). Préface de Louis Dantin.

[28] Dion-Lévesque, *Les Oasis* (Rome: Desclée, 1930), pp. 10-11. Hereafter cited in the text.

[29] Dion-Lévesque, *Vita* (Montréal: Bernard Valiquette, 1939), pp. 13-19. Hereafter cited in the text.

[30] Dion-Lévesque, *Quête* (Québec: Garneau, 1963). Hereafter cited in the text.

[31] See, for example: "Marie et Bernadette," (p. 30), "O Christ!" (p. 32), "Resurrexit," (p. 37), etc.

[32] Paul-P. Chassé, *Et la mer efface . . .* (Somersworth: N.H.: Abbaye de Thélème, 1964). Hereafter cited in the text.

[33] See "Mésanges," pp. 38-39.

[34] Ibid., p. 12.

[35] Paul-P. Chassé, *La Carafe enchantée* (Somersworth, N.H.: Abbaye de Thélème, 1968). Hereafter cited in the text.

A Glance at Three Centuries of German-American Writing

Carl Hammer, Jr.

ABSTRACT

The German colonists in America, numerically next to the English, wrote extensively, from Lederer, the explorer, and Pastorius, the Patriarch of Germantown, on,
but throughout the eighteenth century one finds mainly travel diaries, correspondence, records of settlements and churches, and political and theological writings.
Creative literature began with the religious lyrics of Johann Kelpius and Conrad
Beissel, long before 1776. The nineteenth century produced many German-American
poets, some of them being exiled "Forty-Eighters." Favorite themes were nostalgia
for the homeland, "Landschaftslyrik" celebrating their adopted country, and criticism of Europe's old order. Charles Sealsfield (Karl Postl) and Friedrich Gerstäcker
became preeminent among novelists depicting frontier and Indian life. Nineteenth-
century literature in the broader sense embraces outstanding works by German-
Americans on history, biography, economics, law, and other subjects; instances of
such writers are Carl Schurz and Francis Lieber. The active literary scene of the late
1800's extended into the twentieth century, until World War I caused a hiatus,
gradually overcome in the succeeding decade. Beginning in 1933, a second immigration of political exiles brought a host of prominent German and Austrian authors,
including Thomas Mann, Franz Werfel, and Bertolt Brecht. German-American writing
of the 1970's is noteworthy for a number of gifted lyricists, some of whom are
known in the German-speaking lands. (CH)

The unexpected request for a general lecture on this topic seemed to
offer me a challenge almost impossible of fulfillment, not merely because
of the short notice, but also because of the scope of the subject. An added
difficulty was the fact that, despite my long interest in "Americana
Germanica," my own research and publications in that area have been too
peripheral to justify any claim to authority. Since, however, this occasion
is a commemorative one, with an audience representing many varied cultural backgrounds, rather than a group of specialists in the German-

American field, perhaps the brief sketch that follows will have some informational validity.

A whole series of lectures would be necessary to give an adequate survey of German-American literary activity from the beginnings until the present, for German works produced in America are the most numerous of all non-English writings of different ethnic groups in the United States. This is not to be attributed solely to the Germans' being among the first settlers, nor should it be taken as just an indication of their fondness for committing their thoughts to paper; rather, it shows, above all, what a large segment of the population is of German origin.

In the very earliest period of our country's history, Germans participated in the exploration and settlement of the new land. For example, some came with the group of French Protestants under Jean Ribault who settled at Port Royal, South Carolina, in 1562. And there were several Germans among the English who founded Jamestown, Virginia, in 1607.[1] Eventually they were to be seen in every one of the thirteen colonies, as well as in French Louisiana; in fact, a German settlement on the lower course of the Mississippi is the scene of one of the earliest literary works dealing with America to be published in Germany: *Die Prinzessin von Wolfenbüttel* by Heinrich Zschokke (1771-1848),[2] a popular writer in his time, and one of those earliest known in America.[3]

Large-scale German immigration began in the early decades of the eighteenth century. Probably because then, as now, Germany was ridiculously divided, no colony in America was ever officially German. Nevertheless, Pennsylvania was actually, to a great extent, German, and colonists moving southward from there established numerous German settlements in half a dozen future states. Many Rhinelanders came to New York and settled on the Hudson in the early 1700's, but long before that, in the seventeenth century, the Dutch colony of New Netherland had a German for its first governor, Peter Minuit (Minnewit), and the German-born "soldier statesman" Jacob Leisler not only became governor, but also one of the most influential figures in New York after its seizure by the British.[4] In the nineteenth century further waves of German immigrants arrived at the right time for playing an important role in the great westward expansion of the United States. To a larger extent than many people realize, Texas is among the many states which attracted large numbers of Germans. Estimates of the German element in the white population of this country before World War I range from 24% to 27%, as against 30% for the English. The extent of immigration in the nineteenth century is evident from statistics for the fifty years from 1820 to 1870, during which time some 6,900,000 Germans arrived.[5] Today, just as one hundred years ago, the German element stands, numerically, right next to the Anglo-Saxon among our many ethnic groups. Recent figures indicate that one out of every six Americans is either wholly or partly of German provenience.[6]

The term "German" must be understood in a truly ethnic sense in this connection. It refers to people who were German in speech and customs, no matter under what rule they happened to be as a result of the chaotic state of Central Europe after the Thirty Years' War, which brought on the final disintegration of the medieval German Empire (the so-called Holy Roman Empire of the German Nation). Thus the early German settlers in America came not only from present-day Germany, Austria, and German-Switzerland, but also from such border countries of today as Alsace, Luxemburg, and western Czechoslovakia.

From the beginning, and throughout the eighteenth century, a vast body of material was written by Germans, but it was mainly "literature" in the broadest sense: travel diaries, records of settlements (particularly, church records), memoirs, correspondence, political tracts, and religious works. In part, this pattern continued in the nineteenth century, alongside ever-increasing creative writing.

Johannes Lederer's account of his explorations in the Carolinas, Virginia, etc., in 1669-1670, antedates the year of the Declaration of Independence by more than a century. A few years later (1683) Franz Daniel Pastorius led the first organized group of German colonists to Pennsylvania, at the invitation of his friend William Penn, and became the patriarch of their settlement, Germantown (now a part of Philadelphia). In 1700 Pastorius, with whom German-American writing is customarily said to begin, published a geographical description of the province, his principal work. He is supposed to have been the first known teacher of German in America. Pastorius also kept a remarkable scrapbook which he called his "Bienkorb" (Beehive), and which has been preserved.

At Germantown the first German Bible printed in this country came from the press of Christoph Sauer, as did the first German newspaper, and, beginning in 1738, *Der Hochteutsche-Amerikanische Kalender*. The latter publication was especially influential for a long time. Near Germantown, also, the noted religious leader and adherent of Mysticism, Johann Kelpius, first settled. He and Johann Conrad Beissel, the founder and patriarch of the famous Ephrata Cloisters in Lancaster County, may be called the first German-American lyricists of consequence, by reason of their mystic verse. In Thomas Mann's novel, *Doktor Faustus*, the musicologist Kretschmar quotes his father's praise of Beissel's compositions, which had so deeply moved him years before.

Remarkably enough, Beissel has received much scholarly attention with respect to his mysticism, theosophy, music, and ability as a religious organizer, but disproportionally little recognition of his poetry. Yet Dennis

McCort has recently shown that Beissel's lyrics at their best transcend the banalities which his lesser verse shares with that of Pietism in general.[7] McCort sees in "the panoramic soulscape," for which each one of hundreds of hymns furnishes an additional strand to form "a meticulously wrought spiritual tapestry," evidence of "a mystic imagination" which competes with that of Meister Eckhart or Jakob Böhme. Of special interest is his delineation, in certain poems of the hymnal entitled *Vorspiel der Neuen-welt* (1732), of a "lyrical *Amerikabild*," depicting the new land as an earthly paradise.[8]

The great eighteenth-century leader of German Pietism, Nikolaus Ludwig Count von Zinzendorf (1700-1760), spent several years in America, where he may have written some of his total of around two thousand hymns and religious poems.[9] It seems unlikely, though, that he could have found time for much poetic composition while in the New World, since he was chiefly occupied with two grandiose but unrealizable plans: first, to unite all the Protestant sects in the Colonies; second, to convert all the Indians to Christianity.

As noted already, the records of settlements founded by religious groups constitute a large and valuable part of the immense totality of factual writing in German during the eighteenth century. Whether church documents, letters, or, especially, reports sent to sponsoring organizations in Germany, they are highly important historically, geographically (in that they often contain enlightening descriptions of the country as it was then), as travel accounts, and as faithful, often detailed pictures of the daily life of the settlers. Outstanding examples of German pastors' reports to the home church are the "Hallesche Nachrichten" (Pennsylvania); "Nordcarolinische Kirchennachrichten," or "Helmstedt Reports"; and "Urlsperger Nachrichten" from the Salzburgers' settlement, Ebenezer, in Georgia (visited by the German-Swiss Johannes Tobler on his travels through that section).[10] Of all such records, the most meticulously kept and most complete are those of the Moravians, or "Herrnhuter."[11]

Travel literature, in the broader sense, also includes letters of Hessian officers, some of which were published by General von Riedesel.[12] It must be remembered that the Hessian troops, sold to the British by their tyrannical sovereign, not only fought very unwillingly against the Americans, but often deserted to the ranks of the latter. Some thousands remained after the war ended and, together with their fellow Germans already established in this country, played a significant part in its development.

If religious literature predominated in the German-American sphere during a great part of the eighteenth century, lyric poetry in its manifold aspects came into prominence in the nineteenth—at least, quantitatively, for much of it seems to reflect only faintly the brilliant era of German lyricism in the homeland. Unlike the great singer of *Weltschmerz*, Nikolaus Lenau, who came to the United States in 1832 with high hopes and returned to Europe the following year, disappointed in everything except Niagara Falls, most poetically-inclined *Deutschamerikaner* were firmly entrenched in their new existence. Still, they sought to express not only their thoughts concerning the world around them, but also their nostalgia for "the old country," thus exemplifying the German's oft-cited conflict between his wanderlust and longing for home, or "Fernweh" versus "Heimweh."

The patriotic spirit, already present in German-American poetry, received added impetus from the "Forty-Eighters," those who left Germany after the unsuccessful Revolution of 1848. Having failed to win a more democratic regime and to achieve the reunification of their native land, they were all the more determined to preserve freedom and unity in their adopted country. A note of longing, characteristic of much of the lyric poetry of the German-American element in general, is also prominent in the songs of the "Forty-Eighters." Attachment to the German Fatherland receives notably poignant expression in the frequently quoted poem "An mein Vaterland" by Conrad Krez, of which the opening stanza reads:

> Kein Baum gehörte mir von deinen Wäldern,
> Mein war kein Halm auf deinen Roggenfeldern,
> Und schutzlos hast du mich hinaus getrieben,
> Weil ich in meiner Jugend nicht verstand,
> Dich weniger und mehr mich selbst zu lieben,
> Und dennoch lieb' ich dich, mein Vaterland!

Best known of the lyricists among the 1848 revolutionaries was Ferdinand Freiligrath (1810-1876), who spent his years of exile in England. Plans for his settling in America, actively supported by his friend Longfellow, did not materialize, and Freiligrath returned home, after the long-delayed amnesty, in time to experience the reunification of Germany. Nevertheless, his popularity on this side of the Atlantic was such that a six-volume edition of his collected works was published in New York in 1858 and 1859. Remarkably enough, years before the Revolution of 1848 and his subsequent flight to foreign parts, Freiligrath had written exotic, none too realistic poems about the New World, e.g., "Die Auswanderer," a vivid word-picture of departing German emigrants. Undoubtedly, he exerted a determinative influence on the political lyric of the "Forty-Eighters" in the United States.[13]

These men, outspoken in their liberal convictions, who had worked vainly for a republican form of government in the homeland, probably did not exceed 5,000. Yet they gradually attained an unusually influential position in numerous segments of American public life, ranging from the areas of politics and journalism to those of the sciences, fine arts, and education.

Many who engaged in literary pursuits were also journalists or, in some cases, holders of public office. Only a few representative figures can be mentioned here. An instance is Dr. Franz Lahmeyer, a dentist, who in 1833 published a volume of verse at Baltimore. His poem on Columbus, in which he hails the American ideal of freedom, consists of forty-nine six-line stanzas.[14] Karl Heinzen, a lecturer, journalist, and (as he was called by contemporaries) a "great radical fighter," wrote, beside poems, an autobiography, a novel, and a number of comedies.[15] Other prominent German-American citizens who became well known in their time as poets are Karl Heinrich Schnauffer, Eduard Dorsch, Julius Dresel, and H. A. Rattermann. Gustav Brühl (pen name "Kara Giorg") is the author of numerous ballads under the title *Poesien des Urwalds*. Eduard Leyh translated "The Star Spangled Banner" and Joaquin Miller's "Arizonian" into German. Theodor Kirchoff became known as "the Poet of the Golden Gate," by reasons of poems in praise of his Far-Western home (one of them is entitled "California") and of the Pacific Ocean (example: "Das stille Meer").[16]

In her recent essay on the German-American lyric, Erika A. Metzger[17] takes issue with the viewpoint of Linus Spuler, who, in his standard work on German literature in the United States, distinguishes five successive periods of poetry, represented by "religious," "philosophical and political" verse, that of the "Forty-Eighters," "socialistic," and, finally, from 1919 on, "non-political" writing.[18] She points rather to the anthology of Robert E. Ward,[19] according to which one can designate three major thematic cycles. These are 1) "Heimwehlyrik," or poems expressive of nostalgia for the homeland and friends and/or relatives left behind; 2) "Landschaftslyrik," or poetry descriptive of the American scene, especially its grander aspects—mountains, forests, and rivers—but also including its cities; 3) "Europa-Kritik," expressive of the quest for absolute values under the concepts of religion and freedom, capable of realization only in "the land of unlimited opportunity," after having proved impossible of attainment in Europe.[20]

Many areas of the German-speaking world are represented in the German dialectal poetry which sprang up in various sections of America. For example, Emil Dietsch wrote in the dialect of the Palatinate. F. W. Lafrentz made extensive use of "Plattdeutsch," or Low German, in his works, no doubt inspired by Klaus Groth and Fritz Reuter in the homeland. Lafrentz's writing was surpassed by Carl Münter's *Nu sünd wi in Amerika* ("Now We Are in America").[21] Special mention belongs to the Pennsylvania-German idiom, which is a partially indigenous language, inasmuch as it represents something of an amalgam of Rhineland dialects (especially that of the Palatinate), plus a large component of vocabulary borrowed and/or adapted from American English. Henry Harbaugh (1817-1867) and Henry L. Fisher (1822-1909), both gifted versifiers, have given us vivid pictures of the Pennsylvania-German countryside and people. *Harbaugh's Harfe*[22] might well be styled *the* "classic" instance of poetry in "Pennsylfaanisch Deitsch." The following stanza from his poem "Heemweh" will serve as a characteristic illustration:

> So geht's in däre rauhe Welt,
>   Wo alles muss vergeh!
> Ja, in der alte Heemet gar
>   Fiehlt m'r sich all allee'!
> O, wann's net vor der Himmel wär,
>   Mit seiner scheene Ruh,
> Dann wär m'r's do schun lang verleedt,
>   Ich wisst net, was ze dhu.
> Doch Hoffnung leichtet meinen Weg
>   Der ew'gen Heemet zu.[23]

In the author's English version, "Home-Sickness," the equivalent lines read:

> Such is the fate of earthly loves
>   Where all things die or change.
> Yes, even in the homestead here,
>   I feel alone and strange.
> O were it not for yon bright heaven,
>   With its unchanging rest.
> How heavy would our burdens be,
>   Our life how sore distressed;
> But hope illumes our pathway to
>   The regions of the blest.[24]

No doubt, the most frequently quoted poem by Harbaugh is the first in the *Harfe*, entitled "Das alt Schulhaus an der Krick." Further well known examples are "Der alte Feierheerd," "Die Schlofschtub" (called, respectively, in Harbaugh's English renderings, "The Old-Time Hearth-Fire" and "The Old Sleeping Room"), "Die alt Miehl," and "Das Krischkindel" (i.e., the Christchild, who brings gifts at Christmas).

Fisher's two collections of poems, *'S Alt Marik-Haus mittes in d'r Schtadt* and, especially, *Kurzweil und Zeitfertreib odder Pennsylfanisch-deutsche Folkslieder*, are noteworthy for their depiction of Pennsylvania-German farm life. Many of the quaint old ways, customs, and superstitions, as well as rural festivities described by Fisher, long continued not only in the Quaker State, but also in other regions where Pennsylvania Germans had settled, for instance, in my native section of North Carolina, within my memory.[25]

Other Pennsylvania-German poets of note (to name but a few of the many persons who wrote and published in the dialect from around the middle of the nineteenth century on) are Edward Rauch;[26] Ludwig Wollenweber, born in Germany, but often taken for a native Pennsylvanian because of his expert use of the idiom;[27] Charles Calvin Ziegler;[28] and, especially Charles C. More (1849-1940).[29] The last-named author won late recognition in his eighties, when the German Academy in Munich awarded him its silver medal and Muhlenberg College conferred upon him the honorary degree of Doctor of Letters. His prime achievement is *Die Kutztown Mail*, an *Evangeline*-like story of a betrothed German couple, separated in the wake of the Revolution of 1848 and finally reunited, after long years, by death in Pennsylvania. A dialect writer who acquired widespread prominence as an historian is Israel Daniel Rupp, best known for his *Thirty Thousand Names of German and Other Immigrants to Pennsylvania*.[30]

Among avenues of publication for Pennsylvania-German literary productions, the *Pennsylvania-German Magazine* played an outstanding role, particularly in the early 1900's. Newspapers, early and late, printed innumerable writings of a popular nature, sometimes in a special section, e.g., " 'S Pennsylfawnisch Deitsch Eck" in the *Allentown Morning Call*. Finally, mention should be made of the many translations of High German and English literary works. A striking instance is J. William Frey's Pennsylvania-German adaptation of *Max und Moritz* by Wilhelm Busch.[31]

The two most salient names of novelists who wrote in German about frontier life and the Indians are Charles Sealsfield (pseudonym of Karl Postl, 1793-1864) and Friedrich Gerstäcker (1816-1872). Since John T. Krumpelmann's paper for this symposium deals with them in detail, only brief, general mention seems appropriate here.

Because some of the earlier works of Sealsfield were circulated in both German and English editions, he became known to a broader reading-public than did most German-American writers. Faust emphasizes Sealsfield's unparalleled achievement of capturing, in vivid description, the types of American character belonging specifically to the period between 1820 and 1840. He would rank Sealsfield in this regard with Cooper, Hawthorne, Bret Harte, and George W. Cable, who masterfully portrayed characteristic types in their respective sections of the country. Longfellow, himself of English descent, but a great admirer and mediator of German culture, delighted in reading the novels of "our favorite Sealsfield."[32]

Gerstäcker's firsthand depictions of America, especially of the backwoods and frontier life, have lately been hailed as a convincing refutation of the "Lenau legend," above all, in the controversial novel of Ferdinand Kürnberger, *Der Amerika-Müde*, and in that of Peter Härtling, entitled

Niembsch oder Der Stillstand.[33] Both of these fictional works present the great lyricist (who appears in Kürnberger's narrative as Dr. Moorfeld) as the disappointed "Amerikafahrer" who returns to Europe, broken in spirit and disillusioned in the Utopian longings and hopes with which he had embarked for the New World.

Two contemporaries of Sealsfield and Gerstäcker who dealt extensively in their works with American life as they had observed it, especially in the South, were Otto Ruppius and Friedrich Strubberg.[34] Also contemporaneous with Sealsfield's residence in Louisiana was the visit of Duke Bernhard of Sachsen-Weimar to the southern United States. He was well received generally, and especially in social circles of Charleston and New Orleans. Bernhard, a younger son of Goethe's patron, Duke (later, Grand Duke) Carl August, kept an invaluable record of his travels, which greatly interested Goethe.[35]

Otto Ruppius (1819-1864) spent nearly a dozen years in the United States after having fled from the homeland in 1849 to escape persecution for his inflammatory journalistic activities during and following the Revolution of 1848. His seven novels and thirteen *Novellen* afford a panoramic view of conditions in America shortly before the Civil War, inasmuch as in their totality they embrace the cities of the East, the plantations of the South, and the states of the Middle West, still in the "pioneer" stage. The novel *Drei Vagabunden* even takes the reader to the California gold fields. Exceptionally worthy of note are such shorter narratives as *Die Nachbarn*, *Mary Kreuzer*, and *Vermisst*, which offer genre pictures of life in various frontier settlements of the Middle West. Ruppius attained great popularity both among German-American readers and in Germany.[36]

Reinhold Solger (1817-1864) is likewise a "Forty-Eighter" who became a German-American novelist of distinction, although his premature death prevented the carrying out of numerous ambitious plans. His prize-winning novel, *Anton in Amerika*, was designated by its author as a "Seitenstück," or pendant, to Gustav Freytag's much-debated fictional work, *Soll und Haben.*[37] Solger also won a prize in 1859 for his poem commemorating the centennial of Schiller's birth.

A late successor to Sealsfield and Gerstäcker is Karl May (1842-1912), whose lively narratives of adventure in the West, such as *Winnetou* and *Old Shatterhand*, became extraordinarily popular whenever German was understood. He depicted with surprising accuracy this very region, the Llano Estacado. May's works may be regarded as marking the close of the tradition of exotic fiction which began with Cooper's "Leatherstocking" novels.[38]

Peter Uwe Hohendahl calls attention to the fact that, although Karl May's novels had millions of readers in the German-speaking world and

226

were translated into numerous other languages, they remained almost unknown in America.[39] Hohendahl suggests probable reasons for that scanty recognition, one being that Cooper's fame was too strongly entrenched for a foreigner to be able to compete with him in the same literary genre. Another circumstance is that American readers would have discovered a lot of factual errors of detail which would not have bothered Europeans unfamiliar with the scene. It is Hohendahl's opinion, however, that May's critical attitude toward the whites in relation to the Indians would hardly have aroused any strong antagonism, since that criticism was also evident in contemporaneous Indian stories by American authors; he cites Helen Hunt Jackson's *Ramona*, published in 1884, as an example.[40]

In its broader connotation, nineteenth-century German-American literature includes many distinguished writers in various fields. To cite a few instances, Francis Lieber wrote on international law and social ethics; Carl Follen and Carl Schurz are noted for their speeches and historical works; Friedrich Kapp left biographies of Steuben, Kalb and other German-American patriots; Hugo Münsterberg produced a significant characterization of the American people;[41] and, almost at the end of the century, Kuno Francke wrote a highly important treatment (in English) of German literature in the light of the social conditions prevailing in its various epochs.[42] These writers and many others made their influence felt far beyond the confines of the German language and thus contributed intellectually, as well as practically, to the progress of America.

The most renowned figure among German-Americans of the nineteenth century is Carl Schurz (1829-1906). His remarkable career as a citizen of his adopted country included such highlights as being a friend and adviser of Lincoln, United States ambassador to Spain, a brigadier-general in the Civil War, a senator from Missouri, and Secretary of the Interior during the presidency of Rutherford B. Hayes. With his oratorical ability and eloquent American English, free of accent, Schurz played an important part in the election of Lincoln in 1860. At various times he served as editor of prominent newspapers, including the *Westliche Post* (St. Louis) and the *New York Evening Post*; for a while, also, he was editor-in-chief of *The Nation*. In the first part of his memoirs (*Lebenserinnerungen*) Schurz gives a thrilling account of his escape after the fighting at Rastatt, in the Revolution of 1848, and of his subsequent freeing of his friend and former teacher, the poet Gottfried Kinkel, from imprisonment at Spandau.[43] Above all, in his *Life of Henry Clay*[44] Schurz demonstrated his biographical and historical acumen, his talent as a man of letters, and his almost incredible mastery of the English language.

Among nineteenth-century American authors of German ancestry are Bayard Taylor, Charles Nordhoff (German-born), Joaquin Miller, Henry

Timrod, Owen Wister, and John Godfrey Saxe.[45] While also an original poet and novelist, Bayard Taylor won his lasting fame through his achievements as a mediator of German literature and culture, especially his classic translation of Goethe's *Faust*. Thus he stands preeminent in the fascinating and almost limitless field of literary relations between Germany and America—an area which can receive only passing mention in this brief survey. It should be noted, though, that scarcely a nineteenth-century American poet of importance, from the New Englanders to Walt Whitman, failed to establish contact with German poetry and/or philosophy.[46] Longfellow may be said to have led in the translation of shorter lyrics.[47] As one illustration of literary exchange, his friend Freilingrath rendered a number of Longfellow's poetic works, including *Hiawatha*, into German.

The first few years of the twentieth century appear to a great extent as a projection of the late nineteenth-century literary scene. Perhaps the most salient representative of the younger German-American writers of that time was George Sylvester Viereck. Having come to the United States from Munich in 1897 at the age of thirteen, Viereck began publishing at twenty with poems in German, *Gedichte* (1904). [48] Other works which appeared in the years immediately thereafter are *Ninive und andere Gedichte*[49] and dramas in English, e.g., *A Game at Love and Other Plays*.[50] Viereck subsequently had a long career as a littérateur in New York, engaging not only in original writing but also in translating from the German.

During the early years of the new century a number of German-American scholars and writers were actively endeavoring to make the chief masterpieces of German literature (beginning with the classicism of Goethe and Schiller) available to their fellow countrymen in good English translations. Outstanding examples are *The German Classics*, edited by Kuno Francke with many collaborators (some of non-German descent);[51] Gerhart Hauptmann's plays, in the edition of Ludwig Lewisohn and others;[52] and Margarete Münsterberg's volume of excellent renditions of German lyrics.[53] Of these three gifted interpreters of their literary heritage, the latter two also became American authors in their own right.

The Germanophobia of the years 1917-1918, when in a number of states even the teaching of the language was forbidden by law, was not conducive to new belletristic developments. Consequently, the recovery of German-American equilibrium in the third decade of this century was very gradual. Beginning with the late 1920's, however, a rapid revival of cultural exchange between America and the German-speaking lands became evident.

Somewhat akin to the mass exodus from Germany in 1848 and afterward was the emigration of those German and Austrian nationals who, beginning in 1933, fled from persecution on religious, racial, or political

"Swanhilda," Diana Baker. (Photographed by Meredith E. Aker)

grounds. Inasmuch as there were no less than thirteen Nobel Prize winners in their ranks, they have been called "the most intellectual immigration that America ever experienced."[54] A number of writers among them belonged to world literature as well as to German belles-lettres. One need only cite as instances the novelists Thomas Mann, Franz Werfel (likewise a lyric and dramatic poet), and Erich Maria Remarque, together with the dramatists Bertolt Brecht, Carl Zuckmayer, Fritz von Unruh, and Ernst Toller. Of these and many more, some remained in this country, while others eventually returned to Europe, but their works written in exile bear, in varying degrees, the stamp of their American experiences.

Nowadays, in the 1970's, German-American writers continue their production of short stories, novels, and poems, many of which appear in German-language newspapers. True, much of all this is merely light, ephemeral literature for entertainment ("Unterhaltungsliteratur"), but there are numerous exceptions, especially in poetry. Glancing through such periodicals as *German-American Studies* and *Lyrica Germanica*, or the literary section of the Sunday edition of the *New Yorker Staats-Zeitung und Herold*, one notes that acceptable verse is still being cultivated in German-speaking circles of our land. The following are among the more gifted individuals who frequently contribute poems to German newspapers and periodicals in the United States: Dora Grunewald,[55] Milwaukee; Herman F. Brause, Rochester; Kurt J. Fickert, Springfield, Ohio; Donald Heinrich Tolzmann, Cincinnati; Lowell A. Bangerter, Laramie, Wyoming; Ilse Pracht-Fitzell, Jamesburg, New Jersey; and Bernhard Mock, North Hollywood, California.[56]

Finally, quite recently two poets have each had a volume of verse published in Germany—Lisa Kahn, Houston;[57] and Stuart Friebert, Oberlin, Ohio.[58] Thus, in this Bicentennial year of 1976, the German-American lyric Muse can yet be heard.

Texas Tech University

NOTES

[1] Albert Bernhardt Faust, *The German Element in the United States*, 2 vols. (New York: The Steuben Society of America, 1927), I, 7-9. Hereafter cited as Faust.

[2] See Horst Oppel, "Die deutsche Siedlung in Louisiana im Spiegel des Amerika-Romans der Goethezeit: Heinrich Zschokkes *Prinzessin von Wolfenbüttel*," *Studies in German Literature* [in Honor of John T. Krumpelmann], ed. Carl Hammer, Jr., Louisiana State Univ. Studies, Humanities Series, No. 13 (Baton Rouge, 1963), pp. 18-38.

[3] Cf. Henry A. Pochmann, *German Culture in America: Philosophical and Literary Influences, 1600-1900* (Madison: Univ. of Wisconsin Press, 1957), p. 333. Hereafter cited as Pochmann.

[4] Faust, I, 9, 13, passim.

230

[5] See *Deutsch-Amerikanische 200-Jahr-Feier: Staats-Herold Almanach 1976* (New York: Staats-Herold Corp., 1976), p. 42. Hereafter cited by short title.

[6] Ibid., p. 6.

[7] Dennis McCort, "Johann Conrad Beissel, Colonial Mystic Poet," *German-American Studies*, 8 (Fall 1974), 1.

[8] Ibid., p. 30.

[9] Friedrich Vogt und Max Koch, *Geschichte der deutschen Literatur*, 5th ed. (Leipzig: Bibliographisches Institut, 1934), II, 4.

[10] See Walter L. Robbins, trans. and ed., "John Tobler's Description of South Carolina (1753-1754)," *The South Carolina Historical Magazine*, 71 (1970), 141-61; 257-65, esp. 148-49.

[11] Adelaide L. Fries *et al.*, eds. *Records of the Moravians in North Carolina*, 10 vols. (Raleigh: Edwards & Broughton, 1922-1966). See also Miss Fries's slightly novelized, but historically accurate edition of an eighteenth-century Moravian woman's autobiography, *The Road to Salem* (Chapel Hill: Univ. of North Carolina Press, 1944).

[12] F. A. von Riedesel, *Die Berufsreise nach Amerika: Briefe . . . zur Zeit des dortigen Krieges in den Jahren 1776 bis 1783 nach Deutschland geschrieben* (Berlin: Haude & Spener, 1788).

[13] Cf. Frank Trommler, "Vom Vormärz zum Bürgerkrieg: Die Achtundvierziger und ihre Lyrik," *Amerika in der deutschen Literatur*, eds. Sigrid Bauschinger, Horst Denkler and Wilfried Malsch (Stuttgart: Reclam, 1975), p. 99. Hereafter cited by short title.

[14] See Raymond A. Wiley, "The German-American Verse of Dr. Franz Lahmeyer," *German-American Studies*, 7 (1974), 14-29.

[15] Cf. Katherine and Gerhard Friesen, "Karl Heinzen's German-American Writings: Some Literary Aspects," *German-American Studies*, 7 (1974), 107-29.

[16] Cf. Faust, II, 348-49.

[17] Erika A. Metzger, "Deutsche Lyrik in Amerika," *German-American Studies*, 9 (1975), 2-10. Hereafter cited as Metzger.

[18] Ibid., p. 4. The reference is to Linus Spuler, *Deutsches Schrifttum in den Vereinigten Staaten von Amerika* (Lucerne: Erziehungsdepartement, 1960).

[19] Robert E. Ward, ed. *Deutsche Lyrik aus Amerika* (New York: Literary Soc. Foundation, 1969), p. 7 (cited by Metzger, p. 4).

[20] Metzger, pp. 4-5.

[21] Cf. Faust, II, 350.

[22] Henry Harbaugh, *Harbaugh's Harfe: Gedichte in Pennsylvanisch-Deutscher Mundart*, ed. B. Bausman (Philadelphia: Reformed Church Publication Board, 1870; rev. ed., 1902).

[23] Ibid., pp. 84-85.

[24] Ibid., pp. 104-05.

[25] Cf. Carl Hammer, Jr., *Rhinelanders on the Yadkin: The Story of the Pennsylvania Germans in Rowan and Cabarrus Counties, North Carolina* 2nd, rev. ed. (Salisbury: Rowan Printing Co., 1965), pp. 77-94.

[26] Harry H. Reichard, "Pennsylvania-German Dialect Writings and Their Writers," *Publications of the Pennsylvania-German Society*, 26 (1918), 74-99.

[27] Ibid., pp. 100-04.

[28] Ibid., pp. 284-312.

[29] Cf. Alexander Waldenrath, "Three Studies in German Culture in Pennsylvania, I: The Manuscripts of Charles C. More," *German-American Studies*, 9 (1975), 16-25.

[30] Israel Daniel Rupp, *A Collection of Upward of Thirty Thousand Names of German, Swiss, Dutch, French, and Other Immigrants in Pennsylvania from 1727 to 1776...*, 2nd rev. and enl. ed. (Philadelphia: Kohler, 1876).

[31] J. William Frey, *Jake un Johnny: 'n Buweg'schicht in siwwe Schtreech* (Clinton, S.C.: The Author, 1943).

[32] Cf. Faust, II, 343-44.

[33] See Manfred Durzak, "Nach Amerika. Gerstäckers Widerlegung der Lenau-Legende," *Amerika in der deutschen Literatur*, pp. 135-53; cf. Rüdiger Steinlein, "Ferdinand Kürnbergers *Der Amerikamüde*: Ein 'Amerikanisches Kulturbild' als Entwurf einer negativen Utopie," ibid., pp. 154-77.

[34] Cf. L. H. Woodson, *American Negro Slavery in the Works of Friedrich Strubberg, Friedrich Gerstäcker and Otto Ruppius* (Washington: The Catholic University of America Press, 1949).

[35] Bernhard, *Reise Sr. Hoheit des Herzog Bernhard zu Sachsen-Weimar-Eisenach durch Nord-Amerika in d. Jahren 1825 und 1826* (Weimar: W. Hoffman, 1828); Cf. John T. Krumpelmann, *Southern Scholars in Goethe's Germany* (Chapel Hill: Univ. of North Carolina Press, 1965), p. 7, passim.

[36] Cf. Christoph Hering, "Otto Ruppius, der Amerikafahrer: Flüchtling, Exilschriftsteller, Rückwanderer," *Amerika in der deutschen Literatur*, pp. 124-34.

[37] Cf. Horst Denkler, "Die Schule des Kapitalismus: Reinhold Solgers deutsch-amerikanisches 'Seitenstück' zu Gustav Freytags *Soll und Haben*," ibid., pp. 108-23.

[38] See Hans Plischke, *Von Cooper bis Karl May: Eine Geschichte des völkerkundlichen Reise-und Abenteuerromans* (Düsseldorf: Droste Verlag, 1951).

[39] Peter Uwe Hohendahl, "Von der Rothaut zum Edelmenschen: Karl Mays Amerikaromane," *Amerika in der deutschen Literatur*, p. 230.

[40] Ibid.

[41] Hugo Münsterberg, *American Traits from the Point of View of a German* (Boston: Houghton, Mifflin & Co., 1901); *Die Amerikaner*, 2 vols. (Berlin: Mittler, 1904).

[42] Kuno Francke, *A History of German Literature as Determined by Social Forces*, 5th ed. (New York: Holt, 1927). First published as *Social Forces in German Literature* (New York: Holt, 1896).

[43] Carl Schurz, *Reminiscences*, 3 vols. (New York: McClure, 1907-08); *Lebenserinnerungen*, 3 vols. (Berlin: Reimar, 1912).

[44] Carl Schurz, *Life of Henry Clay*, 2 vols. (Boston: Houghton, Mifflin & Co., 1887).

[45] Cf. Faust, II, 352-57.

[46] See John T. Krumpelmann, *Bayard Taylor and German Letters* (Hamburg: Cram, de Gruyter & Co., 1959); also, Pochmann, pp. 409-74.

[47] Cf. Carl Hammer, Jr., "Longfellow's Lyrics 'From the German,'" *Studies in Comparative Literature*, ed. Waldo F. McNeir, Louisiana State University Studies, Humanities Series, No. 22 (Baton Rouge, 1962), pp. 155-72.

[48] George Sylvester Viereck, *Gedichte* (New York: Progressive Printing Co., 1904).

[49] Viereck, *Ninive und andere Gedichte* (Stuttgart: Cotta, 1906).

[50] Viereck, *A Game at Love and Other Plays* (New York: Jackson Press Inc., 1908).

[51] Kuno Franke, W. G. Howard et al., eds., *The German Classics: Masterpieces of German Literature of the Nineteenth and Twentieth Centuries Translated into English*, 20 vols. (New York: The German Publications Society, 1913-1914).

232

[52] Ludwig Lewisohn, ed., *The Dramatic Works of Gerhart Hauptmann*, 9 vols. (New York: B. W. Huebsch, Inc., 1912-1925). Many of the plays were translated by Lewisohn; the rest, by several others.

[53] Margarete Münsterberg, trans., *A Harvest of German Verse* (New York: D. Appleton & Co., 1916).

[54] *Deutsch-Amerikanische 200-Jahr-Feier*, p. 55.

[55] See Erwin F. Ritter, "Dora Grunewald: Reminiscences," *German-American Studies*, 7 (1974), 5-13.

[56] Poems by these and others are to be found especially in *German-American Studies*; e.g., in vols. 7-9 (1974-1975), passim.

[57] Lisa Kahn, *Klopfet an, so wird euch nicht aufgetan* (Darmstadt: Bläschke-Verlag, 1975).

[58] Stuart Friebert, *Nicht hinauslehnen: Gedichte/Poems* (Munich: Delp Verlag, 1975).

Ethnic Endeavors by Quasi-Residents of Our Nineteenth-Century Southwest

John T. Krumpelmann

ABSTRACT

This study assays to elucidate the accomplishments of those writers of the Southwest, both Americans and Europeans, who, during the nineteenth century, strove, with varying success, to reveal to the world the manner of living of the ethnic groups who inhabited our Southwestern states. By strange coincidence, Timothy Flint, a clergyman from Massachusetts, author of ethnic writings, notably the ethnic novel *Francis Berrian*, took up residence in Alexandria, Louisiana. Shortly thereafter Charles Sealsfield (i.e., the Austrian ex-priest, Karl Postl, better known as Charles Sealsfield) took up abode in that same region and dated the dedication of his exotic novel *Der Legitime und die Republikaner* "Alexandria, La., den 30. September 1831." And Friedrich Gerstäcker, today best known in America as the author of *Germelshausen*, a probable source of *Brigadoon*, but better generally known as a world traveller who visited this country in the middle of the last century and was very familiar with the backwoods folk of Texas, Arkansas and Louisiana, was also in that region. He was the manager of a hotel in Pointe Coupée, Louisiana in Flint and Sealsfield country. (JTK)

It was with much pleasure that I welcomed the honor of being invited by Texas Tech University to participate in the 1976 Comparative Literature Symposium, which, as an event of this institution's observance of the bicentenary of American independence, is dedicated to the current interest in the role of ethnic literatures in our country. I myself am a descendant of maternal grandparents who were Louisiana Creoles, while my father's parents were natives, respectively, of Hanover (Germany) and Ireland, all Roman Catholics. Perhaps on account of such backgrounds, my forebears have always been interested in the literature produced by European travelers who, as a result of residence in the United States, were wont to see America "as others see us." With a family tradition of that sort, I entered all the more gladly into the program outlined for this symposium.

233

Yet at first I felt some trepidation at the thought of labeling the literary productions of our own citizens, or those of our foreign guests and/or visitors, "ethnic." It seems to me in retrospect that I have hitherto avoided using the term "ethnic," substituting "ethnological," "ethnographic(al)," or even "exotic" for it. When, in the course of a conversation with a sometime graduate student of mine at Louisiana State University, I mentioned the invitation and my hesitancy about "ethnic," she told me that her English dictionary defined it as "national." Her statement caused me to begin an extensive lexicographical search.[1]

All of this search prompted further communication with a former colleague, now one of this country's foremost Sealsfield authorities and also a well trained classical philologist, who encouraged me to make the requested contribution and accompanied his advice with an expansive explanation of the evolution of the word "ethnic" and its philological career.

But in the present essay I shall endeavor to concentrate on the ethnic writings of the following authors: Carl Postl (alias Charles Sidons, alias Charles Sealsfield) 1793-1864, an Austrian clergyman and renegade Roman-Catholic priest; Timothy Flint (1780-1840), a Harvard graduate and Protestant clergyman; and Friedrich Gerstäcker (1816-1872), a German traveler and the son of artistic parents.

Sidons (as he called himself then) first set foot on American soil in New Orleans in the late summer of 1823 and evidently remained there throughout the winter. Apparently, he returned to spend his second winter and spring there (from December 1, 1825 till July, 1826). This sojourn in Louisiana resulted in his acquisition of a document in the name of "Charles Sealsfield, citizen of the United States, native of Pennsylvania," which came into his possession before the end of August, 1826.

Remarkably enough, these three writers of ethnic works, Sealsfield, Flint, and Gerstäcker, all resided in Louisiana, and within close proximity of each other, i.e., in the vicinity of the confluence of the Red River and the Mississippi. They were quite familiar with the city of New Orleans, and at almost coincidental dates. Yet we find no record, nor any mention, of a personal meeting of any two of them. But this is no more peculiar than the fact that Charles Sealsfield directed the publishers of his earliest book dealing with this country, *Die Vereinigten Staaten von Nordamerika* (1827), to send a complimentary copy to Duke Bernhard of Saxe-Weimar, who was visiting a resident of New Orleans when Sealsfield was in that city.

It is, however, noteworthy that B. A. Uhlendorf, in his important work on Sealsfield, concedes: "The five novels following next upon *Morton* (1835) form a cycle revolving around life in the southwestern states." He then adds: "Here the author found various racial elements in closer juxta-position than anywhere else in the Union."[2] In other words, in the 1820's the South, and not the industrial Northeast, was what Sealsfield termed the "Schmelztiegel" (in *Bärenhäuter*, 1834), long before the occurrence of the American expression "Melting Pot."[3] Now, before our "citizen of the United States" could venture to write a novel concerning the life and activities of the mixed elements and varied social groups of this new "melting pot," America, he had to familiarize himself with the seething of the different racial components in the process of producing the nation then emerging.[4]

There is evidence of Sealsfield's having been in Saint Francisville, Louisiana, in March 1829. Although there is no certainty regarding the location of his "plantation on the Red River,"[5] it is a fact that the dedication of his novel *Der Legitime und die Republikaner* is dated "Alexandria, La., den 30. September 1831."

It is also a fact that Alexandria on the Red River was at that time the home of Timothy Flint. The record shows that Mr. Flint, "not far from the beginning of the year of 1824," left New Orleans for his semi-permanent residence in Alexandria.[6] There Flint met Judge Henry Bullard, a fellow Harvard man of the class of 1807 and the latter's wife, neé Sarah Maria Kaiser. In the preface to *Francis Berrian, or the Mexican Patriot* (1827), Flint pays tribute to Bullard, who had served several years in Mexico as a soldier-of-fortune. Upon the latter's account of the years of adventure in that country, his friend Flint has based his ethnic narrative.

Sealsfield's first novel appeared in the following three versions: 1) *Tokeah; or the White Rose* (1829)[7]; 2) *The Indian Chief; or Tokeah and the White Rose* (also 1829; a revised and enlarged edition intended for publication in England)[8]; and 3) the more extensively revised edition, *Der Legitime und die Republikaner* (1833).[9] A study of this "trio" reveals that the author underwent a socio-ethnological evolution during the time of his writing the three-fold work.

Initially, Sealsfield produced a romance fundamentally like Cooper's famous novel *The Last of the Mohicans*, and also like Timothy Flint's *Francis Berrian*, a source from which, in my opinion, our novice drew inspiration for numerous features of his own work.[10] Apparently, Seals-field intended to present a romantic novel depicting the exoticism of the American, Spanish, and Indian borderlands in a sentimental vein resem-bling that of Flint's novel. The hero of the latter is a young New England Puritan who rescues, and subsequently marries, the daughter of a high-ranking Spanish official. Similarly, in Sealsfield's novel the youthful Sir Arthur Graham comes to the rescue of the White Rose, who becomes his bride. After the murder of her mother by a band of Indians, she, still a small child, had been adopted by Tokeah, "the Last of the Oconees," and reared as his daughter. It eventually comes to light that she, like Flint's heroine, is a descendant of Spanish nobility, her father being "Don Juan, Chevalier d'Aranza, Count de Montgomez."[11]

Sealsfield was, like Flint, a clergyman and, as every priest must be, a philosopher—whether religious, social, or political. Like Shakespeare, to whom Sealsfield refers in nearly every one of his works, and of whom the young Goethe exclaimed, "Natur, Natur! nichts so Natur als Shakespeares Menschen,"[12] Sealsfield "holds the mirror up to nature." At the same time we see him undergoing a transformation of his philosophy.

Even the changes made in the subtitle of *The Indian Chief* before each republication indicate that the author has developed from a romantic narrator into a cultural-historical sociologist. For Sealsfield now manifests greater interest in the ethnological problems of the "melting-pot" than in the heart-throbs of the young romantic lovers. The sociologist Sealsfield introduces as his leading character Tokeah, the last chief of the Oconees, an Indian who is no idealistic, humanitarian savage, but a creature who distrusts all intruding white men as deadly enemies of his race. Tokeah is by no means a friendly Indian hero of the ilk of Cooper's Uncas or Longfellow's Hiawatha; rather, he is an Indian such as Ferdinand Freiligrath considers all Indians to be, namely, distrustful of the "Whites," whom he regards as annihilators of the Red Man. When Sealsfield revised and enlarged this work for the edition to be published in England, he added, as a subtitle (in addition to the alternate title, *Tokeah and the White Rose*), "A Tale of the Indians and the Whites." This shows his increasing concern for racial relations generally; one notes the beginning of a shift of emphasis from individuals (e.g., Tokeah and Rosa) to categories, in this case, ethnic groups.

In *Der Ligitime und die Republikaner* Sealsfield, the former priest, demonstrates his gradual development into a sociologist. Whereas *The Indian Chief* may still be considered primarily a romance, even though sociological tendencies are also evident, the novel in its last form gives the impression of being an ethnological treatise. No longer does a love story like that of young Sir Arthur Graham and Rosa, the daughter of a Spanish aristocrat, "Don Juan, Chevalier d'Aranza, Count de Montgomez," form the center of interest; rather, the land and the various races inhabiting it are the author's chief concern. *Eros is replaced by Ethos*, as Sealsfield depicts the "classes" and the "unclassed" in the Southern regions of the United States, all undergoing the "melting" process. Here we see Americans, Englishmen, French, Germans, Irish, Spaniards, Indians, and Blacks playing their respective roles in the antebellum Deep South. In this final revision of the novel the dominant character is no longer a chief like Tokeah, but the "Legitime"—a type, rather than an individual.

Sealsfield's first novel, in its three versions, therefore progresses from a sentimental romance (*Tokeah; or The White Rose*), through an intermediate stage *(The Indian Chief)*, to a sociological consideration of the struggle between the aborigines and the white intruders (*Der Legitime und die Republikaner*).

It has long been known that Sealsfield's *Christophorus Bärenhäuter* (1834) owes its origin to Flint's *Jemima O'Keefy—Sentimental Tale,* which had appeared in 1827. Bärenhäuter, "a stupid-heavy German work-horse, but owner of an estate of 300 acres," represents "the honest German," an expression which Sealsfield says (in *Die Vereinigten Staaten* [1827] I, 78) has come to mean the same as "stupid German."

The wife of Christophorus is modeled after Flint's Jemima O'Keefy, a very poor Irish girl, whom Sealsfield calls "Jemima O'Dougherty," and who furnishes the humor characteristic of this ethnic group. Jemima is captured and carried away by the Shawnee Indians. Although she eludes her captors and returns to "Toffel," she finds him wedded to one Dorothea Heumacher. Then, having returned to the Shawnees, she is married by a justice of the peace to "Tomahawk, Chief of the Shawnees." Together they rear a brood of Christian Tomahawks.

It is noteworthy that in his next borrowing from Flint, our so-called "Pennsylvania-German" (Sealsfield) again exploits an ethnic figure of Irish provenience. Flint's *The Host Child*[13] became Sealsfield's "Kinderräuber" (*George Howard's Brautfahrt, Part Three*, 1834). The kidnapper is an Irishman called "Thomas Tutti." The scene of this story is laid in the backwoods of the South Central states.

In Flint's important novel, the above-mentioned *Francis Berrian*,[14] one finds a connection of the same two ethnic elements, the Irish and the German. In the preface Flint ackowledges his debt to Judge Henry Bullard, who, as mentioned previously, had spent several years in Mexico. Flint's daughter married a man named Seip. Descendants of the latter couple still reside in Alexandria, and the record shows that Flint himself held the German people in high esteem.[15]

It may seem striking that in the ethnic works of both Flint and Sealsfield the German and Irish elements have received so much attention, but factual figures, attested to by A. B. Faust in his monumental work, *The German Element in the United States*,[16] confirm that these two nationalities were numerically the largest "ethnic" groups in the United States in Sealsfield's time. This raises the query as to any possible influence *Francis Berrian*, an ethnic novel highly spiced with amiable affection for the German element, might have had on Sealsfield's *Der Virey und die Republikaner* (1835). One even wonders whether Sealsfield perhaps borrowed his "Miko," the main character in *Der Legitime und die Republikaner* (1829), where one reads that Menko, or the Torrent, was chief of the tribe.[17]

"Peasant Bride and Groom," Susan Hopson and Steve Bartell. (Photographed by Meredith E. Aker)

Introducing the last of our triumvirate of authors of ethnic literature in this region, Friedrich Gerstäcker (1816-1872), we must call attention to the dissertation of Erich Seyfarth, *Friedrich Gerstäcker. Ein Beitrag zur Geschichte des exotischen Romans in Deutschland*.[18] The author, who lists the contents of each volume of the *Gesammelte Schriften* (1872-1879), regards Gerstäcker as the most successful of the German group. Seyfarth considers *Die Regulatoren in Arkansas* (1846), *Die Flusspiraten des Mississippi* (1847), and *Mississippi-Bilder* (1847), Gerstäcker's "grossen Wurf." He admits that Sealsfield's *Die Vereinigten Staaten* (1827) sets forth "great cultural and social problems" and designates Sealsfield as a sociologist [i.e. "Forscher"], whereas Gerstäcker is rather a huntsman ("Birscher") who is always on the tracks of the bear rather than endeavoring to reveal the cultural and social problems of the various ethnic groups.[19] It has been appropriately remarked that Gerstäcker's talent was reporting rather than imaginative writing. But let us not forget that Gerstäcker also wrote *Germelshausen*, the famous story of an accursed and sunken village, which has been suggested as a source of Alan Jay Lerner's Broadway hit of the 1940's, *Brigadoon*.[20]

Of course, Gerstäcker was not, like Sealsfield, an ex-priest, nor was he, like Flint, a Harvard man and minister of the Gospel. He was consequently less attracted by the higher social groups of America. But he was an adventurer who succeeded in learning to know the American pioneer settlers. Again we note that the Irish as well as the Germans are depicted in the course of his travels.

In *Die Regulatoren in Arkansas*[21] and in *Die Flusspiraten des Mississippi*[22] "Dayton," alias "Kelly" appears as a "justice of the peace" and as "Captain of the Pirates." Another character, Rowson, is "a Methodist preacher and a horse thief, a robber and a murderer all in one person." To quote Seyfarth (p. 35): "He hastens from murder to preaching, and from preaching to the burial of the man he has murdered."

After Gerstäcker's last hunting trips in Arkansas we find him in October, 1840, installed as the manager of a hotel on Pointe Coupée in Louisiana. Thus he became the third of the ethnic writers who came and saw and wrote in Louisiana, on the reaches of the Mississippi and the Red River (namely, in the vicinity of Bayou Sara and St. Francisville) in the first half of the last century.

Like Flint and Sealsfield, Gerstäcker deals with the German and Irish ethnic elements in this region, but he alone (*Mississippi-Bilder*, in the chapter, "Wandernde Krämer") calls attention to the overwhelming presence of the so-called "Peddlers," with whom, he asserts, the states of Louisiana, Ohio, Pennsylvania, and Kentucky are innundated, adding: "Of all the itinerant German *Krämer* in America hardly one percent are Chris-

240

tians, but the real Yankees offer the Jews considerable competition."[23]
He concludes: "Louisiana is teeming with these people."[24]

So we have, finally, the third of our triumvirate in Louisiana on the Mississippi, where Flint and Sealsfield had spent so much time, evidently without becoming acquainted with each other. Gerstäcker spent almost six years in Arkansas, almost a year in northeastern Texas, and a year in the state of Louisiana. Therefore we may feel well justified in devoting attention to these three and their literary works of ethnic character resting on their observations of the people and life of that era in our section of this nation.

Louisiana State University

NOTES

[1] Consultation of numerous dictionaries of several languages yielded a surprising variety of definitions of the word "ethnic." Further examples were gleaned from newspapers, specifically, the *Baton Rouge Morning Advocate* and the *New Orleans Times-Picayune*. The widely disparate uses of the term included "heathen" or "pagan" and, especially, "foreign" or "exotic" in a derogatory sense.

[2] *Charles Sealsfield, Ethnic Elements and National Problems in His Works* (Reprinted from Deutsch-Amerikanische Geschichtsblätter. Jahrbuch der Deutsch-Amerikanischen Historischen Gesellschaft von Illinois, Chicago), XX (1920-1921), 14.

[3] Attributed to Israel Zangwill, author of the four-act play entitled *The Melting Pot* (New York: MacMillan, 1908).

[4] Cf. Charles Sealsfield, *Sämtliche Werke*, ed. Karl J. R. Arndt et al., *The Indian Chief; or, Tokeah and the White Rose*, ed. John T. Krumpelmann (Hildesheim and New York: Olms Presse, 1972), IV, viii. Cited below as *Sämtliche Werke*.

[5] Cf. Eduard Castle, *Der grosse Unbekannte: Das Leben von Charles Sealsfield* (Vienna and Munich: Manutiuspresse, 1952), p. 265.

[6] See John Erwin Kirkpatrick, *Timothy Flint, Pioneer, Missionary, Author, Editor (1780-1840)* (Cleveland: Arthur H. Clark, 1911), p. 163. Cited below as Kirkpatrick.

[7] In 2 volumes (Philadelphia: Carey, Lea, and Carey, 1829).

[8] Three volumes (London: A. K. Newman and Co., 1829; also issued, under the same date, by the author's Philadelphia publishers).

[9] The full title reads: *Der Legitime und die Republikaner. Eine Geschichte aus dem letzten amerikanisch-englischen Krieg*, 3 vols. (Zürich: Orell, Füssli und Compagnie, 1833). Sealsfield's *Gesammelte Werke* appeared in 15 vols. a dozen and more years later (Stuttgart: Verlag der J. B. Metzlerschen Buchhandlung, 1845-1847). Our text is *Sämtliche Werke*, vols. 6 and 7 (ed. Krumpelmann). Change of emphasis in the third version of Sealsfield's novel is even externally obvious, in that he replaced the motto of the title-page, the opening stanza of Mignon's exotic song in Goethe's *Wilhelm Meister* ("Kennst du das Land," etc., in English translation) with a brief and serious utterance of Jefferson, rendered into German as follows: "Ich zittere für mein Volk, wenn ich der Ungerechtigkeiten gedenke, deren es sich gegen die Ureinwohner schuldig gemacht hat."

[10] Cf. *Sämtliche Werke*, IV, xii.

[11] Ibid., V, 232-44.

[12] Goethe, *Werke*, Weimarer Ausgabe, Series I (Weimar: Hermann Böhlau, 1887-1919), 37, 133.

[13] Published in *Western Monthly Review*, I (May 1829), 9-10.

[14] Timothy Flint, *Francis Berrian; or, The Mexican Patriot*, 2 vols. (Boston: Cummings, Hilliard, 1826).

[15] Cf. Kirkpatrick (p. 251): "But he sees that Germany is to be, and already is, the leader in the search for truth and in cosmopolitan scholarship. He was much interested in, and hopeful concerning, the beginning that was being made by a small group of Harvard men to introduce the German thought and literature into the United States."

[16] A. B. Faust, *The German Element in the United States* (New York: The Steuben Society, 1927), II, 23-27.

[17] Note that the *Dictionary of American English* (1951) does cite two earlier occurrences: "meiko" (1737) and "micco" (1800).

[18] Erich Seyfarth, *Friedrich Gerstäcker. Ein Beitrag zur Geschichte des exotischen Romans in Deutschland* (Freiburg im Breisgau: Jos. Waibel'sche Buchdruckerei, 1930). Cited below (and in the text) as Seyfarth.

[19] Seyfarth, pp. 23-26.

[20] Cf. John T. Krumpelmann, "Gerstäcker's *Germelshausen* and Lerner's *Brigadoon*," *Monatshefte*, 40 (1948), 396-400.

[21] Gerstäcker, *Gesammelte Werke*, 43 vols. (Jena: Hermann Costenoble, 1872-1879), VII, 57, passim.

[22] Ibid., VIII, passim.

[23] Ibid., X, 197-98.

[24] Ibid., p. 203.

James T. Farrell and the Irish-American Urban Experience

William J. Lynch

ABSTRACT

In his major cycles of Irish-American life in Chicago during the first quarter of the twentieth century, James T. Farrell has created two major examples of American urban youth—Studs Lonigan, a death symbol, and Danny O'Neill, a symbol of hope, life, and vitality. The chief contributor to the destruction of Studs is the urban Irish Catholic milieu, whose negative value system, manifest in the Lonigan home and enforced by the local Catholic church and schools, does not permit Studs to grow into a productive American citizen. Farrell portrays with vivid realism the negative forces of Irish Catholicism in the Lonigan trilogy—in family life; in the church itself, with the reactionary dogmatism of the clergy, which extends even to the media with the "radio priest," Father Moylan; and in the schools, with the emphasis on corporal punishment, rote memory, and parochial anti-intellectualism. The progress of Danny O'Neill, culminating in his decision to become a writer, may be seen as a conscious and deliberate gradual rejection of Irish Catholicism for the very reasons that Studs Lonigan accepts it. Consequently, Danny grows in intellect and imagination, but is gradually rejected by and must depart from the narrow-minded Irish Catholic community which will not tolerate dissent. He is thus released from the life-stifling forces of dogma and provinciality, and is able to unleash the creative and intellectual forces which urban Irish Catholicism would deliberately have kept still. (WJL)

William Shannon, in his perceptive book on the Irish in America, has accurately observed that, of the three major Irish-American novelists of the twentieth century—James T. Farrell, F. Scott Fitzgerald, and John O'Hara—only Farrell has made any detailed attempt to recreate and analyze the world of the Irish Catholic of the working and lower middle classes.[1] Fitzgerald and O'Hara, though baptized Catholics, concerned themselves essentially with the middle or upper class Wasp society, leaving Farrell alone in his efforts to describe the plight of the urban Irish Americans and their difficulties in coping with their own conservative, often repressive, culture and the alien Anglo-American value system.

A child of working-class Irish-American parents, but reared from an early age in his Irish maternal grandparents' lower middle-class home, Farrell saw at first hand the problems which the urban Irish of both classes had in coping with life in America in the first third of this century.[2] The big city, Chicago, was his world and that of his people; he chose to make it the early major focus of a lifetime work in fiction, with his Studs Lonigan trilogy and his Danny O'Neill pentalogy.[3]

These works center themselves about the formation of two young men of urban Irish Catholic stock, subject to apparently similar environmental forces—yet one, Studs, is dead at the age of twenty-nine, his life a failure; the other, Danny, only a few years younger, embarks on a writing career; he is filled with hope, vitality and courage. To understand the different fates of the two youths, we must perceive the worlds from which they emerged.

The lot of the Irish Catholic in urban America from 1900-1930 was not an easy one. Though the vicious nativist anti-Catholic violence of the late nineteenth century had ended, the rise of the Irish from the hard-laboring element was still a slow one; only a minority of them were able to move into the middle class.[4] Studs Lonigan's father—a self-made painting contractor—and Danny's Uncle Al, a successful traveling shoe salesman, are typical of this minority. However, old Lonigan came up from a dismally poor Irish home, and Jim O'Neill, Danny's father, dies a pauper's death, trying to raise a large family on a small teamster's income.

The real bleakness of the boyhood world of Studs and Danny, though, is not financial; Farrell, insisting that *Studs Lonigan* must not be judged as a typical slum novel of the thirties, maintained that Studs should be considered an ordinary American city boy from a relatively prosperous environment, who meets disaster for reasons that are more social than economic.

> Studs Lonigan was conceived as a normal American boy of Irish-Catholic extraction. The social milieu in which he lived and was educated was one of spiritual poverty. It was not, contrary to some misconceptions, a slum neighborhood. Had I written *Studs Lonigan* as a story of the slums, it would then have been easy for the reader falsely to place the motivation and causation of the story directly in immediate economic roots. Such a placing of motivation would have obscured one of the most important meanings I wanted to inculcate into my story: my desire to reveal the concrete effects of spiritual poverty. It is readily known that poverty and slums cause spiritual poverty in many lives. One of the most important meanings I perceived in this story was that here was a neighborhood several steps removed from the slums and dire economic want, and here, too, was manifested a pervasive spiritual poverty.[5]

This "spiritual poverty" infiltrates both the worlds of Studs and Danny; the former succumbs to it, the latter overcomes it. Farrell sees such poverty as the failure of four urban forces—the home, church, school, and playground—to bring about the growth of the young to their full intellectual, moral, and physical potential. In Studs' case, in particular, they are not helping to mold him

> ... into the kind of person which society desires him to become. There is, in consequence, a conflict between ideas and reality, and this conflict is translated, as it were, into the concrete and immediate thoughts, dreams of the boy, Studs Lonigan. Out of this conflict, out of the failure of these institutions, we can see how this American is being made, how this destiny is unfolding.[6]

Of the four institutions, it is this paper's contention that the urban Catholic Church—conservative, anti-intellectual, provincial, and authoritative—is the major limitation of Studs' growth, and the central block to Danny's freedom. It unites school, pulpit, and home in a rigid system of indoctrination whose virtues—and there are some—are lost in terms of Studs' behavior, but whose weaknesses are made glaringly visible in the novels.

The elementary parochial school, the initial formal academic ground for both Studs and Danny (and the only one for young Lonigan), is a terrible place. Even though most of Farrell's descriptions of parochial classes are given through the eyes of the youths involved, the system emerges nonetheless as one of an outdated, ineffective, provincial, even cruel operation. Heavy stress is placed on pointless memorization of facts, and subject matter is frequently enforced by periodic beatings by the nuns. The curriculum is unimaginative and centers on dogmatic religion. Boys are not permitted to associate with girls during school, and are encouraged to avoid them after class. The classrooms are dirty, dimly lit, and often cold—small wonder that Studs, at the end of his parochial education, refers to the school as a "jailhouse."

This jailhouse analogy captures completely the effect that Catholicism has had on Studs, though, sadly, he never realizes this. His religion, his education, have made him a prisoner—intellectually and emotionally—through a rigid system of indoctrination from which he has neither the wit nor desire to escape. His life has been lived within a parish structure, his education administered by hostile nuns such as the sadistic Sister "Battling" Bertha, and, worst of all, by his pastor, Father Gilhooley, revered by the adults who surround Studs but, in reality, an arrogant, narrow-minded fool. Andrew Greeley, the Chicago priest-sociologist, notes the power of such a figure over his ill-educated flock:

The parish priest, of course, determined how many collections there were to be on a Sunday, which textbooks were to be used in the school, what time the masses were to be said, when the young people could use the gymnasium, and how the parish books were to be kept.[7]

Father Gilhooley is not averse to using this power— he cruelly casts away from his door a young couple who wish their mixed marriage blessed;[8] he is harsh and unbending with his sensitive and more liberal young curate; he plays upon his superstitious flock with vivid verbal dramatizations of the path of Satan ("Old Nick") in search of the soul of each member of his parish. Studs and his gang jeer at him behind his back, but he has managed to bathe their unconscious in images of death and eternal damnation which haunt Studs up to his last breath.

Gilhooley pays lip service, on graduation day, to the glories of education, but it is only Catholic education to which he refers (and even then, only to elementary and high school)—to risk attendance at a public school would be to risk eternal damnation. It is evident early in the trilogy, however, that Studs' experiences at St. Patrick's have ended any desire for further formal education. He attends Catholic high school briefly and reluctantly. After a long period of absences, he drops out completely and works full time under his father in the painting business.

Gilhooley's pulpit preaching stresses the concept of personal sin (particularly sexual offenses), but it conveniently ignores the common social wrongs within the Irish Catholic community, particularly political graft. Chicago, as most major urban cities with Irish political machines, was rife with financial corruption which, if not condoned by the Church, was never formally condemned. Studs' father accepts the political payoff for city paint jobs as a natural occurrence and corrupt ward politicians such as Studs' friend Red Kelly never let their church duties interfere with their flagrant dishonesty. Both old Lonigan and Kelly are vehement about one recent political event, however—that Catholic Al Smith was defeated by Herbert Hoover in the 1928 Presidential election solely because of the New Yorker's Catholicism.

Father Gilhooley's rhetoric, unctuous and torrid by turn, is not without a certain inflated eloquence. It is complemented by that of another major clerical figure in the trilogy—Father Shannon, a retreat master, who harangues Studs, by then a hard-drinking, whoring young adult, at a parish mission. Shannon's sermons are a terrifying combination of Gilhooley's sulphurous emotionalism, and his own brand of Jansenism and anti-intellectualism. His talks combine a violent attack on contemporary secular sexual mores, with a shockingly ignorant diatribe on secular colleges, on Sinclair Lewis, H. L. Mencken, and H. G. Wells. (He encourages his audience to read G. K. Chesterton, the conservative English Catholic essayist, and in his eyes, "The foremost living writer of this century.") He even advocates physical assault on any secular university student who dares to seek favor with Catholic girls.

But the most sinister influence of all the church figures in the trilogy is the "radio priest," Father Moylan, a figure strikingly similar to the Rev. Charles E. Coughlin, the popular right-wing radio figure of the 1930's.[9] Moylan's radio talks are presented in terms of their effect on Studs and his family, who find their political, religious, and ethnic intolerance fortified by his weekly national broadcasts. Like him, they believe that President Hoover is a tool of the Jewish international bankers, that Hoover personally started the depression, that Communists should be dealt with violently, and that "law and order" is the solution to all of America's problems. The Lonigans, unthinking and meagerly educated, are easy prey for Moylan's demagoguery. They buy his anti-Semitic paper *Christian Justice*, and believe him to be the one honest force for good in America.[10]

Another of Studs' adult connections with the Church is his membership in the Order of Christopher—an all-male Catholic secret society—which provides a pseudo-Masonic ritual air of brotherhood, along with cheap life insurance and an organized sports program. However, the initiation rite, a crude combination of violence and vague Christian symbolism, is a travesty, and leaves Studs with only a superficial sense of belonging. The Christian virtues of charity, patience, devotion and courage, which the rite purportedly illustrates, have no visible moral effect on him. The Order of Christopher is only externally Christian—it does not concern itself with functional moral effects.

The same is true of the Lonigan family life. Studs, his parents, his younger brother, and his sisters have mastered all the externals of Catholic devotion—they attend Mass on Sunday, receive the Sacraments regularly, and contribute to the parish finances; they are generally unquestioning and blindly responsive to clerical authority. They are also racist, religiously bigoted and violent. Studs and his gang delight in beating up blacks, and a sandlot football game between Studs' team and a Jewish eleven turns into a slugging, gouging anti-Semitic pogrom.

Worst of all, as Edgar Branch points out, traits are passed on from each generation—especially the vicious religious, ethnic, and political prejudices.[11] Paddy Lonigan hates the black man and the Jew, both of whom he blames for the Depression—so does Studs. To both men, Socialists are "god-damned Reds," while all priests are intelligent, clean-living paragons of virtue. The Church does nothing to discourage such opinions—if anything, the Reverends Gilhooley, Shannon, and Moylan actively promote them.

The most dramatic example of hypocritical religious display is given, at the trilogy's conclusion, to the women in the Lonigan family—Studs' snobbish sisters, Fran and Loretta, and, worst of all, his mother Mary. Mrs. Lonigan is a whining Irish matriarch whose stock in trade is a desire for bourgeois respectability. Greeley specifically identifies her as a sociological type which he labels "The Respectable Woman."

> Just as the mother of Studs Lonigan could cheerfully contemplate the abortion of Studs' unborn child and at the same time claim to be a paragon of respectability, so her real-life counterpart is more concerned about the appearances of righteousness than about righteousness itself.[12]

When Mrs. Lonigan berates Catherine Banahan, the pregnant sweetheart of the dying Studs, as a fallen woman, her cant is almost too much to bear.

The most forceful, vivid contribution which Catholicism makes to Studs is a terrible fear of death and damnation, which increases as his physical condition deteriorates. Satan and eternal punishment are much more vivid to him than are Christ and eternal salvation, and Studs' pre-confession examination of conscience is always torturous. His final dream in delirium is one in which all the authority symbols of his youth—Sister Bertha, Father Gilhooley, Father Shannon—chase him to damn him forever for his sins of the flesh, the only sins which Studs ever heard really condemned and, consequently, the only ones which ever actually frightened him. He dies ever fearful of hell, although, ironically, the Church's last rites theoretically manage to shove him into heaven. However, as Farrell indicates in his short story "Studs" (out of which the trilogy grew), Studs will probably be bored by eternity where there will be no gangs, poolrooms, brothels, speakeasies or gambling places.[13]

If the negative elements of urban Catholicism are strong enough to help destroy Studs Lonigan, it is certainly reasonable to ask why they do not also bring the same fate, or one approximately like it, to Danny O'Neill, the hero of the next major series of novels written after the Lonigan books. To respond to such a question one must analyze the nature of the role of the Church in the life of Danny, and his reaction to the same.

The fourfold "spiritual poverty" concept is structurally abandoned by Farrell in the O'Neill novels which concentrate on the economic and cultural contrasts which form the life and value system of a future artist—Danny O'Neill. Danny emerges from two different domestic worlds—the poverty of his teamster father's home, and the relative affluence of that of his mother's people—the O'Flahertys. "Spiritual poverty" is replaced by material poverty in the world of Jim O'Neill and his wife.

> What is the meaning of poverty, not expressed in generalizations, but concretely in thoughts, attitudes, in total orientation toward the world, in speech, habits, actions and—let us not forget—health? How do these contrast with a set

of conditions where poverty does not exist? This is a general statement of one of the differences between Danny and his brothers and sisters. And it should serve as an indication of what I mean when I state that the novels are built upon the bases of class controls.[14]

Still, in the world of the O'Neill and O'Flaherty families the Catholic Church plays a very real part. Danny's parents, his brothers and sisters, grandparents, uncles and aunts (his Theosophist Uncle Ned being an exception) are all practicing Catholics; he receives essentially the same parochial elementary education as Studs, and supplements it with a rigid academic curriculum at a Catholic high school. Yet his life is a steady path upward, rather than a decline. Why?

Part of the reason comes from his move as a very young child into the O'Flaherty household, a very different place from the brutally impoverished working-class home of his birth. Besides the luxuries of steam heat, indoor plumbing, nutritious food, and warm clothing, Danny is given genuine, individualized love and attention by his grandmother, aunts Peg and Louise, and especially by his Uncle Al, who treats him like a son.

Removed from his parents' home, Danny sees them and his brothers and sisters only occasionally. His father, a courageous but impoverished working man, dies of a stroke when Danny is in high school, and is buried in a pauper's grave. His mother, Lizz O'Neill, is similar to Mary Lonigan, though there is a tenderness about her which is missing in Studs' mother. She is representative of the emotional, superstitious, over-devout Irish-American women, who spend in church the time which should be used in caring for their home and family; in addition, she throws a disproportionately large amount of her husband's wages into the collection basket. (Greeley characterizes the type as "The Pious Woman.")[15] Prejudiced, vulgar, slovenly, and obese, Lizz mingles pious invocations with crude blasphemies and profanities. She is a born gossip and a virtual failure as a wife and mother—yet her husband loves her, and the children take care of her. The mature Danny can only pity her.

As opposed to the home of the Lonigans, there is a certain cultural air in the O'Flaherty household. Uncle Al, a bromidic traveling salesman, is nonetheless a heavy, if indiscriminate, reader, so that books are at least present in the house. In addition, Danny is able to participate in structured sports in his leisure time. Unlike Studs, he likes school, even though he is unaware of the essential bleakness of the Catholic system of instruction; most of all, he has a healthy sense of introspection, a natural habit of continually questioning, of examining past and present values, discarding some, keeping the rest, adding new ones. One of the elements which he will rationally examine, then discard, precisely because it inhibits his personal and social growth, is the Catholic Church.

Farrell goes into considerable detail to describe the influence of the Church on young Danny. He is an introspective, scrupulous child, afraid of making bad confessions, and, like Studs, terrified of hell. His parochial grammar school training is strongly dogmatic and formal; the nuns appoint themselves guardians of the minds and sexual mores of the students; the better pupils, such as Danny, are asked to inform on offenders against purity. But at least one nun, Sister Magdalen, shows a personal interest in Danny, though she does all within her power to coerce him into the seminary at the age of fourteen. (Fortunately, his father and Uncle Al realize the folly of such a decision and discourage it from the very beginning.)

Danny's secondary school experiences at St. Stanislaus High are not much better. The Carmelite priests are authoritarian, given to capricious punishments, both physical and written. The curriculum is narrow and inflexible with a heavy emphasis on religion and memorization, and student discussion is seldom encouraged, especially during religion lectures which are long on Thomistic apologetics. When the thoughtful Danny attempts to introduce the problem of evil into Father Powers' lecture on the creation of the world, he is curtly silenced:

> That's not a good question. We are not able to conceive either the full character of God's love or the extent and nature of His purpose.[16]

The retreat sermon given during the last year of Danny's schooling is rigidly orthodox, but reasonably literate; it is mercifully lacking in the fiery anti-intellectualism and bigotry of that rendered by the mission priest in *Studs Lonigan*. Both sermons are heavy on the subject of sexual offenses, but their effects are different. Studs concludes the mission with a superficial confession followed by a trip to a brothel; Danny makes an intense general confession, resulting in an exalting sense of spiritual cleanliness such as that experienced by Stephen Dedalus at the close of the Jesuit retreat in Joyce's *A Portrait of the Artist*.

Farrell's own high school experience at Chicago's St. Cyril's High School was not much different, though he does have kind words for one of the teachers, Father Dolan, who encouraged his students to write realistically. However, he still regrets the severe authoritarianism which characterized the Church schools in his time.[17]

When Danny graduates from high school, his career is at a standstill. He has been able to avoid the street corner gang world, for he has been busy with his studies, with organized school sports, and with part-time jobs as a shoe store clerk, and an assistant in the call department of a freight office. Unfortunately, a football injury has ended hopes of a university education at Notre Dame—he is compelled to work full time at the freight office, while attending part-time classes at St. Vincent, a Catholic college whose curriculum, on its own level, is just as provincial as that of St. Stanislaus. Although he is "introduced" to Arnold, Newman, and Huxley, he is discouraged by the lack of intelligent classroom discussion, and is bored by the frivolity of his fellow students and the dullness of his teachers.

The first major step that Danny takes in his path towards intellectual liberation is his decision to enroll at the University of Chicago—the "godless, atheistic A.P.A." institution so vilified by Fathers Gilhooley and Shannon. To do so, he is forced to pump gas by night for Upton Oil and Refining Company, but this hard laboring work does not interfere with his scholastic progress.

At the University, without the dogmatism and the unbending authoritarianism of Catholic schools, Danny swiftly grows intellectually, as he becomes fascinated by his first encounter with the spirit of free inquiry. Courses in medieval history and political science broaden his historical perspective, while readings in the English and American poets and novelists such as Joyce, Dreiser, Lewis, Anderson, and Hemingway—all forbidden in the Catholic schools—give him a desire to write, along with a deep feeling for suffering humanity.

But, as Danny's intellectual horizons expand, his belief in dogmatic Catholicism weakens. He can no longer accept the cut and dried apologetics of Aquinas; he questions the reasoning of Augustine on free will— finally, he doubts even the existence of God. When he attempts to see the missionary Father Shannon during this crisis of faith, the priest curtly dismisses him. He eventually becomes convinced that Catholicism is a militant force of dishonesty, bent on spreading ignorance and superstition. He becomes an atheist, and this spiritual decision results in a great sense of relieved exhilaration and freedom:

> Atheism created a feeling of springtime within himself. It was a new beginning. How weak his faith had really been all these years! How powerless had been the influence of the nuns who had taught him in grammar school, the priests who had been his high school teachers! How painless it was to lose your faith![18]

Danny's rejection of Catholicism alienates him further from his family and from his old friends. It also moves him further away from his Catholic friends at the University; Studs Lonigan and the poolroom gang scoff knowingly at him as a crazy atheist who read too many books for his own good. He knows his departure from the church has hurt his grandmother and Uncle Al, but feels that he must keep his intellectual integrity. He cannot turn back.

There is hope for Danny at the pentalogy's end, because he has been able to reject the very sources of spiritual poverty which have ruined Studs. He has gradually separated himself from his family; avoided the poolroom and the street corner; learned to keep away from drink and whores (after bad experiences with both—delirium tremens and a brief bout with venereal disease); has used sports to develop his reflexes and his body. He has pursued a path of academic growth, and has chosen a profession which will enable him to harness his powers of creativity and purge himself, in his art, of the dark moments of his past. Above all, he has recognized the damage that provincial urban Catholicism has done to his people and, particularly, to himself in its efforts to limit the full growth of a human being—in this case, a potential artist.

Farrell climaxes Danny's growth with the latter's decision to become a writer. He has written of the world of the city, exactly as he has seen it, and his college English instructors have encouraged him to write more. He has done campus reporting for a Chicago newspaper, but finds this type of journalism superficial and trivial. It is only in fiction that he can express his insights into the human scene. Consequently, he makes his final physical break with the Chicago Irish and runs away to New York to become a writer.

Yet he has not really left his family. Far from it, for he conceives of himself as a crusader for a better world—the world which was denied his people because of birth and environment. Though he leaves his family, he becomes closer to them through his art. As Farrell observes, Danny

> ... does not completely destroy his sense of identification with his own people. He feels that he is going to fight not only war but their war. His conception of war, of writing, is a militant one.[19]

Danny's literary career, as Farrell's, will thus have a social purpose.[20] The young writer has overcome the negative forces in his past, and is ready to do battle for the future in an effort to make meaningful the world of the Irish Americans. Many of these may still be being crippled by the institutions such as those which destroyed Studs Lonigan, about whose tragedy Farrell has written

> My attitude ... toward my character here is essentially a simple one. "There but for the grace of God go I." There but for the grace of God go—many others.[21]

Montgomery County Community College

NOTES

[1] William V. Shannon, *The American Irish* (New York: Macmillan, 1963), p. 249. This book is the best written, most objective study of the hardships of the American Irish; valuable sociologically (and divertingly written) is Andrew Greeley's *That Most Distressful Nation* (Chicago: Quadrangle Books, 1972). Other works on the same topic include Oscar Handlin, *The Uprooted* (Boston: Little, Brown, 1951); Carl Wittke, *The Irish in America* (New York: Russell and Russell, 1951); George W. Potter, *To the Golden Door* (Boston: Little, Brown, 1960), and Nathan Glazer and

Daniel Patrick Moynihan, *Beyond the Melting Pot* (Cambridge, Mass.: Harvard–MIT Press, 1963).

[2] Edgar M. Branch, "Of Plebian Origin," in *James T. Farrell* (New York: Twayne Publishers Inc., 1971), pp. 15-35. This chapter contains the most recent and most accurate biographical details of Farrell's life. (Farrell is currently at work on a lengthy autobiography.)

[3] *Studs Lonigan* is the title generally used for the trilogy published initially as three separate volumes: *Young Lonigan* (1932), *The Young Manhood of Studs Lonigan* (1934) and *Judgement Day* (1935). The O'Neill pentalogy consists of five novels: *A World I Never Made* (1936), *No Star Is Lost* (1938), *Father and Son* (1940), *My Days of Anger* (1943), and *The Face of Time* (1953). The last of these novels deals with the pre-school years of Danny; *My Days of Anger* is really the most recent in terms of narrative chronology–it concludes with Danny in his twenties.

[4] Shannon, pp. 1-95. In this section, the author vividly recounts the social and economic difficulties of the Irish in nineteenth- and early twentieth-century America.

[5] James T. Farrell, "How Studs Lonigan Was Written," in *The League of Frightened Philistines* (New York: Vanguard Press, 1945), pp. 86-87.

[6] James T. Farrell, "Introduction," *Young Lonigan* (Cleveland and New York: World Publishing Co., 1943), pp. x-xi.

[7] Andrew M. Greeley, *That Most Distressful Nation* (Chicago: Quadrangle Books, 1972), p. 87.

[8] James T. Farrell, "Reverend Father Gilhooley," in *The Short Stories of James T. Farrell* (Garden City: Sun Dial Press, 1945), pp. 239-53. The mixed marriage motif is central to the story, which also deals with the arrogance, vanity, and ignorance of the pastor. Ironically, his new church, a monument to these vices, is completed just as the parish undergoes a racial change.

[9] Father Moylan's fascism is treated, in more detail, in Farrell's novelette, *Tommy Gallagher's Crusade* (New York: Vanguard Press, 1939). Father Coughlin's career is objectively delineated in Shannon, pp. 295-326.

[10] Ibid.

[11] Edgar M. Branch, "Destiny, Culture and Technique: *Studs Lonigan*" *The University of Kansas City Review*, 29 (December 1962), 105.

[12] Greeley, p. 112. A Catholic critic, he nonetheless is reasonably fair to Farrell, who received less charitable treatment from others of the same faith, e.g., Frank O'Malley, "James T. Farrell: Two Twilight Images," in *Fifty Years of the American Novel*, ed. Harold C. Gardiner, S.J. (New York: Scribner's, 1952), pp. 237-56.

[13] James T. Farrell, "Studs," in *The Short Stories of James T. Farrell*, p. 354.

[14] James T. Farrell, "An Introduction to Two Novels," *The University of Kansas City Review*, 13 (Spring 1947), 223.

[15] Greeley, pp. 110-11.

[16] James T. Farrell, *Father and Son* (Cleveland and New York: The World Publishing Co., 1947), p. 500.

[17] James T. Farrell, "My Beginnings as a Writer," in *Reflections at Fifty* (London: Neville Spearman, 1956), p. 163. In later years Farrell mellowed somewhat in his attitude towards parochial school education, conceding that it gave him a sense of order, of truth, and of self-evaluation. (cf. Branch, *James T. Farrell*, note 2, p. 172.)

[18] James T. Farrell, *My Days of Anger* (New York: Vanguard Press, 1943), p. 222.

[19] James T. Farrell, "Introduction," *My Days of Anger* (Cleveland: The World Publishing Co., 1947), p. xi.

254

[20]James T. Farrell, *A Note on Literary Criticism* (New York: Vanguard Press, 1936), p. 11. Here Farrell states his theory of literature—it is at once "a branch of fine arts and an instrument of social influence."

[21]"How Studs Lonigan Was Written," in *The League of Frightened Philistines*, p. 89.

The Italian Americans: Their Contribution in the Field of Literature*

Aldo Finco

ABSTRACT

For three centuries after Columbus, the New World remained a "terra incognita" to Italians. Except for a few skilled Venetians and Florentines like Mazzei, Bellini, and Da Ponte, there were few Italians in America. In 1870 the number of Italians, most of them artisans from northern and central Italy, was only about three thousand. Toward the end of the nineteenth century, the character of Italian immigration to the United States changed. The time of mass immigration had begun. By 1900, over four million people from Italy had reached the shores of America. They were mainly peasants whose contribution to the new land was chiefly their physical labor. Their ambition was to feed their families and to give their children a better education than they themselves had received. Being without leisure time, guidance, or interest, the Italian Americans were not, for some time to come, aware of their great heritage. Since they were hindered by language and social barriers, their contribution in literature remained superficial and cursory. Only during the last fifty years has the contribution of the Italian Americans in the field of letters become evident and outstanding. Italian-American writers (Pellegrini, Ventura, Forgione, Di Donato, and others) use, as a literary subject, "the alien" as an archetype for the isolated man. In an established society this archetype has the faith to overcome obstacles and to fulfill his destiny. In a subsequent period (Mirabelli, Pollini, Arleo, Puzo, and others), the fictional narration is based mostly on themes stressing the alien's distinctive heritage in the interaction of the two cultures. The "alien" then becomes a member of the national group, a part of the American society and nation. (AF)

Dante, in the xxvi canto of the *Inferno*, presents a great multitude of sinners whose souls are completely enveloped in tongues of fire which remove them from sight, just as in life their ardent speech artfully hid their

*To set the tone for my essay I would like to point out that I also came to this great land as an Italian immigrant, and my American experience may coincide with that of some of the characters I will discuss.

thoughts. One of these flames has two points, and Virgil explains to Dante that the souls of Diomedes and Ulysses are joined in punishment just as their minds on earth were together in fraudulent action. At Dante's request Ulysses related where and how he died. Already old but yielding once more to his burning desire to explore the world, he decides to sail toward the unknown.

> Nè dolcezza di figlio, nè la pietà
> Del vecchio padre, nè il debito amore,
> Lo qual dovea Penelopè far lieta,
>
> Vincer poter dentro da me l'ardore
> Ch'i' ebbi a divenir del mondo esperto
> E de li vizi umani e del valore.

(xxvi. 94-99)

He set out with a few friends on a last voyage of discovery. And they sailed over the entire Mediterranean until they reached the Pillars of Hercules:

> Io e' compagni eravam vecchi e tardi
> Quando venimmo a quella foce stretta
> Dov' Ercule segnò li suoi riguardi
>
> Acciò che l'uom più oltre non si metta.

(xxvi. 106-09)

Ulysses urged his companions to move beyond the Pillars, into the mysterious ocean "Diretro al sol, del mondo sanza gente" because men were not made to live like beasts but to go in pursuit of virtue and knowledge. They made wings of their oars for their foolish flight. For five months they travelled, always heading southward, until they came in sight of a high mountain. Their joy, at sighting land, was short-lived, since a sudden whirlwind arose and caused the small ship to sink:

> Noi ci allegrammo, e tosto tornò in pianto;
> Chè de la nova terra un turbo nacque,
> E percosse del legno il primo canto.
>
> Tre volte il fè girar con tutte l'acque,
> A la quarta levar la poppa in suso,
> E la prora ire in giù, com'Altrui piacque,
>
> Infin che'l mar fu sopra noi richiuso.

(xxvi. 136-42)

The Dantesque narration of Ulysses' last and desperate voyage contains a solitary and melancholic grandiosity. From the very beginning of the trip one has the presentiment of the tragic end. Yet the entire tale assumes a note of hope, of light and of salvation. To the immense waters, which allegorically represent the unknown, the Poet opposes a high mountain, a source of happiness. According to Dante's geography, it is the mountain of Purgatory, emerging from the sea at the antipodes of Jerusalem. He says:

> Noi divenimmo intanto a piè del monte.
> Quivi trovammo la roccia sì erta
> Che 'ndarno vi sarien le gambe pronte.

> (*Purg.* iii. 46-48)

Dante, however, never could have thought that, following the direction taken by Ulysses, he would perhaps have landed on the shores of the New World. Nor could he have guessed that, after many centuries, his name, his *Commedia*, and his beautiful tongue, the language of Florence, "là dove il sì suona," would have appeared in a new land, a land of new vitality and greatness. Dante, the prototype of the uprooted; Dante, the immigrant and the exile.

> Tu lascerai ogni cosa diletta
> Più caramente; e questo è quello strale
> Che l'arco de lo esilio pria saetta.

> Tu proverai sì come sa di sale
> Lo pane altrui, e come è duro calle
> Lo scendere e 'l salir per l'altrui scale.

> (*Par.* xvii. 55-60)

Dante finally reached America, not through the Pillars of Hercules, but by way of England where the Italian language and literature were widespread during the Renaissance. The *Divine Comedy* was partially translated into English in 1782 by Charles Rogers, an art collector and connoisseur. His version, however, contains many distortions, and, at times, even some ridiculous variations without poetic mood. But Rogers' efforts did not go beyond the last canto of the *Inferno*.

> He [Rogers] gave us no information as to what text he used, and his methods are so slapdash that it is often difficult to say whether he understood the original or not.[1]

Studies on Dante and on Italian literature continued in England throughout the eighteenth century, and by way of the English language the Florentine Poet came into the New World. In this new form he crossed the ocean and met his American readers. But it certainly would be difficult to try to establish when and how Dante came to these shores. We are deeply indebted to Joseph G. Fucilla of Northwestern University who discovered an extremely important document. In a very old *New York Almanack for 1697* a certain John Clapp, merchant, planter and perhaps a navigator, speaks of a lunar eclipse of a supernatural force. To succeed in convincing his readers that the eclipse in question was really supernatural he invokes the authority of great people, and, above all, of Dante. He states:

It is said by many divine Authors, that the Eclipse which happened at the Death of our dearest Lord and Saviour, was altogether Supernatural and Miraculous, caused by that same divine *power* and said, *Let this and that thing be done, and it was so*; for it was then the time when the Moon was near her full, and almost opposite to the Sun: so that no Natural Cause could co-operate at that Juncture, as the learned *Italian*, Dante hath it, *A cui Natura non Scaldo, ferro mai ne battel' ancude*, for which Nature did never heat the Iron nor beat the Anvil . . . .[2]

This short translation and its original taken from *Paradiso*, xxiv., 101-02 are like precious gems on two counts—first as the earliest piece of translation now known in America quoted from the *Divine Comedy*, and second as possibly the earliest appearance in this land of words printed in Italian. Another fragment of a translation of the *Divine Comedy* printed in America—also found by Fucilla—appeared in the *New York Magazine*, in the year 1791. It is a thirty-four line translation from the Conte Ugolino episode. The author was, in all probability, a certain William Dunlap.[3]

Italian studies, especially at the beginning of the nineteenth century, assumed a new and more important shape. The *Divine Comedy* became quickly very familiar among the literary circles of Boston where the ground was less hostile to foreign influence. William Ellery Channing, in various articles on national literature, urges his readers to learn to appreciate works of the past. He says:

Let us not be misunderstood. We have no desire to rear in our country a race of pedants, but we would have men explore antiquity . . . to learn its spirit as to accumulate on the present age the influences of whatever was great and wise in former times. . . . We feel our debt to be immense to the glorious company of pure and wise minds which in foreign lands have bequeathed us their choicest thoughts and holiest feelings.[4]

Jared Sparks, in the *North American Review* of March 1817, writes:

It is generally allowed . . . that the Italian language is vastly better adapted to every species of composition than the French; that it has more dignity and strength, a greater facility of expression, and infinitely more sweetness and harmony.[5]

John Chipman Gray, in a long article which appeared in the *North American Review* in 1819, outlines the life of Dante and summarizes the *Divine Comedy* with an account of the vast philosophical, theological and scientific background of Dante's times. He makes a comparison between Milton and the Florentine Poet, and finally insists upon saying that great joy and pleasure are found in the reading of Dante. This observation reminds us of what, years later, T. S. Eliot wrote:

I have found no other poet than Dante to whom I could apply continually, for many purposes, and with much profit, during a familiarity of twenty years. . . . The enjoyment of the *Divine Comedy* is a continuous process.[6]

Thomas William Parson translated in 1843 the first ten cantos of the *Inferno*. Although not too faithful to the original, Parson's work was generally well accepted by the Bostonian circles, which included Ralph W. Emerson, Charles Eliot Norton, and Henry Wadsworth Longfellow. Norton, voicing the opinion of the Boston Danteans, summarized their feeling about Parson's version in the following manner:

> The *Divine Comedy* rendered in this manner [in Parson's translation], remains at least a poem; but its tone is not that of Dante's poem; its merits are its own.[7]

Longfellow, in the *Tales of a Wayside Inn: Prelude*—describes Parson with these words:

> A poet, too, was there, whose verse
> Was tender, musical, and terse;
> The inspiration, the delight,
> The gleam, the glory, the swift flight
> Of thoughts so sudden, that they seem
> The revelation of a dream.[8]

Toward the end of 1843, during his professorship of Modern Languages at Harvard University, Henry Wadsworth Longfellow began the translation of the *Divine Comedy* which was completed in 1865, the sixth centennial of the birth of Dante. Longfellow's version reflects Dante's message, for it is strictly a literal translation, not a comment. Longfellow only translates, he makes no flowery illustrations. His work on Dante was certainly very influential, and played a large role in laying the foundation for future American achievement in the field. Professor Angelina La Piana, in her volume *Dante's American Pilgrimage* in which she discusses the history of the growth of Italian literature in America, writes:

> The influence of Longfellow's version of the *Divine Comedy* upon Dante's fortunes in America cannot be overestimated. The fact that the most famous and most popular of all the American poets of the time turned his talents to making a translation of the *Divine Comedy* was a potent factor in inducing American readers to strike up an acquaintance with the great poem.[9]

Another remarkable person was, perhaps, the first in America to call attention to the beauties of Italian language and literature, and to introduce the Florentine poet to an American public. Lorenzo Da Ponte, the famous librettist of Mozart's *Le nozze di Figaro*, *Don Giovanni* and *Così fan tutte*, after a long and interesting vagabondage throughout Europe as a priest, as a poet, as a libertine and a dramatist, arrived in New York City early in 1807. Professor Arthur Livingston, in his first edition of the translation of Da Ponte's *Memoirs*, with reference to the beginning of Da Ponte's teaching career in New York, says:

> There is no doubt at all that this was an important moment for the American mind. Da Ponte made Europe, poetry, classical lore, a creative classical educa-

tion, live for many important Americans as no one, I venture, had done before. And his classical scholarship, his competence as a creative Latinist, dazzled quite as much as his fame as an Italian poet. . . . And it was not so much Da Ponte, as Da Ponte and his setting–the cultural atmosphere of his home that survived in his children and thereafter. A flare of real genius as a teacher Da Ponte had shown at Portogruaro and Treviso. Perhaps during this year, 1808, and again in the period of 1820 to 1826, Da Ponte was finding his real self. In my estimation it is a greater moment than his casual attachment to Mozart's fame in his *Don Giovanni*.[10]

Almost without help, money, friends and doubtful of success, Da Ponte, with a family to support, stopped along the Hudson and meditated about his future in America:

I began to examine whether I could somehow make a living along the lines of Italian or Latin letters. In a few days I learned that as far as the Italian language and literature were concerned, they were about as well known in this city as Turkish or Chinese. As for Latin I found that it was cultivated generally and that "gentlemen in America thought they knew enough not to need the instruction of an Italian Latinist."[11]

However, toward the beginning of December 1807, Da Ponte initiated his first lessons of Italian with only twelve cultivated youths and maidens in New York, under the most happy auspices and in the house of a very prominent and good friend, Clement Clark Moore, a great scholar in the field of Oriental and Classical literatures, and known to all children for his poem "Twas the night before Christmas."[12] The example of such an illustrious host for Da Ponte could not but cause the most excellent impression upon the rest of the citizens. In fact, in less than a month Da Ponte succeeded in getting an enrollment of almost thirty young people to teach. The interest with which his lessons were listened to, the faithfulness with which they were attended, and the extraordinary favor accorded both to him and to the tongue of his country in a brief time created such an enthusiasm among all his students that, later, he could hardly provide enough room and time for them.

At that time, there were not in New York any booksellers who had Italian volumes on their shelves.

In almost every city one finds the wines and the grapes of Sicily, the oil, the olives, and the silk of Florence, the marble of Carrara, the gold chains of Venice, the cheese of Parma, the straw hats of Leghorn, the ropes of Rome and Padua, the *rosolio* of Trieste, the sausages of Bologna, and even the *maccheroni* of Naples and the plaster figurettes of Lucca. Yet, to the shame of our country, there is not, in the whole America, a bookstore kept by an Italian! All the books in this city, aside from the volumes I introduced myself, have either been brought casually by travelers, or been sold at auction with other books on the death of some foreign inhabitant.[13]

Fully aware of this deficiency, and the extreme need for Italian books, both elementary as well as classical works, Da Ponte, through the assistance of many friends and booksellers throughout Europe, succeeded in establishing a very adequate collection of volumes which he listed in his newly published *Catalogo Ragionato* and could be found in his own bookstore he opened. He says:

> In it . . . I had deposited eight hundred volumes of our classics, costing, bound, not more than twelve hundred dollars, and which were soon to increase in number through the gifts promised me—volumes which each subscriber with his heirs would have the right to read for years and centuries for the very moderate price of five dollars. Yet, who would believe it? Neither through my persuasion, nor through my prayers, and in this rich, cultivated and thickly populated city of New York, where I had fifteen hundred pupils and even more friends, have I been able, in three years of effort, to obtain more than seventy persons willing to disburse five or ten dollars for a foundation so useful.[14]

Although the city of New York, a city of an outstanding commercial and cultural prestige, failed to enrich herself with Italian treasures that she considered practically useless and of superfluous expense, Lorenzo Da Ponte, perhaps through the high and strong recommendations of Clement C. Moore, at that time trustee of Columbia College, had been offered the chair of Italian language and literature at that college. From the minutes of the Standing Board at Columbia one reads:

> May 2nd, 1825. A letter from Mr. Da Ponte was received, asking permission to instruct the alumni of the College in the Italian language and to make use of some part of the building for that purpose. September 6th, 1825. *Resolved*, That a Professorship of Italian Literature be established in this College, but that the Professor be not considered one of the Board of the College, nor subject to the provisions of the statutes.
>
> *Resolved*, That Signore Da Ponte be and is hereby appointed to the said professorship, and that he be allowed to receive from the students who shall attend his lectures a reasonable compensation; but that no salary be allowed him from the College.[15]

Unfortunately, to his deepest disappointment and in spite of all his efforts (he had offered several hundred volumes of Italian works to Columbia College Library upon condition of having a certain number of students), Lorenzo Da Ponte had to renounce the decorative title of professor at the College, together with all hope he had of seeing his most important plan succeed in the future at that institute. He had neither pupils nor salary! Politely declining an invitation to a banquet offered him by the faculty and students of Columbia, Da Ponte wrote an amusing and interesting poem in Latin:

> Sum pastor sine ovibus,
> Arator sine bovibus,
> Hortulus sine flore,
> Lychnus sine splendore,
> Campus sine frumento,

Crumena sine argento,
Navita sine navibus,
Ianua sine clavibus,
Arbustus sine foliis,
Taberna sine doliis,
Olympus sine stellis,
Chorea sine puellis,
Artifex sine manibus,
Venator sine canibus,
Fons sine potatoribus,
Pons sine viatoribus,
Sacerdos sine templo,
Professor sine exemplo.[16]

Toward the end of 1835, Lorenzo Da Ponte, approaching the last days of his life, old, tired and disappointed, says:

Eighteen months have passed since I had a single pupil. I, the creator of the Italian language in America, the teacher of more than two thousand persons whose progress astounded Italy! I, the poet of Joseph II, the author of thirty-six dramas, the inspiration of Salieri, of Weigl, of Martini, of Winter and Mozart! After Twenty-seven years of hard labor, I have no longer a pupil! Nearly ninety years old, I have no more bread in America! [17]

One cannot but admire the indomitable courage of Lorenzo Da Ponte and the priceless contribution that he made to this country. Alone, among people of different culture and tradition, and many times without means, he had promoted the study, the love and enthusiasm for the Italian tongue and literature in a land, in a city where, to use his own words, "Italian was not better known than Turkish or Chinese." However, Da Ponte's enthusiasm, joy and interest for his Italian culture soon had profound and lasting repercussions throughout America.[18]

With the unification of Italy in 1870, and especially before World War I, the Italians were coming to the shores of the New World in large groups, all seeking a better economic opportunity. Most of them, like many other ethnic groups, were unable to communicate in a foreign language. Many of these immigrants came without their wives and children; others were very young and all alone, and in many cases penniless. But in their flight to freedom, to the pursuit of happiness, to a better and brighter future, they all had an immense courage and imagination, they all came with a great dream in their minds: the American dream! They wanted to be Americans, not because of birth, but because of their own choice. They were all poor, but full of desire to work and work hard to form their new lives and the new careers which would not have been possible elsewhere. Angelo Pellegrini, in his book *Americans by Choice*, writes:

Don't be alarmed by our foreign names. We are Americans by choice rather than by the accident of birth. We came to your shores from our birthplace elsewhere. You took us in; you worked us hard; you gave us the means to carve out our future. Forgive us who turned out badly. We were weak where we should have been strong. Such as we are, our careers could not have been possible elsewhere. Our common story is part of the larger story of America.[19]

Pellegrini thus indicates the struggle that Italians have had in finding the identity between their sources within themselves, and whatever these sources might have already contributed to the civilization of the established society in America. The Italians who came to this land had a unique problem: they had to settle underground in a subculture. A longshoreman, a ditchdigger, a shoeshine boy, a winegrower, or a peasant woman might have been illiterate, but they knew about Dante, Petrarch, Da Vinci, Galileo, Ariosto, and others, and would puff with pride and personal dignity. Consequently, the writer who narrates the shoeshine boy's story, whether it is biography or fiction, must always reflect and expose first of all the moral sufferings of these people brought upon them by painful and profound humiliations to their personal dignity. Entering this new land, the Italian immigrants, in their earliest writings, portrayed mainly the first experiences which were encountered in the attempt to define their difficult position in the nation's social and economic areas. At first detailed reports appeared, sometimes in the form of short autobiographies which, later, were developed into subjects of pure fiction. They produced, for instance, vivid and minute narration of the departure from their dear ones, from their village, from their way of life, and the bitterness which accompanied all this. Then they described the treacherous voyage over land and sea. Crossing the ocean was rough, irksome and dangerous. Crowded in a filthy ship where one could eat only smelling cod and drink polluted water all the way, they reached Ellis Island.

A realistic portrait, depicting the near brutality of the first encounter of one culture against another—the alienated, the totally lost, against the established society—is told by Luigi Donato Ventura.[20] In his monograph *Peppino*, he tells the story of a young Italian shoeshine boy who stands at the corner of Prince Street in New York City. He is a poor boy of twelve years of age, and lives with his two young brothers in a ghetto. The entire story is written in French, and published in 1886.

> Je vous mène au coin de Prince Street à l'angle opposé au "Metropolitan." Just au coin stationne un gamin d'environ douze ans, au teint brun, hâlé par le soleil, l'oeil noir, la tête couverte de cheveux frisés et abondants . . . et un je ne sais quoi en toute sa personne qui contraste drôlement avec la boîte a cirer, qu'à l'aide d'une courroie il porte en bandoulière. Peppino![21]

Peppino personifies the American dream, the dream of the poor immigrant, the uprooted and alienated, and reflects to his compatriots the American scene. From his little town of Viggiano in southern Italy, he reached this country with his two brothers Antonio and Philippe. Antonio,

like him, is a shoeshine boy who makes about three dollars per day.
Philippe plays the violin on a boat at Coney Island. Describing their departure from Viggiano, Peppino, almost with tears in his eyes, says:

> A Viggiano tout le monde est joueur de quelque instrument . . . l'on part à six
> ans, le violon sous le bras, sans un sou dans la poche; plus tard on se met
> peut-être une harpe sur le dos, et toujours en jouant l'on ramasse d'abord des
> sous sur le chemin de l'Italie; ces sous deviennent des *lires* quand on est arrivé
> à Gênes. . . . C'est comme cela que nous arrivons en Amérique.[22]

Like Luigi Ventura, who arrived here from Italy with only a few francs in
his pocket and one idea in his head, "je croyais que l'Amérique était un
pays où l'argent courrait les rues," Peppino and his brothers believed that,
by shining shoes, they would one day return to their native village with
enough money to purchase a beautiful home surrounded by flowers and
with a lovely "swell front." In New York Peppino and his brothers live in a
very sad and desolate ghetto:

> La maison occupée par Peppino et par ses frères était d'une apparence triste et
> désolante et située dans la partie de Crosby Street où s'entassent pêle-mêle des
> êtres et des choses sans nom. . . . Je me trouvai en pleine Italie Méridionale —
> Assis par terre des gamins de deux ans, sales et mal couverts . . . des femmes
> assises par terre se peignaient les unes les autres . . . et les hommes assis le long
> des marches de l'escalier s'abandonaient au *dolce far niente*, en fumant des
> bouts de cigars ramassés, et en buvant de mauvaise bière.[23]

Yet, inside the house everything is extremely neat and properly arranged
in a lovely manner. Ventura, who has been invited for a dinner, is welcomed into the small apartment with a jovial "Benvenuto Signore." Peppino shows immediately a deep sense of dignity, honesty and finesse. The
cordiality of the host cannot be fully described. There is a beautiful gera-
nium on the windowsill. The dinner prepared by the three poor Italian
boys is superb and well served. " 'Acceptez' " they say to their friend,
" 'nous sommes pauvres, mais nous sommes compatriotes.' " What the phil-
anthropists by profession could not have done for him had been offered
by some obscure shoeshine boys. Peppino's greatest pride consists in the
privilege of earning a modest living and winning the friendship of those
whose shoes he shines. Then at the end of the day, he would fall asleep,
happy, dreaming of Viggiano and blessing this land, America, that made
him and all his compatriots honest and laborious people.

Americans by Choice is also an autobiography of six characters and the
narrator, Angelo M. Pellegrini, who moved West and settled in California,
Oregon and Washington. The first character we encounter is his mother
"La Bimbina," from Ponte Buggianese, in Tuscany, a peasant mother but
the symbol of devotion to her family.

> Anyone who passed by her house . . . at about five in the afternoon, might
> have seen her at work in the garden: a small, stoutish woman, a little bent with

age, gray hair gathered neatly in a knot at the back of the head, dressed in a plain cotton garment faded by many washings. At about that time she had finished setting out a bed of garlic for her family extended to three generations scattered in various parts of the Northwest. . . . She died appropriately, as if by design, at the end of the day's work. The fall planting had been done. The fruit had been harvested and distributed to the children. The plum jam had been prepared for three generations of offspring. Until the very last she had worked with her hands that those to whom she had given life might have their daily quota of bread and wine, and that she, as a good Christian, might justify her existence.[24]

Louis Martini, called by his friends the "Dean of Winegrowers," is another interesting character in Pellegrini's *Americans by Choice*. He arrived in San Francisco from Pietra Ligure, near Genova. Although the wine-making was very profitable, the Martini family also found pride, joy and dignity in making the best wine in the whole region. Louis never mentioned personal gain in his business, but was only concerned about the perfect wine for the perfect moment and occasion. "Wine-making—he used to say—is one of the greatest arts." He was certainly a man

to whom life is exciting and a constant challenge. Home and vineyard and winery are his laboratory where he works to bring things into being. *This is a beautiful day and a beautiful country and a beautiful vineyard . . . I should like to be twenty again, twenty years old, with the energy and vitality I have now.* To what end? To improve further the quality of the day and the country and the vineyard.[25]

Pellegrini also depicts Guido Sella, the bootlegger, from Castelnuovo, near Florence. Without any formal education (he had gone to school in Italy as a child for only three years), he had acquired a surface polish which set him above his Italian friends. In conversation he would frequently quote from Dante "il divin poeta," and "Così dice Dante." Guido soon abandoned a legitimate business—importing and exporting—to pursue one more profitable and illegitimate. After serving time in a federal penitentiary, he alienated wife and children. He was considered by many of his friends as a good, generous and trustworthy person. He was always proud of selling good stuff. In a rather short period of time he became very rich, but then soon came the disgraceful last years of his life when he had to live all alone in a back alley joint, selling liquor by the drink to miserable bums. One could see him through a small window whose glass was covered with dead flies and cobwebs. A sign was also there on the windowsill "Cigars, Cigarettes, Soft Drinks." Had circumstances been different, he might have become a respectable business or professional man, or even a scholar because he possessed the intelligence, the daring, the imagination and even a great desire for knowledge. Pellegrini assures us that

when Guido Sella decided to sell liquor, he hadn't the slightest idea that he was doing something morally wrong. To him, prohibition was a farce, an inexplicable hoax. . . . Of all the forms of delinquency into which the Italian immigrant was tempted, bootlegging taxed his conscience the least. For him, prohibition had no inhibiting moral basis; hence, he had to make no adjustment of conscience in order to engage in the liquor traffic. Furthermore, he was perfectly at home in the techniques of fermentation and distillation. In the way of life to which he had been accustomed, these processes were salutary rather than criminal. The use of alcoholic beverages was completely integrated with his economy and his religion.[26]

In a letter to his parents back in Castelnuovo, Italy, Guido, after telling them that his business was doing really well, and that money simply doubled in a few years of easy work—$150,000, by the end of 1920—writes:

I must now tell you something incredible. The Congress of the United States of America last December passed an amendment to the Constitution prohibiting the manufacture and sale of alcoholic beverages. . . . It seems very probable that within two or three years drinking a glass of wine will be a federal offense. Can you imagine a law more stupid? You pour a glass of wine. You say *salute* to your friends. You lift to your lips—and you are a criminal! [27]

Guido, of course, wouldn't worry about the prohibition. On the contrary, he knew the Americans would continue drinking, would convert into saloons any hidden place, anywhere, by any means. The federal law would increase rather than decrease the need and demand for liquor. And the topic of Guido's conversation with his friends was: " 'How many bottles have you hidden? How many barrels have you cached away? ' " Therefore he soon decided to invest all his money in liquor. And in one of his letters to his people in Italy, Guido says:

Well, my dear parents, it is not possible for you to imagine what America is like. You must come and see it with your own eyes. Ordinary Italians here— the peasants who do the hard work—eat better than the bishop of the diocese. . . . Father Alfonso used to tell me fabulous stories about Paradise. If he is still living, tell him that I have found Paradise in America and that it is infinitely better than even he supposed.[28]

However, if Guido "found Paradise" in America, if his bootlegging profited him barrels of easy money, to many others America only offered bitter and cruel facts.

The American Experience is more objectively portrayed in Pietro Di Donato's *Christ in Concrete.*[29] Autobiographical in its topic, this novel presents in a dramatic and shocking action the Italian-American bricklayer in New York City. With a touching art, Di Donato discloses the miserable and even brutal conditions documented through visual episodes of these poor Italian immigrants abandoned to themselves. *Christ in Concrete* is the writer's own story. The central character Paulie is a twelve-year-old boy. His father Geremio was killed in the collapse of the building in which he happened to be working. Constructed with faulty material because of the builder's profiteering, the structure crumbled, burying men and construction equipment. Paulie must then take up the duties of a man and follow his father's trade to support his mother and his seven young brothers and sisters. His father's hands were their life, their home and their continuous hope for a brighter future. They brought love, joy and faith. After his father's death there is hardly any food left for them to eat. On the table there are only a few potatoes, two or three onions, five or six large crumbs left from before; around the table are the hungry children: Paul, Annina, Lucia, Giorgio, Joseph, Adela, Johnny. With tears in his eyes, Paulie kneels down and prays:

> You have taken dear father away . . . can you send him back, O Lord? We love him—we are hungry—we need him . . . may I go home and find him seated with the children and mama placing the hot food and macaroni on the table.[30]

But Geremio will never come home again. The icy and wet concrete settled immutably over his entire body reaching his chin, his mouth and his eyes. That Friday afternoon—it was the Good Friday—Geremio did not come home where he used to rest his feet on the chair and his head on his wife's warm and soft breast.

Looking desperately for his father, Paulie reaches the police station, and says to the desk officer:

> "On Friday—Good Friday—the building that fell—my father was working—he didn't come home—his name is Geremio—we want him."
> "What? —oh yeah—the wop is under the wrappin' paper out in the court-yard."[31]

For Paulie and his family, America becomes a land of contradictions, a country of Babel where the poor immigrants must wander about in hungry distress cursing each other in strange languages. Di Donato says:

> Work! Sure! For America beautiful will eat you and spit your bones into the earth's hole! Work! . . .
> O God above, what world and country are we in? We don't mean to be wrong. . . . Born in sin, said the walls. Born in sin, said the dark. Born in sin said the air. Born in sin, said fear. . . .
> Mama! Let us take the kids and run where none can reach us. . . . Mama, we'll build a shelter in the forest and dig fruit of wilderness. . . . Mama, let us find our own world, and never part.[32]

Despite this long and dramatic experience, toward the end Paulie, who personifies the Italian-American dream, will succeed in transcending the values of his parents and will be able to visualize a brighter future. Just before her death, Annunziata, almost prophetic, turning her eyes toward her son Paulie, says:

> . . . son . . . everything in my world is for thee. For thee I desire the fullest gifts of heaven. To thee must the good Dio bestow the world—and lasting health. He must bless thee with the flower of mankind and many-many child-

ren as yourself . . . and joy and peace without measure—for to me—thou art most precious.[33]

For a very long time, through tribulations and vicissitudes of all sorts, the Italian immigrants endured the nostalgic memories of their native villages. The hour came when they had to enter a new phase marking the transition from the state of alienation to assimilation into the established society. But this process had to be an operation of a slow and inward pace if it was going to be successful. There had to be, first, a structural pattern which would involve conflict and isolation, suffering and humiliation.

Louis Forgione's *The River Between* is perhaps one of the most representative attempts at assimilation. All the characters in this fiction are symbols and types. Demetrio, "half man and half devil," this gigantic old man from the small island of Vulcano, north of Sicily, is the guardian of his family's honor and tradition. Old-fashioned and very strict, he would not tolerate his daughter-in-law, Rose, who smokes and goes out alone at night. He calls her names: "Foul, civet, hell-cat . . . Troia." Demetrio feels that he is out of place in this world of noise and people who he does not understand. He should have remained on his island, among the waves, the golden mists and the sunshine. Rose, his daughter-in-law, represents the other side of the coin. She is definitely non-Sicilian; she is Americanized; she was born in Union Hall, and defines herself as "brat of a plodding 'Wop.' " How many times one can see her sitting at the window of the Lyba's house, gazing across the Hudson! How beautiful the other side seems to be, how desirable it appears to this poor changeable creature! And far across the river lies the big city, full of splendor of lights, the immense metropolis, always different, and yet ever the same. The shows are on with the dazzling life, the laughters, the jazz, the fun and a whirl of joy. She exclaims:

> God! God! is there always a river between, always something to separate us from an ideal? Always something to stand between us and the unattainable dream? The River, the Enigma, black, eternal—itself the riddle and the answer—poured beneath . . . and passed out, into the open sea. . . . What is there beyond? A different world, a world of freedom and happiness perhaps?[34]

Rose finally becomes free from the indecisions and gloom of the Lyba's house, propelled in a whirl of pleasures and noise of the great city, in this labyrinth of lights and mundane fun. But soon Rose becomes a lost woman, a bum, a street walker, "a gutter-bird." In her soiled skirt and little battered hat, she wanders all alone along Riverside Drive. Her lips are swollen and her eyes black-ringed; she gazes toward the West and sees the Lyba's house. How peaceful and serene everything appears now in that building created by Demetrio! What a simple portrait of happiness! To be happy, to be contented and at peace with oneself—such bliss could not be found among this maze of ultra-civilization where people seek oblivion through "rum-sodden fun." Certainly, the sole happiness, the real freedom could exist nowhere else but within that peaceful way of life she left behind. Forgione writes:

> But Rose, faltering in the shadow of the city, simply stared, surprised, wondering. . . . Someone was calling her, someone whom she had to comfort, to help, to save . . . someone for whom it was her woman's duty to absorb the shocks of existence with her soft body, to sacrifice, to pay, to expiate—eternally! . . . Someone who she had, above all, to love! [35]

Meanwhile, under her despondent eyes, the Hudson River itself, dark, swift, irresistible, remained forever between her, her unattainable dream, and her illusion.

The Gardella family, in Guido D'Agostino's *Olives on the Apple Tree*,[36] embodies the new type of Italian-American who would not live in "Wop-Roost" village, up on the hill, in the dark and ugly shacks, among chicken coops made from boxes. Federico and Giustina, who became prosperous in construction work, remove themselves and their two children, Emilio who becomes a physician, and Elena, from the Italian ghetto, and settle down in the center of the so-called civilized community where there is a chance to take advantage of opportunities of the New World. Dr. Emilio Gardella, tall, distinguished, well dressed, the real professional type, does anything he can to find favor among the American medical staff of Dr. Stone. He turns his back on everything Italian. His favorite friends are the rich, nice people, the American society. Although he likes an Italian girl, Cristina, who really loves him, Dr. Gardella tries his best to neglect her, to hurt her feelings on any occasion, but spares no efforts to court an American girl of high class, Hazel, who, at the end, will despise him. When she finds out that Emilio is interested in her daughter, Hazel's mother gets very concerned; her conceptions of Italians are based upon those poor creatures living on Park Street "where the charity baskets are delivered on Christmas." When Emilio's sister Elena tells him that the poor people, on the hill, also need doctors, he answers:

> "Jesus Christ, ten years' hard study and work just to be a doctor to a bunch of dump wops! . . . Those goddam Italians up on the hill . . . Oh! Just let me finish . . . Hell, this means more to me than all those wops up there put together."[37]

Emilio, like Rose Lyba in *The River Between*, broke into the new society too fast and became the victim of his own weakness. The immigrant must first make the effort to make himself fit. Emilio is in contrast to Marco, the humble and simple immigrant who makes no effort or attempt to change; he is the isolated reject of a different culture. Marco's great desire is to be with his compatriots, no matter where. He is an Italian and proud of it. He rejects those, who, like Dr. Emilio, came to America just to take and to get rich; instead, he believes that this land needs those who work very hard because only the real and hard labor of the Italians in America makes them Americans. And he warns:

> "If the minute you land here you want to rush to become American, then little by little you kill yourself—and you cheat the land that gives you a home because what you brought with you from your own country to make it richer and better, you have thrown away and forgotten."[38]

Marco, more and more, realizes that for these "bastard Italians" only money counts. They very quickly forget everything from the old country; they soon buy cars, food in cans, and other things, like the Americans they work for. Marco refuses to become a part of American life, refuses to mold and shape to the new form of society. But he does not do so because he despises this land. On the contrary, he came here to find freedom, a new way of life and happiness; he got drunk on the America that so many people from everywhere had helped to make grow. D'Agostino writes:

> "Hell with the money . . . we will never have money. But we will have a good life. We will work. We will produce. . . . And that is better than money which makes the Italian rich. . . . That is happiness—if you out of yourself you give something that would last when you, the man, will be no more. That is the real work of the Italian in America. When he is like this he becomes the true citizen.[39]

Instead, Emilio jumps way ahead too fast. He wants to impress others by using something that does not belong to him, someone that is not a part of himself and his people. He has taken advantage of the friendship of those with whom he comes in contact, people who later would have accepted him. He becomes an olive on the apple tree,

> the olive that jumps to the apple tree. The olive that shouts that it is an apple. There is the mistake. There is the whole trouble. . . . The worry of the immigrant is not to be American. The worry is to work, to produce what you can produce and that is what makes you an American.[40]

Only through strenuous, painful and, sometimes, agonizing work, Lucia Santa, in Mario Puzo's *The Fortunate Pilgrim*, becomes a real and genuine American. In sorrows and in tribulations, the American dream, the dream of happiness and freedom for herself and her family is constantly present in her mind. This formidable woman, a matriarch who forges a place for her six children, is twice made a widow and personifies the great struggle of an ethnic minority, not just to survive, but to achieve social and economic justice and dignity in this land of opportunities. Alone she stands, without fear of life and its dangers, in front of adversities. Illiterate, lacking all the necessary experience in the New World, Lucia Santa, this poor peasant lady, possesses the power of life over any human being near her. All her efforts are centered in the family and are based on love, honor and duty. She never betrays honor and duty; perhaps, at times, she is unable to fulfill them entirely. She knows that there is a heavy price to pay. Yet her dream of happiness can become a reality. There is hope in this land, but none in those villages in the mountains in southern Italy where she had escaped some years ago. Here there is some money in the bank. The children know how to read and write, and, perhaps, one day, they will go to the university. Lucia Santa's family is very well taken care of: the children, in the early morning hours, find their food warm and ready, their clothes neat and pressed. Home from school they find their mother near the kerosene stove; she is enveloped in clouds of steam and tending large pots of greens and meats for the supper. She purchases the best "pasta," the imported "prosciutto" and the most expensive "olio d'oliva." Talking to her sons and daughters, she says:

> ". . . remember this, 'mascalzoni' that you are, I would give anything to have gone to school in Italy. At your age I was chasing goats and digging vegetables and shoveling manure . . . School to me would have been like movie pictures . . . ."[41]

Why should Lucia Santa be concerned about Italy? Most of these Italians on New York's Tenth Avenue from Sicily, Naples, Abruzzi, never really cared for their country. For a long time the Italian government did not care for them. Abandoned to themselves and to their problems, they were spit upon by the rich. Pimps of the North sucked their blood. Back in her village, forty years ago, Lucia Santa would only think of staying alive, of escaping hunger, sicknesses and humiliations. She would not dream about anything else. But in this land, other dreams are possible. Just a roof over the head, some food, good or bad, on the table, clothes enough to cover your body—all that will not be sufficient in America. And always believing in her potentiality, Lucia Santa finally creates a new world, a world of beauty for herself and her family. The magic time for the Angeluzzi-Corbo has come. The great American dream is a reality. Sitting and weeping on her backless kitchen chair, just moments before saying goodbye to the old place on Tenth Avenue for a new home in Long Island, Lucia Santa seems to fall into dreams: she listens for her children to go to bed and for her husband to come through that door and have his warm supper after the hard day's work. She reminisces over her past with all the agonies and joys. She also remembers when, long ago, she left her father and mother and everyone to become a pilgrim and to cross the fearful ocean in search of her mysterious dream. In the midst of these touching thoughts, and with tears in her eyes, she seems to reiterate her strong determination to succeed.

I will live those forty years again. I will make my father weep and become a pilgrim to sail the fearful ocean. I will let my husband die and . . . I will weep beside his coffin. And then I will do it once again.[42]

Like Lucia Santa, most of the Italian immigrants left their land, where there was no room for a self-realization, where the possibility of a permament life of freedom and joy had been removed from them. They came to America, to

a world that was new, both chronologically and ethnically. It would not be an easy world. It would work them hard and relentlessly. It would be frequently and inexcusably cruel. It would be indifferent to the agony and tears of the uprooted. But it was a world in which hope could not be mocked by despair; a world in which they would not be permanently segregated as beasts of burden; a world in which they might aspire to their full dignity as men. Here for the first time they would be offered the possibility of assessing their talents, and of dreaming about growing in the direction urged by their hearts and minds. . . . For those who . . . were young, the opportunity was real; for those who were old, it was no less real for their children.[43]

Texas Tech University

NOTES

[1] Gilbert F. Cunningham, *The Divine Comedy in English: A Critical Bibliography, 1782-1900* (New York: Barnes & Noble, Inc., 1965), p. 14.

[2] Joseph G. Fucilla, "The First Fragment of a Translation of the *Divine Comedy* Printed in America: A New Find," *Italica*, 25 (March 1948), 9.

[3] Joseph G. Fucilla, "The First Fragment of a Translation of the *Divine Comedy* Printed in America," *Italica*, 8 (June 1931).

[4] William Ellery Channing, *Works* (Boston: n.p., 1841), I, 259 and 269.

[5] Jared Sparks, "The Augustan Age in Italian Literature," *North American Review*, 4 (March 1817), 309-27.

[6] T. S. Eliot, *Dante* (London: Faber and Faber, 1929), pp. 11 and 16.

[7] Charles Eliot Norton, "Dante, and His Latest English Translators," *North American Review*, 102 (April 1866), 526.

[8] Henry Wadsworth Longfellow, *The Complete Poetical Works of Henry Wadsworth Longfellow*, Cambridge Edition (Boston and New York: Houghton Mifflin and Company, 1882), p. 206.

[9] Angelina La Piana, *Dante's American Pilgrimage: A Historical Survey of Dante Studies in the United States 1800-1944* (New Haven: Yale Univ. Press, 1948), pp. 109-10.

[10] Lorenzo Da Ponte, *Memoirs of Lorenzo Da Ponte*, trans. Elisabeth Abbot, ed. A. Livingston (New York: The Orion Press, 1929), p. ix.

[11] Ibid., p. 187.

[12] Clement Clark Moore (1779-1863), son of Bishop Benjamin Moore who was president of Columbia College (now Columbia University), was born and educated in New York. He became very well known as a great scholar in oriental and classical literatures. His name is associated with the famous and unique work: *Hebrew and Greek Lexicon*.

[13] Lorenzo Da Ponte, p. 215.

[14] Ibid., pp. 243-44.

[15] Joseph Louis Russo, *Lorenzo Da Ponte: Poet and Adventurer* (New York: AMS Press, 1966), p. 121.

[16] Lorenzo Da Ponte, pp. 237-38.

[17] Russo, p. 133.

[18] For further and more detailed studies on the progress and divulgation of the Italian language and literature throughout America, consult Joseph G. Fucilla's *The Teaching of Italian in the United States* (New Brunswick, New Jersey: American Association of Teachers of Italian, 1967).

[19] Angelo M. Pellegrini, *Americans by Choice* (New York: The Macmillan Company, 1956), pp. 1-2.

[20] Luigi Donato Ventura (1845-1912), born in Italy, came to America, via France, in his thirties and with a good and formal education. He taught Italian at the Sauver Summer College in Burlington, Vermont. Besides *Peppino*, written in French, he is the author of *Misfits and Remnants* (Boston: Ticknor and Co., 1886).

[21] Luigi Donato Ventura, *Peppino* (New York: William R. Jenkins, 1885), p. 9.

[22] Ibid., pp. 37-38.

[23] Ibid., pp. 31-33.

[24] Pellegrini, pp. 7 and 11.

[25] Ibid., p. 76.

[26] Ibid., p. 105.

[27] Ibid., pp. 103-04.

[28] Ibid., p. 100.

[29] Pietro Di Donato (1911-), born in West Hoboken, New Jersey, the son of Annunziata and Dominic, became, at the age of twelve, the orphan of a father who met a violent death on a construction project (while working as a bricklayer). The heavy burden of supporting the entire family fell then on the young boy Pietro who assumed his father's trade. He is the author of *Christ in Concrete* (1939), *This Woman* (1958), and *Three Circles of Light* (1960).

[30] Pietro Di Donato, *Christ in Concrete* (New York: The Bobbs-Merrill Co., 1937-39), p. 77.

[31] Ibid., pp. 39-40.

[32] Ibid., pp. 11, 178, 307.

[33] Ibid., p. 311.

[34] Louis Forgione, *The River Between* (New York: NYT Arno Press, 1975), pp. 189-90.

[35] Ibid., p. 253.

[36] Guido D'Agostino (1906-) was born in the heart of "Little Italy" in New York City. He was an amateur boxer for several years. It was during this period that Guido had the opportunity to come face-to-face with the serious problems the Italian immigrants had to deal with. His books include *Olives on the Apple Tree* (1940), *Hills Beyond Manhattan* (1942), *The Barking of a Lonely Fox* (1952).

[37] Guido D'Agostino, *Olives on the Apple Tree* (New York: NYT Arno Press, 1975), pp. 5, 6 and 10.

[38] Ibid., p. 295.

[39] Ibid., pp. 137-38, 167.

[40] Ibid., p. 295.

[41] Mario Puzo, *The Fortunate Pilgrim* (New York: Atheneum, 1965), p. 149.

[42] Ibid., pp. 299-300.

[43] Pellegrini, p. 93.

The Vision of America in John Okada's *No-No Boy**

Lawson Fusao Inada

ABSTRACT

To speak of war is to speak of places—where the battles happen, the devastation. John Okada's novel takes place entirely in America, but its subject is the effect of war on Ichiro Yamada, one of thousands of Americans of Japanese descent who were imprisoned by their government in their own country during the Second World War. His story is of an ongoing war, as old as this country itself, one which continues in the streets to this day. The theme is alienation. The struggle is for the sense of one's self. (LFI)

The author I speak of is dead, and his only book is out of print. Metaphorically he lives, yes; but, in a way it is hard to reach him. In his absence, then, I hold his book in my hand. It takes the reader into the challenge of chasms, and creates a place to stand, to walk on, live in, a place to go.

John Okada says:

> There is a period between each night and day when one dies for a few hours, neither dreaming nor thinking nor tossing nor hating nor loving, but dying for a little while because life progresses in just such a way. From that sublime depth, a stranger awakens to strain his eyes into focus on the walls of a strange room. Where am I? he asks himself. There is a fleeting sound of lonely panic as he juggles into order the heavy sleep-laden pieces of his mind's puzzle. He is frightened because the bed is not his own. He is in momentary terror because the walls are clean and bare and because the sounds are not the sounds of home, and because the chill air of a hotel room fifteen stories above the street is not the same as the furry, stale warmth of a bedroom occupied by three and pierced by the life-giving fragrance of bacon and eggs sizzling in a pan down below. Then he remembers that he is away from home and smiles

275

smugly as he tells himself that home is there waiting for him forever. He goes to the window, expands his chest, and stretches his arms to give vent to the magnitude of his joys upon being alive and happy and at home in a hotel room a hundred miles away, because home is as surely there as if he had never left it.[1]

They called them "Assembly Centers," "Relocation Camps," and people were taken there by "the Evacuation" as authored and authorized by the "President," "Congress," and the "War Relocation Authority," which is always busy with its powers and euphemisms.[2] In Canada, people of Japanese descent became part of the "Interior Redevelopment Project." But this was America, of Vespucci, the country not the continent, where one can "legislate" people from a community locked-in by fear and hate and actual "regulation," and can lock them up in the interior of their very own country—or rather, the country of their birth.

It can then be demanded that the men join the "American" military to fight "the enemy." And if, for some perverse and peculiar reason, they refuse, they are locked up again and called "no-no boys."[3] Of course, there must be "yes men." "Peace" breaks out. There are no keys in any-one's pockets. What then? Okada says:

> For Ichiro, there was no intervening span of death to still his great unrest through the darkness of night. It was nine o'clock when he woke up and the bitterness and profanity and hatred and fear did not have to be reawakened. He did not have to ask himself where he was or why because it did not matter. He was Ichiro who had said no to the judge and had thereby turned his back on the army and the country and the world and his own self. He thought only that he had felt no differently after spending his first night in prison. On that morning, when he woke up and saw the bars, it had not mattered at all that the bars were there. This morning, for the first time in two years, there were no bars, but the fact left him equally unimpressed. The prison which he had carved out of his own stupidity granted no paroles or pardons. It was a prison of forever. (p. 63)

The prisoner comes "home." He has been gone four years—"two in camp and two in prison" (p. 17). All the ghettoes of the world rolled into one—Seattle. International Town. And yet, even here, something has him feeling "like an intruder in a world to which [he] had no claim" (p. 17)—if he ever did. " 'What the hell have I done? What am I doing back here? Best thing I can do would be to kill some son of a bitch and head back to prison' " (p. 17).

He gets spat on by a friend—Eto Minato in an Eisenhower jacket. Blacks call him "Jap!" and tell him to "Go back to Tokyo, boy" (p. 22). His father has become a sot and a sniveling, lost, destroyed . . . . Mother, well:

> . . . "Where's Ma?"
>
> "Mama is gone to the bakery." The father kept his beaming eyes on his son who was big and tall. He shut off the flow of water and shifted the metal teapot to the stove.

"What for?"

"Bread," his father said in a reply, "bread for the store."

"Don't they deliver?"

"Ya, they deliver." He ran a damp rag over the table, which was spotlessly clean.

"What the hell is she doing at the bakery then?"

"It is good business, Ichiro." He was at the cupboard, fussing with the tea and cups and saucers and cookies. "The truck comes in the morning. We take enough for the morning business. For the afternoon, we get soft, fresh bread. Mama goes to the bakery."

Ichiro tried to think of a bakery nearby and couldn't. There was a big Wonder Bread bakery way up on Nineteenth, where a nickel used to buy a bagful of day-old stuff. That was thirteen and a half blocks, all uphill. He knew the distance by heart because he'd walked it twice every day to go to grade school, which was a half-block beyond the bakery or fourteen blocks from home.

"What bakery?"

The water on the stove began to boil and the old man flipped the lid on the pot and tossed in a pinch of leaves. "Wonder Bread."

"Is that the one up on Nineteenth?"

"Ya."

"How much do you make on bread?"

"Let's see," he said pouring the tea, "Oh, three, four cents. Depends."

"How many loaves does Ma get?"

"Ten or twelve. Depends."

Ten loaves at three or four cents' profit added up to thirty or forty cents. He compromised at thirty-five cents and asked the next question: "The bus, how much is it?"

"Oh, let's see." He sipped the tea noisily, sucking it through his teeth in well regulated gulps. "Let's see. Fifteen cents for one time. Tokens are two for twenty-five cents. That is twelve and one-half cents."

Twenty-five cents for bus fare to get ten loaves of bread which turned a profit of thirty-five cents. It would take easily an hour to make the trip up and back. He didn't mean to shout, but he shouted: "Christ, Pa, what else do you give away?"

His father peered over the teacup with a look of innocent surprise.

It made him madder. "Figure it out. Just figure it out. Say you make thirty-five cents on ten loaves. You take a bus up and back and there's twenty-five cents shot. That leaves ten cents. On top of that, there's an hour wasted. What are you running a business for? Your health?"

Slup went the tea through his teeth, slup, slup, slup. "Mama walks . . . ."

(pp. 25-27)

Mother will always "win," because Japan has "won" the War and "the boat is coming and we must be ready" (p. 32). She has a letter to "prove" it: " 'The day of glory is close at hand' " (p. 33).

It is this same story that makes brother Taro want to join the army, the *American* army. This will atone for his Japanese-American brother, who is not his brother, and for his mother, who is not his mother. Somewhere, he feels, between nothingness and Japan is life, and America. Bobbie

Kumasaka, for instance, met death in Germany to become an American, or to try (p. 52). Okada writes:

> "Ahhhhh." Out of the filth of his anguished soul, the madness welled forth in a sick and crazy scream, loud enough to be heard in the next room.
>
> "What is it, Ichiro, what is it?" His father hovered hesitantly in the doorway, peering into the blind-drawn gloom of the bedroom with startled eyes.
>
> "Nothing." He felt like crying.
>
> "You are not ill?"
>
> "No."
>
> "Not sick someplace for sure?"
>
> "No, goddammit, I'm fine, Pa, fine."
>
> "That is all right then. I thought something was wrong."
>
> Poor, miserable old fool, he thought. How in the world could he understand? "I'm okay, Pa," he said kindly, "hungry, that's all, hungry and . . . and glad to be home."
>
> "Ya, you get used to it. I cook right away." He smiled, relief flowing to his face, and he turned back hastily into the kitchen. (pp. 63-64)

Sure, he will "get used to it," maybe, but can he ever get over it? Can he ever "use" it as a place to stand—firm, flat, and familiar?

Thirty years after, if he can live like that, what will he say when children ask, "What was it like?" Will he say it is the same as now? Or, most likely, will they even have to ask, with that desperation born out of a need for roots and history, "*Where* was it? Can you *tell* us about it?"

For Ichiro, these are the very questions of survival, a place to stand. What is a Jap? What is an American? What is a Japanese-American? He is in-between, incomplete, on the hyphen, and feels he cannot be a man.

And if he cannot feel that, naturally and without question, it is an awful place to be, a dreadful and confusing place of questions and decisions without answers and ways of action. *No-No Boy* reads:

> No, he said to himself as he watched her part the curtains and start into the store. There was a time when I was your son. There was a time that I no longer remember when you used to smile a mother's smile and tell me stories about gallant and fierce warriors who protected their lords with blades of shining steel and about the old woman who found a peach in the stream and took it home, and when her husband split it in half, a husky little boy tumbled out to fill their hearts with boundless joy. I was that boy in the peach and you were the old woman and we were Japanese with Japanese feelings and Japanese pride and Japanese thoughts because it was all right then to be Japanese and feel and think all the things that Japanese do even if we lived in America. Then there came a time when I was only half Japanese because one is not born in America and raised in America and taught in America and one does not speak and swear and drink and smoke and play and fight and see and hear in America among Americans in American streets and houses without becoming American and loving it. But I did not love enough, for you were still half my mother and I was thereby still half Japanese and when the War came and they told me to fight for America, I was not strong enough to fight you and I was not strong enough to fight the bitterness which made the half of me which was you bigger than the half of me which was American and really the whole of

me that I could not see or feel. Now that I know the truth when it is too late and the half of me which was you is no longer there, I am only half of me and the half that remains is American by law because the government was wise and strong enough to know why it was that I could not fight for America and did not strip me of my birthright. But it is not enough to be American only in the eyes of the law and it is not enough to be only half an American and know that is an empty half. I am not your son and I am not Japanese and I am not American . . . . (pp. 34-35)

Or the novel reads:

Was it possible that he, striding freely down the street of an American city, the city of his birth and schooling and the cradle of his hopes and dreams, had waved it all aside beyond recall? Was it possible that he and Freddie and the other four of the poker crowd and all the other American-born, American-educated Japanese who had renounced their American-ness in a frightening moment of madness had done so irretrievably? Was there no hope of redemption? Surely there must be. He was still a citizen. He could still vote. He was free to travel and work and study and marry and drink and gamble. People forgot and, in forgetting, forgave. Time would ease the rupture which now separated him from the young Japanese who were Americans because they had fought for America and believed in it. And time would destroy the old Japanese who, living in America and being denied a place as citizens, nevertheless had become inextricably a part of the country which by its vastness and goodness and fairness and plentitude drew them into its fold, or else they would not have understood why it was that their sons, who looked as Japanese as they themselves, were not Japanese at all but Americans of the country America. In time, he thought, in time there will again be a place for me. I will buy a home and love my family and I will walk down the street holding my son's hand and people will stop and talk with us about the weather and the ball games and the elections. I will take my family to visit the family of Freddie, whom I have just left as I did because time has not yet done its work, and our families together will visit still another family whose father was two years in the army of America instead of two years in prison and it will not matter about the past, for time will have erased it from our memories and there will be only joy and sorrow and sickness, which is the way things should be.

And, as his heart mercifully stacked the blocks of hope into the pattern of an America which would someday hold an unquestioned place for him, his mind said no, it is not to be, and the castle tumbled and was swallowed up by the darkness of his soul, for time might cloud the memories of others but the trouble was inside of him and time would not soften that. (pp. 75-77)

It is not so much a place of "yes" or "no" as it is of "I don't know." And one must have the courage and integrity to even try to find the question. He has to search the interior. Thus, he is still unsure why he said "no-no"; he just did it. And the great difficulty is in being put in that position at all. Under those conditions, what is "right" and what is "wrong"? He thought he was saying "yes-yes" to his mother. He thought he was saying "yes-yes" to his conscience. He thought he was saying "yes-yes" to life, by refusing to kill.

* * *

Kenji is a man of Ichiro's age, but a "war hero," as "American" as any, until the next war, maybe, or "civil disturbance," or "foreign takeover." He is a "credit to his race." He is a man without a leg. The body he inhabits, the new Olds he drives with a left-footed system are a courtesy of the government for a job well done. But he is dying. What is left of his leg has a recurring infection—eleven inches, give or take a few days. He says:

> "They gave me a leg and it worked out pretty well, only, after a while, it started to hurt. I went back into the hospital and it turned out that there's something rotten in my leg that's eating it away. So they cut off a little more and gave me a new leg. As you've probably guessed by now, it wasn't long before I was back in and they whacked off another chunk. This time they took off more than they had to so as to make sure they got all the rottenness. That was five months ago. A couple of days ago I noticed the pains coming back." (p. 89)

His body is forsaking him. Thus, he lives with the abandonment of a man in pain who throws away parking tickets:

> "Is that the way to do it?"
> "My way."
> "Get away with it?"
> "Sometimes."
> They got in and started down the street. Ichiro sniffed the new upholstery and touched a finger to the shiny, spotless dash. "New?"
> "Yes."
> "These things must cost a fortune these days."
> "It's a present."
> "Must be a nice guy," he said, remembering Kenji's father, who had known only poverty and struggle after his wife died leaving six children.
> "He is. Uncle Sam."
> Ichiro turned so that he could see Kenji better and he saw the stiff leg extended uselessly where the gas pedal should have been but wasn't because it and the brake pedal had been rearranged to accommodate the good left leg.
> "I was in, Ichiro, mostly in hospitals. I got this for being a good patient."
> "I see."
> "It wasn't worth it." He started to slow down for a red light and, seeing it turn green, pressed on the accelerator. The car responded beautifully, the power in the engine throwing the vehicle forward with smooth effort.
> Ichiro looked out at the houses, the big, roomy houses of brick and glass which belonged in magazines and were of that world which was no longer his to dream about. Kenji could still hope. A leg more or less wasn't important when compared with himself, Ichiro, who was strong and perfect but only an empty shell. He would have given both legs to change places with Kenji. (pp. 85-86)

It comes down to a question of whose problem is "bigger," who is worse off, not better. It is a moot question, something bad, imposed. What is better or worse: sickness of the body, or sickness of the spirit? The sad thing is that such a question has to be asked at all. But this is life, not fiction, and perhaps there can be occasions to rise to, to shape with vision, to make things happen—if the body and the spirit endure. Looked at in that perspective, life is always worth it.

* * *

A few years back, "before the war," as we always say, Ichiro and Kenji would have been "good Japanese boys," as they were, part of that faceless mass with slide rules in Professor Brown's class on a Gothic campus: " 'You're Su ... Suzu ... no ... Tsuji ... What were you in? Double E? Mechanical? Civil?' " (pp. 80-82).

They took what they got, and called it good. They worked hard for it, too, which is one thing they knew they could do. Of course, there was a lot more they knew they could not do, or they thought that they should not do, and therefore they did not do it. So they worked hard, and got what they could. After all, by comparison to the old folks, it was a good life on this island, albeit with "lotsa Japs," and Chinks, and Niggers, however one had to take them.

Now, through the cruelties of experience, they no longer have the option of that vision, however cozy and convenient. One can see it for what it is, a trap, full of crumbs and ambiguities, one-way hyphens to an island.

But Kenji, who has everything going for him—sensitivity, maturity, a loving family—cannot act. And Ichiro, who has his health, cannot accept himself. His family and closed society is closed to him, leaving him with confusion, shame, and guilt:

> How is one to talk to a woman, a mother who is also a stranger because the son does not know who or what she is? Tell me, Mother, who are you? What is it to be Japanese? There must have been a time when you were a little girl. You never told me about those things. Tell me now so that I can begin to understand. Tell me about the house in which you lived and of your father and mother, who were my grandparents, whom I have never seen or known because I do not remember your ever speaking of them except to say that they died a long time ago. Tell me everything and just a little bit and a little bit more until their lives and yours and mine are fitted together, for they surely must be. There is a time now while there are no customers and you and I are all alone. Begin from the beginning when your hair was straight and black and everyone was Japanese because that was where you were born and America was not yet a country beyond the ocean where fortunes were to be made or an enemy to hate. Quick, now, quick, Mother what was the name of your favorite school teacher? (p. 138)

It is a sad axiom, but true: in a difficult situation, one turns upon what is closest to him; it could be himself.

* * *

So in just this one Japanese-American family, after the war, in a dazzling sequence of inter-related events, Taro, the younger brother, with friends, beats up Ichiro and joins the army; the father gets drunk; Ichiro is offered a job by a "liberal" white man who believes in him; Ichiro turns the job down because he cannot believe in himself; the father gets drunk; and Ichiro haunts himself.

Ichiro meets and makes love to a strong and beautiful woman whose husband is living out his family guilt in Europe. Ralph cannot come home; his brother has joined Japan. To be Japanese-American is to feel responsibility, and shame. She might even love Ichiro; Ichiro cannot love himself. She says good things, but he cannot listen.

His mother gets a letter from her sister, starving and suffering in Japan. Her mind snaps. She stacks and re-stacks the canned goods. Then, the novel reads:

> She was half out of the tub and half in, her hair of dirty gray and white floating up to the surface of the water like a tangled mass of seaweed and obscuring her neck and face. On one side, the hair had pulled away and lodged against the overflow drain, damming up the outlet and causing the flooding, just as her mind, long shut off from reality, had sought and found its erratic release.
>
> Feeling only disgust and irritation, Ichiro forced his hand into the tub to shut off the flow of water. He looked at her again and felt a mild shiver working up his back and into his shoulders. Momentarily unnerved, he found himself thinking frantically that she ought to be pulled out of the water. With movements made awkward by an odd sense of numbness, he bent over to grasp her about the waist. At the touch of her body against his hands, it occurred to him that all he need do was to pull the plug. Calm now, he reached for the chain and pulled it out and over the side. He watched for a while as the water level fell, drawing her tangled hair with it until the sickly white of her neck stood revealed.
>
> Dead, he thought to himself, all dead. For me, you have been dead a long time, as long as I can remember. You, who gave life to me and to Taro and tried to make us conform to a mold which never existed for us because we never knew of it, were never alive to us in the way that other sons and daughters know and feel and see their parents. But you made so many mistakes. It was a mistake to have ever left Japan. It was a mistake to leave Japan and come to America and to have two sons and it was a mistake to think that you could keep us completely Japanese in a country such as America. With me, you almost succeeded, or so it seemed. Sometimes I think it would have been better had you fully succeeded. You would have been so happy and so might I have known a sense of completeness. But the mistakes you made were numerous enough and big enough so that they, in turn, made inevitable my mistake. I have had much time to feel sorry for myself. Suddenly I feel sorry for you. Not sorry that you are dead, but sorry for the happiness you have not known. So, now you are free. Go back quickly. Go to the Japan that you so long remembered and loved, and be happy. It is only right. If it is only after you've gone that I am able to feel these things, it is because that is the way things are. Too late I see your unhappiness, which enables me to understand a little and, perhaps, even to love you a little, but it could not be otherwise. Had you lived another ten years or even twenty, it would still have been too late. If

anything, my hatred for you would have grown. You are dead and I feel a little peace and I want very much for you to know the happiness that you tried so hard to give to me. . . .

Stooping over, he lifted her easily and carried her to the bedroom, where he laid her beside the pile of suitcases. Lingering a while longer, he brushed the damp hair away from her face and pushed it carefully behind her head. Then he made his way through the kitchen and into the store behind the counter to the telephone . . . . (pp. 232-34)

* * *

The most important event in the novel, however, is the death of Kenji. He was the one most alive in the life of Ichiro. He dies in a hospital, with dignity, and his father responds in kind, by living that way; as requested, he will not bury Kenji in a segregated Japanese cemetery. Kenji told Ichiro, at his end:

He paused for a long time, just looking and smiling at Ichiro, his face wan and tired. "There were a lot of them pouring into Seattle about the time I got back there. It made me sick. I'd heard about some of them scattering out all over the country. I read about a girl who's doing pretty good in the fashion business in New York and a guy that's principal of a school in Arkansas, and a lot of others in different places making out pretty good. I got to thinking that the Japs were wising up, that they had learned that living in big bunches and talking Jap and feeling Jap and doing Jap was just inviting trouble. But my dad came back. There was really no reason why he should have. I asked him about it once and he gave me some kind of an answer. Whatever it was, a lot of others did the same thing. I hear there's almost as many in Seattle now as there were before the war. It's a shame, a dirty, rotten shame. Pretty soon it'll be just like it was before the war. A bunch of Japs with a fence around them, not the kind you can see, but it'll hurt them just as much. They bitched and hollered when the government put them in camps and put real fences around them, but now they're doing the same damn thing to themselves. They screamed because the government said they were Japs, and when they finally got out, they couldn't wait to rush together and prove that they were."

"They're not alone, Ken. The Jews, the Italians, the Poles, the Armenians, they've all got their communities."

"Sure, but that doesn't make it right. It's wrong. I don't blame the old ones so much. They don't know any better. They don't want any better. It's me I'm talking about and all the rest of the young who know and want better."

"You just got through telling me to go back to Seattle."

"I still say it. Go back and stay there until they have enough sense to leave you alone. Then get out. It may take a year or two or even five, but the time will come when they'll be feeling too sorry for themselves to pick on you. After that, head out. Go someplace where there isn't another Jap within a thousand miles. Marry a white girl or a Negro or an Italian or even a Chinese. Anything but a Japanese. After a few generations of that, you've got the thing beat. Am I making sense?"

"It's a fine dream, but you're not the first. . . . "

"Have a drink for me. Drink to wherever it is I'm headed, and don't let there by any Japs or Chinks or Jews or Poles or Niggers or Frenchies, but only people. I think about that too. I think about that most of all. You know why?"

He shook his head and Kenji seemed to know he would even though he was still staring out the window. "He was up on the roof of the barn and I shot him, killed him. He wasn't the only German I killed, but I remember him. I see him rolling down the roof. I see him all the time now and that's why I want this other place to have only people because if I'm still a Jap there and this guy's still a German, I'll have to shoot him again and I don't want to have to do that. Then maybe there is no someplace else. Maybe dying is it. The finish. The end. Nothing. I'd like that too. Better an absolute nothing than half a meaning. The living have it tough. It's like a coatrack without pegs, only you think there are. Hang it up, drop, pick it up, hang it again, drop again. . . . Tell my dad I'll miss him like mad."

"I will."

"Crazy talk?"

"No, it makes a lot of sense."

"Goodbye, Ichiro."

His hand slipped off his friend's shoulder and brushed along the white sheet and dropped to his side. The things he wanted to say would not be said. He said "Bye" and no sound came out because the word got caught far down inside his throat and he felt his mouth open and shut against the empty silence. At the door he turned and looked back and, as Kenji had still not moved, he saw again the spot of the head where the hair was thinning out so that the sickly white of the scalp filtered between the strands of black. A few more years and he'll be bald, he thought, and then he started to smile inwardly because there wouldn't be a few more years and as quickly the smile vanished because the towering, choking grief was suddenly upon him. (pp. 207-11)

* * *

Somewhere in the thin space between borders and beliefs, and the imposed order of racial groups, is a place where one cannot be imposed upon. It is a hugh space, where one can respect differences and recognize similarities, retaining one's integrity all the while. America can be a place like that. It is a new country, a state of mind, without the confines of history and tradition. And yet, in the names of unity and destiny, Americans have committed as many sins as people of any other country, starting with the first giant step on a red baby's back. Wherever we go takes us back to that transgression. Wherever we go takes us back to slavery. Wherever we go takes us back to "camp." Wherever we are is contingent upon what we bring, adapt, discard, adopt, and share. This is the real question: where do we go from here? As another great writer, Carlos Bulosan, said, before *he* died: "America is in the heart."[4]

No-No Boy, by its very existence, is an achievement. That it speaks with such force and authority is sheer affirmation. Ichiro, then, can be each of us. But he is particularly the embodiment of the Japanese-American spirit, a people so interiorized, so internalized, it seems we would disappear. We have endured. We are here, with power and conviction. Our words will be heard, through incredible destruction:

The car jumped forward, throwing Bull roughly aside. The motor coughed. There was a hectic jiggling of the gas pedal, and the car screeched through the alley. A pedestrian, about to cross the alleyway, jumped out of the way with comic haste.

"Crazy damn fool," said a voice behind Ichiro.

Ichiro watched the car plunge out across the street. The next instant there was a muffled thud. The car which Freddie drove seemed to jump straight into the air and hang suspended for a deathly, clear second. Then it flipped over and slammed noisily against the wall of the building on the other side of the street. Not until then did he notice the smashed front end of another car jutting into view.

Someone was running to the overturned car. There was an excited shout and another and, soon, people were eagerly crowding toward the wreck from all directions. He stood there alone for a long while, feeling utterly exhausted, knowing, somehow, that Freddie would have to fight no longer.

Over by the club's entrance, Bull was sitting with his back against a trash can; his head hung between his knees.

He went up to him and said: "Bull."

"Get me a drink," he moaned without stirring.

"Sure."

"Damn."

"What?"

"That son of a bitch. I hope it killed him."

The club door was open. Inside, the juke box was playing for one couple at a table and a solitary figure at the bar who was too drunk to move. He went behind the bar and grabbed a bottle.

A Japanese youth, probably about Taro's age, came running in. Flushed with excitement, he exclaimed to Ichiro: "What a mess! Didja see it? Poor guy musta been halfway out when the car smacked the building. Just about cut him in two. Ugh!" He hastened into the phone booth.

Ichiro took a drink out of the bottle and made his way out to where Bull was still sitting.

"Here."

Bull moaned, but made no move to accept the bottle.

He took hold of his hair, pulled him straight, and shoved the bottle against the bloody mouth. Bull drank, coughed, and drank some more. Then grabbing the bottle away from Ichiro, he let his head drop once more.

"They say he's dead," said Ichiro gently.

"So what?"

"Nothing. Just that . . . that . . . I'm sorry."

Bull swung his face upward, his eyes wide with horror, the mouth twisted with rage yet trembling at the same time. The throaty roar was mixed with streaks of agonized screaming verging on the hysterical. "Yeah? Yeah? I ain't. I ain't sorry one friggin' bit. That little bastard's seen it comin' a good long while. I ain't sorry. You hear? I ain't sorry. Damn right I ain't. I hope he goes to hell. I hope he . . . ."

The words refused to come out any longer. Mouth agape, lips trembling, Bull managed only to move his jaws sporadically. Suddenly, he clamped them shut. His cheeks swelled to bursting, and the eyes, the frightened, lonely eyes, peered through a dull film of tears and begged for the solace that was not to be had.

"Aggggggghh," he screamed and, with the brute strength that could only smash, hurled the whisky bottle across the alley. Then he started to cry not like a man in grief or a soldier in pain, but like a baby in loud, gasping, beseeching howls.

A siren moaned, shrieked, then moaned to a stop with a screeching of brakes. A car door slammed. Official voices yelled at the crowd. The murmur of the curious filtered through the alley.

Ichiro put a hand on Bull's shoulder, sharing the empty sorrow in the hulking body, feeling the terrible loneliness of the distressed wails, and saying nothing. He gave the shoulder a tender squeeze, patted the head once tenderly, and began to walk slowly down the alley away from the brightness of the club and the morbidity of the crowd. He wanted to think about Ken and Freddie and Mr. Carrick and the man who had bought the drinks for him and Emi, about the Negro who stood up for Gray, and about Bull, who was an infant crying in the darkness. A glimmer of hope—was that it? It was there, someplace. He couldn't see it to put it into words, but the feeling was pretty strong.

He walked along, thinking, searching, thinking and probing, and, in the darkness of the alley of the community that was a tiny bit of America, he chased that faint and elusive insinuation of promise as it continued to take shape in mind and in heart. (pp. 305-08)

Southern Oregon State College

NOTES

[1] John Okada, *No-No Boy* (Rutland, Vermont: Charles E. Tuttle Co., 1957), pp. 62-63. Subsequent references to the novel will be within parentheses in the text.

[2] During World War II, more than 112,000 Americans of Japanese descent, with over 70,000 American citizens among them, were imprisoned by the government, first in makeshift "Assembly Centers" in California, Oregon, Washington, and Arizona, then in the following "Relocation Centers": Manzanar and Tule Lake, California; Poston and Gila River, Arizona; Minidoka, Idaho; Heart Mountain, Wyoming; Granada, Colorado; Topaz, Utah; Rohwer and Jerome, Arkansas. According to Allan R. Bosworth in *America's Concentration Camps* (New York: Norton, 1967), pp. 20-23, this action had an "unsavory precedent" in American history: The Indian Removal Bill of 1830 in which President Jackson "exchanged" the Choctaws, Cherokees, Chickashaws, and Creeks from their homes in the South to "Indian Territory," at great loss of life. Executive Order 9066, which authorized the Japanese-American removal, was signed by President Roosevelt on 19 February 1942. It was formally lifted by President Ford on 19 February 1976—*thirty-four years* later.

[3] In an attempt to "test the loyalty" of the already incarcerated Japanese-Americans, and to segregate the "bad apples" and secure "volunteers" for service, the War Relocation Authority, in 1943, required a questionnaire to be answered by all men and women over seventeen years of age, including many of the elderly who had *not* been permitted to become American citizens. The most inflammatory and ambiguous questions of this innocuous "Application for Leave Clearance" were:

Question 27: Are you willing to serve in the armed forces of the United States on combat duty, wherever ordered?

Question 28: Will you swear unqualified allegiance to the United States of America and faithfully defend the United States from any or all attack by foreign or domestic forces, and foreswear any form of allegiance or obedience to the Japanese emperor, to any other foreign government, power or organization?

Draft-age men who answered "no-no" became known as "no-no boys" and were segregated or jailed. John Okada, himself, volunteered for military duty and saw action in the Pacific. *No-No Boy* is his only published work of fiction. He died in Los Angeles in 1971, after a career as a technical writer and librarian. As of this writing, *No-No Boy* is still the *only* novel by a Japanese-American to be published by a major firm.

[4] Carlos Bulosan, *America Is in the Heart* (New York: Harcourt Brace Jovanovich, 1946). Carlos Bulosan (1914-1956) was a Philipino-American and a major American writer.

"Who Will Ever Hear What I Suffered and Dreamed": Postwar Latvian Literature in the United States

Valters Nollendorfs

ABSTRACT

The following questions need to be considered when one discusses Latvian literature: (1) What are the main achievements of Latvian literature in the United States
during the last 25 years? (2) Under what conditions did it develop and what changes
has it undergone? (3) What is its relationship to and interaction with life and culture
of the U.S.? (4) What are its future prospects?

Three developmental phases can be distinguished. The older generation of writers
who came to the United States around 1950 regarded themselves as exiles. They
continued the literary traditions of Latvia and wrote for a world-wide exile readership. Life in the United States, if presented at all, was usually treated from an
outsider's point of view. There was hardly any interaction with American culture. A
younger generation entered the scene in the late 1950's. Although still Latvian-
oriented, it broke with the established traditions both in form and content. The
United States usually provided the milieu, but cultural interaction was still minimal.
The youngest—American-educated—generation is still developing. Some younger
writers started their careers in English and are fighting their way into the Latvian
idiom. Their work will probably possess more bicultural characteristics than that of
their predecessors. Since Latvian literature in the United States under the present
political climate cannot interact creatively with the literature in Latvia and since
cultural acclimatization is eroding its bases of existence as a purely national literature, its survival in the United States is questionable. Its best chances for a future
seem to lie in its possibilities to participate meaningfully and creatively in the
developing multi-ethnic cultural scene in America. (VN)

If this paper does not accomplish anything else, it has one accomplishment to its record already—even before it was written!—the completion of
a poem one of whose drafts is cited in the title: "Who will ever know what
I suffered and dreamed?" Aivars Ruņģis, better known as a writer of prose
fiction—I will have occasion to mention his work later—sent me last sum-

289

mer a sketch of an idea of a poem which struck me as a distillation of the
loneliness of the exile poet:

> on this continent of Walt Whitman and Mark Twain
> I still feel guilty
> that I exist
>
> . . . .
>
> as if caught in mischief I ask myself
> who am I?
>
> and in your faces like mirrors
> I read the reply:
>
> —you know, one of those
> immigrants—
>
> never
> will I be able to tell you
> the story of my life
>
> never
>
> for in Latvian
> were my sufferings and
>
> dreams
>
> although—
> it still would be
> so very important for me
>
> loneliness
> is a smoldering pain
> even
> in Latvian[1]

The words of the finished version have changed slightly from the draft but
the idea has remained the same. Ironically, the line quoted in my title has
disappeared, and survives only in my title. I feel somewhat like the poet—
somewhat guilty, somewhat apologetic as if I had been caught in mischief.
And yet—I think the story should be told of a group of immigrants who
reached these shores in the wake of World War II, welcomed by their hosts
as millions before them had been welcomed to become part of them.

   If I, and the poet, feel apologetic it is because we feel that we may have
come—or may have been accepted—under false pretenses. Most Latvian
immigrants considered and probably still consider themselves *exiles* who
came here not because they chose to leave their native land for the
material and political allures of the New World but because their country
had come under the rule of an alien country and ideology. Because
Latvians did not come with an eye toward assimilation but were determined to preserve their national identity and ethnic heritage, I can still
talk about a Latvian literature in the United States. Though time is taking
its toll—the original postwar immigrants are now thirty years older, and,

despite good intentions, many of their children and grandchildren no longer speak Latvian or do so with a heavy accent and broken syntax—there still is Latvian literature in the United States.

But while this exile attitude not only allowed Latvian literature in the United States to survive and renew itself, it also resulted in isolation from the life and cultural processes of this country. Especially among the older generation, the feeling was one of a short-range "hiatus" rather than long-range "readjustment." The roots of exile literature, despite its displacement, were still growing in a different soil, or, to use Ruṇģis' metaphor:

> I swim with the stream
>
> . . . . .
>
> but my feet
> my feet touch deeper springs
>
> . . . . .
>
> my feet in the cool waters
> turn into roots

For the most part, Latvian literature in the United States has had very little interaction with this country and its literary life—both because of its own orientation and because there was little encouragement from the American side for creative exchange. The roots of exile Latvian literature in the United States were—and to a great extent still are—growing in the soil provided by the Latvian exile community which transcends political borders and continents. For that reason, Latvian literature in the United States is a largely artificial designation, some local color notwithstanding. A better unity could be achieved by talking about Latvian exile literature as a whole; there at least the exile experience itself would provide one possible unifying trait. But some politically inclined literati feel even that such a division is remiss and that there is nothing less than one Latvian literature—both in Latvia and abroad—a point vehemently denied by Soviet ideologues as a potential Trojan horse.

If this ideological dispute is even worth mentioning, then it is for a practical reason which may, ironically, lead to a greater symbiosis in the American context. Despite its resiliency and its orientation outside national boundaries to encompass the entire Latvian community in the Western world, a potential public of, who knows, some 100,000 to 150,000 by even the best estimates, exile Latvian literature is undergoing a possibly terminal crisis. This crisis is primarily caused by the isolation of the post-war exile community from the homeland: it is a community that is not enriched by additional immigration and whose intellectual and cultural contacts with Latvia are severely restricted. The crisis, however, is not as much one of creativity as it is of numbers: a dwindling readership makes only popular works financially viable for publishers. And it seems that the readership is dwindling fastest among the younger generation where the discrepancy between the select few capable of handling the language for literary production and the larger mass with relatively crude linguistic capabilities is the greatest.

At the same time the one natural outlet for exile writers—the Latvian population in Latvia—is not allowed to receive exile literary production except by dribbles and even then usually after exacting a heavy political tax from those who consider such cultural exchange important. As long as exiles are not willing to pay that tax—and if they are, they realize that there is no guarantee of creative license—very little creative interaction with the literary life in Latvia is possible. And since cultural acclimatization and old age are eroding the bases of existence for Latvian literature outside Latvia, there are very few choices left for future developments that bode well for its sustained viability. One of these choices may be the way of meaningful participation in the multi-cultural ethnic life in those countries where Latvians live—in our case, the United States.

The trends seem to favor this solution. But it can only succeed if the basic outlook of Latvian exile literature in the United States changes. It does not have to give up anything really: to stay ethnic it has to keep its national/ethnic allegiances. But it has to open up for a much greater interaction with other ethnic literatures and with the culture of the United States than it has had in the past. In turn, of course, there has to be true cultural reciprocity—a willingness to take as well as to give.

Before I enumerate what Latvian literature in the United States has to offer in the way of literary personnel and dowry, I should like to digress briefly and discuss the term "ethnic literature," as I am using it, and present some background information about the Latvian group in the United States.

Perhaps the term "ethnic" is misused for Latvian exile literature because this literature represents the results of some hundred years of literary development—to be sure, on the basis of and with constant reference to, but at the same time *away* from that indigenous literary soil which brought forth the folk songs, the fairy tales, and the proverbs of the oral tradition.[2] In this development, Latvian literature has absorbed various foreign influences and evolved a more cosmopolitan outlook and sophistication in matters literary than during its very first steps in the second half of the nineteenth century so that it can and probably should be judged with generally accepted literary standards. Its ethnicity should not be considered of such nature than an outsider—provided he has reasonably accurate translations and some idea of the literary and ethnic background—could not assess its meaning and literary value. Its ethnicity at this stage should be considered just one and not the only one parameter to be used in assessing it.

The majority of the exile community that produces and reads this literature can be characterized as a middle-class intelligentsia committed to both the idea of free expression of thought (though with constraints imposed by tradition) and to national self-preservation (though not by way of cultural isolationism). In its efforts to preserve its national identity, the exile Latvian community has established and maintains a number of social, cultural, and educational institutions.[3] It is not a community that has to become aware of its heritage but—because of its isolation from the homeland and the dominant social and cultural pressures from outside—is in danger of losing the heritage it has.

In the following I intend to outline some of the developmental characteristics and problems of Latvian exile literature in the United States during the last twenty-five years and three generations by way of several exemplary writers. Furthermore, I hope to show how these characteristics were influenced and determined by certain determinable and measurable factors, both in terms of their ethnicity and adjustment to the American setting (though, as far as I know, few such measurements have taken place). And—last of all—I hope to show how certain of these factors can be altered for the greatest possible benefit of both the U.S. contingent of this small exile literature and its host country.

Three distinct phases can be distinguished in the development of Latvian literature in the United States since World War II. These phases are generational in nature, perhaps more so than under normal circumstances, because they represent simultaneously different levels of adjustment and accommodation to life in this country.

The first phase is represented by the immigration—in the late 1940's and early 1950's—of practicing Latvian writers from the European DP camps. Their literary origins, however, usually extend back to Latvia. Most of them belonged to the pre-1930 generation, were in their thirties, forties, or older, and had a relatively difficult time adjusting to life in the New World. Being the true exiles, they did—and for the most part still do—display certain fixed ideas about Latvia's loss of independence, about the Soviet regime, and about their own suffering and dreams. Exile for them was an interruption, and, on the whole, they never came to terms with it as an extended condition. They continued Latvian literary traditions; their writing changed very little upon arrival and, in general, has shown just as little change since. They did have a rather steady and faithful readership and still have to be considered among the most popular of all Latvian writers in this country. At the same time, their public was and is in no way restricted to the United States. They are read everywhere Latvians reside in exile. Therefore in their attitudes toward and portrayals of the United States—where such are found—they usually take an outsider's point of view or employ commonly held stereotypes.

294

A second phase or generation came into its own in the 1950's and 1960's and is represented by those born in the 1920's and early 1930's. It is important to note that this generation does possess some common and some diverse characteristics, the break being about 1928/1929. Those born earlier still enjoyed most of their schooling in Latvia and brought with them vivid memories; they were too young to participate in the literary life in Latvia, but many of them made their first attempts after the war—in the DP camps in Germany. Yet this group also was hardest hit by the war; the men were of draft age, and many had served in the German-organized Latvian Legion. Those born after 1929 had only elementary school education in Latvia, but most did attend Latvian schools at the DP camps and, until emigration to the United States, enjoyed a lively Latvian cultural life in these refugee enclaves in Germany. What they missed, of course, was the total national environment during their important formative years. Yet, on the whole, these two subgroups did feel closer to each other than to the older generation, both in political outlook and in their ability to adjust to life in the United States. Though they did not give up their Latvian associations and many played an active role in the organizational life of exile Latvians, they did, on the whole, establish themselves in trades or professions and function successfully in American social life as well. At the same time, the exile experience for them became an extended state which could not be overcome by lamenting but finding new, more universally valid forms of expression. They broke with the literary canon and with the exile cultural and political establishment. They also were the first who started searching for passive and active contacts with the cultural life in Soviet Latvia.

The third exile generation—those who were born in the late thirties, in the forties and even later—is actually the first purely exile, and at the same time non-exile, generation. If its members enjoyed any Latvian schooling at all, it was incomplete, either in Latvian schools in the DP camps and/or in Latvian Saturday schools, summer camps, and high schools in the United States. They have no memories of Latvia even if, indeed, they were born there. As far as their Latvian disposition is concerned, however, the decisive factor—on intuitive evidence, to be sure—seems to have been their family background and its influence. It is a rather diverse group, still in its formative stage, and it would be precipitous to try to characterize it too firmly. In terms of linguistic competence, it ranks from seasoned to precocious. Some of the younger writers started out in English and are only now fighting their way into the Latvian idiom, while there are others who display a surprisingly rich linguistic palette. That they do at all is to some extent to be credited to exile Latvian ethnic consciousness and educational efforts, but probably even more to the recent notion in the United States that ethnic is beautiful. If the middle generation was still cautious in its approach to cultural exchange with Soviet Latvia, the younger one is much more direct and even less respectful of the wishes of its elders, although no less forceful in its rejection of the Soviet regime's anti-Latvian attitudes and policies. The ethnic element takes precedence over political ideology. For them visits to Latvia are a search for the cultural soil in which they never could grow. Their readership, however, is limited, though even this generation, despite its closer ties to the United States, is internationally oriented when it comes to their Latvianity. Despite the educational efforts, many of their peers, who would understand them, either cannot or do not read Latvian; the older generation, who could read them, does not because it cannot empathize with or understand them and thus publication is problematic.

The three groups, of course, exist side by side. Only a fourth generation—if it materializes—in some ten to fifteen years—will no longer have to contend with those who came here in the wake of World War II, bringing with them the literary traditions of their homeland, outsiders in a strange country.

If we ask for the substance of the literary activities of these three groups in the last twenty-five years, we are entering a realm of value judgment. Since I, myself, belong to the middle generation—youngest wing—my bias may show; I only hope that I can provide it some justification. For I feel that the middle generation in many ways is crucial in any future developments, particularly in the direction of cultural symbiosis. The middle generation, too, possesses a greater distance from the events that indelibly scoured the literary psyche and social/political attitudes of the older one.

Instead of trying to present a long list of strange-sounding names, I will pick out a few writers who in my opinion would pass the judgment of even non-Latvian critics, who at the same time in some way combine the uniquely ethnic, exile-ethnic, with certain universal human values. Quality, not quaintness, is what I have tried to pick foremost, though some quaintness, I hope, will still show. Let me proceed chronologically once again.

The older generation did not land many renowned names on these shores. And not all of those whose names already meant something continued to produce literature of high caliber. The older generation, after all, did have a public to satisfy, and—let me quote the ascerbic but fair critic Jānis Rudzītis: ". . . the publishers demand thick manuscripts. The publishers' demands are in tune with the public's desires for thick books. It is not literary quality but the thickness of a novel that sometimes determines sales, and this factor leads to fateful results."[4]

Some of these publishers of thick novels landed in the United States and are still in business. Helmārs Rudzītis of Grāmatu Draugs (The Friend of Books), now celebrating its fiftieth anniversary since its founding in

Latvia, started a newspaper *Laiks* (Time) in New York, which has become the leading Latvian newspaper outside Latvia with still about 12,000 subscribers. By effectively using the advertising potential of the newspaper, Rudzītis built up a thriving book publishing house whose specialities are popular Latvian novels and Latvian translations, particularly of the popular Scandinavians. It must be said that occasionally Grāmatu Draugs publishes volumes of poetry and less than overwhelming popular choices. The bulk, however, is not geared to literary but consumption considerations. Hugo Skrastiņš, the flamboyant entrepreneur and publisher of an illustrated magazine, *Tilts* (Bridge), settled in Minneapolis. Combining a discount coupon promotion through the magazine and direct mail techniques, he, too, built up a thriving publishing house also called Tilts. A great deal were and are republications of once popular works and, in the sixties, of Soviet Latvian authors, but a good number of originals, too, appeared with his imprimatur. The story of Latvian publishing houses in the United States and elsewhere in the West has not been told yet, and it would not be easy to do since hard data on finances, press runs, and sales is almost impossible to obtain from publishers who claim that they are working for a pittance to further the cause of Latvian culture. But it would be a story worth telling since publishers crucially affect the type of literature produced and read and the literary attitudes developed, especially among a group limited in number and sales potential.

If Jānis Rudzītis' assessment of the bulk of Latvian prose fiction is correct, and I have no reason to doubt it, then this genre does not particularly abound in valuables but glitters mostly with costume jewelry. Most of the practitioners from the older generation continued writing according to formulas that had been successful before and proved still to be successful. The exile situation, the suffering and the dreams were and are explored in many of the works, but too often the quintessence of suffering is not touched; it usually appears and immediately gets defused by release in humor upon encountering strange lands and people, or trivialized and psychologized away by stressing its symptomatic aspects. They, after all, would be passing states.

The best and most productive author—practically in the employ of Grāmatu Draugs and *Laiks*—is Anšlavs Eglītis (1906-   ), who resides in Pacific Palisades, California, and is the only exile author earning his living professionally as a writer. Eglītis, educated as a pictorial artist, came into the Latvian literature in the thirties with novels about artists' lives, the Riga Boheme. His works are full of characters bordering on caricature and abound in grotesque juxtapositions. He has a facile narrative style and a penchant for the exotic. These are qualities that even in formula writing sustain enough interest.[5] Carried on the wave of popularity, Eglītis has endured and, though very little new of substance has come from his pen, the novelty of new variations of the old has always been there. Eglītis is also deservedly known as the best Latvian playwright in the United States, a genre that still persists despite the lack of professional Latvian theaters and only a few good professionals in basically amateur groups continuing the art.

Voldemārs Kārkliņš (1906-1964), who had started his career in Latvia as translator for Grāmatu Draugs, developed into another house novelist for the publisher, and some of his work has been praised as among the best produced. Kārkliņš is typical of the accomplished latecomers on the literary scene, a phenomenon that seems to be rather frequent among exile Latvians. The well-known paintress Margarita Kovaļevska (1910-   ), too, produced her first novel, an accomplished work, late in her life.[6] And just recently the seventy-year-old Arturs Baumanis (1905-) came out with his life's work, an eight-volume historical novel of the first Moravian congregations in Latvia in the eighteenth century.[7]

Lyric poetry seems to be the one genre Latvians write best and with the greatest devotion. Most of the truly outstanding poets of the older generation—Veronika Strelerte, Andrejs Eglītis, Pēteris Ērmanis, Velta Toma—did not settle in the United States. Only Zinaīda Lazda (1902-1957), who lived and died on the West coast, in Salem, Oregon, belongs to this group. Her poetry incorporates some of the simplicity, gentleness, economy, and striving for wholeness that is characteristic of Latvian folk poetry.[8] But she can also be forceful in her accusation of injustice, as in the following poem which in three terse stanzas sums up the post World War II refugee problem:

> Look, Europe's slaves, the DP's:
> Buy them, take them who wills;
> The simple and the refined,
> Both can be got.
>
> Asia is on the one side,
> On the other there is the ocean;
> This is no dream nor delusion—
> All can be got.
>
> Once, for large sums of money,
> They bought various luxuries here;
> Now you can get them themselves—
> Europe's slaves, the DP's.[9]

A major lyric prize, awarded biannually, is named after Zinaīda Lazda, and some of the lyric poets I mention later in this paper have been recipients of the award.

But it was up to the younger generation to establish an "American school" of Latvian poetry. Its center was the now urbanely renewed Westside Manhattan area known as Hell's Kitchen, a Latvian Boheme of sorts with Linards Tauns (Arnolds Bērzs, 1922-1963) as its pulsating heart. Tauns is the second great city poet of Latvian literature, which otherwise has strong pastoral tendencies; as city poet he was the follower of Riga's own Aleksandrs Čaks. But Tauns, despite his slender oeuvre,[10] has his own characteristic signature. He lacks the bravura and emotional amplitude of Čaks, but is more consistent, more sustained, penetrating the cityscape, becoming absorbed in it and thus transcending it simultaneously. For, as has been remarked, Tauns can be in many cities and many times at once.[11] Thus New York for him—though alluded to realistically enough, with its sounds, its smells, and the characters of Hell's Kitchen—is only a point of departure, but such lines as these are striking:

> I want to test if my city is such
> As it appears in my dreams.
> . . . . . .
> And I went to the city and put my dream
>   on obstinate stones
> And saw—they are even older than my
>   own previous lives.
> In them Pharaohs doze and the suns
>   surrounding them.
> We don't dream the city; the city dreams us.[12]

He also writes:

> A woman is walking.
>
> She comes out of a cafe
> And now goes toward downtown.
>
> There is something significant about her gait
> As if she—all alone—
> Were forming a procession or a parade,
> As if she—walking downtown—were not,
> But instead were walking to some beginning
>   or end.[13]

As Tauns had lived the city, the city took Tauns—at much too early an age. His posthumous work was carefully edited and published by his friend and companion from the New Jersey side, Gunārs Saliņš (1924-   ). Saliņš himself is to be counted among the best Latvian poets in the United States, and Hell's Kitchen also has nourished his writing. More intellectual, less intense than Tauns, Saliņš dazzles with his imagination. If Tauns succeeds in synthesizing the discrete parts of his poetic vision, Saliņš lets them stand side by side in surreal images. Just as in Tauns, however, New York serves as a symbol of the exile experience. But whereas for Tauns New York is a poetic point of departure, for Saliņš it is a point of arrival: he brings the Latvian world to New York and superimposes it upon the city. In a poetic epistle to a poet friend he says:

When you will arrive in naked New York,
you will agree with us:
it must be forested!
    And this might be how:

Fast growing birches on Times Square,
oaks along the fashionable avenues,
in Greenwich Village mountain ash, mountain ash,
weeping willows in Harlem,
in the harbor district—spruce and pine;
junipers around the slaughterhouses.

But as New York is forested, it also becomes Latvianized:

The young ones will later roam the woods,
will leave carved hearts in the trees
for their Latvian children and grandchildren.[14]

Aina Kraujiete (1923-   ), whose poetic career postdates both Tauns and Saliņš, but whose productivity starts exceeding both, seems to be a synthesis of the two. On less intimate terms with her poetic objects than Tauns, she nevertheless manages to overcome the surrealistic/intellectual distance that Saliņš interposes and manages to approach the essential core of human experience. Her last collection, *Ne bungas ne trompetes* (Neither Drums nor Trumpets), ends with this re-affirmation of the poet's mission in a political world:

Much louder and stormier than drums
and much
much longer than trumpets
even through eternities,
the poet's voice can resound.
They say.
    I see: a young minstrel,
a blond-bearded bard,
is coming with an electronic guitar
and, his strings pulsing excitedly
hoarsely begins—
    "as time passes all
is fairytales and myths."
    Flocks
of birds and laurel leaves
fall from the branches—

branches and blossoms
    blossoms and sun and lizard—

it is noon.
    Buls.[15]

In her world, however, there is the ethnic referent even in the image of the modern musician; as the lonely minstrel he also stands for the poetic soul of the nation, and in another poem he is portrayed as the lonely shepherd boy who overcomes the drums and trumpets of power politics.

300

Baiba Bičole (1931-), also a product of Hell's Kitchen, is different;
she is both more subdued formally and much more passionately personal,
or, as Astride Ivaska has pointed out, elemental.[16] All experiences end in
the human being as the final recipient and measure. But in her writing,
too, the glance moves away from the present to the past, to the lost dream
world of childhood:

> Woodstock, New York: old sleighs, saddles and halters,
>   butter churns, pestles and roosts,
>   ancient Sanskrit letters,
>   the smell of lacquer and wood—
>   in the antique shop
>   patinized—as if my childhood's dreams
>   walk tiptoe
>   touching my lids and my cheeks—
>   I smile.
>   —A statuesque, overdone woman stops,
>   asks
>   "Found what you've been looking for?"
>   —"Yes!"
>   —and from my overflowing palms
>   rain the shimmering signs of
>   excavated days, years, and times.[17]

If Hell's Kitchen has justifiably become a concept in Latvian literature
not only in the United States, it was by no means the only place where
literary activity thrived. Two poets who live elsewhere deserve mention.
Astrīde Ivaska (1926-), formerly of Minnesota, now in Oklahoma, and
Olafs Stumbrs (1931-) in Los Angeles.

If New York's facade serves as a point of departure for many of the
preceding group, there is little of the Midwestern landscape in Ivaska.
Reminiscences of childhood images from Latvia and the Scandinavian
landscape, where she and her husband, the Estonian poet Ivar Ivask, like to
spend as much time as possible, dominate her delicately personal lyrics.
She is less fierce than Bičole, achieving more by mood and suggestion than
direct expression; she is probably closest to Zinaīda Lazda, whose prize she
received for her first collection. She seems like a lonely wanderer in search
of the one landscape denied her, be it in Northern European forests or in
the hot Midwestern city:

> Awakening
> from the indifference of things
>   feeling in their eyes
> as a three-year-old
> unable to reach the shelf.
>   With a sweaty forehead
> the heart climbs the glass mountain
>   to stand at the princess'
>   empty coffin.

We both
in this sultry
godforsaken city
without salvation
from the indifference of things,
clanking windows,
and dusty wind.[18]

The great event in Stumbrs' poetic life was his first visit back to Riga in
the late sixties. If his poetic activities in the early sixties included participation in the poetic life of Southern California's Little Venice—he has a
slender volume of English poems to show for it[19]—his production ever
since has been homeward-directed with strong personal undercurrents that
he tries to hide under a mask of irony and a style of expression that, on
the whole, eschews typical lyricism only to make place for such lyrical
lines as:

That night we walked
from loneliness to Rīga.
In some verandas lights were burning,
but you cannot judge the house by its veranda,
but you cannot divine the morning from a lamp,
neither mine, nor yours, nor Grieg's—
. . . . . .
Someone draws a long line on the horizon
with a green and wide piece of chalk
from loneliness to Riga.[20]

The advent of this lyric generation is to be dated in the mid- to late
fifties. It was reinforced by the publication, since 1955, of a magazine
Jaunā Gaita (The New Way) which eventually became the prime outlet for
the younger generation with its—for Latvians—avant-gardist and experimental tendencies.[21] The magazine, first published under the auspices of
the American Latvian Youth Association, succeeded in achieving what
previous similar ventures had not been able to—regular and sustained publication and the establishment of a new readership as a sound practical basis.
Above all, the magazine was independent of the literary establishment and
canon and dared tread where others were unable or unwilling to, both in
matters political and literary. *Jaunā Gaita* was the first to start acquainting
its readership with literary developments in Soviet Latvia, particularly its
younger generation, and to analyze Soviet Latvian literature without the
usual general dismissals as "Socialist Realism." *Jaunā Gaita* also dared to
be innovative, even iconoclastic in its literary program. It was clear that a
new generation was asserting itself here, met by scepticism if not outright
enmity by some exile social and political groups. The matter came to a
head in 1959, after excerpts from an "irreverent" fairytale, by one Jānis
Turbads (Valdis Zeps, 1932-), were printed together with an editorial

concerning the "youth week" of the American Latvian Youth Association with the theme referring to the exile relationship with Latvians in Latvia: "Let Us Not Grow Apart." Turbads' iconoclastic and totally unserious journey through the Latvian mythologic, literary, cultural, social, and political landscape[22] was viewed as an attempt to "subvert exile Latvian values"; and the editorial, with its call for reassessing attitudes toward communism and Soviet Latvia, was denounced, together with editorial policies, as an attempt to infiltrate the enemy viewpoint. The American Latvian Association passed a resolution denouncing the magazine for "not adhering to common Latvian aims and morality" and barring the magazine from a modest subvention by its Cultural Foundation. The magazine survived, however, and—now in Canada—has just finished its twentieth year of continuous publication. The critic Jānis Rudzītis derived the term *jaungaitnieki* for those publishing in *Jaunā Gaita*, and this term has stuck to the literary generation of the 1950's and 1960's.

If the 1950's came with lyricists, such as Tauns, Saliņš, Stumbrs, followed by Bičole and Ivaska, to recapitulate the poets in the United States, the 1960's brought a renaissance in prose writing as well. Turbads' modern fairytale led the way, followed, on the American side, by Ilze Šķipsna (Ilse Rothrock, 1928-   ) from Fort Worth, Texas, and Aivars Ruņģis (1925-   ), from Kalamazoo, Michigan, as the most notable innovators of prose fiction. In particular their accomplishment was to overcome the plot-bound psychological novel of the earlier generation. Both Šķipsna and Ruņģis deal with the problem of exile in their works, and yet each one of them has a distinct style and approach.

Ruņģis attacks the problem more directly than Šķipsna. His novel, *Pats esi kungs, pats* (Be Your Own Master, Your Own, 1967) is, on the surface, a kaleidoscopic twenty-four-hour journey through the Latvian community of Toronto. In its primary intent it is a search for identity by an exile group and its individuals. One of the key passages in the novel reads:

> . . . I, being a Latvian in the midst of other nations, experience the fate of an individual in modern civilization, in which more and more of all kinds of borders will dissolve, creating the great question: how to endure with one's own characteristics and traits . . . .[23]

As the passage indicates, however, the novel is more than the exile's simple search for identity: the exile situation and the situation of a small nation in a world dominated by large nations are at the same time connected to the problems of humanity in the modern world. This connection breaks the self-imposed isolation and surface treatments of exile so common in the prose of the older generation.[24] Like James Joyce, with whom he has been compared, though he denies ever having read Joyce, Ruņģis employs a variety of styles and points of view to achieve his purpose.

Ilze Škipsna's prose lacks this display of overt virtuosity; her virtuosity is much more in condensation and penetration. Where Ruņģis analyzes, she synthesizes. There is little overt action, philosophizing, or symbolism in her works. But she succeeds by subtle indirection at creating, beneath a seemingly realistic surface, an inner landscape, at times with Kafkaesque undertones, that assumes all the power of a symbol of separation, isolation, loneliness. In her *Aiz septītā Tilta* (Beyond the Seventh Bridge, 1965[25]), this separation is symbolized by two distinct, separate—not schizophrenic!—women of opposite character who, however, can only exist as an entity, and that means—death. Ojārs Krātiņš finds that the theme of one's proper place is characteristic of Škipsna and ties this theme to the exile situation: "The nation is the critical element that guarantees the individual's proper place. As a concept of belonging it seems to be more viable than society. Severed from his nation, the individual seems only to be able to struggle for a substitute sense of belonging which has no existence outside the mind."[26] That is why Škipsna's American city and landscapes—New York, or the Texas plain are among her favorites—appear distant and strange in her work. Under her married name, Rothrock, Škipsna, incidentally, has also published original prose fiction in the English language.[27]

Both for Stumbrs and Škipsna English is an acquired language. But for the younger generation in the U.S., English is, if not the first, then certainly the strongest language of expression. Some of the 1970's generation started writing in English and are only now attempting to develop a Latvian idiom capable of accommodating their ripe poetic fruit. Since some of them developed and matured away from the ethnic Latvian environment in the U.S.—no matter how insufficient and unable to replace the native country this environment might be—they are coming unto the Latvian literary scene with a completely new set of cultural experiences, some of them quite exotic. Andris Kārkliņš, known as flamenco guitarist André el Leton, lived for some years with the gypsies in Spain and was accepted as their own; on his travels he also stayed with several African tribes. And Laimons Juris G. (for Gārskis) with his patriotic verses has become a celebrated poet of Bangladesh.[28]

Of the poets who have grown up in a more traditional manner, I would like to mention only two, Baiba Kaugara (1943-   ), whose father was an accomplished poetic craftsman, and the daughter of Ruņģis, who publishes under the pen name of Dīna Rauna (Sniedze Ruņģis, 1951-   ). Both possess an uncommonly rich poetic idiom in Latvian and an uncommon depth of expression.

Dīna Rauna has, in my opinion, succeeded in doing what no Latvian writer—here or there—has been able to do: to give poetic shape to the

Siberian experience of untold numbers of Latvians in Stalin's labor camps.
She has never been there, and maybe for that very reason she has been able
to transcend the transitory individual expression of physical suffering in
apocalyptic visions that can touch all of us:

TO EVE, STILL A MAIDEN, THERE APPEARS A YET UNBORN
GRANDDAUGHTER IN SOME SIBERIAN TUNDRA

Don't start, grandmother; why call on God, what do you
cross yourself for? Better take these dice in your hand
                                        my jewelry—
how white are my uplifted arms, these towering elephant tusks.
This eternal forest: what mighty coffin!
I lie
on the black back of a whale washed ashore.

Hark, how the grass hums around my feet!
Like a swarm of blue icicles—
for already my veins are letting out roots.
Overhead the auroral flames are burning the roof-beams of heaven,
        grandmother.
Indeed, in these storm-clouds birds burn and a hail of stars falls
silently, mercilessly on my body.

Do dream my death—
let me enter the Other Realm as you will once help your daughter
burst forth from your body.
For I cannot remember
what she was called
and my name sounds
like a fool's riddle.
Let me!
Let me!
Let me be reborn
in stone.[29]

In Kaugara, the mysticism of the concurrence of time and place bridges
the gap between exile and native land which she never had:

i hope to
enter the realm of the dead
dive into the waters of the daugava
flow through streams
ascend springs surface in wells
from all waters
i hope to look at myself alive
facing the sun.[30]

But who reads these lines? And who understands these voices? The
young—though more distant from the suffering and the remembrances that
dreams are made of—seem to be better able to express their own and their

elders' tragedy in universal terms. They deserve to be listened to and to be read. But, as I noted earlier, most of them exist in a strange kind of isolation: between their elders, who could read them but who for the most part fail to understand the very universality and expression of their concern, and their own generation, who despite all efforts seem to be more at home in English than in Latvian.

Here, between two cultures, however, may also lie a tenuous solution for the dilemma of the endangered species, the Latvian ethnic group in the United States. In the current refashioning of the American melting pot into a mosaic, a place perhaps may be found even for a small stone chip of Latvian poets. What that small stone chip looks like, I have tried to show. But what may the new mosaic in turn contribute to the preservation of the uniqueness of the small stone chip itself? Whatever sharing and conceptualization of ethnic cultural experiences and values will occur among the different ethnic groups—through the common medium of English—will also have a reciprocal effect on those among the Latvians who did not, could not, or could only partially develop the primary idiom in which these values are preserved and transmitted. For some, I can envision the chance of a late development of this idiom to maturity; for many, however, the ability to belong—even through the medium of English—may become a viable alternative.

And thus the poet, the doors of his native home slammed shut in his face, may still, and for a long time to come, have someone who will hear what he suffered and dreamed—even in Latvian—and—understand.

University of Wisconsin-Madison

NOTES

[1] Aivars Ruņģis. *Slīdošajās kāpēs* (Madison, Wisconsin: Latviešu Rakstnieku Apvienība, 1975). Poetry Folder 5, published by the Latvian Writers' Association Translation mine. The original reads "jo es šai Valta Vitmana un Marka Tvēna kontinentā / vēl joprojām jūtos vainīgs / ka eksistēju / / . . . / / kā nedarbā pieķerts sev prasu: / kas esmu es? / / un jūsu sejās kā spoguļos / atbildi lasu: / / —ziniet / viens no tiem / imigrantiem— / / nekad / nevarēšu pastāstīt jums / savas dzīves stāstu / / nekad / / pa latviski / bija manas ciešanas un / / sapņi / / kaut gan— / man tas tomēr būtu/ tik ļoti svarīgi / / vientulība / ir gruzdošas sāpes / arī / pa latviski" Lines quoted later: " . . . līdzi straumei peldu / . . . / / bet kājas / kājas man dziļus avotus skaŗ / / . . . / / manas kājas / vēsajos ūdeņos / par saknēm top."

[2] Latvians seem to be more folklore-oriented than their neighbors, the Lithuanians and the Estonians, observed Ivar Ivask in his address to the Third Conference on Baltic Studies. See Ivask, "Baltic Literatures in Exile: Balance of a Quarter Century," *Baltic Literature and Linguistics*, Arvids Ziedonis et al., eds. (Columbus, Ohio: Association for the Advancement of Baltic Studies, 1973), p. 14. The paper gives a useful survey of the three literatures as they developed outside their countries after the Second World War (pp. 3-19). For a useful introduction into Latvian literary

306

folklore, see Jānis Andrups' essay "Folklore-Poetry and Early Writings," *Latvian Literature* (Stockholm: Zelta Ābele, 1954), pp. 11-46.

[3] A rather uneven compilation of anecdotal facts is *The Latvians in America 1640-1973*, compiled and edited by Maruta Kārklis, Līga Streips, and Laimonis Streips, Ethnic Chronology Series 13 (Dobbs Ferry, N.Y.: Oceana Publications, 1974). The 1970 census figures quoted in this book give as total number 86,413 Latvians in the U.S. who either were born abroad (41,707) or whose parents were foreign-born or of mixed parentage (44,706). Although the postwar Latvian immigrants did not establish national neighborhoods, several cities in the U.S. have sufficiently large numbers of Latvians to support active cultural and educational enterprises. Among the larger Latvian settlements are New York City, Boston, Philadelphia, Washington, D.C., Cleveland, Grand Rapids, Kalamazoo, Indianapolis, Chicago, Milwaukee, Minneapolis, Lincoln, Los Angeles, San Francisco, Seattle, and their respective metropolitan areas. Among the educational enterprises that should be mentioned are schools, usually meeting Saturdays or Sundays to teach Latvian language, literature, history, geography, and related subjects; summer high schools—there are three of them—meeting on a full-time basis up to six weeks; several summer camps; an intensive cultural/political camp for young people—peripatetic but meeting every summer; and Latvian language, literature, and political science courses at Western Michigan University every summer. Most of these enterprises are supported by the participants and by the Latvian society in the U.S.; little if any public funds are used. Among the cultural activities only the major ones can be mentioned: the Cultural Foundation administered by the American Latvian Association, and the Latvian Foundation, an independent non-profit corporation, both in the business of providing funding for cultural activities; the Cultural Bureau and the newly organized Latvian Institute under the auspices of the American Latvian Association; and regular song-and-culture fests drawing attendances of up to 15,000 every few years. Local activities are too numerous and too varied to mention.

[4] Jānis Rudzītis, *Starp provinci un Eiropu* ([Västerås]: Ziemeļblāzma, 1971), p. 162. Translation mine.

[5] For a brief characterization of Eglītis, see Vitauts Kalve, "The Fortunes of Latvian Literature in the Last 100 Years," *Latvian Literature* (Stockholm: Zelta Ābele, 1954), pp. 177-79 and 183-84. The only available translation is that of his adventure novel *Ajurjonga*, by L. Parks ([Stockholm]: Daugava, 1955), 231 pages.

[6] Her first novel, *Posta puķe* ([Brooklyn]: Grāmatu Draugs, 1962), received the Jānis Jaunsudrabiņš Prose Prize in 1965.

[7] There is no overall title. The series consists of three parts, three, two, and three volumes respectively. Each of the three parts and each of the eight volumes has a separate title. The first two parts and five volumes were published by Ceļinieks, Ann Arbor, Michigan, 1975. The last part was published in 1973 but released in 1975. See my review in *Books Abroad*, 50 (1975), 208-09.

[8] Kalve, p. 163.

[9] Ibid., p. 164. Translation by Ruth Speirs.

[10] Only *Mūžīgais mākonis* ([Västerås]: Ziemeļblāzma, 1958) appeared during his lifetime; *Laulības ar pilsētu* was a posthumous collection by Gunars Saliņš in 1964. The two together, in a recent combined edition *Iesim pie manas mīļās* ([Brooklyn]: Grāmatu Draugs, 1972) comprise 135 pages of poetry. Some translations by Ruth Speirs are to be found in *Translations from the Latvian*, Exeter Books 17 (University of Exeter, 1968), 28 pages.

[11] Gundars Pļavkalns, "Pilsēta Linarda Tauna dzejā," *Jaunā Gaita,* No. 59 (1966), 43-44. See also Valda Melngaile, "Real and Symbolic Landscapes in Exile Latvian Poetry," *Books Abroad*, 47 (1973), 682-88.

[12] "Es gribu pārbaudīt, vai mana pilsēta ir tāda, / Kā manos sapņos rādās. / . . . . / Un es iegāju pilsētā un uzliku savu sapni uz akmeņiem spīviem / Un redzēju–tie vecāki pat par manām aizsenām iepriekšējām dzīvēm. / Viņos dus faraoni un saules, kas viņus apņem. / Mēs nesapņojam pilsētu. Mēs esam sapnis, ko pilsēta sapņo." *Iesim pie manas mīļās*, p. 7. Translation mine.

[13] "Viena sieviete iet. / / Viņa iznāk no kafejnīcas / Un tagad iet centra virzienā. / / Viņas gaitā kaut kas tik ievērojams, / It kā viņa viena pati / Veidoto veselu procesiju vai parādi, / It kā viņa, ejot uz centru, neietu uz centru, / Bet ietu uz kādu sākumu vai galu." Ibid., p. 106. Translation mine.

[14] "Kad iebrauksi kailajā Ņukorkā, / būsi ar mums Tu vienis prātis: / tā jāapmežo! / Un varētu apmēram tā: / / Ātraudžus bērziņus Taimsskvērā, / ozolus lepnākās avēnijās, / Greničas ciemā pīlādžus, pīlādžus, / sēru vītolus Harlemā, / ostas rajonā priedes, egles, / kadiķu cerus ap lopkautuvēm, / . . . . / / Jaunie pēcāk pa mežu klejos, / atstās latviskiem bērnu bērniem / koku mizās iegrebtas sirdis. / . . ." Gunārs Saliņš, *Melnā Saule* ([Brooklyn]; Grāmatu Draugs, 1967), pp. 7-8. Translation mine. The collection was awarded the literary prize of the North American Latvian Cultural Foundation for 1967. For additional reading, see Astrid Ivask, "Gunars Saliņš: Poet of the Two Suns," *Books Abroad*, 43, No. 1 (1968), 55-58. See also Speirs, n. 10 and Melngaile, n. 11.

[15] "Par bungām skaļāk un brāzmaināk / un daudz, / daudz ilgāk par taurēm, / pat veseliem mūžiem cauri / varot izskanēt dzejnieka balss. / Tā saka. / / Es redzu: jauns dziesminieks, / gaiši bārdains bards, / ar elektronisko ģitaru nāk / un, stīgām satraukti pulsējot, / piesmacis iesāk– / 'ar laiku viss / mīti un pasakas'. / Bariem / nokrīt putni un lauru / lapas no zariem– / / zari un ziedi / ziedi un saule / saule un ķirzaka– / / ir pusdienlaiks. / Buls." Aina Kraujiete, *Ne bungas, ne trompetes* ([Brooklyn]: Grāmatu Draugs, 1974), p. 94. Translation mine. The last word, "buls," to my knowledge has no English counterpart. It describes the depressive, hazy calm that oftentimes precedes a thunderstorm. This collection shared the 1975 prize of the Cultural Foundation of the World Association of Free Latvians.

[16] Astrīde Ivaska, " 'My Age-Old Hidden Voice': The Poetry of Baiba Bičole," *Lituanus*, 16, No. 1 (1970), 33-42.

[17] "Woodstock, New York: vecas ragavas, segli un sakas, / sviesta ķērnes, piestas, laktas, / seni sanskrita burti, / lakas un koka smaržā– / / veclietu tirgotavā / nosūbējuši–it kā manas bērnības–sapņi / uz pirkstgaliem staigā, / pieskaras plakstiem un vaigiem– / es smaidu. / / –Stalta, izgleznojusies sieva piestājas, / prasa: / 'You found what you were looking for?' / / –'Yes!' / –un no manām pāri plūstošām saujām / līst atraktu dienu, gadu, laiku / vizošās zīmes." Baiba Bičole, *Ceļos* ([Brooklyn]: Grāmatu Draugs, 1969), p. 7. Translation mine.

[18] "Pamosties / no lietu vienaldzības, / justies to acīs / ka triju gadu vecumā, / nespējot aizsniegt plauktu. / Norasojušu pieri, / sirds kāpj stikla kalnā / stāvēt pie princeses / tukšā zārka. / Mēs abi / šai karstajā / pamestajā pilsētā / bez glābiņa / no lietu vienaldzības, / šķindošiem stikliem / un puteklļainā vēja." Astrīde Ivaska, *Solis silos* ([Stockholm]: Daugava, 1973), p. 43. Translation mine. This collection earned the literature prize of the Cultural Foundation of the World Association of Free Latvians for 1974.

[19] Olafs Stumbrs, *Variations* ([Chicago]: Alfred Kalnajs & Son, 1970), 65 pages.

[20]"No vientulības uz Rīgu / tai naktī mēs nostaigājām. / Dega dažā verandā ugunis, / bet no vernandas nespriež par mājām, / bet no lampiņas nezīlē rītu, / ne Tavu, ne manu, ne Grīga– / - - - - - / Kāds pamalē gaŗi velk strīpu / ar zaļu un platu krītu / no vientulības līdz Rīgai." Olafs Stumbrs, *Vasaras brīvlaiks* (Madison, Wisconsin: Latviešu Rakstnieku Apvienība, 1975), Poetry Folder 3 published by the Latvian Writers' Association. Translation mine.

[21]The magazine was edited by Valters Nollendorfs from 1955 to 1959, except for six issues in 1956/57, which were edited by Aivars Ruņģis. The editor since 1959 has been Laimonis Zandbergs. The publisher, since 1958, has been Latvian Youth Literary Society "Ceļinieks."

[22]The "fairy tale" has since appeared as a book: Jānis Turbads, *Ķēves dēls Kurbads* (Ann Arbur, Michigan: Ceļinieks, 1970), 143 pages. For the controversy surrounding the work and *Jaunā Gaita* see, Valters Nollendorfs, "The Demythologization of Latvian Literature," *Books Abroad*, 47 (1973), 669-71.

[23]Aivars Ruņģis, *Pats esi kungs, pats* ([Brooklyn]: Grāmatu Draugs, 1967), pp. 111-12. Translation mine.

[24]For an analysis of Ruņģis' prose see Valters Nollendorfs, "The Lonesome Patriot in the Prose of Latvian Writer Aivars Ruņģis," *Lituanus*, 20, No. 3 (1974), 12-27.

[25]For her first collection, *Vēja stabules* ([Minneapolis]: Tilts, 1961, Šķipsna received the initial Jānis Jaunsudrabiņš Prose Prise. *Aiz septītā tilta*, too, was published by Tilts.

[26]Ojārs Krātiņš, "Society and the Self in the Novels of Ilze Šķipsna and Alberts Bels," *Books Abroad*, 47 (1973), 677-78.

[27]See Ilse S. Rothrock, "A Ship for the Flood," *A Part of Space: Ten Texas Writers*, ed. Betsy F. Colquitt (Fort Worth: Texas Christian Univ. Press, 1969), pp. 141-47.

[28]His first American collection appeared recently under the title *i.e. (New Years; Return of the Life Force)* (Topanga, Cal.: Poet Papers, 1975).

[29]"IEVAE, ESOT MEITĀS, SAPNĪ PARĀDĀS VĒL NEDZIMUSI MAZMEITA KĀDĀ SIBIRIJAS TUNDRĀ. / / Netrūksties, vecomāt; kam piesauc Dievu, kur tu met / to krustu? Ņem saujā labāk šos kauliņus–manas rotas– / cik baltas manas paceltās rokas, šie izslietie ziloņa ilkņi. / Šis mūža mežs: kāds varens šķirsts! / Es guļu / uz krastā izskalotas valzivs melnās muguras. / / Klau, kā zāle dūc ap pēdām! / Kā zilu lāsteku spiets– / jo manas dzīslas jau sāk izlaist saknes. / Virs galvas kāvi lauž debess spraišļus, vecomāt. / Jā, šais padebešos sadeg putni, un zvaigžņu krusa krīt / klusi un nežēlo miesu. / / Jel nosapņo manu nāvi–tā ielaid mani aizsaulē, kā reiz līdzēsi meitai / izšķelties no savas miesas. / Jo nespēju vairs atcerēties, / kā viņu sauca, / un mans vārds skan / kā nelgas mīkla. / Laid mani! / Laid mani! / Lai spētu atdzimt / akmenī." Dīna Rauna, *Klauna āda* (Madison, Wisconsin: Latviešu Rakstnieku Apvienība, 1974), Poetry Folder 1 of the Latvian Writers' Association. Translation mine.

[30]"es ceru / veļos ieiet / ienirt daugavas ūdeņos / pietekas attekāt avotus izpētīt / uznirt akās: / no visiem ūdeņiem / raudzīties sevī dzīvā / pret sauli." Baiba Kaugara, *aizcirstas durvis* ([Västerås]: Ziemeļblāzma, 1970), p. 14. Translation by Astrīde Ivaska. Kaugara received the lyric prize of the Zināīda Lazda Foundation for her collection. An analysis of Kaugara's poetry: Astrīde Ivaska, "Is the Voice in Me a Maimed Whisper: Young Latvian Exile Poets of the Seventies," *Journal of Baltic Studies*, 5 (1974), 26-33.

Three Intellectual Lithuanian Poets

Rimvydas Šilbajoris

ABSTRACT

After World War II, a large number of Lithuanian writers made their home in the United States. In their works, many poets fed upon their nostalgia for home and their anguish of dispossession. Others lived again in their art as in another country, without any visions of paradise found or lost. Jonas Mekas (b. 1922), Liūnė Sutema (b. 1927) and Algimantas Mackus (1932-1964) are three poets who occupy a tenuous middle ground, where new poetic language arises from complex relationships between fresh experiences in the adopted land and the old images of home. Jonas Mekas escapes the limbo of exile by shifting his loyalty from places in his past to his own enduring emotions evoked by them, so that in the end he depicts his own mind as it moves through time. In this way, Mekas can speak with an American voice enriched by echoes of his Lithuanian inheritance. Liūnė Sutema seeks to belong to her new land through a kind of "spiritual symbiosis," where memories of the past permeate and transform the experiences of the present. She is, however, wary of poetic images which might claim too much for themselves and endanger her personal integrity, her lonely freedom. The most somber voice is that of Algimantas Mackus. He experiences exile as a universal human condition. For him the ultimate physical and spiritual union with the new land bears the name of death. This total alienation, however, does echo in its own way the young American voices of protest and disillusion. (RS)

Among the many voices of America, that of the Lithuanian writers had its origin in an exile's cry of pain. The year was 1944, and the place—the ruins of Germany where a great many Lithuanians, including intellectuals and writers, were deported or had escaped from the advancing Soviet troops. After the war, these writers found it difficult and sometimes impossible to come to terms with their dispossession. Some sank into the trauma of silence, others voiced their sorrow and anger against the Soviets, but most continued to write of their country as she continued to live in their minds. Among such writers were some of the best-known names in

Lithuanian letters, people who had achieved creative maturity at home but who afterwards could not find a new artistic language commensurate to their catastrophic new reality. Typical in this respect was the poet Bernardas Brazdžionis (b. 1907),[1] whose passionate and melodious lyrical rhetoric was pushed to the edge of distress as he strained to use it in protest against the injustice done to his God and country and to lament the fate of exiles and martyrs. When the war came, the poet Jonas Aistis (b. 1904)[2] was doing research in France, and the novelist Antanas Vaičiulaitis (b. 1906)[3] lived in the United States. The realization that the events of 1944 had turned them into exiles struck like a shock wave across great distances. Aistis, a complex and intensely personal writer on the themes of love, both sacred and profane, an experimenter with native folk idiom in relation to French-inspired modernistic imagery, and a disturbed thinker on the very nature of art, was drawn gradually away from all this to patriotic themes, intimate landscapes of home and tragic, accusatory visions about the nation's future. Vaičiulaitis, a highly refined stylist in prose, had written delicately of love in his novel *Valentina* (1936), while in his short stories he unfolded warm, poetic visions of simple country life. As an exile, Vaičiulaitis continued his village stories, but two of his latest books, in 1957 and 1966, are in the fairy tale genre, as if he were trying to build a never-never land which could embrace and console his longing for the home he had lost.

Some younger writers also turned inward to dwell on their longing and sorrow during the first days of exile. The poet Kazys Bradūnas (b. 1917)[4] was especially effective in conveying the farmer's agonizing sense of loss in his book *The Alien Bread* (1945), where every surrounding detail in the foreign countryside pierces the heart with memories of home. Later Bradūnas developed his poetry to a point at which the experience of dispossession blended with the Christian mystique of life as a continuous sacrifice; the troubled history of Lithuania became a sacred vision of both the pagan and the Christian rite, a sacrament of blood and earth.

For most of the young writers, however, the experience of exile, instead of forcing them into a protective shell, became a broadening, challenging thing. Even though the sight of Europe in ruins may have opened their own inner spaces to despair, they also felt the excitement of an encounter with new ideas and new devices in art. One of their discoveries was that Western Existentialism had extended the concept of exile to include the human condition in principle. This discovery opened a possibility that they could use the images of art as a link between alienation and dispossession, between the universal and the particular experience of human loss.

The anguish of the poet's ultimate solitude in a world full of his own visions and dreams is especially painful in the work of Alfonsas Nyka-

Niliūnas (b. 1917).[5] In prose, Antanas Škėma (1911-1961)[6] was the most dramatic exponent of the tragic perception that we often perish at the highest point of our creative consciousness, when we become rebels against the inherent meaninglessness of the universe. Both Škėma and Algirdas Landsbergis (b. 1924)[7] turned not only to prose but also to drama, as if to illustrate the proposition that Lithuanian literature was strengthening its narrative and dramatic voices in the time of cruel conflicts and epic events.

Landsbergis, however, does not pursue the images of despair as far as did Škėma, who drove them to the point of man's insanity. Landsbergis prefers a well-mannered challenge to the universal void and a hopeful confrontation with human smallness. This approach often enables him to soften the impact of his tragic plays and to write puckish comedies on the collapse of our dreams.

A somewhat special place in this development belongs to an older writer, the poet Henrikas Radauskas (1910-1970),[8] and a younger one, the playwright Kostas Ostrauskas (b. 1926).[9] Fortunately for Lithuanian letters, Radauskas did not conform to the image of a middle-aged expatriate writer who eventually drowns his muse in a pool of stagnant rhetoric. After his first book in 1935, others came out abroad, in 1950, 1955 and 1965, and he kept developing as a poet until his death. His work shows no direct traces of the exile syndrome, although it does encompass the experiences of alienation, solitude and death on a level where they enter the structure of art as component elements, placed in an esthetically productive relationship with the feelings of beauty, humor and of sheer creative joy. Radauskas' main concern was the language of art itself, the design and texture of words, their multifaceted and subtle interplays which, by the force of creative imagination, can become everything that it should mean to us to be human.

The actors on Ostrauskas' stage impersonate certain general aspects of the human condition, mostly those that have to do with the comedy and drama of our encounters with death. Ostrauskas really belongs to exile literature only in the sense that he writes in Lithuanian instead of English, and also because death in exile, in its many themes and variations, constitutes the underlying reality of the refugee community as such.

The foregoing was meant to set a general frame for discussing three relatively young poets, Jonas Mekas (b. 1922),[10] Liūnė Sutema (b. 1927),[11] and Algimantas Mackus (1932-1964).[12] In émigré letters they occupy a certain tenuous middle ground, touching upon all the facets of exile as these have been reflected in the work of other artists, but striving themselves for a synthesis of experience, a poetic universe which can exist on its own terms. In the work of all three, but particularly Mackus, the new realities of an alien land, as well as the receding memories of home, often present themselves under the aspect of death. For all three, reality and memory may survive or perish only in their embodiment as language, that is, as the specific idiom of their art.

Mekas and Sutema are old enough to know Lithuanian well, but they share with the rest of the émigré community the problem of adjusting and expanding their native language to meet the realities of their complex new world. In attempting to do this, the artist must work as a creator of language, even on the pre-literary level. Algimantas Mackus left Lithuania at the age of twelve, and his command of the language was less comprehensive. Paradoxically, this enabled him to achieve some striking effects in his poetry, as he struggled to adapt his imperfect tools to a modern and cosmopolitan poetic idiom. The very difficulty of his efforts may have caused him to feel more acutely the decay and disintegration of the Lithuanian language in exile.

As poets, they also inherited the entire superstructure of Lithuanian poetic traditions with its predominantly romantic and nationalistic view of history observed from an inner sanctum of intimate lyrical sorrow. This tradition had acquired so much meaning and substance of its own that, instead of being modified by new circumstances, it itself transformed the image of exile. The nation's catastrophe could be depicted as an event which the past generations of Lithuanians, schooled in suffering, would have understood equally well and in the same way. It could be written about in the same language (and tone) of moral indignation combined with humble piety and enduring hope. Most of the established poets proceeded to write in this traditional way, but the young ones felt that the entire superstructure of inherited poetic language had collapsed together with the premises of Western civilization in their own country and perhaps throughout the world. An entirely new model had to be built, and all they had to work with was a poetic tradition which permitted no true conception of the magnitude and essence of this radical turn in history. Their individual poetic universes, with their own ideas, emotions and images, could only take shape concurrently with and as a result of their developing new language.

While still in Germany, Jonas Mekas was the first to publish a book of verse (1947). Its title, *The Idyls of Semeniškiai* (Semeniškiai is Mekas' own native village) certainly did not seem to promise any clear break with the established tradition, unlike, for instance, the first book by Nyka-Niliūnas, in 1946, entitled *The Symphonies of Dispossession.* Yet, even a fairly superficial first reading of Mekas was enough to reveal a very important new direction. What had previously been the poetic model of idyllic Lithuanian countryside had developed into a set of abstractions, where references to concrete things were used to do no more than signal the names of emotions originating not in a poet's contact with the land itself, but in his remembrance of feelings evoked in him by those who had described it before. Mekas, on the other hand, systematically deprived all such objects of their previous poetic connotations, and the Lithuanian readers were shocked to see what seemed to them like plain country prose. Instead of the expected melodious cadences about golden-haired maidens in green meadows, Mekas spoke of "women, their hair over their eyes, their arms cut and bruised by the straw."[13] Or again, rather than describe how the tears of heaven fall on patient tillers of the soil as they cross the melancholy native plain, Mekas wrote about "wagons with axle-trees that creak and splash across the oozing mud of torn and trampled potato patches."[14] This scratchy, filthy homespun reality, it seemed, would not permit poetic emotion. It took some time to perceive that this emotion was there the whole time, that it suffused the coarse, plain surface of the verse and made the lost country compellingly and poignantly real in memory. It was, after all, not a new language, but a very old one indeed, often used by country folk to great poetic effect but without a conscious artistic purpose. In Mekas' poetry, as in peasant usage, the plane of everyday reality intersects with that of art to communicate a perception of life which shows that man has understood and accepted his close organic relation with the hard and the beautiful facts of nature. His accomplishment was to make explicit the implicit poetry of country speech, producing verses such as the following:

> Old is the smell of the clover,
> the horses whinnying in the summer nights,
> the chirp and chime of harrows, rollers, plows,
> grindstones of the mills,
> the green smells from the meadow, steeping flax.
> white gleem of kerchief of the weeders in the garden.
> Old is the hush of rain over the branches
> of underbrush; and the hoarse cries of the black cocks
> are old in the red summer dawn
> —old this our speech.[15]

It was rather ironic that this old speech should be rediscovered by Mekas just at the time when he had lost the soil from which it grew. But in a sense, it was also proper that this should be so at this historic turning point of Lithuanian letters, because the very first work, at the dawn of written Lithuanian poetry in the eighteenth century, was also a peasant epic called *The Seasons*, by Kristijonas Donelaitis,[16] a country pastor who spoke in a similar plain language of daily peasant labors and conveyed a poetic and a sacral sense of life.

In the United States Mekas became interested in film.[17] In this new medium he also showed immediate concern with the source of esthetic experience, in opposition to the established Hollywood myth. His highly unorthodox experiments in movie-making eventually produced a movement known as the New York underground cinema. This movement occurred in an altogether American context and it very quickly expelled him from the émigré Lithuanian culture. It seemed as if Mekas had become a new voice of America in its hippie-artist subculture which had nothing whatever to do with the rainy seasons of potato harvests back in Semeniškiai. Actually, there was a very strong bond between the two worlds, consisting of Mekas' own highly personal approach to art as a fundamentally autobiographical experience. What he sought was a direct and truthful image of his soul as a reality outside of time but in an intimate contact with every changing frame of his existence.

Mekas' next book of verse, *The Talk of Flowers* (1961), seems a kind of interlude in a private place inside the heart, where the author is contemplating his intimate perceptions of fragile things: the shape of a blossom, an impulse of love, a passing shadow of memory. He uses poetic language as if it were a closeup camera, to focus precisely and delicately upon such nuances of meaning as will describe for him his own self-awareness as an atom of consciousness making an effort of loyalty to his love for the eternal in all passing things. Several years later, in his book *Words Apart* (1967), Mekas intensified the process of minute observations to the degree that both the image of reality and the movement of language depicting it seemed frozen in their isolated facets, each work or even each syllable taking up a separate line, like the frames of a film strip. In one place he says:

> I
> seek
> new
> forms
> which
> would
> permit
> permit
> to open
> all
> the memory
> of
> my
> experience.[18]

In this effort, the book becomes like a microscopic film of some very difficult inner process, an effort to go deep into the irreducible fragments of awareness in order to piece together a sense of lasting identity. Airborne and alone, Mekas comes to a standstill:

> Far
> from

earth,
O—
ver
the clouds
I put
a question:
what
am
I?
No
answers.
No
questions.
Falls
the light
of the moon
on
the wings
of the plane.[19]

Mekas wrote these lines on an airplane to Europe—a tiny dot in space in search of his roots on the home continent. The situation is reversed in his next book, *Reminiscences* (1972). There he writes of his postwar years in Germany—a time and space existing nowhere but in his memory, and he uses direct, concrete language full of warm intimacy with every detail of his past but avoiding any conventional signs which would tell the reader: "this is poetry." The plain, prosaic surface of the poems actually conceals intricate sets of devices aimed at intensifying the esthetic experience through a perception of time which is simultaneously static and dynamic—frozen moments in memory which in themselves signify a completed course of events. Here, for instance, is a description of one cycle in the life of a young German soldier, leading from his childhood dreams to the death of all hope:

And a young German soldier—still like a child,
still as if a child—was standing
in the burned-out Hanau station, looking
at the pile of bricks and stones, at the steel skeleton,
the black tree trunk, consumed by fire, and at the chimney, at the dust
a window frame torn off, and at the dangling
chunk of reinforced concrete—
the broken pieces, the remainders of his childhood,
and tears were streaming down his face, just like water,
just like water.[20]

Some critics say that life is significant and society is human to the extent that it is sustained by a flow of warm feeling toward both people and things running under the surface of the impersonal social structures we must devise in order to function. If so, then the voice of Mekas belongs among such other American voices as that of James Agee, or Carl Sandburg, or even Mark Twain, all of whom have spoken of the secret warm-blooded pulse of humanity.

The work of Algimantas Mackus is very different. No other Lithuanian poet writing abroad had such a bleak and lucid understanding of the close affinity between exile and death in all its aspects: the physical dismemberment of the émigré community, the evanescence of its native language, the fading of memory and the loss of hope and faith. For a comparison one might look at Sylvia Plath and her people in bell jars. Mackus himself, looking with irony and anguish at the hopeful world of fairy tales, uses the image of a glass coffin:

> —What do I carry in this glass coffin?
> —All the things gathered up which I used to possess.
> The dead things have pushed through their roots into me.
> —Will you not then discard this piercing dead weight?
> —With nothing to bury, a man is alone.
> —So be.[21]

One of these dead roots was the inherited language of Lithuanian poetry. In 1950 Mackus had written a book of poems called *Elegies*, full of traditional patriotic phrases, and it was a total failure. The next book, *His Is the Earth* (1959), began a process of semantic reversals in poetic language. Travelling across the Arcadian landscapes of traditional imagery, Mackus changed the metaphorical values of its shapes, substances and colors so that all signs of life and hope became the messengers of death. This produced brooding *nature morte* poems like the following:

I

In the green water
(as it moves to the black and the tenebrous forest)
are reflections of our tired bodies.

In the green water
(its surface is pierced by the silvery bow of the moon)
the soul of our boy is playing.

In the green water
our bodies are cold
and in the green water
the soul of our boy is now also dead.

II

Above the green water
(it reaches the black and the tenebrous forest)
the death of all trees, of all forests has lighted its fire.

Above the green water
(which our small boy now holds in his hand)
slowly rises the pillar-like torso of red conflagration.

> In the green water
> our bodies are but extinguished fire
> and in the green water
> we are dead guests.[22]

Green color and water, signifying life, in the context of this poem acquire the meaning of death which is intensified through the repetitions like an incantation. In later poems, the colors silver and black and the image of fire establish sets of image relationships in which they catch and hold a bleak and death-bound vision. Green water and black earth have their substance transformed into glass and are framed in stained glass windows to deny us the hope of religious consolation. The dead soul of the child grows into an ambivalent image of the Lord's angel, an angel of death. This angel-child is one of the basic explicit and implicit images in Mackus' next book, *The Generation of Unornamented Language and the Wards* (1962). He becomes both a symbol and a victim of our time, carrying the burden of the older exiles' fading dreams and also exuding the cadaverous smell of their decaying reality. Sometimes this child becomes personified in the image of young Theresa, a saint of masochistic love. In this shape she is buried and defiled by the generation of her parents who, lonely, maudlin and cruel, still believe themselves to be idealists. In a longer poem within the book this child becomes the black preacher John of Africa, the prophet of its emerging nations betrayed in their inception by the self-deceiving dreams of its former white masters. A second narrative poem speaks of Jurek, a Jewish child in Lithuania, killed by the Nazis, who dies mercifully without having understood the horror of his age. Removed from such specific references, the child-angel image stands black and green as a coldly luminous symbol of all-pervading death:

> By Lord's Angel awakened
> I look at stained glass in the chapel.
> The face of the Angel of the Lord . . .
> Angel, it's green and it's black,
> Angel, rest thou in peace.
>
> I shall sleep through Lord's Angel
> I shall sleep through stained glass in the chapel,
> Through the face of the Angel of the Lord.
> Through, Angel, the black and the green,
> Angel, through rest eternal.
>
> Green is Angel, the land,
> Green is the earth being taken away and divided,
> Angel, it weeps rest eternal,—
> Birth-giving mothers
> Sing thus and sing in their cry,
> It is, Angel, black before sleep.[23]

318

The impulse for Mackus' last book of poems was the death of Antanas Škėma, a writer close to Mackus in many ways. The book, entitled *Chapel B*, includes intense personal sorrow augmented by meditations upon the death of his own country and of the community of exiles, and then expands into a complex relationship with the images of the American continent, broadening out still more by free-borrowings of poetic themes and idioms from Federico García Lorca, Dylan Thomas and Paul Celan.

Škėma died in a highway accident on the Pennsylvania turnpike; he was run over by a truck. On that morning, his crushed and mangled body, as it lay on the concrete pavement, was one among hundreds of traffic fatalities all over the globe. In order to be a significant artistic fact, this death had to be related in terms of poetic images to those fatal moments in modern history in which Mackus saw emerging a grim pattern of doom. First, there was the desperate guerilla war in Lithuania. Stubborn farmers held on to their land for years against the Soviets until they and the land were torn to shreds and soaked in blood. This, for Mackus, was one of the faces of death:

> Death is fanatic tillers of the soil,
> the blinded sacrament of blood and earth;
> like wounded beasts arising from their lairs
> they shatter in the evening against cement.[24]

So ended freedom for one of the world's nations. Was the birth of freedom for others a new face of death? Mackus believed so:

> Death is the names of the new republics
> in Africa, ensnared inside the trap of history;
> exhausted Negro Mary fell to earth
> still holding a narrow amulet between her palms.[25]

The American promise also contained, for Mackus, the fulfillment of death deep in its soil, in the coal mines, where early Lithuanian, Polish or Irish immigrants worked and perished, together with their fading ethnic identities:

> In the mines they dig the coal And they bury
> the hair Hail Mary Diminishing numbers of men
> on Sundays go out to the tavern Hoarse their voices
> sing of how Nemunas flows At midnight they read
> letters from home Hail Mary[26]

This Lithuanian death becomes intertwined with a similar death of the Poles and then reaches out to the tragic continent of Africa. The image of the Virgin Mary, a mother and a child of God, connects these different fates into a single human agony:

> In a gray postcard from Łomża
> she sends goodnight Hail Mary
> she tells you to grit your teeth

she orders to cry Hail Mary
that Poland has not perished yet in a gray postcard Mary
cutting whips you say
like serpents are scourging Mary
on the hardened ground of plantations
you lay down your shoulders and breast
you lay down from your naked body
into the African race Mary
I'll go to the land in the timeless hour
black Mary Diminishing numbers of men
on Sundays go out to the tavern There drinks death
Singing how Nemunas flows In the gray postcard from Łomża
goodnight sings Hail Mary[27]

From such a vantage point, the bloody collage of Škėma's body comes to represent, for Mackus, the map of the continent, reflecting man's damnation by God:

The voice of the continent, at dawn, having become
both sex and body, cries hysterically;
on copper plate—intaglio—
the furious God, in midst of ritual,
recalls salvation thrown out to the crowds.[28]

Mackus uses the refrain "a las cinco de la tarde" from Federico García Lorca's poem *Lament for Ignacio Sanchez Mejías*, changing it to "seven o'clock in the morning," the time of Škėma's death and surrounding it with the implications of the Spanish context acting together with the Lithuanian frame of reference to produce an image of the death of God, or rather, the image of God as death. Similar contextual use was made of Paul Celan's *Todesfuge* and Dylan Thomas' poem "And Death Shall Have No Dominion," to which Mackus provides the antistrophe:

And death shall have its dominion.
Dead men will no more turn around,
leaning on skeleton elbows.
The soul will remain, but there'll be no more soul.
And death shall have its dominion.[29]

Mackus himself was killed around Christmastime, in another traffic accident in Chicago, in 1964.

Liūnė Sutema was a good personal friend of Mackus, and the strongest bond between them as poets was the same stark honesty of vision in which the entire myth of exile as a temporary condition disintegrates and turns to ashes. This bond informs their work with the images of death on many levels of experience. For Sutema, however, death also means the unwillingness or inability to perceive oneself as a participant, a contributor to the life of the new country. Her poetry in many ways also resembles the funeral of dead things in a glass coffin, but it speaks with the voice of one who is a determined survivor and who does not wish to retreat into a deathlike isolation. Rather, her solitude resembles more that of a hermit who withdraws himself in order to reconstitute his image of the world so that she can ultimately accept it again with the kind of faith and hope which is truthful because it permits no illusions.

The prevailing category of images in Sutema's poetry, her view of the world, might be called organic; like some hardy plant from a distant clime, she protects herself with needles and armor, while at the same time seeking some sort of symbiosis with the alien growth around her. Two different organic textures, the native sinew and leaf preserved in memory, and the body and blood of the new land palpably interact and interweave in the design of her poetry. A stanza from her first book of poems, *No More Is Anything Alien* (1962), illustrates this attitude:

> No more is anything alien,
> the tree I never knew has grown
> and spread its twigs in my eyeballs—
> the woven texture of its prickly leaves
> is breathing in my palms
> spun out in tangled filligree.
> My lips have grown accustomed
> to its untasted, succulent fruit.[30]

It may seem strange to say that this metaphor of the new land growing into and becoming part of the poet's identity expresses a highly unorthodox poetic belief, but it is so in émigré Lithuanian letters, where the accepted image of exile is that of a dying branch, torn from the native tree. Sutema stands stubbornly alive, letting the image of her lost country shrivel up and die instead. "I am not to be tamed by death," she says in one of her poems. The point is not that Sutema is switching her allegiance from the old world to the new, but rather that she wishes to protect and preserve that which is of true value in the myth of her native country by freeing it from the traditional and no longer valid systems of symbols and images which have also ceased to exist in the native country itself, because it has changed, and has been changed, by others in the cataclysmic events of the war and of foreign occupation. The ultimate true exiles, in other words, are really the old poetic images of home, and it is to them that Sutema refuses to return, nor would she give them shelter in her own heart. Love for the native land remains and is more intense than before, but, to be true, it must also be, as Sutema puts in in one poem, a faith in Humanity and a faith in Life as well. In her second book, *Land Without Name* (1966), the path to that faith is represented as a liberation, as freedom to doubt again:

> Now I can doubt again
> my subconscious has washed on the shore,
> to the sun-filled day of Summer

the heavy unnecessary things
which I had carried in myself:
just like a lake washes up
dead fish, grass and roots, branches
and sometimes a human body.
Now I have everything in front of me
(everything of which I had been sure)
Now I am free again
and I can doubt.[31]

This must not be understood as a contradiction but rather as a logical continuum with the words of another poem in this book:

I will not give anything away —
I will disclaim to have possession.
I will carry within myself,
will guard inside the catacombs
to end this game *my* way.[32]

In the final analysis, this letting go and this refusal to give up represents an extension of the struggle for one's own poetic language into the realm of the deepest emotional loyalties on the existential plane. Sutema was actually trying to reach beyond the language in which love for one's fatherland had always been expressed toward the sources of that love, the ancient loyalties and fresh emotional responses which the native landscape had also awakened in the older generations of Lithuanian poets, even though they spoke of them in the traditional way. Sutema understood that her search for a new poetic idiom was not a search for something external, that it was an inner transformation as well, a struggle for a new idea, new conception of herself as a person and as a poet. Her latest book, *The Time of Famine* (1972), expresses this point succinctly:

It is time to burn. Time to burn
the words for which there are no more things
like the nutshells after the kernel falls out,
like the pods of flowers and trees
after the seed has fallen,
like the steeds of war without their riders,
like the homes, deserted for decades,
without their owners.[33]

The organic imagery so frequent in Sutema's work passes over in this stanza to historical references about ancient Lithuanian warriors fallen in battle whose steeds were burned with them on the funeral pyre, and to the modern fate of the nation, the abandoned homes of the refugees in which no one now will ever live again, no matter what strangers should come and inhabit them.

The tenacious quality of Sutema's poetry thus comes through, paradoxically, in a series of renunciations, as if she had decided of her own will to complete the process of dispossession begun by her exile. While seeking new language in which to come to terms with new realities, she actually achieves an embodiment of one of the most ancient character traits of the Lithuanian people, well noted by the older poets in their own type of language, namely, an infinitely patient inner seclusion in the face of adversity. In this aspect of her poetry Sutema echoes in a rather special way an American voice, that of William Faulkner, who said in his Nobel prize acceptance speech that humanity shall not only endure, but that it shall also prevail.

In what sense can one speak about Mekas, Mackus and Sutema as "intellectual poets"? This term does not apply very much to their works, because their works' complexity and depth are not of the intellectual order. The fragmentation of language and of self-perception in Mekas' *Words Apart* is not a by-product of some rational analysis, but is more like a close-up view through the magnifying glass of emotion and in this respect no different from his declarations of love for the reality lost in time and space in his *Idyls of Semeniškiai* or *Reminiscences*. The consistent reversal of the images of life to signify death in the poetry of Mackus is not carried out in the philosophical dimension, but represents for him an act of moral courage in a world which has betrayed all its hopes. Sutema's renunciations as well as her stubborn defense of spiritual values are accomplished in the realm of poetic imagery rather than in that of intellectual propositions. In calling these writers "intellectuals," we are actually speaking of their reputation among the broad masses of émigré Lithuanian reading public. So used, this term describes a sense of remoteness, almost to the point of irrelevance, which the ordinary readers feel toward these poets. It thus means a certain solitude, an exile-within-exile caused by the readers' failure to understand, even sometimes to seek understanding, of a poetic language which is not familiar to them. The reading public still shares the basic premises of the older writers with respect to poetic imagery, form and emotional clues pertaining to moral and patriotic values. Consequently, these three poets appear to many of their readers as puzzling and distant figures, people who do not speak in moral categories, nor in those of familiar emotions. They seem, in other words, like builders of obscure, even cold, poetic structures devised in the mind rather than born in the heart.

In addition to this, the critics who attempt to analyze the work of these poets inevitably follow their own mental habits of constructing morally and emotionally noncommital rational structures. The result is that we see in the end not so much the true profiles of these poets as sets of analytical models pertaining to them, and this critical treatment is what gives the reading public one more reason to think of them as "intellectual poets."

Finally, some confrontation with the question of what these poets have contributed to this continent, to its voice, seems in order. It is difficult to compare them with American expatriates in Paris, because those voices were in essence cosmopolitan, contributing to the general life of belles lettres more than to any specific trends in French culture. On the other hand, these poets' commitment to America does not compare with that made by T. S. Eliot to his vision of England. In many ways these Lithuanian writers remain an isolated enclave in the American cultural stream, not in the least because they write in an exotic minor tongue. What they have accomplished, however, is a formulation of the inner world of many young Lithuanian-Americans whose value systems derive equally from both cultural traditions. For them, such vision of exile in itself provides a key to the traumatic experiences of America, a country which is renewing itself on its 200th birthday through a similar process of dispossession, the loss of an idyllic American dream and the search for a new, often painful, but truthful American vision. In this, the cry of exile may well become a voice speaking to many other Americans, hyphenated or not, of a return to the home of their own indomitable spirit, both old and new.

Ohio State University

NOTES

[1] For a general discussion of Brazdžionis' poetry in English, see Rimvydas Šilbajoris, *Perfection of Exile: 14 Contemporary Lithuanian Writers* (Norman: Univ. of Oklahoma Press, 1970), pp. 302-17.

[2] Ibid., pp. 77-93.

[3] Ibid., pp. 56-76.

[4] Ibid., pp. 243-51.

[5] Ibid., pp. 161-83. See also Viktoria Skrupskelis, "Alfonsas Nyka-Niliūnas: A Poet of Dualities," *Books Abroad*, 47 (Autumn 1973), 708-15.

[6] *Perfection of Exile*, pp. 94-111.

[7] Ibid., pp. 135-60.

[8] Ibid., pp. 25-55. See also R. Šilbajoris, "Henrikas Radauskas—Timeless Modernist," *Books Abroad*, 43 (Winter 1969), 50-54; R. Šilbajoris, "The Arts as Images in the Poetry of Henrikas Radauskas," *Baltic Literature and Linguistics* (Columbus, Ohio: Association for the Advancement of Baltic Studies, 1973), pp. 29-35.

[9] *Perfection of Exile*, pp. 112-34. See also R. Šilbajoris, "Some Structural Principles in the Theater of Kostas Ostrauskas," *Lituanistikos darbai* (Lithuanian Studies), issue III, Item 6 (1973), 173-97.

[10] *Perfection of Exile*, pp. 271-84. See also R. Šilbajoris, "The 'Reminiscences' of Jonas Mekas: Poetic Form and Rooted Sorrow," *Journal of Baltic Studies*, 4, No. 4 (1973), 327-34.

[11] On the existential tension between home as a poetic universe and home as the land remembered in the work of Sutema and Mackus, see R. Šilbajoris, "Lithuanian Poets—Strangers and Children of Their Native Land," *Lituanus*, 17, No. 1 (1971), 5-17.

324

[12] *Perfection of Exile*, p. 184-217.

[13] Jonas Mekas, *Semeniškiu idiles*, Second Printing (Brooklyn, N.Y.: *Aidai* magazine, 1955), p. 47.

[14] Ibid., p. 49.

[15] Translation by Clark Mills in Algirdas Landsbergis and Clark Mills, ed., *The Green Linden: Selected Lithuanian Poetry* (New York: Voyage Press, 1962), pp. 103-04. All other translations of poetry in this article are my own.

[16] At various times, Donelaitis' poem *The Seasons* has been translated into English, German, Russian and Hungarian.

[17] For Mekas' work on film, see C. Tomkins, "All Pockets Open," *The New Yorker*, 6 Jan. 1973, pp. 31-40.

[18] Jonas Mekas, *Pavieniai zodziai* (Words Apart [Chicago: Algimantas Mackus Book Publishing Fund, 1967]), p. 19.

[19] Ibid., p. 54.

[20] Jonas Mekas, *Reminiscencijos* (Reminiscences [United States of America]: Privately printed, 1972), n. p.

[21] Algimantas Mackus, *Neornamentuotos kalbos generacija ir augintiniai* (The Generation of Unornamented Speech and the Words [Chicago: Santara, 1963]), p. 7.

[22] Algimantas Mackus, *Jo yra zeme* (His Is the Earth [Chicago: Santara, 1959]), p. 68.

[23] *Neornamentuotos . . .*, p. 8.

[24] Algimantas Mackus, *Chapel B* (Chicago: The Algimantas Mackus Book Publishing Fund, 1965), p. 11.

[25] Ibid., p. 12.

[26] Ibid., p. 33.

[27] Ibid., p. 34.

[28] Ibid., p. 23.

[29] Ibid., p. 60.

[30] Liūnė Sutema, *Nebera nieko svetimo* (No More Is Anything Alien [Chicago: Gintaras, 1962]), p. 29.

[31] Liūnė Sutema, *Bevardė šalis* (Land Without Name [Chicago: Santara-Sviesa Federation, 1966]), p. 14.

[32] Ibid., p. 40.

[33] Liūnė Sutema, *Badmetis* (The Time of Famine [Chicago: Gintaras, 1972]), p. 14.